THE CALIPHATE OF MAN

THE CALIPHATE OF MAN

Popular Sovereignty in Modern Islamic Thought

Andrew F. March

The Belknap Press of
Harvard University Press

Cambridge, Massachusetts / London, England / 2019

Printed in the United States of America

First printing

Library of Congress Cataloging-in-Publication Data

Names: March, Andrew F., 1976- author.
Title: The caliphate of man : popular sovereignty in modern Islamic thought / Andrew F. March.
Description: Cambridge, Massachusetts : The Belknap Press, Harvard University Press, 2019. | Includes bibliographical references and index.
Identifiers: LCCN 2019010887 | ISBN 9780674987838 (alk. paper)
Subjects: LCSH: Islam and politics. | Islam and state. | Ummah (Islam) | Caliphate. | Islamic fundamentalism. | Islamic countries—Politics and government.
Classification: LCC BP173.7 .M3769 2019 | DDC 320.55/7—dc23 LC record available at https://lccn.loc.gov/2019010887

To Tamir and Ayla

Contents

Preface

"The People Wills . . ."

On February 18, 2011, one week after popular protests forced the downfall of the Egyptian President Hosni Mubarak, an estimated 2 million Egyptians assembled in Cairo's Tahrir Square for a "Day of Victory" celebration. This was a Friday, the Muslim day of communal prayer. Leading the prayer and delivering the sermon that day was 84-year-old Egyptian scholar Yūsuf al-Qaraḍāwī, who had lived in exile in Qatar since 1961 and was probably the single best-known global intellectual figure associated with the Islamist movement.[1] Qaraḍāwī's presence that day was less a symbol of a returning demagogue come to proclaim Islamist triumph over a fallen secular dictatorship. Rather, it represented the tragically short-lived unity of purpose of all those who had participated in the eighteen days that stunned the world. As such, Qaraḍāwī addressed not just Islamists or even Muslims, but "O Muslims and Copts! O children of Egypt!" and spoke of "these youth from all regions in Egypt, from all social classes, rich and poor, educated and illiterate, workers and cultured . . . They became, they fused into, one melting-pot: Muslims and Christians, radicals and conservatives, rightists and leftists, men and women, old and young, all of them became one, all of them acting for Egypt, in order to liberate Egypt from injustice and tyranny."[2]

Qaraḍāwī's ecumenical sermon is a window into a certain political theology. Although a sermon is not a political treatise, Qaraḍāwī could not avoid invoking a vision of dual popular and theocratic sovereignty over political life. This Friday was a commemoration of the victory of the people, and Qaraḍāwī duly honors "the Egyptian spirit, the spirit that encompasses all. I hope from the people of Egypt that it sticks to this unity." Moreover, he warns the as-yet-untoppled Arab dictators that "the Arab world has changed from the inside. So, do not stand against the people. . . . It is not possible that the people shall remain silent. Dialogue with them in a real dialogue, not to patch things up, but with constructive actions that put things in their places, respect the minds of people [*al-nās*] and respect the minds of *the* people [*al-sha'b*]!"

But what is the essence of this people, and what is the source of its power? For Qaraḍāwī, the victorious multitude is a *believing* people: "This is the unity of a line of people praying. Let there be no fanaticism! We are all believers. We have to believe in God and deepen our faith. We are all Egyptians. We are all rising up against falseness. We are all angry on behalf of the Truth!" And it is a believing people that has the power to move even the divine will: "It was inevitable that Egypt be liberated, because these youth willed it, and when the youth will, their will participates in the will of God. . . . Nobody will be able to fight the divine decrees, nor to delay the day when it rises. This world has changed and the world has evolved." Without entering into practical questions of law and sovereignty over a new legal order, Qaraḍāwī expresses a political theology whereby the world is moved by a harmony of popular and divine will, a dual sovereignty according to which the people's supremacy over its governors is absolute. That popular sovereignty is constrained by a higher, divine sovereignty. But this is not only a relationship of hierarchy and restraint. It is a relationship of harmony and representation. The people not only realizes its own essence through obedience to God; it in some way represents and advances divine purposes.[3]

This book argues that this vision of popular sovereignty is not merely demagogic flattery in homiletic form, but rather reflects a genuine intellectual revolution in modern Islamic thought, from a view of politics as just guardianship and pious representation by rulers and scholars to a distinctive vision of democracy whereby a just and pious people governs itself while also representing God's instructions to humanity. This intellectual revolution involved more than political pragmatism or superficial adoption of democratic language. It consisted in a comprehensive reformulation of Islamic political philosophy, built in particular on a theological claim about mankind's status as God's vicegerent—or caliph—on earth. That reformulation involved not only reducing rulers to their proper status as agents of the people but also implicitly raising the people to the ultimate arbiters of God's law. If Islamism as a political theology represents a grand idea, one that is meant to challenge and replace others in the modern Muslim public sphere, it is this. The 2011 Arab revolutions were both a unique opportunity for this grand idea to be tested politically and, perhaps, the historical event that consigned this idea to the realm of the ideal. What was the ideal, where did it come from, and what were its theoretical conditions of possibility? If it is now a matter of history, and intellectual history at that, does this not leave Islamists with a kind of intellectual crisis as they seek to define what distinctive approach to political life Islam has to offer?

The Arab Spring and Islamist Parties

From the winter of 2010 through the spring and summer of 2011, not just Cairo, but the capitals and major cities of Tunisia, Syria, Libya, Jordan, Yemen, Morocco, and Bahrain erupted in popular demonstrations.[4] This alone was not unprecedented. But in this case the unprecedented did happen. Two of the longest ruling, and apparently most stable, rulers in the Arab Middle East were forced out of power by popular will and intransigence. In other countries of the "Arab Spring," governments successfully co-opted or suppressed nascent protest movements. In others (Libya, Syria, Yemen), the initially nonviolent protest movements descended into devastating civil wars.

Tunisia and Egypt stand out from these events for clear historical and political reasons. In both countries, mass protests and sit-ins succeeded remarkably quickly, in the face of severe state repression and considerable loss of life, in forcing the resignations of previously untouchable rulers, if not the regime and state behind those rulers. I do not wish to overemphasize the religious meaning of these revolts. In both countries, the protests were not primarily driven by the numbers and organizational power of the main Islamist movements. But the importance of Islamic discourses for the revolutions, and of the revolutions for Islamic discourses, should also not be underemphasized. Religious symbols of sacrifice and forms of solidarity were particularly important in the Egyptian context—most famously when Muslims and Christians took turns forming protective walls during prayers. Moreover, regimes were quick to deploy official religious authorities to condemn anti-regime demonstrations.[5] And in response to this, and to the requests for guidance on the part of some participants in the revolutions, pro-revolt scholars responded with their own impromptu justifications for anti-regime mobilization (as, it must be said, did some official scholars, as in the case of al-Azhar's 2011 "Wathīqa," which attempted to propose guidelines for a democratic transition[6]). A neologism even emerged for this discourse: *fiqh al-thawra*, or the "jurisprudence of revolution." Important statements in support of the demonstrations' religious legitimacy included those of the well-known Moroccan legal theorist and political activist Aḥmad al-Raysūnī,[7] the renowned Saudi Islamist scholar Salmān al-'Awda,[8] and of course Qaraḍāwī himself.[9]

Nor were the protests ideologically "secularist" or anti-Islamist.[10] Instead, they tended toward fervent declarations of popular sovereignty, most memorably through the Egyptian chant: *al-Shaʿb yurīd isqāṭ al-niẓām!* ("The People Wants [or *Wills*] the Fall of the Regime!"), and demands for "Bread, Freedom, Social Justice." They were not necessarily "liberal revolutions." Many of the youth activists harbored ideas of an open-ended politics outside of the familiar script of elections, parliaments, and representative governments.[11] This is, of course, part of what many outside of these countries found so inspiring, as well as what allowed many to see in these protests what they wished.[12] They seemed spontaneous, organized from below by networks of youth and labor activists,[13] with a prominent role for the women's movement.[14]

The meaning of the revolutions would be revealed in time through the transformation of the corrupt states they intended to topple.

Like electricity, popular power has to go somewhere. It either dissipates and leaves the prior regime in place, or helps to constitute something new. But that something new is, if not a seizure by some narrow group, often merely a form of ordinary, banal politics, even when it involves the drafting of new constitutions.[15] It is precisely the difficulty of sustaining the magical and inspiring nature of the revolutionary moment that is, above all, not so many other things—banal, petty, boring, corrupt, ordinary, tyrannical—that so often causes the disappointing crash after the high of the victory, that feeling of the "lost treasure" when everything was possible and everyone was sincere.

Thus, the heady, intoxicating, open-ended days of revolution (particularly in Egypt's Tahrir Square, which has become a synecdoche for a specific kind of politics and revolutionary moment) gave way to the disillusionment of the all-too-ordinary politics of the extraordinary. Revolutionary moments are supposed to be moments of political refounding and reconstitution. And so it was in both Tunisia and Egypt. Indeed, both countries elected directly some of the most representative and democratic constituent assemblies ever tasked with forming new constitutions. Depending on one's politics and vantage point, the transformations of the spirit of January 2011 into electorally representative constituent moments were either the fulfillment of their democratic potential or the betrayal of the revolutions.

Once the energy and passion of the multitude in the streets turned into the organization of elections to constituent assemblies the logic of representation and demographics took over.[16] Pro-democracy activists speak with much justice about the caution of Islamist leaders in joining anti-regime protests, about their willingness to negotiate during the transitions with former regime elements, and about their different priorities from those of the "revolutionaries" who brought the first victories.[17] But a democratic revolution can only argue with the numbers so far. Between 2011 and 2013, Egyptians voted in two constitutional referenda (March 19, 2011, and then December 15 and 22, 2012) elections for a new parliament (between November 28, 2011, and January 11, 2012) and a new Shūrā Council (January and February 2012), and two rounds of presidential elections (May and June 2012), each of which resulted in a victory for Islamist parties or candidates. Tunisia's experiment goes on, with political support for Islamists and others much more balanced. Since 2011, Tunisians have voted in a constituent assembly election (October 23, 2011), a parliamentary election (October 26, 2014), two rounds of presidential elections (November 23 and December 21, 2014), and local elections (May 2018), with parliamentary and presidential elections scheduled for 2019. In contrast with Egypt, the sole relevant Islamist party in Tunisia has never attained more than 41 percent of the seats in elected bodies, and thus has always shared power with ideological rivals.[18]

Whatever the origins of the revolutionary moment unleashed in January and February 2011, and to whomever credit is due, the representative character of the constituent assemblies meant that political Islamists would either be *the* or *a* dominant force in the drafting of new constitutions. To be sure, these were not radically open revolutionary moments, particularly in Egypt. The existing regime may not have stacked the assembly, but the full state apparatus continued to preside over the entire political, security, and economic situation during this period. The process in Tunisia was more open and democratic by comparison. But in neither case should we imagine a condition of radical freedom for a sovereign people to determine its own essence, as political theorists sometimes romanticize constituent politics to be.[19]

The events of July and August 2013 in Egypt, of course, are the proof of this constraint, or even that there never had been a revolution at all.[20] The violence and brutality of 'Abd al-Fattāh al-Sīsī's crackdown on all opposition after August 2013, not to mention the farcical propaganda campaign and cult of personality that emerged afterward, have almost guaranteed that 2011 will come to stand not for a wave of democratization throughout the Arab world, but for a cruel joke—much like the original "springtime of nations" (1848), or like Prague 1968, which gave us the modern tendency to brand uprisings against authoritarian regimes as "springs." Only in Tunisia (and decreasingly in Turkey) does the initial hope for a post-authoritarian democratic politics involving open and free political cooperation as well as competition between Islamist and non-Islamist parties still endure.

Having said that, part of what many found inspiring and hopeful in the events of early 2011 was the way the likelihood of an extended revolutionary moment seemed to reopen the question of what it means for a Muslim society to be ruled legitimately and to force Islamist parties to account for their visions of sovereignty and authority in the public sphere. The longer the revolutionary and constituent moment seemed to last without a single entity seizing absolute power, the more the ubiquitous and vague idea of the "civil state" spoken of by both Islamists and others[21] would have to be given concrete religious and political content. In this sense, the Arab Spring promised to bring the political back into political Islam, and Islamic political thought back into history.[22]

More substantively, there was a hope (again, still alive in Tunisia) that the rhetorical and doctrinal affirmations of constitutionalism and democracy issued by Islamist parties while out of power in the previous decades would be revealed as authentic commitments in post-revolutionary conditions. In both Egypt and Tunisia, the prerevolutionary constitutional order appeared to be the most important factor in determining the content of the postrevolutionary order, rather than the ideal ideological aspirations of the dominant parties. Even in Egypt the defunct 2012 constitution drafted by the Islamist-dominated constituent assembly was most notable for its relatively minor departure from the prerevolutionary text.[23] The constituent assemblies in both countries were formed as relatively inclusive, representative bodies, and the dominant (non-Salafi) Islamist parties in both Egypt and Tunisia have unfailingly insisted that their objective was a civil state in which the people held sovereignty. Indeed, even the Salafi parties that contested elections also endorsed in their party manifestos some version of the claim that "the people is the source of political authority."[24]

However, in the decades preceding 2011, Islamist thinkers had articulated theories of legitimate governance and ideal constitutions that reflected not just democratic commitments but a kind of dual divine and popular sovereignty.[25] These theories were represented in very diluted form in the defunct 2012 Egyptian constitution.[26] The Preamble to this constitution stated as its first principle that "the people is the source of all [political] authorities; authorities are established by, derive their legitimacy from, and are subject to the will of the people." Article 5 reinforced this principle: "Sovereignty [*al-siyāda*] belongs to the people alone and it shall exercise and protect this sovereignty, and safeguard national unity, as the source of all authorities." Longtime Muslim Brotherhood activist and Freedom and Justice Party vice-chair ʿIṣṣām al-ʿAryān (Essam el-Erian) was thus on firm ground when he pleaded that "the new constitution has delegated sovereignty [*siyāda*] to the people [despite] the existence of those who place God in opposition to the people."[27] The latter can be read as a reference perhaps to both some secularists as well as some radical Salafis. On cue, Muḥammad al-Ẓawāhirī (brother of al-Qāʿida leader Ayman al-Ẓawāhirī) denounced elections under the authority of the new constitution as putting "sovereignty in the hands of the people and not God."[28]

But at the same time ideals of divine sovereignty were enhanced in the 2012 text. Most important was Article 2, a holdover from the 1971 (1980) constitution that remained unaltered in the 2012 version (as well as in the 2013 replacement): "The principles of the Islamic *sharīʿa* are the main source of legislation." As is well known, the phrase "principles of Islamic *sharīʿa*" leaves plenty to the jurisprudential imagination and the *sharīʿa* friendliness of legislation depends thoroughly on the theory developed by the judges charged with adjudicating this.[29] Although it is a mistake to view constitutional courts as inherently prone to adopt secularizing theories of compatibility between religious and secular law,[30] the 1971 Egyptian constitution left that determination entirely in the hands of judges appointed by the autocratic head of state. However, in a new, more democratic regime, over time the identity of those judges might change, and with that their jurisprudence of *sharīʿa* compatibility.

The 2012 constitution included two new articles that seemed to expand the commitment to a pre-political sacred law. Article 4 created a role for al-Azhar that did not exist in the prior constitution: "Al-Azhar Senior Scholars are to be consulted in matters pertaining to Islamic law." More controversially, Article 219 clarified that the "principles of the Islamic *sharīʿa* include general evidence, foundational rules, legal maxims, and credible sources accepted by the Sunni legal schools." (It is not clear to me whether the verb "include" means that all of these must not be excluded from judicial consideration, or that the definition of the "principles of the Islamic *sharīʿa*" must be narrowed to these sources and that the Supreme Constitutional Court must draw from them.) This article was removed entirely from the August 2013 post-coup constitution.

There was obviously not enough time from the adoption of the new constitution to the July 3 coup to assess the effect it would have had on legislation and judicial review in any systematic way. (The debate over the Islamic bonds *(sukūk)* law, and the role of al-Azhar in amending it, was the sole instance of a debate at the legislative stage involving *sharīʿa* compatibility issues.[31]) But the 2012 constitution nonetheless can be read as a reflection of specific theory, even theology, of a hybrid conception of political and legislative sovereignty. The movement that popularized the slogan "Islam is the solution" and divine sovereignty *(ḥākimiyyat Allāh)* as the sole source of legitimacy saw itself as the true voice of popular sovereignty. That movement also saw the constitution as a site for enhancing the supremacy of divine law.

What does it mean to hold that both God and the people can be said to be "sovereign"? Imperatives of the divine and the popular, the theocratic and the democratic, often speak in different voices. Divine sovereignty is the language of transcendence and alterity. Whatever the place of human nature in knowing God and embracing His law, the Islamic conception of the divine law locates it outside of us—not as written in our hearts, but primarily written in texts and signs. God's command is addressed to humans, and their initial obligation is entirely passive: to receive, hear, submit, obey. Responsive action is in the first order a matter of trust and faithfulness.

By contrast, much of what is involved in popular sovereignty involves the absence of God. God (for Sunnis) has not designated a ruler and so Muslims have a collective duty to choose and appoint one. God's law may in theory be comprehensive, but it is silent or imprecise on countless particular questions, and so the people have to judge and act in the spaces left by that silence. If to speak of divine sovereignty is often to speak of that which is fixed and constraining, popular sovereignty often refers to the indeterminate spaces of judgment and uncertain consequences of action.

But a core thesis of my analysis is that the divine and popular elements in Islamic democratic theory are often derived from the same commitments and materials. Divine command is not just a constraint on human freedom, and human freedom is not just the absence of divine command. Rather, the foundation of Islamic democratic theory is the same as the foundation of Islamic theocratic theory. That foundation is the relationship between divine address and the divine delegation. The political theology of popular sovereignty in Islam is that the *umma* has been entrusted by God with the realization of His law on Earth. God is the principal agent and actor, and the first response of the people-as-deputy is a passive and receptive one. But the force of God dignifying mankind as His caliph is that He has deputized no one else in between God and man—no kings, no priests, no scholars. Adherence to the covenant of vicegerency is also synonymous with human virtue and perfection. But above all, the idea of the universal caliphate of mankind points beyond the mere fulfillment of the law to the popular creation of the law, the ultimate marker of sovereignty.

But this ideal leaves unresolved certain paradoxes and uncertainties. Which specific aspects or powers of sovereignty is the "people" said to enjoy? Are they fully sovereign powers, or are they constrained? What are the implications for traditional conceptions of the divine law and those agents who claim to represent it? What kind of "people" is imagined to be sovereign; what are the conditions for it to claim this authority; and how is this sovereignty represented and enacted? These are the questions addressed by the present book.

"The Caliphate of Man": Outlining the Argument

More specifically, this is a book about the invention of popular sovereignty in modern Islamic thought. My focus is almost exclusively on Sunni thought, apart from some occasional comparisons or references to Shiʿa thought. Note: This is not a book about the invention of popular sovereignty in modern Muslim societies, as that history is not simply the history of Islamic thought. Admittedly this requires selection and identification of what texts and discourses constitute the relevant genealogy. My aim here is not to be exhaustive or encyclopedic, but instead to focus closely on some important intellectual moments in the modern tradition of political Islam. This book is thus a kind of intellectual history and critique. However, I seek to be mindful of the political, historical, and institutional context in which Islamist political thought has developed. Chapter 1 thus puts Islamist political theology in the context of the political experiences of Islamist movements and the parallel constitutional and legal developments of the states they have sought to transform. Because this book, as a work of political theory rather than historiography, proceeds through close readings of a few specific thinkers, this chapter also seeks to present a synthesis of contemporary Islamic constitutional theory for which the doctrine of the caliphate of man provides the deep political-theological foundation.

The first premise of this book is that if popular sovereignty is an important commitment for modern Islamist thinkers, it required inventing. To say that it required inventing is neither to say that I am judging Islamic thought by some external standards related to democratic legitimacy (this is not a work of normative theory or critique[32]) nor that commitments to popular sovereignty or democracy are historically necessary developments. It is to say, however, that if certain thinkers find themselves compelled to argue that Islam does support some form of popular sovereignty, this is not a mere application or light repurposing of Islamic tradition prior to the nineteenth century. There are indeed resources, particularly within Sunni thought, that make certain aspects of popular sovereignty easier to accept or justify. But to the extent that we can speak about sovereignty in premodern Islamic theory and practice, it was largely a matter of a kind of power sharing between various elites or experts. Chapter 2 introduces my theoretical-conceptual framework for studying sovereignty and what I understand to be the legacies of premodern Islamic political and constitutional theory.

Certain ideas related to popular sovereignty did begin to emerge in the nineteenth century, particularly within what is sometimes referred to as the Arab "Awakening" *(al-Nahḍa)* and Young Ottoman reform movements. A few important precursors to the rise of popular sovereignty in Islam are introduced here, but I argue that the umbrella of the Ottoman caliphate overshadowed constitutional theory during this period. Indeed, the idea of the caliphate as the necessary focal point of public life and law endured at least until the 1920s (and in some cases beyond). Thinkers like Rashīd Riḍā and ʿAbd al-Razzāq al-Sanhūrī drafted treatises on the caliphate during this decade, arguing for its compatibility with limited government and the rule of law. Riḍā's text in particular is a fascinating exploration of a kind of public, deliberative *sharīʿa* that receives focus in its own right as an exploration of the sovereignty of law and the enduring rule of unelected experts and elites. Chapter 3 is devoted to this moment, showing that popular sovereignty was far from taken for granted in Islamic discourses, even during the decade when nation-states were being formed after the collapse of the Ottoman and Qajar empires. Importantly, this chapter helps us appreciate the ideological innovations that were to follow this period, particularly the reinterpretation of the Qurʾānic verses that refer to God's appointment of a "caliph on earth."

Chapter 4 turns attention away from the Mediterranean littoral to South Asia and the thought of Abu'l-Aʿlā Mawdūdī. Mawdūdī is widely regarded as the founding thinker of modern Islamism, with extraordinary influence not only in South Asia but throughout the Muslim world, including on Arab Islamist thinkers. His ideas on divine sovereignty are widely appreciated, and this chapter explores the meaning and implications of divine sovereignty in some detail. It is here that sovereignty truly becomes a problem in modern Islamic thought and the terrain of argument shifts. But Mawdūdī also plants the seed for later populist developments in Islamist thought. It is Mawdūdī who first begins to emphasize the caliphate of man as a central concept in Islamic political theory, as central, I argue, as the imperative of divine sovereignty. Although he does not refer to this as "sovereignty," and he tries to restrict the authority of the people, there is no doubt that the ground shifted with the move to thinking of politics as resting on a universal popular vicegerency. It is here that this idea fully enters the intellectual bloodstream of modern Islamic thought, with revolutionary consequences.

Sayyid Quṭb is usually regarded, along with Mawdūdī, as the arch-theorist (or propagandist) of a strict understanding of divine sovereignty and a radical anathematization of any voluntary reliance on non-Islamic sources of value or law. That is true, but this is not where his most profound contribution lies. Quṭb, of course, takes on the concepts of divine sovereignty *(ḥākimiyya)* and the universal caliphate. But he also develops in much more depth another idea found in Mawdūdī's thought, namely, that the divine law is the path to collective social happiness and emancipation. For him the divine law is designed by God with the average human self in mind and is perfectly matched to the innate human disposition *(fiṭra)*. There is no clash between moral obligation and moral psychology because God designed both in harmony.

I argue that although this is primarily a defense of the sovereignty of divine law, it is also related to the incorporation of popular sovereignty into even radical Islamist thought. The discourse around the *sharīʿa* and human nature, I suggest, is an attempt to show why Muslims ought to choose the *sharīʿa*. But even more than that, it is an attempt to bridge the alterity and heteronomy of the divine law. It is an argument that Muslims can be both free and governed under the *sharīʿa*. Instead of saying, with social contract theories, that freedom is when people give themselves a law in the right conditions, Quṭb argues in effect that in the right conditions the *sharīʿa* is the law we would give ourselves. Without arguing for popular sovereignty directly, and without ever denying God's sovereignty and lordship as the ultimate grounds of politics, I contend in Chapter 5 that Quṭb implicitly makes popular identification with the law (if not authorship of it) an important part of the law's justification.

Chapter 6 picks up from my survey in Chapter 1 of the wider body of literature on Islamic constitutional theory. But this chapter focuses in close detail on the most famous theorist of the harmony of Islam and democracy, the Tunisian intellectual and party leader Rāshid al-Ghannūshī. This chapter attempts to present and analyze what I regard as the culmination of Islamic democratic theory, which is ultimately built on the political theology of the caliphate of man. I argue that

Ghannūshī represents the theorization of a distinct form of regime type, Islamic democracy, and reveals which assumptions about moral unity and collective virtue make it possible to theorize a sovereign people governing itself while remaining committed to upholding God's ultimate sovereignty.

In Chapter 7, I turn back to the contemporary post-2011 political context. This is a context not only of violent authoritarian counterrevolution, but also Islamist co-authorship of a pluralist, democratic system that does not embody the ideals of "Islamic democracy." This is acknowledged by the embrace by Ghannūshī and his party of the label "Muslim democracy." I conclude this book by outlining some of the core concepts that characterize this post-Islamist ideology of "Muslim democracy," noting also its relative thinness in comparison to the sophisticated ideal theory of an "Islamic democracy."

But more than this, I ask whether the regime-type of an Islamic democracy must remain at the level of ideal theory. I argue that not only certain persistent oligarchic features of Muslim states make it exceedingly difficult to radically reconstitute political life through popular constituent power, but that there are also some basic contradictions between the theory of Islamic democracy and the composition of modern Muslim societies. The vision of an Islamic democracy theorized by Ghannūshī and others requires a level of moral consensus around religion that can no longer be assumed in modernity. This vision is only possible through extensive forms of coercion or long-term subject formation through education and social discipline. Instead, I suggest that the language and imaginary of sovereignty (whether divine or popular) can no longer structure an Islamic approach to political life. The future of Islamic political thought may need to be, in a deep sense, post-sovereigntist and post-statist.

THE CALIPHATE OF MAN

1

The Idea of Islamic Democracy

Islamist Movements in History

The post-2011 period was far from the first time Islamist movements had demonstrated in practice "moderation," pragmatism, or compromise. The story of Islamists engaging with democratic or merely consultative or representative forms of government is a long one, dating back to debates within the Muslim Brotherhood in the 1940s[1] and the Jamāʿat-i Islāmī after the independence of Pakistan.[2] There are vast and rich literatures on the effects of Islamist parties on political processes,[3] on the question of an Islamist electoral advantage,[4] and on how semi-authoritarian political systems affect Islamists in turn.[5]

Of course, Islamism is not just a political theory, but the sum of many social movements comprised of political parties, public intellectuals, non-governmental organizations (NGOs), militant groups, think tanks, professional associations, charities, and humanitarian organizations. All of these real-world actors display not only a considerable degree of ideological variation but also a range of political attitudes and judgments about how to act politically within the world.[6] This spectrum ranges from rejection and refusal to participate in systems regarded as "non-Islamic" to competing in elections within semi-authoritarian political regimes. Islamist movements have on occasion expressed both opposition to authoritarian regimes and a vision for a consensual, pluralist political process in cooperation with non-Islamist oppositional movements. In Tunisia, for example, a very specific precursor to the political process after 2011 was the so-called "Collectif 18 octobre pour les droits et des libertés en Tunisie," a forum for dialogue between Islamist and secular opposition groups, which resulted in a series of joint declarations on a shared commitment to gender equality, freedom of conscience, a "civil state" that nonetheless does not seek to suppress or monopolize religious expression, and other basic aspects of good governance and political freedoms.[7]

One major debate pertains to the so-called "inclusion-moderation hypothesis," which holds "that political groups and individuals may become more moderate as a result of their inclusion in pluralist political processes."[8] Major case studies for this debate include Yemen, Jordan, Morocco, Egypt, Pakistan, and Turkey, countries with limited democratic elections in which Islamist parties had competed for years.[9] Other countries, including Tunisia, have sometimes been referred to as evidence for an "exclusion-moderation hypothesis."[10] Moreover, the political behavior of Islamist groups is rarely reducible to a religious, ideological appeal. Islamist political parties, for example, often appeal to voters on the basis of local, organizational bonds of trust, social service provision, or a reputation for honesty and good governance, rather than high ideology.[11]

Alongside this empirical literature, there is a sizable literature on the doctrinal and ideological shifts within the Islamist movement.[12] Scholarly attention to the question of "Islam and democracy" has been a mainstay of writing about political Islam for decades,[13] but particularly since the 1990s, when there was an explosion of scholarly attention to this question.[14] More interesting for political theorists than the brute question of whether "Islam is compatible with democracy" are questions related to particular versions or modifications of democracy in an Islamic political context.[15] Many theorists have been interested in how the evolution of political Islam points to unique models of democracy with a "religious referent" or with a more public role for religion than recent liberal democratic theory would prefer, often referred to as a vision or ideology of "Muslim democracy" (as opposed to secular democracy or a utopian Islamist state).[16]

However, in a more or less radical rejection of an ideology-centered approach, some argue that political Islam *is* political practice. Islamism is what Islamism does and so "democratic Islamism" or "post-Islamism" ought to be descriptions of political praxis rather than political philosophy. Asef Bayat has argued that, by looking beyond theology and even ideological dogma, it was possible to observe a "post-Islamist" phase of pragmatic, pluralist Islamic political action in practice from the 1980s and 1990s, although one that did not conform to any doctrinaire liberal secularism.[17] Even without claiming a formal moderation of Islamist political doctrine, some scholars have noted that Islamist groups have a long-standing "demotic praxis,"[18] or that Islamist groups have long formed an important countervailing force against secular authoritarian states.

So, in some important ways, the Arab Spring was less a revolutionary break with a past characterized by a conflict between illegitimate authoritarian states and utopian Islamist ideologues and more a continuity with pre-2011 politics. Before 2011, regimes employed a range of strategies of co-optation and resistance to democratic accountability, and Islamist movements exhibited a variety of forms of political and social behavior and multiple registers of ideological opposition. But none of this changes the fact that the context of relatively open political competition to help define and give character to new regimes, both in the form of extended constituent moments and the founding elections that accompanied them, represents new challenges to a political movement that, for all its pragmatism and variation, is fundamentally defined by its grand moral and ideological alternative to state secularism.

This present historical moment, which is characterized most notably by the severe counterrevolutionary suppression of Islamists (Egypt, the Gulf), the transformation of Islamists into post-ideological authoritarians (Turkey), or the indefinite acquiescence to a democratic system characterized by pluralism and resilient secularism (Tunisia), is an occasion to reflect upon the origins, development, and prospects for modern Islamism as a political philosophy. This book is about the development of a particular ideal theory of a regime type distinct from both the classical Islamic condominium of authority between rulers and scholars and the modern sovereign nation-state. It is a regime type that I refer to as "Islamic democracy," at odds with a few notable alternatives within modern Islamic religious discourse, namely, a kind of "neo-Traditionalist" quietism represented by an alliance between authoritarian rulers and an official religious bureaucracy, and a radical Islamist rejection of the language of "democracy" and insistence on absolute divine sovereignty. Modern democratic Islamism is, from a political philosophical standpoint, particularly interesting because of its ideal theory of politics, and our present moment is an occasion to take stock of that vision and, perhaps, its permanent loss.

The Legacy of Modern Islamic Constitutionalism

Similarly, 2011 was hardly the first time that questions of Islamic constitutionalism had been raised in Muslim-majority countries. Quite the opposite. Much of the modern political history of Muslim states is the history of attempts to demonstrate religious legitimacy through constitution making.[19] In addition to this, efforts to realize an "Islamic state" or an Islamic legal order did not wait for Islamist political movements to take power. The idea of "political Islam" should not be restricted to social movements seeking to attain power or to those revolutionary governments brought to power by Islamist activism (Iran, Sudan, Afghanistan).[20] The goals of political Islam, above all Islamizing domestic legislation, have been co-opted by many states, including Pakistan, Egypt, Morocco, Malaysia, Indonesia, and Nigeria.[21]

The first written constitutions in Muslim countries, namely in Tunisia (1861), the Ottoman Empire (1876), and Egypt (1882), came about in the context of European imperial pressure and the desire of various local elites to form strong, centralized states capable of resisting that pressure.[22] For present purposes, it is fair to note that, unlike in the case of European revolutions in 1789, 1830, and 1848, the first constitutions in the Muslim world were the products of efforts to stabilize and strengthen existing state structures. As such, the defenses of constitutionalism and legal reform written by intellectuals during the nineteenth century were often modest, aiming mostly to defend limitations on traditional sovereign executives as compatible with the true commitments of Islam and to define the political aspects of the *sharīʿa* as whatever advanced justice and the public interest.[23]

The Persian constitutional revolution of 1906–1911 was the great exception to this and thus represents, particularly in its 1907 Supplement, the first constitution with the true hallmarks of twentieth-century Islamic constitutionalism. There, high-ranking religious authorities (Grand Ayatollahs) were arrayed on both sides of the struggle, and the polemics produced in favor of and against a written constitution are some of the most complex and sophisticated works of modern Islamic political thought. They prefigured not only the debates after the 1979 Islamic revolution in Iran but also much twentieth-century constitutional thought throughout the Muslim world.[24]

The key feature of that constitution was found in the 1907 Supplement that, after considerable conservative and clerical opposition to the first version, revised the legislative powers of the National Consultative Assembly in a new Article 2: "At no time must any legal enactment of the Sacred National Consultative Assembly . . . be at variance with the sacred rules of Islam or the laws established by His Holiness the Best of Mankind (on whom and on whose household be the Blessings of God and His Peace)."[25] In order to guarantee the *sharīʿa* compatibility of all enacted laws, Article 2 also provided for a council of religious scholars to review legislation: "It is hereby declared that it is for the learned doctors of theology (the *ʿulamāʾ*) . . . to determine whether such laws as may be proposed are or are not conformable to the rules of Islam; and it is therefore officially enacted that there shall at all times exist a committee composed of not fewer than five *mujtahids* [scholars of the highest rank] or other devout theologians, cognizant also of the requirements of the age." Once constituted by the National Assembly with the advice and consent of the scholars, this committee would be authorized to "carefully discuss and consider all matters proposed in the Assembly, and reject and repudiate, wholly or in part, any such proposal which is at variance with the Sacred Laws of Islam, so that it shall not obtain the title of legality. In such matters the decision of this ecclesiastical committee shall be followed and obeyed and this article shall continue unchanged until the appearance of His Holiness the Proof of the Age."

The Iranian constitutional experiment was short-lived, although some of its innovations were to be resurrected in the postrevolutionary constitution of the Islamic Republic of Iran.[26] However, a few universal features of modern Islamic constitutionalism (including in Sunni countries) can be observed here. First, because modern Islamic constitutional theory is a response to the development of the modern state, it begins with a commitment to a representative, consultative body with some legislative and policy-making authority. Second, what makes this Islamic constitutional theory is the commitment to some form of authority for the *sharīʿa*. Third, the authority of the *sharīʿa,* however, can range from a consultative role to outright sovereign superiority over any enacted positive law. Fourth, the meaning of the *sharīʿa* has to be defined, or some kind of body has to be given the right to define it. Fifth, although the presumption is that the custodians of the meaning and interpretation of the *sharīʿa* are the classically trained scholars of Islamic law, modern Islamic constitutional theory often divides that authority with other kinds of legal experts.

For variation on these themes, consider the various iterations of the Pakistani constitution. The 1949 "Objectives Resolution" issued at the birth of Pakistan declared that "sovereignty belongs to Allah alone; but he has delegated it to the State of Pakistan through its people for being exercised within the limits prescribed by Him as a sacred trust."[27] However, it did not provide institutionally for any guarantee of the supremacy of the *sharīʿa* over any positive law. It was the 1956 Constitution that added the clause "no law shall be enacted which is repugnant to the Injunctions of Islam as laid down in the Holy Quran and the Sunna." But at this point, no institution was created to adjudicate this. The 1980 amendments to the constitution created a Federal Shariat Court (FSC) with the powers "either of its own motion or on the petition of a citizen of Pakistan or the Federal Government or a Provincial Government, to examine and decide the question whether or not any law or provision of law is repugnant to the injunctions of Islam, as laid down in the Holy Quran and Sunnah of the Holy Prophet, hereinafter referred to as the Injunctions of Islam."[28]

But, as noted above, the mere idea of *sharīʿa* compatibility only opens up a series of more complex questions: What is meant by "the injunctions of Islam"? Who defines it? And how can the conflict between positive law and "the injunctions of Islam" be resolved? In the case of Pakistan, these questions are resolved in a number of fascinating ways. As to the composition of the FSC, it is composed of eight judges, all appointed by the president, but not more than three of whom may be traditionally trained Islamic scholars *(ʿulamāʾ)*. So, an important feature of much modern Islamic constitutional practice is that the authority to speak in the name of the divine law is not monopolized by religious scholars, and those religious scholars who are appointed are chosen by the state rather than on the basis of their own epistemic claims.

While the paradigmatic feature of Islamic constitutions is some form of "downstream" review of legislation, another important Pakistani constitutional innovation is the creation of an institution to reform legal codes to bring them into conformity with the *sharīʿa* at the legislative stage. Founded in 1962, the Council of Islamic Ideology is assigned by Article 230 of the constitution the following powers: "(a) to make recommendations to [Parliament] and the Provincial Assemblies as to the ways and means of enabling and encouraging the Muslims of Pakistan to order their lives individually and collectively in all respects in accordance with the principles and concepts of Islam as enunciated in the Holy Quran and Sunnah; (b) to advise a House, a Provincial Assembly, the President or a Governor on any question referred to the Council as to whether a proposed law is or is not repugnant to the Injunctions of Islam; (c) to make recommendations as to the measures for bringing existing laws into conformity with the Injunctions of Islam and the stages by which such measures should be brought into effect; and (d) to compile in a suitable form, for the guidance of [Parliament] and the Provincial Assemblies, such Injunctions of Islam as can be given legislative effect."[29]

Finally, consider the various constitutional reforms in Egypt in 1971, 1980, and 2012. The 1971 constitution introduced an Article 2 declaring "the principles of the Islamic *sharīʿa* are a principle source of legislation," which was amended in 1980 to read, "the principles of the Islamic *sharīʿa* are *the* principle source of legislation."[30] This language reveals at least two core questions about Islamic constitutionalism: Is the *sharīʿa* one among many sources, or the primary and sovereign source, of law? And what aspects of the "Islamic *sharīʿa*" have this status—the principles, traditional rulings, or something else? One possibility is for the constitution itself to answer these questions, as we saw with the 2012 constitution. The pre-2012 Egyptian constitution, however, assigned this interpretive task entirely to a Supreme Constitutional Court (SCC), comprised of judges appointed by the president.

Thus, we see that "Islamic constitutionalism" in Egypt represents an even further twist in the direction of ultimate "secular" (or at least state) control over the meaning of *sharīʿa*. Whether laws are constitutional in the sense of being sufficiently based on the *sharīʿa* is a question that is decided by judges trained not in al-Azhar, but in modern state universities. Accordingly, the entire question of what it means for laws to have the *sharīʿa* as their primary source is decided by judges who may have a range of political motivations, epistemic qualifications, and ethical sensibilities. Of course, this is also true about so-called "religious" authorities, whether traditionally trained scholars or "movement" activists and intellectuals. But it is nonetheless noteworthy for a theory of Islamic constitutionalism to assign the definition and adjudication of *sharīʿa* compatibility to judges with no pretense to traditional religious authority.[31]

Many constitutions throughout the Muslim world gained an increasingly "Islamic" character throughout the second half of the twentieth century, sometimes through revolution or coup (Iran, Sudan), sometimes through political pressure on the state and the state's strategic effort to co-opt religious opposition (Egypt, Pakistan, and Malaysia), and sometimes through elite bargaining after foreign occupation (Iraq, Afghanistan). In all cases, the form that "Islamic constitutionalism" takes is some combination of or variation on the above features.[32] Thus, the post-2011 constituent moments took place neither in a vacuum without political constraints from the prior regimes or the global political order, nor on a blank slate with no script for constitution making.

The Basic Structure of Late-Twentieth-Century Islamic Constitutional Theory

But during the period roughly from the 1950s to 2011, there was not only a lot of constitutional law (particularly in Egypt and Pakistan) but a voluminous discourse of constitutional theory that cumulatively created an ideal of a modern Islamic constitutional state that exists nowhere exactly in reality. This discourse takes a variety of forms and is elaborated through different genres of writing. Some influential mid-century works attempted to bring the classical theory of "religiously legitimate governance" *(siyāsa shar'iyya)* (discussed more in Chapter 2) up to date with modern concerns, the pioneering works being that of ʿAbd al-Wahhāb Khallāf (d. 1956)[33] and Muḥammad Ḍiyā al-Dīn al-Rayyis.[34] Prominent Egyptian jurist and legal scholar Aḥmad Kamāl Abū al-Majd's 1962 lectures on "constitutional jurisprudence" *(fiqh dustūrī)*[35] are not the first effort to treat Islamic constitutionalism in comparative terms or address the question of an ideal Islamic state's relationship to democracy,[36] but are nonetheless often treated in the subsequent literature as a starting point and touchstone for Islamic constitutional theory.

The concern to distance the idea of an Islamic state from associations with tyranny and totalitarianism, not only by portraying it as regulated by law and responsible to the people, but also as safeguarding "civil freedom" or "public liberties," also began fairly early.[37] By now, this literature includes dozens (if not hundreds) of scholarly monographs on Islamic constitutional jurisprudence *(fiqh dustūrī)* in a comparative framework,[38] "the principles of government" *(uṣūl al-ḥukm)* or "system of government" *(niẓām al-ḥukm)* in Islam,[39] as well as some that continue to frame the inquiry in terms of "religiously legitimate governance" *(siyāsa shar'iyya)*[40] or even the caliphate,[41] written by professional academics. One sophisticated recent work even frames the study of comparative constitutional law around the concept of constituent power.[42]

Alongside this technical academic literature on Islamic constitutional law lies the discourse developed by Islamist public intellectuals. Although Ḥassan al-Banna' himself wrote on "the system of government" in Islam,[43] and an entire chapter of this book is devoted to constitutional theory of Mawdūdī, the need for intellectuals of the Islamist movement to clarify their position on democracy and the rule of law took on particular urgency after Quṭb and the violence of certain offshoots of the Muslim Brotherhood. Since the 1970s, many Islamist thinkers have written treatises on the kind of Islamic state Islamists should be striving for. These include activist intellectuals such as Muḥammad al-Ghazālī,[44] Ḥasan al-Turābī,[45] Yūsuf al-Qaraḍāwī,[46] 'Abd al-Salām Yāsīn,[47] and Rāshid al-Ghannūshī,[48] the last of whom is one of the central subjects of this book. This set might also include treatises written by independent intellectuals sympathetic to political Islam, such as Muhammad Asad,[49] Faḥmī Huwaydī,[50] Muḥammad 'Imāra,[51] Muḥammad Salīm al-'Awwa,[52] and Ṭāriq al-Bishrī.[53] The "Draft Islamic Constitution" drawn up by al-Azhar's Academy for Islamic Research in 1978 to be made "available to any country that wishes to model itself after the Islamic *sharī'a*" also deserves mention in this context.[54] This discourse is also represented in diluted form in some of the public pamphlets, communiques, platforms, and constitutional proposals issued officially by Islamist groups like the Brotherhood[55] or the reformist party that splintered from it, known as the *Wasaṭ* (the "Middle" or "Center").[56]

This is a vast and diverse body of writing and discourse. However, it is possible to summarize some points of general consensus that together form a kind of modal modern Islamic constitutional theory.

- Governance itself *(ḥukm)* is a necessary condition for mankind, and this can be known through both reason and revelation. Whatever freedom Muslims have to extend and revoke authorization for rulers, they are not free to choose to not be governed at all.[57]
- The Islamic *umma* preexists any particular political regime or contract of rulership.[58]

- The *umma* is almost always portrayed as the "source of all political authorities" *(maṣdar al-sulutāt).*[59] Islamic constitutional theorists often refer to the "sovereignty of the people" (*siyādat al-umma* or *siyādat al-sha'b*) on the basis of it being the source of the legitimacy of all political authorities and having effective rights of appointment, supervision, and removal over the government.[60] In some cases it is stressed that it is a "*believing* society" that is the source of all authority.[61]
- Moreover, the grounding of the *umma*'s status as the source of political legitimacy on its collective status as *God's caliph,* entrusted by God with the execution of law and political power on Earth, has become essentially canonical. The doctrine of the *caliphate of man* is an almost ubiquitous trope in contemporary Islamic political and constitutional theory.[62]
- Whatever the status of a particular executive office (e.g., the caliphate, sultanate, or simply public authority [*wilāya 'āmma*] as such), the holder of the office is seen by Sunnis as a legally constrained and accountable officer or civil servant. Government is a form of contract, and the ruler is an agent of the people chosen by some form of consultation among the people or its representatives. It follows that the ruler is constrained by law and is accountable to the people (or their representatives), and subject to removal when his violation of his duties exceeds certain boundaries.[63]
- Government in general is characterized first and foremost as the application of a preexisting law, the *sharī'a.* The social contract between the ruler and the ruled is largely seen as a pact between a principal (the *umma*) and an agent (the ruler) for the latter to execute the former's divinely imposed obligation to implement divine law in the world. Thus, the law is portrayed as largely preexisting the political sphere and there to be discovered more than made, particularly through an independent judiciary.[64] In constitutional terms, since the *sharī'a* is declared to be the supreme law and the source of all legislation, there are certain ordained limits on the legislative authority of any state office or institution.[65]
- This principle also implies limitations on the sovereignty of the people itself, which is not free to violate God's law and its

moral commands. This is the most commonly cited difference between Islamic and "Western" democratic theory by thinkers who wish to assert some kind of democracy within Islam and who frequently see non-Islamic democratic theory as resting on a completely limitless (and thus amoral) popular sovereignty.[66] It is very frequent for theorists to describe sovereignty in Islamic political theory as "dual": divided between God and the people, but never the rulers, who are mere agents assigned the administration of government.[67]

- Of course, no one holds that the *sharīʿa* has legislated fixed and unalterable preexisting rules for every conceivable area of social life. The task of government is not only to apply the law that the jurists discover (*fiqh* law) but to issue policy and administrative directives in areas left over or intended to be flexible. Thus, (modern) Islamic constitutional theory explicitly anticipates a realm of lawmaking that is distinct from law derived from classical *fiqh,* including in the area of constitutional design itself. Almost always, this kind of lawmaking is framed in terms of the Qurʾānic concept of "consultation" *(shūrā).*[68]
- But such laws are not legislated without limitations. They must aim at the welfare of the *umma (maṣlaḥa ʿāmma)* and they must not violate the *sharīʿa.* Thus, a major theme in modern Islamic constitutional theory is the idea that all laws made and enforced by a state must either be compatible with the *sharīʿa* or otherwise not repugnant to it.[69]
- Modern Islamic constitutional theory stresses the participatory role of the *umma* not only in electing and appointing the government but also in whatever process is imagined for institutionalizing *shūrā* and policy-oriented lawmaking.[70]
- Finally, an important feature of modern Islamic constitutional theory is that constitutions are often used as important sites for declaring ideologically transformative goals within society. Moral goals related to the family, social solidarity, religious education, social welfare, public dress and modesty, and the ethical conduct of politics are often articulated as constitutional obligations of an Islamic state.[71]

Thus, the aspects of constitutionalism that are more or less subject to agreement in modern Sunni Islamic thought are that the people is, broadly-speaking, the source or origin of the legitimacy of political institutions; can elect and supervise political officers; and can participate in various forms of consultation and lawmaking. Similarly, it is broadly agreed that elected rulers are agents or civil servants subject to the law and limited in their authority, and that all laws and enactments are subject to some kind of *sharīʿa* review. This is what is meant when some contemporary Islamic constitutional theorists claim that the state in Islam is neither theocratic nor fully secular, but rather a "civil state."

But any scheme that is capable of garnering so much agreement across the full ideological spectrum of modern Islamic thought must be masking some significant ambiguities. The points of disagreement and debate within modern Islamic constitutional theory include the following:

- How far does the constituent authority of the *umma* extend? Is the *umma* free to create new institutions and forms of governance suitable to its time and place? Or is the specific office of the Caliphate a permanent obligation of the *sharīʿa* in principle?
- How broadly based must the election of the ruler or other representatives be? Although Sunni legal thought has always held that the caliph is an elective office (by *ikhtiyār* rather than the Shiʿa *naṣṣ*, or designation), it does not follow that participation in the election of the caliph needed to involve a wide segment of the population. Technically, the election was by the "People Who Loose and Bind" *(ahl al-ḥall wa'l-ʿaqd),* which could be an ad hoc council of notables, or even just the sitting caliph, who could "elect" his successor on the grounds that he was best placed to know what was in the *umma*'s interest. By and large, modern Islamic constitutional theory is not comfortable with limiting the election of the ruler to a limited group of "People Who Loose and Bind," but this nonetheless remains an issue of disagreement.
- Similarly, there is disagreement about the source of authority of other intermediary or representative bodies. Traditionally,

scholar-jurists and whoever constituted the People Who Loose and Bind of the time stood in between the ruler and the people, and to that extent mediated the ruler's power. But they occupied this role on their own authority, whether epistocratic (in the case of the scholars) or functional (in the case of military and other bureaucratic elites who claimed to fulfill the role of the People Who Loose and Bind), rather than by any authorization or consent of the people, and thus are often said to be the ones who represent sovereignty. It is an active point of debate whether the source of their practical political authority is only the consent and authorization of the people or whether it can be imposed on the people because of their intrinsic capacity to govern in the people's interest.

- Although all Islamic constitutional theorists make some kind of "application of the *sharīʿa*" central to the understanding of political legitimacy, there is substantial disagreement about what it means to apply the *sharīʿa,* what is timeless and what is flexible in the *sharīʿa,* and whether the *sharīʿa* is more or less identical to the classical *fiqh* tradition or is instead a living process of reinterpreting the meaning of revelation based on present circumstances *(ijtihād).* Thus, there is ambiguity as to the core constitutional question of how free political authorities are from pre-political legal and moral constraints to legislate about public matters.
- Related to this problem, there is disagreement about the meaning and institutionalization of *sharīʿa* adjudication. What is modern codified state law evaluated against for *sharīʿa*-compatibility purposes—traditional *fiqh* law as found in the compendia and summaries of the legal schools, some new direct evaluation of what the primary sources of revelation require, or some combination of the two? Are all bodies of law treated equally in terms of the requirement of *sharīʿa* compatibility? Or is there a distinction between areas of law where the *sharīʿa* is thought to speak directly, and possibly definitively, and areas of the law where the *umma* and its representatives have greater freedom to pursue the public interest *(maṣlaḥa)?*

- There is a further dimension to the question of *sharīʿa* adjudication, namely, who decides on the question of the compatibility of state law with the *sharīʿa* and what is the implication of a finding one way or the other for the bindingness and validity of law within a given state? There is significant disagreement on who holds the authority to speak in the name of the *sharīʿa* in the modern state. But more intriguing perhaps is the question of the authority of the *sharīʿa* as such. Suppose a new law is held to be in violation of *sharīʿa* principles. Does this immediately invalidate a law, or does it merely subject it to further scrutiny or revision? When other branches or authorities of government override an initial judgment of *sharīʿa* incompatibility, should this be seen as governing beyond the limits of the "*sharīʿa*," or rather might the overall dialectical process of enacting law and policy in consideration of revealed texts, traditional scholarly knowledge, and temporal considerations of the *umma*'s best interest *(maṣlaḥa)* itself be what it means to govern within the *sharīʿa?*

This, I submit, is the important intellectual context for understanding the rise of popular sovereignty in modern Islamic thought, and the invention of a distinct ideal regime type within which democracy is not only formally tolerated but also an important moral commitment. But in order to understand this intellectual revolution, it is necessary to step back briefly and appraise how it emerged from a distinct Islamic tradition of thought on power, law, and representation.

2

The Question of Sovereignty in Classical Islamic Political Thought

Imagine a king than whose sovereignty no more perfect sovereignty can be conceived. He rules either by right of his own conquest and will or by irrevocable divine delegation. He owes his rule to no actual or fictive delegation of authority from any more original source of authority. No command has the force of the law unless it issues from his will. To be law, a command only has to accord with his will or pleasure; there is no requirement for it to harmonize with or answer to any higher natural, divine, or customary law. All offices of state, including judicial ones, derive their legitimacy from his creation and appointment. Any uncertainty in the interpretation or adjudication of his laws, including arbitrating apparent conflicts between laws, is ultimately resolved by him alone. All powers to enforce law receive their legitimacy from his appointment and authorization alone. Finally, he is entitled to order exceptions to the enforcement of specific laws or the suspension of an entire normally functioning legal system. His use or authorization of violence is not bound even by his own prior commands or promises.

This brief illustration is meant to do two things. First, I would like to identify a core, if flexible, meaning to the concept of sovereignty in political theory. I use the term "sovereignty" to refer to the following problems in the theoretical study of politics: *constituent authority,* or the original source of legitimate government and the power to authorize or constitute specific regimes of governance;[1] *ultimate lawmaking authority,* both in the preceding sense of the power to constitute and authorize regimes of governance but also the ultimate authority to give law within a constituted regime of government;[2] *ultimate interpretive or adjudicative authority,* because to enforce sovereign command one must know what is being commanded;[3] and *supreme legitimate coercive power.*[4] To these powers, we might also add dimensions of sovereignty implied by the Schmittian concept of the exception and extra-legal violence: the suspension of the entire legal order of a regime (without attempting a revolutionary transformation of its legal foundation) and decisions about the boundary between law (or civil society) and war (or the state of nature) in relation both to other communities and to individuals within the political community.[5] All of these extensions of the concept of sovereignty are meant to admit inclusion of a variety of answers as to their location or possession: the people, the king, God, the Pope, the party, parliament, and so on.

Second, although this work devotes considerable attention to the question of constituent power and takes the so-called sovereignty-government distinction seriously, I think it is clear that certain powers of government clearly fall under the proper understanding of sovereignty.[6] Although it might be coherent to refer to an agent (a king or a people) as "sovereign" if they only have the authority to create and give legitimacy to a political regime, and leave ordinary government to institutions and offices that derive their authority from that principal's sovereignty, it is also coherent to point out that a purer and more complete form of sovereignty would be that in which the most important powers of government (legislation, adjudication, coercion) are gathered into the same hands.

The preceding paragraphs are only intended to fix ideas by identifying a generic list of powers and claims that tend to characterize struggles over sovereignty. In the rest of this chapter, I adapt this scheme based on certain distinct features of the classical Islamic constitutional and juridical tradition. My aim here is to identify both a more or less common Islamic constitutional tradition and also the distinct tensions, problems, and sources of crisis inherent to that tradition. Not only are modern debates on sovereignty informed by this tradition, but we can also track crucial modern moves and innovations only with knowledge of the contours of this inherited legacy.

Sulṭān and Scholar: Introducing the Dualism of Classical Islamic Constitutionalism

In this section, I wish to give an account of what is common and what is unique in the way Islamic discourses tend to treat these powers. For Islamic thought is not only unique in still preserving an active theocratic impulse, but also in the particular forms that this impulse does, and doesn't, take. I suggest that three properties in particular are the most important. The first two are the most familiar. Islamic legal and political thought tends to refer to a positive revealed law that precedes and constrains politics, as opposed to a more abstract "natural law" that often haunts theories of sovereignty in Christian and post-Christian political thought. But second, there is no agreed-on institution or agent (a king, a pope, a church) that speaks authoritatively in the name of that law. However, a third distinguishing feature complicates the picture even further: premodern theories of legitimate governance in Islam tend to be dualist in that they recognized not only two kinds or sources of political power but also two forms and rationales of law.

The problem of sovereignty in Islam begins with the question of the rule of the divine law. But what does that question ask exactly? The idea that only God has the right to command and create laws does not result in an order in which the divine law rules in an unmediated, self-interpreting, self-enforcing way. It does not even result in an order in which all commands or edicts are justified as applications of norms derived from revelatory texts. And yet the notion that there are legal orders that strive to uphold divine sovereignty and those that do not remains. In order to pose the right questions, I submit that we must begin before a singular, monistic use of "sovereignty" became the prime ideological litmus test in Islamic discourses.[7] What follows is a brief conceptual introduction to legal and political authority up to the nineteenth century (and in some cases well beyond).

Before the consolidation of the modern, sovereign state in Islamic countries, legal-political arrangements in both Shiʿa and Sunni regimes can be characterized as "dualist" in the following way. Governance begins with the rule of the divine law, the *sharīʿa*. The custodians of the divine law were not priests or an organized church, but scholars. They administered courts in the name of their own epistemic authority, and the law enforced by courts was drawn from the scholars' tradition of interpretation, which was almost entirely outside the authority of the executive. It is true that sultans reserved the power not only to execute that law but also to adjudicate its application in the name of public welfare or expediency. But they would never claim to be the ultimate source of the *sharīʿa*'s authority.

The scholars were collectively the "heirs of the prophets" in their possession of religious and legal knowledge.[8] In some accounts this was taken to its logical conclusion. If authority in Islam was only authorized to protect the worldly and otherworldly interests of the Muslim *umma*, those interests were known primarily through the law, and if the scholars were the custodians of the law, then the rulers derived their authority from the approval of the scholars. In the words of one important scholar from the post-ʿAbbasid and pre-Ottoman period (Ibn Qayyim al-Jawziyya, d. 1350): "Properly speaking the rulers are obeyed [only to the extent] that their commands are consistent with the religious sciences. Hence, the duty to obey them derives from the duty to obey the jurists. Obedience is due only in what is good [*maʿrūf*], and what is required by the religious sciences. Since the duty to obey the jurists is derived from the duty to obey the Prophet, then the duty to obey the rulers is derived from the duty to obey the jurists. Furthermore, since Islam is protected and upheld by the rulers and the jurists alike, this means that the laity must follow these two."[9] This even appears in some treatments of fundamental creed: "Obedience to the leaders of the Muslims [is obligatory] whether the holders of authority or their scholars."[10]

However, with almost no exception in Islamic history,[11] scholars did not rule directly in the sense of holding coercive power. They participated in a kind of power-sharing agreement with executive rulers. During some periods of Islamic history, this worldly, coercive power *(sulṭa)* was represented and fully executed by someone claiming the office of the caliphate. During other periods (most notably, the ʿAbbāsid era from the tenth century to the Mongol conquest, and then in Cairo during the Mamlūk period), worldly power was fictitiously delegated by the caliph to a sultan with actual executive and coercive power. But in most times and places, Muslims were ruled by "mere" sultans (kings, shahs, beys, khans, etc.), and there followed juridical theories that explained why their coercive authority was just as valid and obedience-worthy (if not as exalted) as those of caliphs.[12]

Worldly *sulṭa* (power or authority), however, represented not only executive, coercive force but also a distinct kind of legislative and judicial power. Beyond the letter of what the religious law can prescribe or legislate with any specificity lies the entire realm of public order, administration, and welfare. The ruler is not only required to hear grievances against his own policies and underlings *(maẓālim)* but is entitled to issue commands in administrative and other policy matters. The ruler's discretionary authority (often referred to simply as "*siyāsa*") might be compared to the "royal prerogative." The sultan's legislative sovereignty here is constrained but also purer than that of the scholars. He is, of course, a unitary actor: law issues from his own will or judgment, and the power of execution is united with the power of command.[13]

This realm of discretionary "*siyāsa*" law was traditionally uncodified and ad hoc. (In Persia, the uncodified, discretionary law of the Shahs tended to be referred to as *ʿurf*, or "custom."[14]) But that changed in the fifteenth century under the Ottomans, who inaugurated the tradition of promulgating codes (*qānūn;* Turkish: *kānūn*) in the name of the *will (irāde)* of the sultan.[15] Most rulers in premodern Muslim states could be referred to as sovereign in a number of ways: They held exclusive coercive authority; they were seen as the font of the legitimacy of all delegated offices, especially judges; they held discretionary power over war and peace, life and death; they intervened in the application of the *sharīʿa* on a discretionary basis on grounds of *raison d'état;* they claimed (particularly in their caliphal moments) the right to final adjudication of intra-*sharīʿa* legal disputes;[16] and their person was exalted and many charismatic tropes were associated with them. But in addition to all of these, Ottoman rulers claimed a kind of legislative authority completely independent from any source other than their own will and judgment, even if *in practice* the sultanic *kānūn* and the jurists' *fiqh* were not always greatly at odds or if the sultan attempted to formulate law in harmony with the *sharīʿa*.[17]

If the scholars were the "heirs of the prophets," the sultan was the "shadow of God on Earth,"[18] or possibly the "caliph of the Messenger of God." But a good Hobbesian would not regard even the Ottoman caliph-sultan as fully sovereign. Not only did he not seek to restrict the freedom of his subjects to argue about religious truth or the requirements of justice in public, but his legislative pretensions were severely curtailed. The sultan (and here we are not limited to the Ottoman case) derived his legitimacy from the application and enforcement of a law that he did not make and could not alter.

One name for this dualistic arrangement is *al-siyāsa al-sharʿiyya*. Literally meaning "religiously legitimate governance" or "governance in accord with the *sharīʿa*," the term refers to the authorization of discretionary public policy exercised by public authorities beyond the letter of the *sharīʿa*.[19] This is partly a division of labor. Most areas of social and economic life are in the hands of jurists who derive their legitimacy from their administration of the *sharīʿa*. Their authority is moral and epistemic, and derived not from popular or even sultanic authorization but from the general moral obligation to "Obey God and obey the Messenger and those in authority among you" (Q. 4:59; *The Study Quran*[20]). On this view, the scholars are at least part of what is meant by the "powers that be" appointed as God's and the Prophet's lieutenants on Earth.

However, they in turn recognized the right and obligation of the holders of coercive power to craft and enforce policies in many areas in order to preserve the welfare *(maṣlaḥa)* of the people. Handling public order and security, currency policy, food and water supplies, discipline within the ranks of the state itself, policies toward enemies, and the enforcement of justice, to name just the most obvious, was to be conducted without direct supervision by the scholars.[21] However, this was in theory subject to two caveats: policies beyond the letter of the divine law are only authorized if they advance the public interest, and in principle even this *siyāsa* law *(qānūn)* is supposed to be harmonious with the *sharīʿa*. Insofar as the scholars retained the prerogative of vetoing a sultanic edict or policy on *sharīʿa* grounds, there is a sense in which they made a claim to ultimate legislative sovereignty. In theory, sultanic *siyāsa* law could be said to be in force at their sufferance, but the *sharīʿa* could never be said to be an indulgence or prerogative of the sultan.

The Fault Lines of Sovereignty in Classical Islam

On my reading of classical Islamic legal and political theory, the problem of sovereignty in Islam is more complex than in a legally unitary system and involves at least the following distinct questions.

1. *The scope of constituent authority:* Are specific offices and institutions seen as ordained by God, thus locating all constituent authority in the interpretation of divine law, or are powers to create and authorize new institutions undetermined by revelation?
2. *The exercise of legitimate political authority:* How is the right to occupy and exercise the supreme offices of authority acquired? Are public offices (especially the supreme one of the Imamate or caliphate) strictly elected or appointed offices, or can they be acquired by force or claims to divine right? When they are seen as elected or appointed offices, to whom does the authority to elect or appoint fall? What is the foundation of that authority? How is supreme coercive authority lost? Who is entitled to make this judgment and authorize resistance or rebellion?
3. *Legislative Authority 1:* Who holds the right to represent and execute God's law *(sharīʿa)* in political life? Is there a difference between the right to speak in the name of the divine law (engage publicly in interpretation) and the right for those interpretations of God's law to be regarded as authoritative and enforced?
4. *Legislative Authority 2:* Who holds the right to express, formulate, and enact temporal *(siyāsa)* law on the grounds of the welfare *(maṣlaḥa)* of the community?
5. *Adjudicative Authority 1:* Who holds the right to decide on the location of the boundary between law as the enactment of *sharīʿa*

(Legislative Authority 1) and law as the sphere of temporal policy enactments (Legislative Authority 2)?

6. *Adjudicative Authority 2/Coercive Authority:* Given the previous judgment, who holds the right to decide on the implications of judgments about the *sharīʿa* (in)compatibility of temporal policy enactments? In other words, is the right to speak in the name of the divine law the right to speak about legal sovereignty as such, or is it merely an advisory statement about one of many sources of legality? Can the very question of *sharīʿa* compatibility be suspended, thus subordinating the *sharīʿa* to judgments of expediency and public interest?
7. *Divine Violence:* Islamic law, of course, has both ordinary criminal punishments prescribed by the revelatory texts (the *ḥudūd* punishments) as well as a general authorization for public authorities to punish as they see fit for the preservation of public order and morality (the *siyāsa* or *taʿzīr* punishments). Some crimes and punishments are particularly laden symbolically as representing the very boundaries of Islam and the preservation of the Muslim community. Public apostasy, blasphemy, ostentatious denunciation of the Islamic rules of worship or morality, treason or sedition against the public order, or violent incursion from outside all strike at the heart of what it means to defend the integrity of a Muslim community both physically and morally. In a theocratic imaginary, the right to represent and enact divine sovereignty in the use of violence against enemies and traitors (apostates), that is, the right to enforce through violence the boundary between the sphere of law and civil society and the sphere of war and enmity is a salient dimension of the exercise of sovereignty. Which agents legitimately exercise this aspect of sovereign power?

Who Is Sovereign in Islam? The Traditional Answer

What is of interest for this book is not the full range of diversity and disagreement around politics produced in Islam between the seventh and nineteenth centuries, but rather what modern Muslims have received as premodern Sunni Muslim tradition. For the most part, that consists in a few sets of canonical materials, including a certain narration of the practice of the Prophet and the first caliphs. Eventually a juridical literature on the rules of government developed during the ʿAbbāsid period after the crystallization of the Sunni-Shīʿa sectarian boundaries. This is represented in particular by the figures Abū Bakr b. al-Ṭayyib al-Bāqillānī (d. 403/1013),[22] Abū Manṣūr ʿAbd al-Qāhir Ṭāhir al-Baghdādī (d. 429/1037), Abū Yaʿlā Ibn al-Farrāʾ (d. 458/1065),[23] Abū'l-Ḥasan al-Māwardī (d. 450/1058),[24] ʿAbd al-Mālik b. ʿAbd Allāh al-Juwaynī (d. 478/1085),[25] and Abū Ḥāmid al-Ghazālī (d. 505/1111).[26] After the ʿAbbāsid period, particularly under the Mamlūks, a theory of the relationship between discretionary executive authority and religious law *(al-siyāsa al-sharʿiyya)* was formulated by thinkers such as Shihāb al-Dīn al-Qarāfī (d. 684/1285), Taqī al-Dīn Ibn Taymiyya (d. 728/1328), Badr al-Dīn Muḥammad Ibn Jamāʿa (d. 733/1333), and Ibn Qayyim al-Jawziyya (d. 751/1350). The way these norms were institutionalized in premodern polities (particularly the Ottoman Empire) also informs our understanding of this constitutional tradition. In this section, I want to simply bring attention to those elements of the classical Islamic treatment of these questions that are relevant for our story.

First, much of classical Islamic political thought held that God has ordained for Muslims not only the obligation to obey the powers that be (with Q. 4:59 taking over from Romans 13:1) but also certain specific offices, particularly the caliphate. Islamic constitutional theorists from the origins of Sunnism began their investigations by asserting that the specific office of the unitary caliphate is a collective religious obligation for the Muslim community, known through reason *(ʿaql)* and certain *ḥadīth* reports, but most importantly through the consensus of the earliest Muslims. The necessity of this office is, in fact, a point of creed *(ʿaqīda)*, not only law, and so, on some accounts, denying the necessity of the caliphate might be regarded as an act of heresy, if not apostasy.[27] In short, traditional Islamic constitutional theory (or political theology) by and large recognized no scope whatsoever for any significant constituent authority on the part of any human actors, whether caliph, sultan, scholar or the *umma* at large.

Second, in addition to the necessity of the office, certain aspects of the office are held to be known by law and are thus not a matter of political judgment or negotiation. Sunni jurists from the tenth century onward more or less agreed on the conditions of eligibility for the caliphal candidate[28] and on the caliph's legally ordained duties. The point at the moment is not about how "sovereign" the caliph was, but rather about the fact that jurists held these constitutional essentials to be known through the law, the fact of which constrains in some way the freedom of the Muslim community to create and authorize new institutions.

Third, the people did not need to be directly involved in appointment to political office or in recognizing the authority of scholars to speak in the name of divine law. For Sunni Muslims, the ruler's authority is derived from the appointment and the consent of the *umma* in a sense. But in fact the people are represented directly by an amorphous group of electors known as the "People Who Loose and Bind" *(ahl al-ḥall wa'l-ʿaqd)* or the "People of Consultation" *(ahl al-shūrā).* On idealistic accounts of this scheme, the People Who Loose and Bind derive their representative authority from their religious knowledge or their proximity to the popular mood. On realist accounts, they are the elites who hold actual power and influence in a society and are thus the ones able to guarantee obedience to a new ruler.[29] It is not farfetched to say that the People Who Loose and Bind are described in Islamic constitutional theory in quasi-sovereign terms: they enjoy their right to delegate and appoint nominally in the name of the *umma*, but without any appointment by or accountability to it.

The status of these elites as guardians of the community is already realistic enough. But Sunni scholars generally had little difficulty in recognizing the legitimacy of rulers who came to power through their own force. Governance was seen in terms of its functions rather than the strict legality of its acquisition, especially after the fall of the ʿAbbāsid caliphate. Legitimacy was as legitimacy did: provide security and order, appoint judges to *sharīʿa* courts, hear grievances *(maẓālim)*, give people their rights, and provide for the common good through discretionary public policies.[30]

A sine qua non of this realist theory of executive power is that the ruler not encroach on the scholars' right to enunciate and enforce the divine law. But from where do the scholars get their authority to interpret and impose the law? Not the people. The scholars themselves were eventually able to establish that they are the referent in the Qurʾānic phrase "obey those in authority" (or at least share this status with the worldly rulers), and they stressed and circulated the *ḥadīth* report "the scholars are the heirs of the prophets." It may be the case that the scholars' authority is in a sense derived from the people insofar as it was the consensus of the *umma* that to be a community of Muslims was to be governed by God's law, and the scholars emerged organically from the people. But this is, at most, a kind of delegatory authority. The people can (in theory) choose which scholars to endorse and follow in law and custom, but they cannot do away with this arrangement entirely.

Fourth, the relationship between the authority of the rulers and that of the scholars was never definitively delineated. Beyond some very clear areas of law or policy, there are many areas that might be seen as falling either under the authority of the scholars (*fiqh* law) or under the authority of the rulers (*siyāsa* law). There is nothing definitive to be said here as this question simply points to the inherent possibility for crisis in Islamic constitutional theory. This is not only a matter of whether a substantive area of the law belongs to one legal sphere or the other; it is also a question of a contest of knowledge and authority within each legal rationality.

In constitutional theory, the ideal ruler was supposed to be one of the "people of knowledge" who held enough religious expertise to act as the final court of appeal in legal (but not creedal) questions. The ideal caliph was not quite a philosopher-king, but was definitely something of a scholar-statesman, with the virtues of character necessary for rulership (resolve, courage, self-restraint, *phronesis*), as well as the moral virtues necessary for justice (including religious knowledge up to the *ijtihād* level). So the ruler not only had his own sphere in which he could legislate or make policy, but in theory he also had a role to play in the administration, interpretation, and adjudication of the *sharīʿa*.[31] By all accounts, though, this was a limited authority. He was a jurist of final resort, not a sovereign legislator, and the claim was always that the sultan's authority to interfere in the *sharīʿa* in this way was itself derived from the *sharīʿa*.

But his own sphere of law (*siyāsa* law) was also not immune from interference by the scholars. The *siyāsa* law may derive solely from the sultan's will or judgment, but in principle it is not unlimited or irreproachable, as it is subject to the two constraints that it advance the general welfare *(maṣlaḥa)* of the Muslim community and that it not violate the *sharīʿa*. Consultation on *maṣlaḥa* is open to any person with the kind of knowledge necessary for this judgment. But judgment of *sharīʿa* (in)compatibility is the domain of the scholars. In principle, this judgment might be a prior check on the issuance of a command, edict, or code, and thus we might say that the sultan's legislative authority is already shared with the scholars. Alternatively, judgment of *sharīʿa* (in) compatibility might occur after the fact, resulting not in a conflict over legislative authority, but over moral legitimacy or over adjudicative authority.

Historically speaking, the relationship between the scholars and sultan is more one of cooperation than conflict. Ottoman religious scholars expended great efforts not only on guarding their own autonomy but also on reforming the *kanun* law and harmonizing it with Ḥanafī legal doctrine, with the full endorsement of the sultan.[32] But the fact remains that the tradition and convention of cooperation between the class of scholars and the class of sultans does not mean that there is no latent possibility for conflict over the right to determine legal authority over a particular sphere. We can observe the existence of a principle that executive action should be constrained by the *sharīʿa* and that the scholars are the ones entitled to make that judgment. This is a principle with the capacity to generate a genuine constitutional dilemma once Muslims prioritized the regulation of political power through written constitutions. It is a statement of latent scholarly sovereignty if a *sharīʿa* violation is always capable of imposing a legal impediment to executive action. At the same time, the scholars themselves never exercised coercive authority and never sought to deprive the executive of his authority to contribute to the formation of legal norms in both spheres.

This is, in fact, a deeper question of the very meaning of the *sharīʿa*. What does it mean to say that a law is repugnant to the *sharīʿa?* On some accounts of *siyāsa sharʿiyya,* the rationales of power and prerogative are themselves values internal to the *sharīʿa*. The public interest *(maṣlaḥa)* and necessity *(ḍarūra)*, the core rationales of political judgment, are precisely concepts employed by Islamic legal theory.[33] Sometimes considerations of utility or public interest in the law are routine applications of rules that modify other rules. Other times they are permissible applications of judicial judgment or discretion in particular cases.

But such interventions in the normal functioning of Islamic legal norms is not only the domain of the scholar or judge. Insofar as the primary function of the ruler is to execute the divine law, it is also the responsibility of the ruler to exercise discretion and prerogative. The ruler has the right (indeed, obligation) to make judgments about social facts and conditions that bear on the justice, prudence, or expediency of applying legal norms provided by the scholars.

These judgments are in a way both inside and outside of "the *sharīʿa*." They are inside in the sense that the scholars approve of this discretion and regard such caliphal prerogative as called for by the divine law. Some particular cases may also be incorporated into the normal rules of *fiqh* as a standard exception or sub-rule, like the case of killing human shields as an undesired double effect or suspending pilgrimage during a public health or security crisis. But they are in a sense outside of the *sharīʿa* in that judgments of justice, prudence, or expediency are unpredictable, irregular—and ubiquitous. Such judgments could be brought to bear on *any* case or circumstance. Who judges that they, in *this* case, do not warrant replacement of the normal rule?

Now the question is less whether the *sharīʿa* can suffer rules or policies made in the name of expediency or public policy, but rather whether the application of the "norm" (*fiqh* rules) is in fact always at the mercy of judgments of the immediate public interest. We have here a twist on the Schmittian "deciding on the exception": one aspect of sovereignty in Islam is the power to "decide to suspend the *problem* of *sharīʿa* incompatibility," for certainly *sharīʿa* compatibility is one dimension of legality in an Islamic legal order (although now we see that it is not the only one). One register in which sovereignty might speak in that legal order is not only to ignore or neglect the *sharīʿa* (that is common), but to pronounce the right to judge or command purely on the basis of political judgment, regardless of *sharīʿa* incompatibility.

Again, all we can say here is that this is a deep, unresolved problem in Islamic constitutional theory. A judgment that an act or policy justified on grounds of expediency or welfare is violative of the *sharīʿa* is just a judgment rather than a fact in the world. Someone has to decide how weighty that judgment is, all things considered, even conceding the point that the policy enactment is *sharīʿa* violative. Surely whoever decides on that (whether worldly ruler or religious scholar) is exercising a profoundly important aspect of sovereignty in an Islamic legal order. In practice, the weight of evidence suggests that this aspect of sovereignty belonged to the sultan. After all, he commanded coercive force (that's what *sulṭa* means), and crises of legitimacy are habitually decided in the favor of the sword.

But the problem that I am identifying is thus less a key to understanding historical constitutional crises and more an argument about how to read Islamic political and constitutional theory. Is Islamic governance ultimately "*maṣlaḥa* all the way down" in the sense that interpretations of the *sharīʿa* will always be advisory or applied at the discretion of sovereign power after all considerations of utility, prudence, and expedience have been weighed? And if so, is there no such thing as a law or command being "outside the *sharīʿa*" as long as it is made by a legitimate official on the basis of utility, prudence, or expediency? Alternatively, must an Islamic political order have some way of subordinating utility, prudence, and expediency to morality and the divine law, and how is this institutionalized as actual sovereign power? To foreshadow a later argument, there is a third possibility: that the conceptual and practical distinction between utility, prudence, and expedience, on the one hand, and "*sharīʿa*," on the other, is collapsed and dissolved. In its place is a kind of unitary, public, deliberative lawmaking where the "applied *sharīʿa*" is what emerges from popular deliberation about all of those rationales together.

The Sleeping *Umma*

Notably, the "people" figure very modestly in this tradition. In the broadest sense, Sunnism is the following of "the Prophet's example and the community *(al-jamāʿa),*" and in a very broad sense the Caliph derives his authority from "election" rather than divine designation. But the consent of the people to a legitimate ruler is expected. If the ruler fulfills the conditions of eligibility for the office and performs the basic tasks expected of him, he has a right to the people's loyalty, obedience, and support, particularly after the pledge of allegiance to the ruler by the close elite of the polity (the so-called *bayʿa khāṣṣa*). The only other agent or body diluting the sovereignty of the sultan and the scholars was the amorphous People Who Loose and Bind. In principle, certain elites who stood between the ruler and the people had powers of appointment, removal, and consultation. But the assumption seemed to be that this was less an aspirational body than a factual one: it will be known in any given situation which people have sufficient power or influence to supervise the succession to power. But they derived this "constitutional" role from their actual power and influence, not from their designation by the people or their ideal qualifications. Thus, if the people is to be seen as sovereign in any way in modern Islamic thought, that will have to be argued for on the basis of resources that were never used in that way.

This is not to say that "the people" itself is an invented concept, including in a political sense. The "*umma*" of believers is a subject of address in the Qurʾān itself and is charged not only with believing in the revelation brought by Muḥammad and submitting to his (and, of course, God's) authority, but with certain kinds of action in the world. Consider, for example, Q. 3:110: "You are the best community brought forth unto mankind, enjoining right, forbidding wrong, and believing in God" *(The Study Quran).* In a nontrivial sense, the idea of collective "commanding the right and forbidding the wrong"[34] is the foundation of all Islamic political thought insofar as all political authority is justified as the discharging of this obligation. It also explains some of the important features of Islamic public authority: it does not exist merely to restrain the worse behaviors of a fallen humanity and thus to secure the minimal goods of this world, but also to bring about morally good aims and suppress evil.

The *umma* is exhorted to act collectively in more specific ways as well, most notoriously in matters of war and peace. Q. 2:190 commands the believers to "fight in the way of God against those who fight you, but do not transgress," whereas 9:7 instructs them that "if they remain true to you, remain true to them" *(The Study Quran)*. And so, along with the Prophet individually, the believers are addressed collectively as the agents of God's power on Earth. Politically speaking, although the believers are commanded to "obey those in authority among you" (4:59), they are also described as those whose "affair being counsel among them" (42:38), and the Prophet himself is instructed to "consult them in affairs" (3:159). As we have seen, "consultation" *(shūrā)* was the language used after the death of the Prophet to treat certain caliphal appointment procedures.

The vision of an early Islamic ethos of rule by consensus and consultation remains a kind of founding myth of a lost paradise. After executive power became irremediably dynastic and patrimonial, the role of the "people" was increasingly seen in its collective memory of the Prophet's practice (eventually codified in the collections of *ḥadīth* reports). This idea of the Prophet's teaching persisting after his death in the collective memory and knowledge of the community provided the basis of Sunni identity once it crystallized.[35] This was also the source of authority for communal consensus *(ijmāʿ)* as a "source of the law." If no single successor of the Prophet (ruler or scholar) could be considered as infallible for Sunnis, certainty was to be found in the collective agreement of the community. This principle had a Prophetic foundation (famously, "my community will not agree on an error"), but might be thought to resemble also Aristotelian and Condorcetian arguments for the epistemic advantages of larger groups.

But once law became professionalized, the authority of the community was reduced to a largely retrospective status. It is then possible to speak about the "dualist" distribution of authority between rulers and scholars that this chapter outlines. There may have been exceptions that proved this rule. For example, Ovamir Anjum has recently argued that the Syrian Ḥanbalī jurist and theologian Ibn Taymiyya (d. 1328) was not only crucial for the synthesis of political judgment and *sharīʿa* legitimacy (portrayed earlier in this chapter) but for resurrecting a community-centered vision of politics and *sharīʿa*. On Anjum's reading, Ibn Taymiyya "grounded all political authority in the qur'anic arch-obligation of commanding right and forbidding wrong, an obligation that appears in the Qur'an as the mission of the entire Community. . . .

If the justification of the state is based on an inalienable mission and prerogative of the Community, the state is justified primarily as a representative of the Community." But even more radically, "if political authority is based on the practice of commanding and forbidding, the entire Community now becomes the site of political authority. It is not the Community that owes unqualified obedience and service to the Islamic state, but the state that derives its *raison d'être* from its fulfillment of the Community's mission."[36] Although even his later interpreters were to overlook some of the more radical implications of this view, it anticipates much of the invention of popular sovereignty in modernity that this book analyzes.

"I Am Placing a Caliph upon the Earth": Premodern Understandings

However, I will argue that the twentieth-century thinkers organize their argument for popular sovereignty not only around the normative example of the early Muslim community (although this is a crucial leitmotif) but also around the specific Qur'ānic notion that the people has been designated as God's vicegerent—His caliph—on Earth. I close this chapter by noting the dominant premodern interpretations of this Qur'ānic idea in order to establish the novelty of the modern popular-political repurposing of it.

The term "caliph" or "caliphs" (*khalīfa, khalā'if, khulafā'*) occurs in the Qur'ān nine times—twice in the singular and seven times in the plural, with other verses employing various verbal forms derived from the same root (most notably 24:55[37]). When used in the singular, the verses in question (Q. 2:30[38] and 38:26[39]) appear to refer to the prophets Adam and David, respectively. However, it is common for 2:30 in particular (the "Adam verse") to be read as referring collectively to all mankind, the children of Adam.[40] Although this is somewhat morally ambiguous in some of the early exegesis, with some early exegetes interpreting it to refer to humankind as replacing or succeeding the jinns, angels, and even devils on Earth,[41] it is this verse that is the most prominent proof-text for moderns seeking to formulate a political theology of popular sovereignty. When used in the plural (6:165,[42] 7:69,[43] 7:74,[44] 10:14,[45] 10:73,[46] 27:62,[47] 35:39[48]), the verses tend to refer to a particular people that has taken the place, substituted, or succeeded a previous people that perished or was deprived of God's favor because of its iniquity, disbelief, or impiety.

The terms derived from the root *kh-l-f* (translated uniformly as "vicegerent" in the recently published *Study Quran*) have been interpreted in a variety of ways. Much early exegesis of these verses places them in the context of Abrahamic salvation history: God designates certain nations on Earth (often known according to the prophet who leads them); as these nations all successively go astray and neglect the prophets God has sent to them, He destroys them and then replaces them with new peoples: their *khalā'if* or *khulafā'*. Thus, insofar as a present people is the successor of past ones, it is not *God's* vicegerent, although it may have certain divine charges as well as a general grant from God to "inherit the earth" and all that that implies by way of the cultivation of the earth and accepting it as a sacred trust.[49]

When all humans (or at least all Muslims) were taken to be God's *khulafā'*, this meant, in the first place, a universal charge to behave righteously. Wadad al-Qadi quotes a report attributed to the Caliph ʿUmar canonized in the exegetical literature: "Our Lord spoke the truth; He did not make us *khulafā'* except in order to see how [we carry on with] our deeds. Thus, show (pl.) God the goodness of your deeds by night and day, in secret and in public."[50] Insofar as it is a collective charge to obey God, it includes both rulers and ruled. But this is not sufficient to establish a more specific right of the people over their rulers.

The earliest exegetes did, however, connect these verses to political power in the general sense of those who govern or are in charge, although al-Qadi shows that the connection between the Qur'ānic *khalīfa* and the office of the Sunni caliphate was not made until the end of the Umayyad period or the beginning of ʿAbbāsid rule.[51] The notion that the status of caliph in the "Adam verse" (2:30) might refer to "God's caliph" is not attested until later exegetes, beginning with al-Ṭabarī (d. 923). Of course, it is not possible to speak about man "replacing" or "succeeding" God, and so the term had to be glossed as referring to acting as God's "deputy" in certain matters.

Medieval Sunni exegetes from the tenth to fourteenth centuries tended to connect the Qur'ānic verses more closely to the specific office of the caliphate. Ṭabarī explicitly connects the Qur'ānic idea of peoples succeeding one another "so that We might behold how you would behave" with the office of the "the supreme ruler [who] is called *khalīfa* because he replaces the one who was before him, and takes his place in the affair, and his is successor."[52] Ṭabarī partly justifies this interpretation by connecting the office of the caliphate to Adam's designation by God as "a *khalīfa* on My behalf on Earth to act on My behalf in judging between My creatures . . . this *khalīfa* was Adam and those who took his place in obeying God and judging with justice between His creatures."[53] Adam here is less the forefather of all humans than the forerunner of all universal political rulers, who thus succeed to the status as God's vicegerent, or of all prophets, who thus function as mediators between God and humans.[54] Indeed, it is humankind as Adam's offspring that is used to solve the problem of explaining how God's deputy could be responsible for "spread[ing] corruption [on the earth] and shed[ding] blood" (2:30). For Ṭabarī, the *caliphate* refers to Adam and his righteous successors in rulership, whereas spreading corruption and shedding blood refers to his offspring. He expressly rejects early claims that the caliphate refers to all the children of Adam, made by earlier scholars like al-Ḥasan al-Baṣrī (d. 728).

Ṭabarī's interpretation of the caliphate as referring to Adam and his righteous successors in rulership (including, of course, the ʿAbbāsid caliphs) was to form the template for future commentaries. The Qur'ānic *khalīfa* is taken to refer to righteous and just rulers in the prophetic tradition, including the Sunni caliphs from Abū Bakr on, by exegetes including al-Thaʿālibī (d. 1038), al-Māwardī (d. 1058) and al-Wāḥidī (d. 1076).[55] Adam and his successors in supreme rulership are thus God's caliphs, which can only be taken to mean God's vicegerents in "the establishment of His rulings *(iqāmat aḥkāmihu)* and implementation of His injunctions *(tanfīdh waṣāyāhu)*."[56] Sarra Tlili notes that "Al-Rāzī and al-Qurṭubī also state that one of the reasons God calls Adam *khalīfa* is because he 'represents *(yakhluf)* Him in ruling over the *mukallafīn* [i.e., those who are required to follow religious precepts].'"[57] Thus, insofar as it authorizes quasi-sovereign power in the implementation of divine law and justice, the vicegerency of God is an office, occupied by specific men, rather than a status enjoyed by the multitude. This is an association that was to last well into the nineteenth century, and even in the debates on the caliphate in the 1920s, despite the general universalization of the "caliphate of Adam" in exegetical literature during this period.

The later exegetes do refer to the possibility of the caliphate as the collective inheritance of nations who are charged with the dual task of establishing truth *(iqāmat al-ḥaqq)* and cultivating the Earth *(ʿimārat al-arḍ)*. But although this may refer to mankind enjoying certain of God's favors on Earth in addition to weighty obligations of obedience, it is not a basis for a claim of popular authority over rulers. The "Adam verse," once connected to the Sunni caliphate, is precisely a theological refutation of the view that "if the people in the community maintain right order and establish the truth, they would then free themselves of the necessity of appointing a caliph."[58] It is thus a firmer Qurʾānic proof-text for the office of the caliphate, buttressing the "proof" from the universal consensus of the community *(ijmāʿ)*, which dominated in earlier jurisprudence (as seen above with Māwardī).

In some philosophical and theological ethical discourses, the term *"khalīfa"* did come to refer to believers individually or collectively, but as part of a kind of theological anthropology of excellence. The tenth- and eleventh-century philosopher (and chancery official to the Buyids) wrote in his treatise on ethics (mostly inspired by Aristotelianism) that "if the rational soul realizes its own nobility and perceives its rank with respect to God, it will fulfil well its task as His deputy [*caliph*] in ordering and tending these faculties and will rise up with the help of the power bestowed on it by God to its place in His esteem and to its own level of sublimeness and honor."[59] In Abū Ḥāmid al-Ghazālī's complex ethical theory in his *Mīzān al-ʿamal* (which drew on Sufism, philosophy, theology, and law alike), he at times advanced a Platonic analogy between the human self and the city or a kingdom. But here the Qurʾānic notion of a "caliph of God" serves as his metaphor for the perfection of virtue.[60] In Ebrahim Moosa's recent formulation: "Just as the sovereignty of an earthly monarch requires the optimum functioning of all organs of government to secure justice and order, similarly, all the bodily organs must be disciplined so that the monarch of the body, namely, the spirit, may reign supreme and turn the person into a true vicegerent *(khalīfa)* of God on Earth."[61]

Similar to this is the view of one of the great synthesizers of (Greek) philosophy and orthodox Islam, al-Rāghib al-Iṣfahānī.[62] In an important work of philosophical and religious ethics, *Kitāb al-dharīʿa ilā makārim al-sharīʿa (The Path to the Noble Virtues of the Sharīʿa),* al-Rāghib attempted a kind of orthodox Islamic transformation of Aristotelian ethics. Al-Rāghib's theological anthropology and ethical doctrine is recognizably Aristotelian in form but Islamic in content. Following Aristotle, al-Rāghib seeks to identify man's purpose by identifying his unique function or activity (*fiʿl; érgon*). But whereas other Muslim philosophers writing in the Aristotelian ethical tradition continued to identify man's distinctive activity as reason-directed action, al-Rāghib identified three specific activities particular to man and thus for which man had been created: to cultivate and civilize the earth *(ʿimārat al-arḍ),* to worship God *(ʿibādat Allāh)* and to accept the vicegerency of God *(khilāfat Allāh)* on Earth.[63] Whatever its precise origin, this becomes a standard trope of Islamic thought, present, for example, in Ibn Khaldūn's (d. 1406) fourteenth-century universal history and summary of the Islamic sciences.[64]

Al-Rāghib's tripartite account of man's function—*ʿimāra, ʿibāda, khilāfa*—does not allow for cultivating and civilizing the earth to be an explanation of what being God's *khalīfa* means. Instead, we should see the vicegerency of God *(khilāfat Allāh)* as an *aspiration,* something individual humans might lay claim to at the end of their struggle for self-purification and virtue. The concept preserves its traditional reference to the worldly ruler of Muslims—the caliph—but individual self-mastery becomes the primary qualification for the political ruler: "He who cannot rule over his own soul is not suitable for ruling others."[65] Moreover, the status of God's caliph is generalized as an aspiration for all humans without being universalized as the inherent dignity or authority of all humans: "Only he who is pure of soul is suited for the vicegerency of God, because this vicegerency is the imitation of God according to man's capacity to strive for divine actions."[66]

Thus, the idea of mankind as God's vicegerent is a standard theological doctrine in Islam that was given a variety of moral and political interpretations—from specific people as successors to previous ones, to mankind's general dominion over the earth (cf. Gen. 1:26), to a notion of collective responsibility to be faithful to God lest the community lose His favor. However, it was not (to my knowledge) used as a basis for justifying the Muslim community's derivative political sovereignty over its worldly rulers and custodianship of the *sharīʿa*. Subsequent chapters of this book show precisely how this is the dominant concept for many twentieth-century Islamic political theorists, with important implications not only for the relationship between rulers and the ruled but also for the relationship between politics and the divine law.[67]

3

The Crisis of the Caliphate and the End of Classical Islamic Political Theory

The Crisis of the Caliphate

Two events in the period following the First World War can be identified as particularly important in sparking an intense debate within Islamic political theory, one political and one intellectual. The political event is the abolition of the caliphate in the name of "national sovereignty"[1] by the Turkish National Assembly on March 4, 1924 (although the Sultanate had been abolished and the last Sultan, Mehmet VI, had departed in November 1922).[2] And indeed, at least one well-known Turkish nationalist defended this national popular sovereignty on the basis of the doctrine of the caliphate of man. Ziya Gökalp, one of the primary intellectual architects of Kemalism and post-Ottoman nationalism, declared in a poem in 1922 that "God's representative (on earth) is the people. . . . Authority belongs to the people and not to the Sultan. . . . To it belongs all power—legislative, judicial and executive."[3]

The intellectual event is the 1925 publication of al-Azhar-trained scholar ʿAlī ʿAbd al-Rāziq's *al-Islām wa uṣūl al-ḥukm: Baḥth fī'l-khilāfa wa'l-ḥukuma fi'l-Islām (Islam and the Foundations of Governance: A Study of the Caliphate and Government in Islam),* which claimed that the Prophet Muḥammad had only been sent as a religious messenger to the world and did not reveal a political doctrine, and thus called for a strict removal of religious claims from political life.[4] In the 1920s, a number of works forced to justify Islam's claim to priority over the political sphere thus continued to take the form of defending the obligatoriness of the office of the caliphate. These include Rashīd Riḍā's *al-Khilāfa,*[5] the critiques of ʿAbd al-Rāziq's treatise by such *ʿulamāʾ* as Muḥammad al-Khiḍr Husayn (*Naqḍ Kitāb al-Islām wa uṣūl al-ḥukm*[6]), Muḥammad Bakhīt al-Muṭīʿī (*Ḥaqīqat al-Islām wa uṣūl al-ḥukm*[7]), and Muḥammad al-Ṭāhir bin ʿĀshūr (*Naqd ʿilmī li-kitāb al-Islām wa uṣūl al-ḥukm*[8]), as well as the great Egyptian jurist ʿAbd al-Razzāq al-Sanhūrī's French doctoral thesis on the caliphate, translated much later into Arabic.[9]

I begin with this moment, but I do not want to exaggerate its importance as the beginning of modern Islamic political thought. States in the Ottoman, Arab, and Persian spheres had been "modernizing" since the eighteenth century. Apart from (largely unsuccessful) efforts to constitutionalize state authority during nineteenth century, it is important to note the much more successful and impactful process of both codifying Islamic legal norms as well as importing foreign legal codes.[10] The best-known case of Islamic legal codification is that of the Ottoman *Mecelle* (Digest), in the area of civil law, announced in 1868 and completed in 1876. At roughly the same time, the Ottoman state adopted new legal codes in the areas of commerce (1850), criminal law (1858), commercial procedure (1861), maritime commerce (1863), and criminal procedure (1879). This process of transplanting foreign legal codes, codifying Islamic law, and expanding the authority of the ruler's *siyāsa* jurisdiction[11] is one of the primary hallmarks of the accelerated, compressed process of state modernization in the Middle East.

Constitutional theory during the period before the fall of the Ottomans arguably did not undergo the same revolution that occurred in such areas as law and legal theory, education, and administration, not to mention finance, infrastructure, medicine, and technology. The constitutions themselves (Tunisia in 1861, the Ottoman state in 1876, and Egypt in 1882) are historically important landmarks but are not great sources for studying theories of popular sovereignty. They are mostly concerned with limiting the discretionary power of the executive and are not preoccupied with questions of constituent power. It is true that the Ottoman constitution of 1876 enunciates the sovereignty of the sultan while creating a popularly elected legislative assembly. But because it was short-lived, this constitution did not allow for the basic conflict of authority between the executive, the people's representatives, and the representatives of the divine law to be tested.[12]

It is also true that some very imaginative thinkers of the nineteenth-century Young Ottoman and Arab Nahḍa (Renaissance) movements penned important and visionary works of political theory that embraced the idea of popular sovereignty. Whereas earlier figures like Rifāʿa al-Ṭahṭāwī (1801–1873),[13] Aḥmad Ibn Abī al-Ḍiyāf (Bin Ḍiyāf; 1804–1874),[14] and Khayr al-Dīn Pasha (c. 1820–1890)[15] largely justified written constitutions as necessary for good governance and justice in the classical framework of power sharing between rulers and scholars or other advisors, later thinkers, like Namık Kemal (1840–1888)[16] and ʿAbd al-Raḥmān al-Kawākibī (1855–1902),[17] explicitly endorsed the idea of popular constituent power and ongoing popular control over government as the only safeguard against tyranny. Although some scholars begin a modern genealogy of reformist or even "democratic" Islamic thought in this period,[18] this book begins in earnest with the 1920s because I am primarily concerned with the Islamist discovery of a commitment to popular sovereignty *given* their rejection of the sovereignty of modern nation-states.

What I am calling the crisis of the caliphate, coming directly in the wake of European conquest of core areas of the former Ottoman Empire, might reasonably be regarded as marking the end of one phase of Islamic modernity, a phase characterized by reform and modernization growing out of existing political structures and intellectual traditions. But this is still very much a liminal period. The thinkers discussed here (as well as the other scholars who participated in the various international conferences during this period designed to explore the possibility of refounding the caliphate) were still largely focused on premodern juridical sources of authority and had not yet fully grappled with the place that mass politics and popular participation might have in an Islamic political order. It is precisely this liminality—trying to resuscitate the caliphate with one eye on the new world of republics and nation-states—that makes it necessary for understanding the subsequent turns within Islamist ideology.

Rashīd Riḍā's Theory of the Caliphate on the Eve of Its Abolition

Muḥammad Rashīd Riḍā (1865–1935), Syrian by origin, was the most important student and collaborator of Muḥammad ʿAbduh, in whose orbit Riḍā spent much of his political and intellectual career. Riḍā was, if anything, a more rigorous and systematic expositor than ʿAbduh of the reformist legal theories associated with the school of Salafiyya modernism.[19] Riḍā's political writings go back to the late nineteenth century, when he published in the journal *al-Manār* on topics ranging from political intrigue in specific countries, from France to Yemen; to the preconditions and requirements of civilizational reform in the Muslim world; to his own understanding of the principles of law, morality, and politics in Islam.[20] A flexible, even opportunistic, thinker and activist who participated in drafting and ratifying a short-lived secular and liberal constitution for Syria in 1920,[21] the primary constant in his life was a concern for Arab-Islamic political independence and strength.[22] After the death of ʿAbduh, Riḍā gradually moved toward a more conservative, even "Wahhabi" understanding of Islam and was thus influential not only on subsequent modernists (who range from political liberals to Islamic revivalists after the founding of the Muslim Brotherhood) but also on *ḥadīth*-oriented scholars like the Syrian Naṣr al-Dīn al-Albānī.[23]

Riḍā's most elaborate and systematic work of political theory was his study of the caliphate, first serialized in *al-Manār* and then published as a book.[24] Because of the identity of the author and the centrality of the questions involved for later Muslim political thinkers, it stands out as deserving careful treatment. On my reading, this text represents an important statement of the political and intellectual imaginary of a thinker writing at a time when the authority of the traditional juridical canon was in crisis enough to need defending, but before the abolition of the caliphate, the entrenchment of postcolonial nation-states, and the emergence of mass political parties calling for a new ideological formulation of the Islamic approach to politics. The body (of the caliphate) was on the slab, and Riḍā's urgent attempts to justify its resuscitation have something to teach us about the vision of sovereignty and legitimacy available to him in the immediate postwar period. This moment thus also puts into relief the novelty of moves made shortly thereafter by political Islamists like Mawdūdī and Quṭb.

Riḍā's text is crucial both for what it does and what it doesn't contain. Riḍā evinces acute awareness of the most important dilemmas of sovereignty in an Islamic legal order. Yet he only anticipates the later Islamist concern to portray the Islamic *sharīʿa* in ways conducive to mass politics. He is also reticent about the status of the people while being aware of the need to portray the people as sovereign in some sense. Importantly, the doctrine of the caliphate of man had not yet been fully adopted and repurposed for an Islamist theory of popular sovereignty. Where Riḍā does refer to the Qurʾānic verses on God's vicegerent on Earth, this theme is not yet connected to the *umma*'s possession of original authority over its rulers.

Riḍā, in fact, opens his book by quoting two of the primary Qurʾānic verses in question: Q. 24:55[25] and 6:165.[26] The opening lines of the book follow these epigraphs:

> The Book of Truth and human history both direct us to consider the succession [*khilāfa*] of peoples, one after the other, in sovereignty and rulership [*siyāda wa ḥukm*] on the earth, and the succession [*khilāfa*] of individuals and families within peoples, and what they demonstrate in terms of ordained right [*ḥaqq mashrūʿ*] and usurped traditions. They have guided us to what belongs to God Most-High in this by way of governance and social laws, as well as revealed rules, the contract of general rulership given to certain apostles, and the promise to deputize and inherit the earth to those righteous servants. Amongst these social rules is the setting of some peoples against others in a test to reveal which of them is most upright and closest to justice and truth.[27]

There is no hint here that the Qurʾānic verses where God has appointed a caliph on earth imply collective authority over a political regime and the implementation of divine law within it.

Here I discuss Riḍā's characterization of legitimate political and legal authority in a duly-constituted Islamic caliphate around six core themes and problems: (1) the status and function of the caliph, (2) the subordination of the caliph to law, (3) the relation of the caliph's "prerogative" to the legal order, (4) the place of lawmaking within a caliphate governed by the pre-political *sharīʿa* law, (5) the nature of the *umma*'s authority and agency, and (6) the status of the amorphous representatives of the *umma,* known as the "People Who Loose and Bind" *(ahl al-ḥall wa'l-ʿaqd).* I discuss these themes in turn and then conclude this chapter with some reflections on the general crisis of the caliphate and the dilemmas of refounding a political order in a state of exception.

The World the Caliphate Makes

This text is, by and large, preoccupied with stressing the necessity and importance of the unitary (if not fully sovereign) executive authority—the caliph, or Imam—and with restoring its legal foundation after centuries of usurpation. Riḍā devotes his core chapters to proving the necessity of the caliphate (in the lead-up to its abolition by the Turkish Republic) and then recapitulating the classical juridical rules for electing, controlling, and removing the caliph. But in an age of ascendant nationalism, a fragmented *umma,* and colonial occupation, why did he hold that the office of the caliphate remained obligatory?

First, all defenses of the office of the caliphate begin with its foundation in divine law, proven in this case by the legal principle of communal consensus *(ijmāʿ).* In addition, Riḍā points to the necessity of the caliphate for fulfilling other divinely commanded obligations, on the basis of the legal maxim "that without which an obligation cannot be fulfilled is also an obligation." The caliphate is necessary because without it the *umma* cannot preserve public order, enact the ordained criminal punishments (the *ḥudūd*), and defend Muslim territory.

But most of the text is devoted to the specific political and moral circumstances of the Muslim *umma.* As a spiritual and political community, the *umma* has interests related to both worlds. A virtuous caliph represents the unitary guardianship over the *umma*'s spiritual, religious, and political interests. Without this guardianship, the protection of those interests is endangered; they may be set against each other, and the *umma* is faced with the greatest of social evils: sedition and chaos *(fitna)*. Crucially, it also follows from this that the caliph must hold actual, supreme coercive power of command, and not figure merely as a symbol of unity to be accorded honor without obedience. As Riḍā writes, "there is no meaning to calling a man the caliph of the Muslims unless he is their *imām* in religion and head of their government, making obedience to him obligatory and rebellion against him an offense that renders it permissible to shed [the rebels'] blood."[28]

It is not just the multiplicity of rulers that is the cause of moral chaos and corruption. Riḍā thinks that the only cure for these various vices, corruptions, and errors is the renewal of the true caliphate, because a legitimately elected caliph will of necessity be one with the full panoply of moral and intellectual qualifications. A caliph genuinely worthy of obedience will be one capable of generating the political unity that is the precondition for moral regeneration.[29]

But the relationship of the caliph to the *umma* as a political community is often portrayed as much in symbolic (even metaphysical) terms as in functional ones. Riḍā's appeal to the notables of the Muslim community of his day was to bring back the caliphate in fully legal form in order to "reconstitute the *umma* and its unity."[30] We should not confuse this with a more radical Hobbesian claim that the political community (commonwealth, *umma*) is only created or instituted "when a multitude of men do agree, and covenant, every one with every one, that to whatsoever man, or assembly of men, shall be given by the major part the right to present the person of them all, that is to say, to be their representative."[31] The *umma,* of course, already exists as a political community prior to any constituted regime of governance *(ḥukm),* including the caliphate. This is, indeed, why the caliphate can be lawfully constituted in a nonarbitrary way. Nonetheless, the political unity of the *umma* is represented and embodied, according to this view, in the office of the caliphate.

Riḍā writes, in a rich section on the meaning of "legislation" in a regime that exists to uphold divinely ordained law, to which I return at length below, that "the caliphate is the focal point of unity, the source of legislation [*ishtirāʿ*], the path to order, and the guarantor of the execution of rulings and laws."[32] Riḍā is insistent that the figure of the caliph is necessary for the unity of the *umma* as a political body. The *umma* exists without a caliph but is in a state of sin, or pagan ignorance, when one is not installed.[33] Such statements might be read as implying that wherever sovereignty is ultimately located (God, the law, the scholars, the caliph, the *umma*), the *unity* of this sovereignty is necessarily represented in the singularity of the office of the caliph.

The caliph's role in guaranteeing the rule of law, as Riḍā sees it, is the final piece of the argument for the necessity of this particular form of government. The focus of obedience and loyalty is, of course, the divine law itself. It is adherence to the law that defines and constitutes the *umma*. However, the law must not only be applied and enforced but also interpreted. More to the point, the boundary between the private areas of the law (where Muslims are free to follow their conscience) and the public areas of the law must be adjudicated. This is a twofold adjudication: when a matter is public and thus must be decided authoritatively, and then which of the many possible *sharīʿa* rulings will be enforced.

Riḍā thus stresses the traditional qualification, as expounded in the classical manuals of constitutional jurisprudence, that the caliph should have education in the legal sciences up to the level of an independent scholar *(mujtahid)*. He writes that although "every religious person holds himself or his conscience to account according to what he believes is right," respect for the rule of *sharīʿa* requires obedience to the ruler in matters affecting public order.[34] The caliph is thus something like an *ex officio* chief justice of a supreme court: capable not only of rendering competent constitutional decisions in their own right but also of deciding on when an issue pertains to the ordinary application of the law or when the public policy justifies overriding the law. He writes that because the caliph is duly appointed both to uphold religion and to safeguard the affairs of this world,

> obedience to him is an obligation in everything pertaining to public welfare that is not clear, established disobedience to the text of the Qurʾān or an authentic tradition, and it is not permitted to oppose him in anything related to that on the basis of independent reasoning [*ijtihād*] that contradicts his

> independent reasoning on the basis of fidelity to another authoritative religious scholar. For his reasoning in matters of public welfare has preponderance over the religious reasoning of any other when he [the Imām] is one of the people who has attained independent religious authority [*min ahl al-ijtihād*], as is required of him. For it is only allowed to follow one's own independent religious judgment, or the *fatwa* of one's heart or the comfort of one's conscience in those personal and private matters on which there is disagreement amongst the opinions of the scholars, like whether this money [acquired gain or profit] is permitted or forbidden.[35]

Riḍā, I think, imagines for the role of caliph a kind of constitutional lawyer cum chief executive (perhaps a Barack Obama figure in certain liberal imaginations). But this discussion raises directly the question of the location and extent of legislative and judicial sovereignty in Riḍā's theory. For him, the caliph's use of his own *ijtihād* in public policy matters is less a right to decide on the exception and more the normal application of his constitutional authority. Thus, for all that this treatise is about the necessity of a supreme office, occupied by a specific man with the personal qualifications to safeguard religious and mundane interests, the primary emphasis in the text is on the rule of law rather than the sovereignty of a particular office.

However, the understanding of law in this text is somewhat complex. Riḍā treats the *sharīʿa* ambiguously, both in terms of a set of rulings *(aḥkām)* located in the corpus of traditional Islamic jurisprudence and in terms of a dynamic, living process of negotiating revelatory texts, the exigencies of time and place, the tradition of derived rulings, and the deeper objectives of revelation. The rule of law in an Islamic caliphate in Riḍā's theory can mean both a set of pre-political rulings that constrain the holders of power (including the caliph) and also the promise of dynamic *ijtihād* that the caliph oversees but also breathes life into.

The Contractual, Limited Office of the Caliphate

Riḍā never fails to stress that the caliphate is not to be confused with European conceptions of divine right.[36] He is a mere agent of the people charged with enacting the law that is the patrimony of all Muslims. Even though judges, religious scholars, and caliphs claim to represent the divine law, "God did not grant them the slightest authority over doctrines or creeds, or over determining rulings. Any authority granted to any of them is purely civil [*madanī*] and was established by the Islamic revealed law. It is not permitted to any of them to claim the right to control belief, worship or engage in a mode of inquisition over any one."[37]

It is, however, far from clear that Riḍā has presented a vision of the caliph that is fully expunged of the charismatic associations that he associates with European theocracy. Remember from above that the caliph represents the *umma*'s unity, its political existence and agency, and its pursuit of both religious and worldly well-being. The *umma* is not fully complete without being led, commanded, and guided by a caliph. The caliph resolves legal disputes and judges in discretionary matters related to the *umma*'s welfare. Questioning and admonishing him may be a religious obligation, but rejecting or rebelling against him can be apostasy.

Riḍā's text does not engage these questions at any length. Instead, large sections of the text are given over to recapitulating the rulings governing the proper election of a caliph. Riḍā here draws directly on classical jurists like Māwardī (d. 1058) and Taftāzānī (d. 1390) to discuss such issues as the meaning of the caliphate, the knowledge of its necessity, the reasons for its necessity, the method of electing and deposing the caliph, his qualifications, and the rights and obligations of the caliph and the *umma*, respectively. It is worth observing in this context that although Riḍā subjects traditionalist jurists who hold to their respective schools' doctrines in law to withering critique throughout this and other works, and calls throughout for the resuscitation of lawmaking through active *ijtihād* rather than pragmatic rule-swapping *(talfīq)* within the confines of the *fiqh* tradition, he does not treat the basic constitutional structure of the caliphate as a matter of *ijtihād*. His elaboration of the caliphate (as well as, e.g., the treatment of non-Muslim People of the Book) within the *sharīʿa* is fully indebted to the traditional rules as elaborated by prestigious classical scholars and preserved by the *madhhab* tradition. Moreover, Riḍā appears to treat these areas of the divine law (the caliphate and the *dhimma* rules) as more or less fixed and permanent despite the many places (discussed below) where he suggests that virtually all areas of the law pertaining to social relations, as opposed to the worship of God, are justified by the way they advance the well-being of the *umma.*

Although Riḍā is still writing in a pre-apologetic phase (he is not compelled to show how Islam already anticipates democracy or human rights, e.g.[38]), he does proclaim at the beginning of his treatise that the "government [prescribed by Islam] is a kind of republic within which the successor of the prophet is not superior under its rules to the weakest individuals of the flock but is only the executor of the revealed law and the public opinion of the *umma,* preserving religion and worldly interests, joining ethical virtues and material benefits, leading to the universalization of human brotherhood by unifying the moral basic principles of nations."[39] The traditional canon of Islamic jurisprudence on public authority serves for Riḍā as a kind of latent constitutional tradition there for recuperation. Indeed, the caliphate is, in its legal form, a kind of (social) contract because it comes into effect through the offer and acceptance of the oath of loyalty *(bayʿa).* The traditional qualifications a caliph must fulfill,[40] the role of the *bayʿa* in authorizing his rule,[41] the qualifications of the electors,[42] the obligatory duties imposed on the ruler,[43] the obligation of the caliph to consult on matters not determined by revelation, and the right of the ruled to remove him for certain transgressions[44] all establish that the duly-appointed caliph is not an absolute ruler because he is subject to the law in how he attains his office and the scope of his authority within it.

However, this text is perhaps surprisingly uninterested in the institutional arrangements by which the rule of law in general and the supremacy of the *sharīʿa* would be preserved. By the time he was writing the essays that eventually comprised this book, the Muslim world not only had the experience of written constitutions in the Ottoman realm (including Tunisia and Egypt), not to mention the short-lived 1920 Syrian constitution that Riḍā helped draft, but also the 1906 Persian constitution, which introduced two notions that were to dominate twentieth-century Islamic constitutionalism: the idea of a *sharīʿa* compatibility clause written into a constitution and the idea of a body created to adjudicate the compliance of any positive law with the *sharīʿa.*

Riḍā's characterization of the rule of law remains more abstract (and, perhaps, traditional) than the experiences of his time required. Nonetheless, I think two themes stand out here: his treatment of the space for the caliph as executive to make discretionary judgments of public policy and his idea of how a government under the overall authority of a caliph might make new law despite its subordination to the *sharīʿa.*

The Caliph's Prerogative: Judgment and Discretion Beyond the Letter of the Law

The theory of *siyāsa sharʿiyya* ("religiously-legitimate governance") has always authorized the executive to employ a certain measure of discretion and prerogative in the making of public policy. The notion of a legitimate form of rule being measured by the extent to which a pre-political law (the *sharīʿa,* as understood by the tradition of juridical interpretation) is applied, rather than made, has always been qualified by the space left for discretionary policy making where the texts of revelation are silent or indeterminate. This is part of the space that allows for a more democratic imaginary in later Islamic political theories, on the presumption that where God has not determined something, humans are free to pursue their welfare, and that God has specifically commanded mutual consultation *(shūrā)* in government. These themes are present in Riḍā as well, but at this stage he also emphasizes the space left simply for what I am calling the "caliph's prerogative." In his terms: because most political and judicial questions are matters of judgment, even the religious scholars are obligated to obey the Imam in any command that does not violate a clear text of revelation, especially where no reference is made to creed or worship.[45]

As noted above, candidates for the caliphate and the electors themselves are supposed to possess both normative religious knowledge and practical wisdom. The tendency of the *siyāsa sharʿiyya* model is to stress the (temporary) supremacy of practical wisdom or political expertise over fidelity to textual religious knowledge, the notion being that God's community must be thriving, independent, and strong in order for the world to be safe for God's law. This has some important implications for political theory. One is that it is not always possible to anticipate the kinds of knowledge that will be required in any particular period. In moments of weakness and danger, the martial virtues may take precedence over moral ones. In times of stability and prosperity, the *umma* can afford to prioritize honesty and moral virtue. In this context, then, Riḍā notes that that when looking for the right persons to elect the caliph (more on this below), the kinds of knowledge needed by the electors can differ with the change in time and circumstances.

Another implication is that the divine law cannot be expected to anticipate with any precision the kinds of executive decisions that might be regarded as legitimate. Riḍā points to the *locus classicus* for this discussion: the actions of the second caliph ʿUmar in meting out or suspending punishments as the times required. (The classical example is ʿUmar's suspending of the *ḥadd* punishment for theft during a famine.) Riḍā sides with the view that such decisions do not set precedent for rules to be applied in the future, but only figure as examples of the kind of political *ijtihād* that can be used by the ruler in pursuit of the welfare of the community.[46]

This sounds obvious, but isn't. For one, Islamic legal theory *(uṣūl al-fiqh)* recognizes the judgments or *fatwas* of early Muslims, particularly caliphs, as an additional source of law. Moreover, there were periods at the height of Islamic theological and jurisprudential accomplishments when some of the most prestigious scholars went to great lengths to show that some of these early caliphal decisions (like setting the punishment for drinking wine) were evidence not of the caliph's prerogative, but of the capacity of Islamic legal theory to provide the right answer in all cases.[47] Between a Hobbesian or Schmittian theory of sovereign prerogative and a Dworkinian theory of a master judge ("Hercules") able to arrive at right answers, Islamic political jurisprudence contains a range of answers. Riḍā here seems to side with a view of the caliphal prerogative either as reflecting (Aristotelian) *phronesis* (the unification of a variety of kinds of knowledge and virtue around a master capacity to choose the right virtue at the right time) or as the need for a sovereign decision when the law does not yield a specific determinate ruling.

This raises at least two crucial questions: What are the limits of this space for executive discretion, and how far does this create an independent realm of politics? As to the first, Riḍā endorses the traditional views that the obligation to obey "the Imām of the House of Justice" extends up until the point where he commands clear, unequivocal disobedience to God known by a perspicuous proof-text not subject to *ijtihād*.[48] But it is not permitted to oppose him in anything pertaining to public welfare on the basis of a contradictory bit of independent reasoning by an authoritative religious scholar. The reason for this is that the caliph's reasoning in matters of public welfare preponderates over the religious reasoning of any other when he himself is one of the people of religious knowledge, as is required of him.[49]

Arguably, what is a casual point for Riḍā (that the ruler can make policy not forbidden by the texts) contains the entirety of the problem of sovereignty in Islamic constitutional theory. Revelatory texts do not speak for themselves. They must be interpreted, and someone must be authorized to do this. So, someone must decide when there is a clear textual norm at stake that might raise questions about executive authority. But more importantly, there must be a political decision about when the textual norm is strong enough to be a potential veto over a public policy. However, virtually any textually based rule is subject to considerations of equity or public interest. We have here multiple dimensions of sovereign adjudication: when a text speaks to a specific social context, what that text indicates juridically, how strong that implication is epistemically and morally, and when the textually derived ruling may or may not be superseded by a human judgment of public interest in a specific circumstance. None of these complexities and ambiguities is discussed at any length as a problem in Riḍā's text.

If we are dealing, then, with a potentially expansive realm of political judgment that is in conflict with the realm of *sharīʿa*-based norm application, who is entitled to speak in this realm? Riḍā is open to an active role by the elite People Who Loose and Bind, but his focus is still largely ruler centered. Part of the reason is precisely his commitment to the authority of the *sharīʿa* and anxiety about its neglect. He registers his concern that "abandoning acting and judging according to the *sharīʿa* in some questions or matters leads to abandoning it in others or makes it impossible [to apply] once it becomes corrupt . . . this then seeps into the thoughts, morals, habits and minds of Muslims until it results in a big change in their constitutions and personalities. The Islamic community has lost that which preserves it from deterioration." The point here, though, is that the preservation of the integrity and authority of the *sharīʿa* is less a matter of strict preservation of rulings frozen in time than the kind of flexible adaptation that "establishes for it the stages of ascent and progress, [by] developing rulings for it appropriate for each time." On his reading of Islamic history, "the kind of extrapolation and law-making that was permitted to the leaders of the Muslims" made room for flexibility in designing new rules in the areas of the laws of social relations. We know that he has a fairly ambitious notion of *ijtihād*-based lawmaking in mind in this context, because he criticizes the practice of designing new legal codes merely by patching together rulings from various legal schools, giving the examples of how Ottomans and Egyptians departed from Ḥanafī rules on marriage, divorce, and other areas in modern codification but only by uncreative, rote borrowing from other schools.[50]

Riḍā here is speaking about a kind of lawmaking that overlaps with executive prerogative in policy making and more formal legislation. I turn to his views on the space for legislating in an Islamic caliphate shortly, but a few points are worth noting here. The first is that he regards the kind of discretionary, political semi-sovereignty as primarily concentrated with the holders of authority, not the *umma* at large. But it is also worth noting that the force of the argument for elite discretion in revising and adapting traditional Islamic legal rulings is that this is what allows the divine law itself to survive and preserve its self-sufficiency. Muslims have no need to borrow or import foreign laws, Riḍā is arguing, because Islamic legal principles already allow for changing certain areas of the civil law without losing any of the benefits or virtues of being part of the divine law. His way of guaranteeing this trick is less through a specific method of legal reform or reinterpretation and more by insisting that it be performed by the virtuous, properly disposed people: the rightful holders of authority, the authorized "people of consultation," or those identified as the People Who Loose and Bind.

This points to an important aspect of what it means to speak of sovereignty in Islam: not just deciding when this or that *sharīʿa* rule is to be suspended in the name of necessity, but deciding what the question of *sharīʿa* compatibility means or when the very question as a standard of legitimacy is suspended. The guarantee of the *sharīʿa* compatibility of laws or policies enacted in public is partially who is doing the enacting: persons with thorough knowledge of the textual tradition of the divine law as well as the moral commitment to the flourishing of the *umma* as a pious community of the faithful. Religiously legitimate interpretations the law based on the exigencies of the time are interpretations enacted by the persons endowed with the right kinds of intellectual and moral virtues. But then, if almost any kind of command can be portrayed as a good-faith judgment of what is in the public interest, then what remains of the application of the *sharīʿa* as a law that exists through time separate from any particular judgment of equity or welfare?

Riḍa and What It Means to Change the Sharīʿa

The central feature of Riḍā's apologia for the preservation of the rule of the *sharīʿa* in Muslim societies is that "the renaissance of the Muslims" is said to depend not on the restoration of classical *sharīʿa* rules, but on the renewal of *ijtihād* in the *sharīʿa*.[51] For Islam to claim its rightful status as "the religion of sovereignty and power" and not further descend into its present crisis of weakness, Muslims must reclaim the use of *ijtihād* in law. "Independent *ijtihādī* knowledge is what will establish for this government and the whole world that the Islamic *sharīʿa* is the most capacious and most perfect of all the laws, and that from its sources it has prohibited all that has been established as harmful and permitted all that has been established as beneficial."[52] In the past, the practice of *ijtihād* has been suppressed or stymied by the vested interest the legal schools had in obedience to their traditional doctrines and by the fact that for so long rulers and their advisors have been ignorant of the law. But, Riḍā argues, a real Islamic government would revive *ijtihād*, and in fact the Islamic *umma* will not be able to climb out of the pit it is has fallen into without the renewal of *ijtihād*. Indeed, even the very existence of the true Imamate depends on the existence of *ijtihād*.[53]

Riḍā sees himself as responding to the canard, which some Arab secularist newspapers were circulating at the time, that "Islam does not allow humans to legislate because its *sharīʿa* is derived from the Qurʾān, in which civil and political rulings are few and limited, and the Sunna, the little of which is found there being appropriate for the state of Muslims at the beginning of Islam and not for other times, especially ours today."[54] For Riḍā, this purely scripturalist understanding of law in Islam confuses multiple categories that he insists the proper understanding of the *sharīʿa* separates: religion (as such) versus the revealed law; the basic principles of creed, wisdom, and ethics versus judicial and practical rulings; the rules of worship versus the rules of social relations, and religiosity versus adjudication.[55] As a basic rule, the former concepts in the preceding dichotomies all have the higher status in terms of signifying permanent, unchanging expressions of the human relationship to the divine. The latter are contingent upon their usefulness for human well-being in particular times and places. But crucially, the distinction is not between "religious" and "nonreligious" norms. Rather, the distinction between unchanging norms and their contingent application is something internal to religion itself.

As noted earlier, Riḍā sees many of the political decisions of the Prophet (and early caliphs) not as establishing juridical rules that would then become part of legal doctrine on the basis of precedent. Given that the Prophet was only a man and himself distinguished between revealed knowledge of religion (command) and his own opinions, "it is not possible to have fixed rulings for a system of consultation that befit all times and places. Had the Messenger set down temporary ordinances for it he would then have feared that people would take hold of what he set down solely for that era as precedential, as an element of the religion to be followed in every circumstance and in every era, even if it should be at odds with the public welfare . . . thus [the Prophet] was satisfied with God's revealed law on consultation, and with instructing the *umma* to act in accordance with it."[56] The rule that the Prophet established in his decisions as a political and military leader was one of constitutional principle. As the conditions and circumstances that affect the *umma*'s development, social composition, and welfare change, so may laws and regulations pertaining to (many) areas of social life.

But Riḍā emphasizes that even the contingent, malleable rules of social practice "are referred to as 'religion' in consideration of the fact that their existence is owed to God Almighty, and so they are binding in the spirit of submitting to His commands and prohibitions."[57] Laws derived from divine sources are flexible and useful, but they enjoy a more profound legitimacy in the eyes of the people subject to them, and so they are also superior in their capacity to engender willing, uncoerced obedience. As he writes later in the text, "Another difference between the Islamic revealed law and human legislation, the government of which is not constrained by religion . . . is that every Muslim believes that a ruling from the divine law is a divine rule and that obedience to it involves getting closer to God and will be rewarded in the afterlife, and that disobedience to it is disobedience to God and will be punished in the afterlife." This is true even if the political decision to apply one out of many possible rulings is not itself infallible, and the applied ruling does not constitute a permanent legal doctrine, as the judgment of the ruler serves to ensure that *some* just norm is applied. It remains the case that "every religious person holds himself or his conscience to account according to what he believes is right," but respect for the rule of *sharīʿa* mandates the duty to obey the ruler even if one's own personal conscience is not persuaded.[58]

Thus, there are two related errors Muslims (and others) must avoid: one, thinking that the traditional rules of jurisprudence are sacrosanct and, two, thinking that active, engaged processes of legislation on the part of humans are not part of the *sharīʿa*. But the ambiguity does not go away. Humans are not radically free to legislate even in the areas of social relations.[59] Certain aspects of social relations are said to have a properly "religious aspect," such as those rules relating to "respecting people's lives, honor and property; advising them sincerely; and forsaking sin, injustice, aggression, cheating, treachery, and invalidly appropriating the property of others." Others are said to implicate merely administration, adjudication, politics, taxation, and the waging of war in ways that do not pertain to worshipping and approaching God. But Riḍā does not elaborate with any precision how one knows whether a particular practical question belongs to the first or second category, or what methods of forming legislation each prescribes.

So the ambiguities relate both to the drawing of the line between "religious" and "administrative-policy" matters, and the methods that constrain legislation in social areas that are determined to implicate core questions of religious moral concern. What matters for Riḍā above all is that the practice of extracting or deducing rulings pertaining to public order and welfare be affirmed as a legitimate and necessary form of legislation within Islam. Even if these rulings change with time and place, there can exist no civil government without this kind of legislative enactment, no improvement in the *umma*'s level of civilization without a government that guarantees just legislation appropriate for its historical circumstances. But this does not resolve the question of what makes an enacted law or policy part of the *sharīʿa*.

Riḍā's vision of the practice of legislating at the beginning of Islam recalls less the classical *siyāsa sharʿiyya* distinction between *fiqh* rules that are fixed or certain and rules of *siyāsa* that change based on the ruler's judgment of equity or welfare, and more the vision of a "living *sharīʿa*" that is created dynamically in the interaction between the revealed text, the Imam, and his practice of consultation *(shūrā)* with expert members of the *umma*. He writes that the model was established by the Prophet, who was a "legislator on the basis of his own *ijtihād* and in consultation with the *umma*, especially the elite holders of authority, who are entrusted with the *umma*'s welfare and represent its will."[60] What is important is that Riḍā insists on this being referred to as "legislation" (both *ishtirāʿ* and *tashrīʿ*) and pertaining to the sphere of Islamic governance.

Thus, on one plausible reading of his vision, this form of consultative lawmaking collapses the distinction between *law* (divine, textually grounded) and *policy* (subjective, discretionary). That distinction arguably reserves the practice of "legislation" proper to the formal methods of Islamic jurisprudence for deriving rules, and limits the scope of human discretion to temporary exceptions to the rules. In the spirit of the modern Salafiyya reformist school, Riḍā imagines an original period before the hardening of legal doctrine, during which the boundary between law and policy was less important, or perhaps nonexistent. Texts had their force, but they did not anticipate all social problems. It was thus the norm for social problems to be addressed through the dialectic of text-*ijtihād* consultation, and this process generated *law.* This kind of "living *sharī'a*" was lost not only because the doctrines of the legal schools hardened and the jurists acquired a vested interest in monopolizing the representation of law, but also because the caliphate lost its capacity to guide, nourish, and legitimate the public process of norm generation.

The caliphate thus represents not only public Islamic power but also public Islamic reason, capable of restoring the original kind of living *sharī'a* that characterized the time of the Prophet and the earliest caliphs. This restoration of active, authoritative *ijtihād* is ultimately what seems to lie behind Riḍā's passion for the restoration of the caliphate.[61] To be sure, he primarily sees this kind of public *ijtihād* as the prerogative of the part of the caliph and elite experts. However, his discussion of the questions of consultation and legislation also includes the assertions that "legislation is delegated to the *umma.* . . . For authority in truth belongs to the *umma,* and if it were possible to ask them collectively about a matter, and they all agreed about it, then there would be no alternative to it. And it is not for the Caliph, never mind any lesser ruler, to veto their agreement, to oppose it or even to oppose their deputies and representatives from the People Who Loose and Bind."[62] What scope for popular sovereignty can a thinker like Riḍā imagine at this point in the development of modern Islamic political thought?

Latent Populism?

The metaphor of the "sleeping sovereign," based on the distinction between sovereignty and government, and according to which "a sovereign democracy need not be involved at all in the ordinary business of government [but] could simply determine who should rule on its behalf and how in general they should behave, and then retire into the shadows, just as a monarch might appoint a vizier to govern in his place before going to sleep,"[63] is a tempting one to use to describe the place of the *umma* in Riḍā's theory. He writes that "general leadership is a right of the *umma* and it is thus up to it to remove the Imam if it regards something necessitating removal"[64] and "the *umma* . . . is the one that installs [the caliph]. So the *umma* is the possessor of the right to control him and the one who creates him when it sees its own benefit in so doing. So he is a civil ruler in all aspects."[65] However, on my reading, the authority of the *umma* in Riḍā's account is both potentially stronger and also tangibly weaker than the sleeping sovereign metaphor suggests.

Certain passages, like some of those cited above, suggest that the *umma* is meant to take a more active role in actual government and legislation. Call this a theory of "latent" or "embryonic" popular legislative sovereignty. Riḍā prefers to speak about active governance or legislation in terms of the agency of the ruler and the *umma*'s elite representatives. Yet Riḍā gives no clear account of why the participatory role of the *umma* at large could not in principle be broader. Given his focus on the flexibility of most public areas of the *sharīʿa* and the role of *ijtihād* in reviving the applicability of the *sharīʿa* to new areas, his reason cannot be primarily the epistemic one that the many are necessarily unqualified to judge how the divine law should be applied to novel problems. He also does not invoke the claim that moderns are too busy with private or commercial affairs to engage in public life (although there is, naturally, much less collective memory of an active democratic past in his context). However, the notion of a more active popular role in legislation remains a mere latent possibility.

But it is also not quite true that the *umma* is assigned the same kind of sovereign status that Tuck has in mind with early modern European political theory. In those theories, a people enjoys full constituent authority. All power is in its name, and it has the freedom to create and dissolve government. Some of Riḍā's dogmatic statements affirming the popular origins of governance in the Islamic caliphate do indeed have this flavor. A representative statement comes at the beginning of *al-Khilāfa:*

> Among the basic principles [of Islam] is that authority over and command of the *umma* belongs to it itself and that its affairs are a matter of consultation within it. Its government is a type of republic within which the successor of the Prophet is not superior under its rules to the weakest individuals of governed

> but is only the executor of the revealed law and the opinion of the *umma,* preserving religion and worldly interests, joining ethical virtues and material benefits, leading to the universalization of human brotherhood by unifying the moral basic principles of nations.[66]

Throughout the text the *umma* is referred to as the source of authority *(sulṭa)* or the "rights-holder" *(ṣāḥibat al-ḥaqq)* in political affairs. But this popular authority is not fully self-originating or self-authorizing. The right of the *umma* to authorize, supervise, and remove its guardians is itself a merely "ordained right" *(ḥaqq mashrūʿ).* The *umma*'s authority over any rulers it may set up is more a charge than an act of sovereign choice. Moreover, the institutions and the rulings governing them are more or less fixed by divine revealed law (as elaborated in this very text):

> As far as civil and social governance is concerned, Islam laid down its foundation and principles, and prescribed for the *umma* that it employ judgment and discretion in this area, because it changes with the change of time and place, and it advances with advances in civilization and knowledge.[67]

The *umma* may employ judgment and discretion in authorizing government, but only on top of foundations already laid down by God.

In fact, in the one place where Riḍā refers to the notion of "popular sovereignty," he does so in order to distinguish the condition of Muslim peoples from that of Europeans. He objects to the Turkish path under Ataturk, claiming that when Ataturk decided to modernize and get rid of tyranny, he assumed that the only way to achieve this was by imitating the Europeans in separating religion from the state and establishing "*ḥākimiyyat al-milla*"—the sovereignty of the nation.[68] Riḍā's entire book is an effort to preempt this conclusion by proving that because the correct interpretation of the Islamic caliphate is as an anti-despotic, legally instituted, civil office ultimately dependent on and accountable to the authority of the Muslim *umma,* Muslims do not need to secularize their political life in order to achieve accountable and representative government.

The Constituent Authority of the People Who Loose and Bind

Where Riḍā actually tends to look for active participation in legislative sovereignty and, more importantly, for the authority to form and constitute a legitimate political order out of a state of lawlessness is in the amorphous group of People Who Loose and Bind. This is the final piece of his theory of legitimate governance in an Islamic caliphate. Although Riḍā stresses (what, as a Sunni Muslim he must) that the caliph derives his authority from the *umma* and is its agent, he is primarily interested in deriving from this less the need for broad popular participation in politics than the authority of the *umma*'s traditional representatives, the People Who Loose and Bind. It is they—particularly classically trained religious scholars—whom Riḍā imagines restoring the rule of law and virtue in a renewed Islamic caliphate. Where he mentions the authority of the *umma* in the Islamic polity, it is as much to ground its obligation to choose a ruler, bind one another to him and the community, and commit itself to religious virtue.

And yet Riḍā's views on constituent power are complex and unclear. For obvious reasons, he cannot subscribe to a Hobbesian view whereby the multitude only comes to be a body politic that can be represented when the sovereign is formed. The *umma*—not just as a body of the faithful but as a political community—always predates the formation of a particular pact of governance. There is no paradox of founding that threatens the Islamic social contract because it is not constitutively democratic. Riḍā says as much shortly after his statement about the necessity of the caliphate: if the caliphate is the effective cause of the *umma*'s actual political unity, the prior religious, creedal, and moral unity of the *umma* is the material, formal, and final cause of the unity of the caliphate.[69]

And yet at the same time he calls for the restoration of the mediating, representative body—the People Who Loose and Bind—as those who can bring about the reconstitution of the *umma* and its unity through legalizing the election of the caliph.[70] In fact, the right of the People Who Loose and Bind to represent the *umma* in restoring the rule of the *sharīʿa* and the legal office of the caliph precedes any actual political designation of them by the *umma*. They—whoever they are in practice—simply have this right and obligation. In Riḍā's words: "So we ask here: do any People Who Loose and Bind exist today in Islamic lands who can resurrect this matter? And if there is not, then who has this power and influence in actuality, or does there not exist anyone with this power? Then is it not possible for Muslims to create a system to make coercive power into true authority?"[71] Might must resolve itself into right through the subsequent legality of its actions, but right also must reveal itself through the initiative taken to represent the *umma* in restoring the caliphate.

Thus, while there is no deep paradox of democratic founding in operation here, there might be a paradox of legal self-constitution. Riḍā is against force and usurpation with regard to the caliphate, but who can lawfully constitute the electoral body that appoints the caliph, particularly among Sunnis? They must appoint themselves in an act of will that cannot itself be fully legal. We will see that this problem is solved somewhat later by "democratic" Islamists for whom the *umma* is always already sovereign in a sense.

Closing the Curtain on the Caliphate

As it happened, not long after the publications of his book, Riḍā and scholars from around the Muslim world had an opportunity in practice to solve the theoretical problem of founding a political order through legal means. The idea of addressing such questions as Muslim unity in the face of Western encroachment and the need for an authoritative voice to legitimize necessary reforms to Islamic legal doctrines emerged in various quarters in the nineteenth century.[72] At times this was instigated by the Ottomans in an effort to bolster their own claims, but more often calls to assemble a transnational group of scholars to speak in the voice of the *umma* emerged to challenge Ottoman authority. The idea of a congress as the site for the election of a new caliph emerged in certain late Ottoman-era reformist tracts (notably ʿAbd al-Raḥmān al-Kawākibī's semifictional *Umm al-Qurā* [1900]) and then during the war among certain Ottoman scholars anticipating the possible overthrow of the sitting sultan. It was also during the war that certain reform-minded scholars of the Salafiyya modernist school began to contemplate a post-Ottoman Arab caliphate to be reconstituted on consensual foundations through the agency of a pan-Islamic congress.

Immediately in the wake of the abolition of the caliphate in Istanbul and before Mecca itself was taken by Ibn Saʿūd, ending Hashimite rule in the Ḥijāz, the Sharīf Ḥusayn of Mecca had briefly claimed the title of caliph for himself. There was in fact a *shūrā* council organized in Jerusalem on March 10, 1924, to endow this claim with a consensual veneer.[73] The mostly Palestinian delegates who had been appointed by al-Ḥājj al-Amīn al-Ḥusaynī of Jerusalem as the People Who Loose and Bind on this occasion did endorse Sharīf Ḥusayn's claim to the caliphate, subject to the conditions that he govern by consultation *(shūrā),* not violate the public interest *(maṣlaḥa)* of Muslims, and not undertake any decisions with regard to the status of Palestine or the occupation of any other Muslim lands without consulting the peoples of those lands first. The prospect of a Sharifian caliphate was threatening to French interests in the region, who took various measures to prevent the acclamation of Ḥusayn from the pulpits of mosques under French Mandate control. But it was ultimately the Najdī conquest of Mecca by ʿAbd al-ʿAzīz ibn Saʿūd that put an end to the Sharīf's claims.

In the wake of this episode, the idea of a grand and inclusive international conference to appoint a new caliph had the greatest appeal for many Muslims of a pan-Islamist persuasion, particularly those who may have had reservations about the rulers who were tempted to claim the mantle of the caliphate with only local support (e.g., King Fuʾād of Egypt, who was not seen as representative to the Muslims of India and elsewhere).[74] Such plans were realized finally in Cairo in 1926 in the form of the General Islamic Congress for the Caliphate.[75] Of interest for present purposes is less the politics around the Congress than the reflections of the scholars involved on the necessity, and yet elusiveness, of a fully consensual, noncoercive, "legal" foundation for any new claim to the caliphate.

An important source for these debates are the notes preserved by Riḍā and published in his collected political writings.[76] Invitations went out in the name of the Shaykh of al-Azhar to representatives of all Muslim communities, including various Shiʿa sects and Ibāḍīs.[77] A total of 610 invitations were sent out to Muslim leaders in every country with a significant Muslim population (including Argentina and the United States), although only forty-four attended in the end. Important to note first about this effort to ground the legitimacy of a political founding moment in the inclusivity of a representative body is that this body was not charged with creating norms or institutions ex nihilo. All of the scholars involved emphasized the prior (and permanent) religious obligatoriness of the office of the caliphate in Islam and the basic rules outlining the qualifications for the office. What was at stake in terms of jurisprudential interpretation *(ijithād),* rather, were issues like the precise distinction between a future caliph's political and religious authority and the basis on which Muslims should be represented in a quasi-constituent assembly like the Caliphate Congress (e.g., on the basis of nationality, region, religious school, etc.).[78]

However, the key aim and assumption relevant to the present study is that, although the caliphate was seen as the necessary solution to the problem of Muslim disunity, prior Muslim unity around the caliphate was also seen as a necessary condition for the reinstitution of a legitimate caliphate. The scholars (commanding no armored divisions themselves) argued that it was some preexisting Muslim unity that allowed for the greatness of the caliphate in times past, rather than the coercive strength of certain dynasties being that which allowed for unitary governance under a single head. Delegates asked whether it was even possible to refound the caliphate at that time in the face of outside threats, not because it might be difficult to unite around a single man and combine forces, but because peace and unity were structural and legal preconditions of a legitimate caliphate.

In fact, Riḍā began his introductory address with a denunciation of certain recent pretenders to the office who had first declared their caliphate and then announced the obligation of Muslims to declare allegiance to them, acts that only generated alienation between those pretenders and the Muslim people, and degradation of the prestige of the office. Riḍā even declared that the Ottoman sultanate had never been a true caliphate because the regime had been founded on force rather than consent.[79] The congress was thus built on a faith in persuasion and consultation as a path to consensus and on the need for strict procedural legality as the foundation of any universal pan-Islamic governance. The unity of the group's will must precede political unity backed by force.

The path through procedural legality runs through the identification of the People Who Loose and Bind. For Riḍā and the scholars associated with the Caliphate Congress, the consensus of the *umma* is identified through the consensus of its legitimate representatives. But who are they; how are they identified; and how are they delegated this authority? The curious feature of the Caliphate Congress is that it was as much about the reconstitution and recognition of a permanent body of representatives and a system for their communication and cooperation as it was about a one-time appointment of a ruling caliph. Indeed, it was part of Riḍā's vision that a stable body of People Who Loose and Bind would also establish a permanent school (or, more appropriately, *academy*) that would train persons qualified to assume that caliphate in the future. Partially this gestured toward the esteem in which they held the ideal of the caliphate, but it referred more explicitly to the political dilemma of securing universal consent in current geopolitical conditions. The idea was to train future guardians who had all of the requisite scholarly, political, and moral qualifications for the office so that no one could reasonably withhold consent and allegiance *(bayʿa)* from a future caliph.

But there was a sense that, in the absence of a recognized institution or organization that constituted the People Who Loose or Bind, there was a chicken-and-egg problem that these scholars themselves were not competent to solve by their own will. One Egyptian delegate, Muḥammad al-Ẓawāhirī (an ancestor of the future head of al-Qāʿida, Aymān al-Ẓawāhirī), lamented the apparent dilemma that this body of scholars would have to conclude that establishing a legitimate caliphate is impossible today because of the absence of prior consensus around who formed the People Who Loose and Bind that could themselves agree on the appointment of a caliph. But he himself could only call with greater emphasis for future councils or organizations of Muslims to solve this problem. The caliphate was necessary, and thus they could not say that it was an impossibility, so instead emphasized that the collectivity of Muslims *must* fulfill this duty. But there was no clear sense of the agency or will that could bring it about.[80]

Defending the Caliphate in the 1920s

Riḍā was one of a number of Arab scholars in the 1920s who structured inquiries into the foundational political principles of Islam around an investigation into the office of the caliphate. The most notorious by far was the treatise by al-Azhar scholar ʿAlī ʿAbd al-Rāziq, *al-Islām wa uṣūl al-ḥukm: Baḥth fī'l-khilāfa wa'l-ḥukuma fi'l-Islām (Islam and the Foundations of Governance: A Study of the Caliphate and Government in Islam),* the arguments of which were so radical in the judgment of his fellow scholars that they led to something like a "heresy trial" and his eventual expulsion from the ranks of the *ʿulamāʾ*.[81] In my view, ʿAbd al-Rāziq's own text is much less interesting than some of the prominent refutations it provoked.

Although they were obliged to spill lots of ink showing that the Prophet did in fact exercise executive and judicial authority, the responses also met ʿAbd al-Rāziq on the modern terrain of popular consent and accountability. Islam may require as a matter of doctrine the establishment of public coercive authority, but "Muslims were the first to establish the norm that the people is the source of all political authorities."[82] More intriguing still, the treatise of Muḥammad al-Khiḍr Ḥusayn (a Tunisian scholar who later served as the Chief Muftī of al-Azhar), *Naqḍ Kitāb al-Islām wa uṣūl al-ḥukm,*[83] casts the debate as one about Hobbes and Islam's anti-Hobbesian conception of executive authority. Whereas ʿAbd al-Rāziq erroneously portrays the traditional, Islamic theory of sovereignty in Hobbesian terms as endowing the sultan with absolute authority and honor, al-Khiḍr Ḥusayn corrects him in the following way:

> Whereas Hobbes says "every individual must submit his will to the ruling sultan," the scholars of Islam say "there is no obedience to a ruler except when he commands justly and with right." Whereas Hobbes says "the submission of the ruler to

> any individual from his subjects is contrary to the requirements of nature," the scholars of Islam say "the ruler must submit even to a person of the lowliest station if he commands the right of him and forbids the wrong of him." Whereas Hobbes says "rejecting the will of the ruler is considered revolution or rebellion," the scholars of Islam say "if the will of the ruler is to order any of the *umma*'s public affairs in a way contrary to its welfare, or if he judges on a matter in a way that contravenes the code of justice, then there is no restriction on the *umma* from rejecting his will in a wise manner, and it is not proper for him to consider their resistance revolution or rebellion." . . . Whereas Hobbes says "religion must be subjected to the will of the ruler," the scholars of Islam say "the ruler must submit to the law of Islam both by the letter of the Text and by what is implied by it, and he is obligated to open the way for various groups to enjoy freedom in their religions and to uphold their rituals, it not being permitted to him to interfere with them in the matter.[84]

This account of a limited, restrained, bound executive implies a conception of sovereignty focused on the supremacy of the law. To this end, he deploys not only the Islamic tradition of constitutional jurisprudence (up to and including modern writers like Kawākibī and Riḍā) but also Aristotle and Montesquieu in defense of the view that kingship is not equivalent to tyranny if it is constrained by the rule of law.[85]

Al-Khiḍr Ḥusayn is not averse to the language of popular sovereignty or the will of the people, but this is largely limited to something like the power to withdraw consent to a specific ruler within a governing system that the people have no choice but to consent to. He writes that the Islamic vision of a limited caliph is best realized when the caliph sees his authority as derived strictly from the *umma*'s power of will. When the *umma*'s will is the source of power, then its rights are naturally respected and protected, as opposed to when the sultan relies on brute force. "Even every armed power knew that the will of the *umma* was a fortress that could not be conquered and an army that could not be defeated."[86] Although he is speaking in the language of the "popular will," the scope of this will is restricted to the choice of a person to rule over them virtuously and in accord with the divine law.

Similarly, the people's freedom to authorize general systems of rule is constrained by the people's own immanent identification of its own will with the existence of the *sharīʿa*. There is no freedom in this view for a Muslim people except what is established according to the requirements of the *sharīʿa:* "Islam is not an antiquated system that Muslims must submit to in a humiliated way, but rather in the basic principles of their *sharīʿa* are to be found the sources of what will provide them with laws that are superior to human laws and take into account their interests and well-being in a wise and capable way." The people's will that oversees the system of governance is identical to the ruler's obligation to obey the *sharīʿa:* "If the head of state departs in his governing policies from the *sharʿī* perspective then he becomes accountable before the *umma* in this world and before God on the Day of Judgment."

His view of popular sovereignty is essentially that Muslims have the right to manifest forcefully the only will they can possibly have: to be ruled by God's law. "Muslims do not submit to foreign, positive laws in their hearts. The principle of freedom is that peoples are governed by laws and systems in accordance with their own will. Muslims will only accept the *sharīʿa* . . . those who want to import laws crafted in Rome, London, Paris or Berlin on eastern societies do not know that in front of them lie principles of a *sharīʿa* that have been revealed from horizons free of imagination or error, bringing benefits and repelling harms."[87] Al-Khiḍr Ḥusayn's is, in fact, something like the modal position on sovereignty in modern traditionalist Islamic thought: the people exercises ultimate control over the legitimacy of the rulers but is seen as having no foundational legislative sovereignty of its own.

ʿAbd al-Razzāq al-Sanhūrī's Jurisprudence of the Caliphate

At the same time as many of the most senior scholars of the Muslim world were attempting to refound the caliphate on the basis of their own constituent authority, perhaps the greatest twentieth-century

Arab jurist was completing a doctoral dissertation in France on the jurisprudence of the caliphate. ʿAbd al-Razzāq al-Sanhūrī is best known as the drafter of the modern civil code that is in force in a number of Arab countries until today.[88] Little can compare with the import of his work in civil law, but Sanhūrī's writing on public law is a creative work of conceptual synthesis as well as an anticipation of themes that were to gain in importance for Muslim thinkers writing on sovereignty and constitutional theory. While it is best known today for its vision of the caliphate as kind of confederation in the form of an "Eastern League of Nations" (anticipating something like the Organization of Islamic Cooperation were it to exercise powers more along the lines of the European Union), this text is of more interest here for its discussion of the relationship between the authority of religious scholars and that of the multitude.[89]

Much of what Sanhūrī summarized on the caliphate is familiar from preceding thinkers. Valid Islamic government rests on a consensual and representative foundation for the benefit of those ruled, for government is a responsibility and a charge rather than a right to power and domination. The caliph is not a sovereign, but a limited executive officer with no legislative sovereignty. The office is a contract and involves very specific religious and political obligations (e.g., the ten "*sharʿī* duties" laid out by Māwardī), and there can be no comparison to Catholic ideas of papal authority. The caliph has no ultimate power of pardon, excommunication, divine blessings *(barakāt),* individual holiness, infallibility, or a right to pronounce interpretations of theological issues.[90] Whatever discretionary public policy authority he enjoys is also subject to legal restraint and regulation. In fact, Islamic law calls for a complete separation between the legislative and executive powers to a degree unattained by modern parliamentary systems.[91] In a sense, then, the legislative power is completely separate from the state itself, because the legislative power is held by the highest-ranking scholars *(mujtahidūn)* of the *ʿulamāʾ*.[92]

The source of the authority of the highest-ranking scholars is a subtle area of analysis for Sanhūrī, and one where divergences between the French original and the much later Arabic translation are particularly instructive. Sanhūrī writes that although the Islamic system has a similar foundation to the "the modern parliamentary regime," it is "with this difference, that in the Islamic system the representatives of the nation are not elected; rather, they are designated by their personal juridical qualification *(ijtihād);* Islamic government is a government of the scholars [*savants*]."[93] In one sense, Sanhūrī remains fully on the terrain of traditional Islamic constitutional theory, as we have seen up through Riḍā. He responds to some contemporary critics (one Professor Édouard Lambert and the famous nineteenth-century Orientalist Snouck Hurgronje) who deny that scholars can be regarded as representatives of the people without express appointment or election in the following way:

> It appears to us that the vagueness of the expression "representation of the people" is what leads to confusion. If one means that the scholars have received from the people an explicit or even tacit mandate to legislate, this is clearly inaccurate. But it appears to us correct to maintain that the Muslim scholars, in their consensus, act on behalf of the entire nation. There is in this a kind of management of affairs by the most competent men, a management that is always ratified by the people. In other terms, the people, having confidence in the conformity of the consensus of the scholars with the principles of Islamic law, accept this [management] voluntarily. At the foundation of this agreement one finds the tacit acceptance of the people.[94]

Sanhūrī in this text is laying the groundwork for more radically popular and democratic turns in Islamic political theory, but the status and authority of the scholars is one crucial area in which he acknowledges epistocratic claims.

The issue is not only how representation is verified (which is how Sanhūrī portrays his disagreement with Édouard Lambert), but also the question of what about the people is being represented: their will, their interests, or their will to realize their true interests. It is here that he poses the question of sovereignty in a technical sense to Islamic constitutional theory. Noting that in constitutional and political theory the idea of sovereignty is a question of ultimate legislative authority and that there is in modern political thought wide agreement that sovereignty belongs to the people (recognizing Rousseau's idea of popular sovereignty and the social contract as paradigmatic), he writes that from a *sharīʿa* perspective, there is no sovereignty in the sense of a human agent with unlimited authority. All human authority is limited by God because only God is the possessor of ultimate authority, and His will is the law that represents sovereignty in society.[95] There is thus ample evidence in Sanhūrī's theory for the view that when all government (including interpretation of the divine law) is seen as representation of the people, the people is represented primarily in its interest in fulfilling God's covenant.

Here Sanhūrī wants to hold that the ideals of divine, scholarly, and popular sovereignty are not in conflict because they all reflect a shared will. The rule of the "savants" is not domination because, as quoted above, "the people, having confidence in the conformity of the consensus of the scholars with the principles of Islamic law, accept this [management] voluntarily. At the foundation of this agreement one finds the tacit acceptance of the people." Thus, the forceful assertion of popular sovereignty one also finds in this work in the form of Sanhūrī's elevation of the juridical principle of *ijmāʿ* should also not be seen as in conflict with any authority assigned to unelected epistocrats. Of course, Sanhūrī acknowledges as "its source and expression God's Word revealed in the Qurʾān and the infallible Sunna of the Prophet," but he is particularly invested in the consensus *(ijmāʿ)* of the *umma* as a source of the divine law—perhaps the ultimate source of it.

For Sanhūrī, the sovereignty of the *sharīʿa* is identical to the sovereignty of the *umma* because the meaning of *ijmāʿ* (one of the sources of the *sharīʿa*) is that the *umma* is the possessor of sovereignty. "Divine sovereignty and the right to legislate settled, after the cessation of revelation and divine communication, in the hands of the *umma,* not in the hands of absolute monarchs as some tyrants claimed."[96] He argues that the scholars derived their authority to interpret the law ("legislate") as representatives of the people not only because the law is applied in order to benefit the people but also on the grounds of *vox populi vox Dei*: "the *umma,* and not the caliph or ruler, expresses the divine will through its consensus. The consensus of the *umma* is one of the forms of expressing divine will. . . . The right to legislate is only for the collectivity of Muslims." For Sanhūrī, divine, epistocratic and popular sovereignty are thus not in conflict, but rather their fusion into a single will represents a more perfect form of democracy: "What could be more democratic than affirming that the will of the people is the expression of the very will of God?"[97] "The agreement of our [human] wills expresses the divine will, and becomes also binding law."[98]

There are also areas where Sanhūrī emphasizes the sovereign constitutional status of the people, even where his views might not be strictly considered doctrinal innovations. For example, while judges are appointed by the caliph, their appointment does not end with his death because judges ultimately derive their authority from the *umma,* and not the Caliph. The caliph's own power to appoint is only by virtue of his capacity as an agent or representative of the *umma.*[99]

Sanhūrī thus provides a deeper political theology to explain the political status of the people, beyond just pointing to law or tradition as the foundation for the authority of collective popular *ijmāʿ*. To wit, we see here the emergence of something like a view of the people's collective vicegerency of God, although the difference in Sanhūrī's French and the translators' Arabic six decades later must be acknowledged. In the well-trodden passage where Sanhūrī refers to God not having left humans without guidance after the death of the Prophet and the cessation of active revelation, he clarifies that this guidance is not only in the form of revelation preserved in text, the custodianship of the scholars, or even the collective memory and wisdom of the *umma,* but in the fact that God "has accorded us the privilege of representing Him on the Earth, in as much as the agreement of our [human] wills expresses the divine will, and becomes also binding law. . . . In a word, sovereignty in Islamic law resides in God alone, but it is delegated by Him to the entire nation rather than to any individual, be he the caliph or even a privileged [closed] religious group."[100]

This doctrine of collective, popular representation of God, I submit, is a theological turn not seen even in thinkers as contemporary to Sanhūrī as Riḍā. Importantly, even where nineteenth-century thinkers (like Kemal and Kawākibī in particular) articulated fairly radical theories of popular sovereignty, they did not endow them with this political theology. Intriguingly, Sanhūrī himself simply asserts this claim in passing as fact, citing not the Qur'ān or theological tradition, but a contemporary work of Islamic jurisprudence in English, one Abdur Rahim's *The Principles of Muhammadan Jurisprudence.*[101] It is thus noteworthy that Sanhūrī's translators (his daughter and son-in-law, the prominent jurist Tawfīq al-Shāwī), after more than a half a century of Islamist thinking on divine and popular sovereignty, interpret Sanhūrī as expressing here the doctrine of the "caliphate of man." Where Sanhūrī moves freely between both the language of European public law and that of Islamic law in transliterated Arabic when he wishes to express a technical concept from the Islamic tradition, and the translators have no shortage of literal translations for words like "representation," in this case they simply render Sanhūrī's "Il nous a accordé le privilège de le représenter sur terre" as "*istakhlafanā fi'l-arḍ*" ("He deputized us on Earth as His vicegerent") and, for emphasis, "He endowed us with the honor of His caliphate [*khilāfatahu*]."

I am not sure how important this difference in language is, even if I am right in claiming both that Sanhūrī could have easily used the language of "caliphate" in the French original or made reference to the theological foundation of this doctrine and that the translators could have rendered "représenter" with one of the more common modern Arabic calques for this political term (*tamthīl* or *niyāba* perhaps). I am not claiming that this is a case where the translators distorted Sanhūrī's meaning or intent. He clarifies in the same passage that what this means is that God's sovereignty "est déléguée par Lui à toute la Nation," which is rendered here as "a deposit in the hands of the entire people," although other terms for "delegation" (e.g., *tafwīḍ*) are frequently used in later Islamist language. Perhaps "God's representative" is one way of expressing "God's caliph" alongside "vicegerent" or "lieutenant," whether or not Sanhūrī made clear the provenance of this idea.

What I am claiming, however, is that by the time of the Arabic translation the trope of the people as "God's caliph" had become ubiquitous in Islamic political theory and that this rhetoric and doctrine has particular force, implications, possibilities, and also limitations. Although Sanhūrī himself was to largely neglect public law after this period, devoting himself mostly to the reconstruction of a modern civil law informed by (among many other impulses) the tradition of Islamic legal rulings, preoccupation with the problem of sovereignty in Islam was to shift first to the oppositional ideology of political Islam and then later to a renewed, technical, scholarly interest in Islamic constitutional theory in the second half of the twentieth century. The rest of this book is on this development and particularly the continued invention of an ideal of popular sovereignty in modern Islamic thought based on the political theology of the universal caliphate.

The period of the 1920s between the abolition of the Ottoman caliphate and the entrenchment of post-Ottoman nation-states was far from the last time that the caliphate was debated or held up as a permanent religious obligation for Muslims. The ideology of the transnational Islamist organization Ḥizb al-Taḥrīr is primarily oriented around the restoration of a caliphate uniting all Muslims and the special legal status of the person occupying the office of caliph.[102] More notably, the 2014 declaration of the "Islamic State of Iraq and Syria" to have restored the "caliphate" and that entity's claims to henceforth represent all of the Muslim world brought to public attention the persistence of the view that installing a caliph is a timeless religious obligation in Salafi-Jihadi discourses.

But for most of the twentieth century, the far more compelling and salient cry was less for a particular office and form of government than for upholding God's sovereignty in the form of restoring the *sharīʿa.* The founding of the Muslim Brotherhood by Ḥasan al-Bannā in 1928 (known to be inspired by Riḍā as well as Muḥibb al-Dīn al-Khaṭīb[103]) is traditionally identified as the origin and wellspring of this new kind of religiously inspired mass politics and reformulation of Islamic political ideology. For all of Bannā's historical importance, in my view it is more in the arena of organization and charismatic leadership than in ideological and doctrinal formation. For this reason, I turn next not to Bannā and the early ideological statements of the Egyptian Muslim Brotherhood, but to the Pakistani thinker and party leader Abū'l-A'lā Mawdūdī, whose writings were in any event to exert extraordinary influence on the ideological development of the Muslim Brotherhood and others in the Arab world.

4

The Sovereignty of God and the Caliphate of Man

The crisis of the caliphate in the 1920s stood at the boundary between the fall of the old world and the birth of mass politics in the Muslim world, including the Islamist movement. As is well known, the central rallying cry of the Sunni Islamist movement during the middle of the twentieth century was the proclamation of God's exclusive sovereignty *(ḥākimiyya)* over the world and human legislation. As formulated most popularly by the Pakistani Abū'l Aʿlā Mawdūdī (1903–1979) and the Egyptian Sayyid Quṭb (1906–1966), what I call "high utopian Islamism" (rather than the less accurate "fundamentalism") was skeptical of (if not outright contemptuous toward) any form of identification with modern Western ideals of governance.

More germanely, the writings of the main Islamist thinkers of this period are characterized by a much more explicit concern with discussing the *concept* of sovereignty in Islam. What I am concerned to note here, first, is the establishment of something called "divine sovereignty" (which I suggested was merely tacit in the thought of Riḍā) as the arch-standard of legitimacy for all political, legislative, and moral action. The statements of Sayyid Quṭb on the rigorous demands of a commitment to divine sovereignty remain among the most influential:

> If we look at the sources and foundations of modern modes of living, it becomes clear that the whole world is steeped in *jāhiliyya* [pagan ignorance] . . . based on rebellion against the sovereignty of God on earth. It attempts to transfer to man one of the greatest attributes of God, namely sovereignty, by making some men lords over others . . . in the more subtle form of claiming that the right to create values, to legislate rules of collective behavior, and to choose a way of life rests with men, without regard to what God has prescribed.[1]

In short, the common Abrahamic belief in God's cosmic, creative sovereignty—what we might call divine sovereignty as fact—leads to an uncompromising insistence on God's exclusive legislative and normative sovereignty, or divine sovereignty as norm.

But, as is well known, Quṭb himself was influenced by reading Mawdūdī in Arabic translation.[2] Born in Aurangabad, India, Mawdūdī received training in a local *madrasa,* but began his professional life as a journalist. He was the editor of the official journal of the Association of Indian *'Ulamā'* from 1924–1927, around which period he was also active in the Khilafat Movement, an Indian anticolonial movement (1919–1924) dedicated to supporting the preservation of the Ottoman Caliphate.[3] From 1932, he edited the monthly journal *al-Tarjumān al-Qur'ān,* where he developed and published his ideas for most of the rest of his life.[4]

It was here, as he later reflected, that the distinctive features of modern Islamist thought emerge, specifically in the ideas of Islam as a comprehensive code or system that required nothing from alien systems of thought. It is this belief in Islam's systematicity, comprehensiveness, and self-sufficiency that leads to an insistence on establishing the state on the foundations of divine sovereignty. To this end he founded in 1941 the *Jama'āt-i Islāmī,* which he led until 1972 and through which he exerted extraordinary influence on those constitutional developments in the early years of independent Pakistan that enunciated a commitment to divine sovereignty and the supremacy of the *sharī'a.*[5]

Mawdūdī's writings were voluminous, ranging from his commentary on the Qur'ān (*Tafhīm al-Qur'ān,* translated as *Towards Under-*

standing the Qur'ān) to works on law, Islamic philosophy, history, economics, and theology. What concerns us here are his main works of political theory, including an early lecture on the political theory of Islam, a collection of writings published as *The Islamic Law and Constitution*, and a later work entitled *Caliphate and Kingship*. This chapter explores the contours of this authoritative articulation of some of the core features of modern Islamist political theology, in particular the interaction of his assertion of divine sovereignty alongside the politicization and popularization of the doctrine of the caliphate of man.[6]

Mawdūdī was not the first to argue for some form of popular sovereignty with an Islamic referent. We saw in the previous chapter that ideas of popular sovereignty were in circulation around the time of the transition from the Ottoman caliphate to postwar nation-states (with even some secular nationalists describing the nation as God's representative on earth). In an early (1908) essay by the great twentieth-century Indian-Pakistani poet and philosopher Muhammad Iqbal, he writes that in Islam "Political Sovereignty *de facto* resides in the people; and that the electorate by their free act of unanimous choice embody it in a determinate personality in which the collective will is, so to speak, individualised, without investing this concrete seat of power with any privilege in the eye of the law except legal control over the individual wills of which it is an expression." Without here invoking the doctrine of the universal caliphate, Iqbal adds that "the idea of universal agreement is, in fact, the fundamental principle of Muslim constitutional theory. 'What the Muslim community considers good,' says the Prophet, 'God also considers good.'"[7] Also, as I stressed in my introduction, the history of modern political thought in the Islamic world is not simply the history of Islamic, or Islamist, thought. Muslims were not waiting for religious scholars or Islamist intellectuals to "invent" popular sovereignty. Rather, my claim is twofold: First, that popular sovereignty is a crucial development within a particular ideological tradition, one so crucial, in fact, that it is often denied or downplayed within the discourses of that tradition. Second, that what matters are less isolated declarations of support for popular sovereignty than more systematic theoretical accounts of how it is an important commitment given other commitments, specifically to divine sovereignty.

It is the growth of the ideal of popular sovereignty within a politically and intellectually influential *theocratic* movement that is the concern of this book.

The Introduction of Divine Sovereignty

For many scholars of modern Islamic thought, the political and ideological assertion of "divine sovereignty" as the master principle of Islamic political thought was less an inevitable consequence of Islam's radical monotheism and theological voluntarism than a modern discovery. The least that might be said is that modern Islamic political theory foregrounds (without inventing) the symbolic question of where sovereignty ought to lie in the state. As we saw in previous chapters, the theorization of public authority and the rule of law in the nineteenth and early twentieth centuries did not require extensive declarations of divine sovereignty. Thus, there is a problem to be addressed of how the rhetoric and centrality of "sovereignty" in the juridico-political sense enter into modern Islamic thought.

This chapter thus proceeds on the widely shared understandings that Mawdūdī's writings represent the emergence of a particularly clear and stark articulation of the demand for God's sovereignty to be acknowledged and upheld in modern Muslim states[8] and that Mawdūdī's theories are not only of South Asian significance but shaped heavily the thinking of Arab and other Muslim thinkers.[9] But we also arrive in this chapter at the emergence of the central theme of this book, the importance of the doctrine of the "universal caliphate" for political theory. It is here, rather than in a supposed invention of divine sovereignty, that modern Islamist thought takes its crucial turn of insisting on humankind's (or at least the *umma*'s) collective custodianship of God's sovereignty.

This chapter explores the simultaneous development of commitments to divine and popular sovereignty in Mawdūdī's political theory. Although I submit that Mawdūdī does introduce (or at least make mainstream) some of the core theological innovations that underpin a kind of vision of popular sovereignty, his political theory remains weighted much more heavily on the side of an anti-democratic assertion of divine sovereignty. I argue that this political commitment to divine sovereignty entails (1) a view of divinity as defined as the giving of law; (2) a critique of non-divine claims to legal sovereignty as a form of idolatry and, in fact, the source of domination; (3) a moral and epistemic critique of secular democracy; (4) an account of the fundamentally emancipatory qualities of the divinely revealed law; and finally (5) an assertion of the undelegated authority of experts (in the religious law) over the legislative aspects of sovereignty. Collectively, these understandings of the meaning of God's sovereignty give shape to the anti-popular elements of Mawdūdī's political thought.

But these anti-democratic elements are only part of his overall theory. As is well known, Mawdūdī refers to his own vision as "theo-democracy," and my aim in this chapter is largely to chart the way in which Mawdūdī facilitates the rise of a kind of political theology of popular sovereignty in modern Islamist thought. Although it is less developed and less fulsome in its endorsement of popular sovereignty than what is to be found in later thinkers, I argue that Mawdūdī advances this conception of "theo-democracy" through the following themes: (1) the common Sunni view of the people as the origin and effective cause of any executive power; (2) the role of the people in modifying, updating, or filling in the gaps of the divine law; (3) the political interpretation of the doctrine of the universal human vicegerency—the caliphate of man; and (4) the vision of a perfectionist political order that is at least in part sustained and governed by a people united in a conception of virtuous political action.

Divine Sovereignty and the Limits of Politics

Mawdūdī's political theory is cosmological at its foundation. Mawdūdī stresses a few familiar doctrines: that God is the Creator of the universe and everything in it, including man and the things of the world from which he benefits; that God is the king and ruler of this creation and everything that occurs within it; that sovereignty over this creation belongs to none other than God, which leads to an awareness of

God's creative and governing sovereignty over all that exists in the universe; that God is capable of all things, controlling of all things, and the owner of all things; and that God is unaccountable for whom He rewards or punishes in the afterlife.[10]

This statement of God's effective sovereignty over everything that occurs in the world leads in quick succession to affirmations of "divine sovereignty" *(al-ḥākimiyya al-ilāhiyya)* over humans. This sovereignty is now defined less as a metaphysical fact about why things occur in the way they do than as a moral right that God possesses, one that He exercises not through physical compulsion, but through speech.[11] Mawdūdī's concern with the theological and metaphysical aspects of God's sovereignty is exactly as brief as this. The cosmic dimension of the fact of God's sovereign power and control is but a foundation for addressing his true concern: God's ethical and legislative sovereignty.

Divinity as Law

Mawdūdī's elaboration of the meaning of sovereignty as a concept is radically voluntarist. To speak of sovereignty is to speak of "absolute overlordship or complete suzerainty." Sovereignty is the

> undisputed right to impose his orders on all subjects of the State, and the subjects are under an absolute obligation to obey. . . . No outside agency, but his own will, imposes any limitations or restrictions on his power to rule. No subject has any rights against him or in contravention of his orders . . . every right in law comes into existence only because the Law-Giver desires it to be so. . . . Laws come into existence by dint of the will of the Sovereign and place all subjects of the State under an obligation to obey them; but no law binds the sovereign himself . . . in relation to his orders, questions of good and evil and right and wrong cannot and should not arise at all. Whatever he does is just and no subject of his can question his conduct or his orders and their enforcement, even by declaring them evil. His behavior is the criterion of right and wrong, and none can question it.[12]

Mawdūdī's moral argument for divine sovereignty can be formalized in the following way:

1. Sovereignty is the absolute right to command without being questioned;
2. Any human who claims sovereignty will inevitably be asked about the origin of his right to rule;

Thus:

3. Because only God can command without being asked for a justification, only God can be considered morally sovereign.

Mawdūdī himself seems to recognize that this argument is not valid in a logical sense. He entertains the idea that democratic authorization might be invoked for the exercise of legislative sovereignty. "The question will inevitably be asked: What justification is there for the investment with those powers and for that sovereign authority? The most that can be said in reply to this would be that a general consensus of opinion justifies such a course." This would be the claim of popular constituent power. But Mawdūdī in this case uses Rousseau's own democratic argument against Grotius to refute democracy itself: "But are we prepared to accept such a contention? Suppose a person willingly auctions himself. Does the purchaser really become his owner? If it is not so, we may well ask: How can the mere passive acceptance by the people of such an investment justify this alleged sovereign status?"[13] Of course, Rousseau had used this example to refute Grotius's claim that because a person may voluntarily submit to slavery, *a fortiori* a people can submit to an absolute monarch. Because a person may not submit to slavery for life, a people may not submit to a monarch with no power to revoke his authority.[14] Perhaps Rousseau would agree with Mawdūdī that the passive acceptance by an entire people of an absolute monarch's rule does not provide justification for *this kind* of government. But Mawdūdī does not entertain arguments for democratic legitimacy in any serious way here. His point is to prove that any human form of sovereignty is necessarily illegitimate domination.

People have a right to not be illegitimately dominated, not to collective self-rule.

But despite his confidence in this logical deduction, Mawdūdī relies almost entirely on verses from the Qur'ān that he regards as self-explanatory to establish God's absolute and exclusive right to be obeyed by humans. Q. 10:32–33[15] prove simply that "the lord of the universe is the lord of mankind and must be submitted to." Q. 42:10[16] and 12:40[17] are evidence that "No one else has the right to rule [*ḥukm*] and determination [*qaḍā'*] but God, and mankind is simply required to obey and worship." Q. 3:54[18] establishes God's exclusive right to rule and judge [*ḥukm*] from His act of creation. Q. 5:40[19] in turn grounds God's exclusive right to rule and judge [*ḥukm*] from His being the lord or king [*mālik*] of the universe and all that is in it. Finally, Q. 2:216[20] and many others establish God's exclusive right to issue commands and laws on the grounds of His sole knowledge of the truth, His determination of man's true goal and the identification of the sound path to this guidance.[21]

The full expression of this right is "God's legal sovereignty" (*ḥākimiyyat Allāh al-qānūniyya),* which Mawdūdī explains in the following way:

> The Qur'ān establishes that obedience must be rendered to God alone and that only His law [*qānūn*] must be followed. It is forbidden for man to neglect or abandon this law and follow the laws of others, or his own law [*shir'a*] or whims. . . . Similarly, the Qur'ān says that every rule or judgment that opposes the law of God is not only a mistake or a sin, but is unbelief, error, injustice, and depravity. Any such law is the law of pagan ignorance [*jāhiliyya*].[22]

Mawdūdī is also not particularly interested in (or adept at) any more technical theological or meta-ethical questions related to the implications of divine ethical voluntarism. Rather, what matters for him is that God's creative, causal, moral, and legal sovereignty obviously lead to a principle of political legitimacy based on this sovereignty: "The correct form for human governance in the view of the Qur'ān is that the state believes in the legal sovereignty of God and the Prophet and renounces its own sovereignty in favor of them. It must also believe that the caliphate is the deputy of the true Ruler and that its powers must be limited in accordance with what was stated earlier, whether those powers be legislative, judicial or executive."[23] "A system of government that turns its face from God and becomes a free system governing itself by itself is not a caliphate, but an insurrection against and a usurpation of the true authority."[24]

Implicit in the very understanding of what it means to recognize one's Creator is to recognize that lawgiving is not an accidental aspect of divinity, but rather intrinsic and necessary to it. Divinity *means* lawgiving. But beyond the conceptual imperative, what does divine sovereignty mean in practice? It cannot mean that humans do not wield coercive power or authority unless it were believed that God executes His own laws and commands in this world, carrying out the punishments and rewards for disobedience or faithfulness immediately. Rather, belief in the unity and sovereignty of God means "no one is entitled to make laws on his own authority and none is obliged to abide by them." Taking divine sovereignty seriously means that "no man, even a Prophet, has the right to order others in his own right to do or not to do certain things."[25]

More importantly, it means that no people can fully legislate for itself collectively. The principle of divine sovereignty, when articulated in the twentieth century, is often mobilized in opposition to (secular) dictatorships, but its primary force is as a refutation of democracy and popular sovereignty. A nation of believers is not morally free to give itself "totally independent legislation nor can they modify any law which God has laid down, even if the desire to effect such legislation or change in Divine laws is unanimous." Rather, a people's freedom should only extend as far as authorizing state power to enact God's law, and such a state will be entitled to obedience in its capacity as a political agency set up to enforce the laws of God and only insofar as it acts in that capacity, as "command is the exclusive prerogative of God," . . . "a State becomes Islamic only when it recognizes in clear terms the political and legal sovereignty of God and binds itself to His obedience and acknowledges Him as the Paramount Power, Whose commands must be upheld."[26]

The political and legislative agency that this conception of divine sovereignty authorizes is a somewhat complex issue that I untangle in the following sections. But one important principle established—at least at the level of a theoretical norm—is that the sovereignty of state authorities is undermined by the idea of divine sovereignty. For Mawdūdī, the right of divine sovereignty does not only vest in the law in the abstract sense, nor in the state as the concrete manifestation of law's authority, but also in the community and individual believers: "if [state authorities] rule in contravention of the teachings of the Qur'ān and Sunna, the Muslims must disobey them," Mawdūdī writes.[27] This is a first glimpse at the way in which a radical turn to divine sovereignty in Islamist thought also enables popular political agency.

Lawgiving as Idolatry

If divinity is defined as the right of lawgiving, non-divine claims to legislate are thus forms of idolatry, pretensions to divinity. Mawdūdī speaks about humankind's will to divinize itself through lawmaking. Animals, never mind inanimate objects, do not make claims to divinity or lordship:

> It is only man who can, and does, claim godhood in relation to his fellow-beings. It is only man's excessive lust for power and desire for exploitation that prompts him to project himself on other people as a god and extract their obedience; force them to bow down before him in reverential awe, and make them instruments of his self-aggrandizement. The pleasure of posing as a god is more enchanting and appealing than anything else that man has yet been able to discover. Whoever possesses power or wealth or cleverness or any other superior faculty develops a strong inclination to outstep his natural and proper limits, to extend his area of influence, and to thrust his godhood upon such of his fellow men as are comparably feeble, poor, weak-minded, or deficient in any manner.[28]

To claim the right to make law is to claim the right to command a fellow creature, which is to set oneself over him as a master over a slave. This will to self-divinize is an erotic impulse—men claim godhood partly for the pleasure of command and superiority. But there is an important reversal of Freudian or Nietzschean genealogies of religion: it is not man who creates a God after his own desires, needs, or fantasies. Rather, man intuits these desires and fantasies out of the knowledge of God's attributes.

Historically, Mawdūdī sees two classes of tyrants who have aspired to this form of godlike domination: kings and priests. His vision of the essence of kingship is not far at all from Hobbes's ideal of sovereignty. The sovereign is like a "mortal god": "it is not necessary for a man who claims godhood that he should openly declare himself to be an *ilāh* or *rabb*. All persons who exercise unqualified domination over a group of men, who impose their will upon others, who make them their instruments and seek to control their destinies in the same manner as Pharaoh and Nimrod did are essentially claimants to godhood."[29] Priests exercise similar domination to kings, but not in their own name. They invest some inanimate object with godhood or claim that they are the sole intermediaries between humans and god. When priests "proclaim themselves to be bearers of the Book of God," their claim amounts to domination and self-divinization because "they deliberately keep the common people ignorant of its meaning and contents. Constituting themselves into mouthpieces for God, they start dictating to others what is permissible and what is forbidden. In this way their word becomes law and they force people to obey their own commands instead of those of God."[30]

But today the primary manifestations of idolatry are the theory of popular sovereignty and the divinization of the state. Human whims and desires,[31] as well as attachment to the ways and customs of tribal ancestors,[32] are denounced as no less idolatrous rejections of God than sacral kingship. If the powers of the secular state are akin to the false gods and idols described in the Qur'ān, and if "power relations are the substance of life, closely interwoven into it . . . the basis and texture of all social relations and institutions [and] no life can be God's without bringing all of them under God,"[33] then "can a Muslim be a Muslim without striving to demolish them and wrest all power from these powers to bring it under God? Is that not politics?"[34]

Thus, although Mawdūdī shares with many democrats and republicans the concern with domination in political life, for him secular democracy is another form of domination—indeed, one with its own distinct ills and risks. The problem is not domination alone, but that human rule is always inherently a form of domination. This is also the essence of Mawdūdī's philosophical explanation of the origin of evil. "The root-cause of all evil and mischief in the world is the dominion of man over man, be it direct or indirect. This was the origin of all the troubles of mankind and even to this day it remains the main cause of all the misfortunes and vices which have brought untold misery on the teeming humanity. God, of course, knows all the secrets of human nature."[35] The troubles that flow from one person's lordship and domination over other people include "tyranny, despotism, intemperance, unlawful exploitation, and inequality."

Of course, this requires some explanation: if man-made law and rule is inherently a kind of usurpation of God's rights, and thus a form of idolatry then this alone doesn't explain why it is also a cause of these further evils. In addition to the illegitimacy of humans commanding other humans, we need an account of why man-made law will be substantively evil. Moreover, it is difficult to see domination as the *root* cause. What is it that causes humans (who, generally in Islamic thought, are not characterized by original sin) to choose their own values or laws when the option to accept God's law is available? The "excessive lust for power and desire for exploitation" and "pleasure of posing as a god" seem more radical than "the dominion of man over man." The latter seems more plausible as the outcome or symptom of some more radical defect.

Mawdūdī's Critique of Democracy

In addition to the charge that democracy is usurpation and idolatry, he advances a further principled and theoretical objection on the grounds of the insufficient rationality and epistemic virtue of the people:

> The common people are incapable of perceiving their own true interests. It is in the natural weakness of man that in most of the affairs concerning his life he takes into consideration only

> some one aspect of reality and loses sight of some other aspects. His judgments are usually one-sided, and he is swayed by emotions and desires such that rarely, if ever, can he judge important matters with the impartiality and objectivity of scientific reason. Quite often he rejects the plea of reason simply because it conflicts with his passions and desires.[36]

As radical a critique of the rule of the people as this is, it is partial and limited in an important way. Humans are not completely incapable of judging on questions of means and ends, or entirely lacking in knowledge of what might benefit their social condition. But we are fallible judges of our ultimate, true interests, not necessarily because of any inherent cognitive incapacity to know our true interests (as in Plato, e.g.), but because our judgment is burdened by passions. We suffer from a kind of *akrasia* of judgment.

It is noteworthy that this present argument of Mawdūdī's is not far from Rawls's argument about the "burdens of judgment" for political liberalism[37] or Hume's view of reason as a "slave of the passions." Mawdūdī rejects the liberal conclusion that because of this general condition of human reason political power must be as impartial as possible when it comes to endorsing truth in these most "important matters." Rather, because ordinary people are prone to mistaking their true interests, "man is not competent to become an absolute legislator." For Mawdūdī this kind of absolute sovereignty that man is denied would especially include the judgment that politics should aspire to neutrality because of reasonable doubt or pluralism about God's guidance. That itself would be an idolatrous, self-divinizing usurpation of God's right to determine and declare our ultimate purposes and values. Our epistemic and affective condition authorizes precisely "limitations on human freedom, provided they are appropriate and do not deprive him of all initiative." Such limitations "are absolutely necessary in the interest of man himself."[38]

Instead politics should be seen as thoroughly perfectionist:

> The purpose of the state visualized by the Holy Qur'ān is not negative but positive. The object of the state is not merely to prevent people from exploiting each other, to safeguard their liberty, and to protect its subjects from foreign invasion. It also

> aims at evolving and developing that well-balanced system of social justice which has been set forth by God in His Holy Book. Its object is to eradicate all forms of evil and to encourage all types of virtue and excellence expressly mentioned by God in the Holy Qur'ān. For this purpose, political power will be made use of as and when the occasion demands; all means of propaganda and peaceful persuasion will be employed; the moral education of the people will also be undertaken; and social influence as well as the force of public opinion will be harnessed to the task.[39]

The Islamic state is precisely distinguished by "the fact that it has to encourage and popularize those good practices that Islam desires humanity to adopt and to discourage, eradicate, and crush with full force all those evils from which Islam aims to purge mankind."[40] But if there is a revolution in Mawdūdī's thought, it is not the idea that Islam informs in some way every aspect of life, but rather with the further idea that the Islamic *state* "seeks to mould every aspect of life and activity in consonance with its moral norms and program of social reform. In such a state no one can regard any field of his affairs as personal and private. Considered from this aspect, the Islamic state bears a kind of resemblance to the Fascist and Communist states."[41]

Although later writings do attempt to stress a balance between the individual and the state, Mawdūdī always insists that in an Islamic state the individual must be denied the kind of absolute freedom that would allow him to "become an enemy of himself." Whatever individual freedom to develop free from state power is preserved, it is the essential mission of "the state [to] help the individual bind himself to the principles of morality" and advance "mutual cooperation in the good."[42] As a goal about which there can be no rational or reasonable disagreement, this is a goal that in its essence can have no restriction or qualification.

But how will an Islamic political order itself (even if one accepts in principle that being ruled by the *sharīʿa* is just) escape oligarchic capture and corruption? Any political order, not just democratic ones, is subject to the risk of degeneration into oligarchy or tyranny. What are the superior mechanisms by which Mawdūdī thinks that his own ideal regime will avoid oligarchic decay or capture? Ironically, as I will elaborate below, much of his account of justice, virtue, and rule of law in an Islamic state rests on certain *democratic* precepts.

Sharīʿa as Emancipation

Although God's right to command and legislate is fundamentally derived from His creation and ownership of the world (including man), and He is thus not answerable for the law He prescribes, He is also supreme in His knowledge and wisdom. Divine sovereignty is thus also justified in relation to what the divine law does for humans. We saw above that whenever humans claim sovereignty and dominion, this leads not only to the wronging of God but also to the harming of humans. Under human domination, "the human soul is inevitably deprived of its natural freedom; and man's mind and heart and his inborn faculties and aptitudes are subjected to such vexatious restrictions that the proper growth and development of his personality is arrested."[43]

Applying the *sharīʿa* is a positive project of human emancipation for Mawdūdī, as much as a project of removing or preventing injustice and corruption. The promise that the rule of *sharīʿa* in society will unleash human freedom and facilitate the full flourishing of man's moral and intellectual potential depends on a vision of the *sharīʿa*'s restrictions on human behavior as productive and enabling. The notion that true freedom depends on certain externally imposed restrictions is not hard to identify with and need not reflect some totalitarian perversion of language. But it does depend on a certain account of the authentic human self and how ordinary humans might prefer these restrictions even from the standpoint of their non-emancipated selves.

In Islam, that account depends on the concept of *fiṭra,* or the innate human condition. We humans are born with a certain nature that both defines what our thriving or flourishing looks like and also provides for our capacity to attain it. In traditional Islamic theology, the concept of *fiṭra* was closely linked to assumptions about mankind's inherent monotheism. Whatever the status of certain demonstrative, logical proofs for the existence of God, it is claimed in such verses as Q. 7:172 that humans have an innate, instinctual intuition about the existence of an omnipotent, omniscient Creator.[44] (A plausible comparison perhaps is to Kant's "fact of reason," or the way in which the moral law cannot be reasoned out from prior data, but instead "forces itself upon us of itself."[45])

For the modern Islamist apologetic project, the meaning of *fiṭra* is broader than this innate apprehension of the existence of God. It is also related to man's moral and psychological health and flourishing. The embrace of monotheism is itself psychologically and emotionally emancipatory, because it "released the human soul from its fetters and set man's intellectual and material powers free from the bonds of slavery that held them in subjection."[46] If the alternatives to monotheism—materialism or some form of idolatry—involve misrecognition of the self and its essential ontological condition, then the acknowledgment of metaphysical reality itself might be experienced as emancipatory. But the more important assumption here relates to man's relationship to God's law. Although God is unconstrained by a preexisting moral order, His law is not received as arbitrary or frustrating, but rather as identical to happiness and flourishing. "God has retained the right of legislation in His own hand not in order to deprive man of his natural freedom but to safeguard that very freedom. His purpose is to save man from going astray and inviting his own ruin."[47]

In the case of *sharīʿa* rulings in the realms of economics, gender relations, or homicide, "God has provided a permanent and immutable code of behavior for man, and it does not deprive him of any essential liberty nor does it dull the edge of his mental faculties." These rulings come at no moral or psychological cost to humans, but Mawdūdī still portrays the law as external to us and fixed. Because the code is obligatory and unchangeable, "you can, if you like, rebel against it, as some Muslim countries have done. But you cannot alter it. It will continue to be unalterable till the last day. It has its own avenues of growth and evolution, but no human being has any right to tamper with it. Whenever an Islamic state comes into existence, this code would form its fundamental law and will constitute the mainspring of all its legislation."[48]

The view of human nature here is somewhat mixed. On the one hand, man is made to be uplifted and to excel. The law is not only about constraining man's desires and impulses but also about realizing human intellectual and material powers. True freedom is the successful realization of human capacities while minimizing acts of sin and rebellion. But on the other hand, Mawdūdī portrays man as in severe need of instruction and incentive to follow the path that leads to freedom. Mawdūdī thus seems to waver between a view of man as a being that merely needs help and one that needs salvation from himself.

This frequently leads to a complex balancing of the tropes of Islam's lenience and its severity. Islam is, first, relatively undemanding and forgiving: "except for a few things specially prohibited by the *sharī'a*, everything under the sun is permissible for a Muslim."[49] At the same time, the *sharī'a* is an all-comprehensive, all-embracing social order that lacks nothing, but is an organic whole that requires everything being included and functioning together.[50] But I would submit that this is less a matter of inconsistency or about the apologetic claim that the arduous or unforgiving elements of the law "are to be viewed in the background of the whole system of life covering the economic, social, political and educational spheres of human activity." It is not just a matter of what can be fairly demanded of humans before they are liable for punishment. It is about resolving the paradox of politics given humankind's dual nature: If we need the *sharī'a* to make us free, how can we choose the *sharī'a* before we are free? Although our nature may incline us to Islam, we need to be socialized into virtue through the law before we can fully apprehend the *sharī'a*'s emancipatory quality.

But the law alone does not work miracles. What is required is also a comprehensive social and psychological revolution alongside, but not reducible to, the creation of the legal order. Thus we see that the task of whomever is called upon to rule in the Islamic state is infused with the perfectionist mission of subject formation. In his later work on Islamic constitutional theory, the function of the executive in Mawdūdī's Islamic state is not only "to enforce the Directives of God conveyed through the Qur'ān and the Sunna" but also "to bring about a society ready to accept and adopt these directives for practical application in life."[51] The people here appears to be portrayed somewhere in between the classical guardianship model of the passive flock, or *raʿiyya,* and the democratic ideal of "ruling and being ruled in turn." The people are governed and are an object of political discipline and formation. But why is it so important that the people be morally transformed in this way? This clearly goes beyond the need to secure compliance or obedience with state power. There is a vision of popular acceptance and even participation, as hinted at in the notion that the governed also play a role in adopting and applying the divine plan in ordinary life. Mawdūdī not only reveals an assumption that the sovereignty of God will depend on the collective agency of the *umma* (rather than a guardian caliph or class of scholars), but also that the heteronomy and alterity of the divine law is bridged by law's congruence with human flourishing and power.

The theme of the moral perfection of the people as the path to social revolution exemplifies my argument throughout this book that divine sovereignty and popular sovereignty are less antagonistic principles of modern Islamist thought than mutually constituting commitments. Note how the people is portrayed here as a passive recipient of both moral command and formation, with "Islam" as the active agent: "Islam builds a higher system of morality by virtue of which mankind can realise its greatest potential. Islam purifies the soul from self-seeking egotism, tyranny, wantonness and indiscipline. It creates God-fearing men, devoted to their ideal, possessed of piety, abstinence and discipline and uncompromising in the face of truth. It induces feelings of moral responsibility and fosters the capacity for self-control. Islam generates kindness, generosity, mercy, sympathy, peace, disinterested goodwill, scrupulous fairness and truthfulness toward all creation in all situations. It nourishes noble qualities from which only good may be expected."[52] But this is immediately transformed into an authorization for collective political agency and moral responsibility: "Nor is Islam content only to make a man good: in the words of a Hadith, it makes him 'the key to good and the barrier against evil'. In other words, it has been entrusted with the mission to spread good in the world and prevent evil. Such is the beauty and magnetism of Islamic morality that if some organised group possesses it and actively works toward the mission Islam has set it, then no power in the world can stand against it." Divine sovereignty is a theology of both popular constraint and popular power.

At the same time, this turn to collective political responsibility functions as both authorization and alibi. God's law is weak in the world today because Muslims have not embraced their own sovereign power. Into this vacuum non-Muslims have rushed with their own cunning. "The law of God regarding the granting of leadership . . . is this: if there is no organized collectivity that combines the Islamic moral attributes with the basic human moral attributes and which also has the capability to use material resources, then the leadership necessarily passes to that group which, although lacking Islamic moral virtues, is more advanced in its development of the basic human moral qualities and material resources than other existing groups."[53] Mawdūdī is calling not only for popular virtue, but also for popular *virtù*.

Custodians of Law, Guardians of Politics: The Rule of Scholars

But for all that, by far the strongest emphasis in Mawdūdī's constitutional theory is on the unmediated right of a certain kind of expert to represent the sovereignty of the divine law in political life. If politics is defined largely in terms of law, and that law is seen as received with significant precision prior to political life, then it is likely to follow that politics will be seen as subordinate to a certain kind of expert knowledge rather than public participation and contestation. Mawdūdī's thought introduces certain concepts that contribute to the invention of a kind of popular sovereignty in modern Islamic thought, but this contribution in his own thought remains embryonic and constrained—much like his conception of politics itself.

When Mawdūdī asserts that "the entire code of life has been decreed by the All-Powerful Sovereign of the universe," part of his assumption is that many laws have been laid down in explicit and unambiguous terms in the Qur'ān or Sunna, or "unalterable mandatory provisions of the Islamic Law which determine the complexion of the Islamic social order."[54] But no one thinks that this represents the bulk of the law, and Mawdūdī is no exception. Much of the *sharī'a* is composed of guiding principles, broad limitations on behavior that allow for further regulation within those limits, and extensive space for modification or extension of the law according to changing needs and requirements of the specific time and place. Mawdūdī mentions a number of the techniques and methods that have been developed for these purposes throughout the history of Islamic jurisprudence: disciplined interpretation of the texts of revelation *(taʾwīl),* analogical reasoning *(qiyās),* creative reinterpretation or extension of the law *(ijtihād),* and weighing the application of legal rulings in light of equity *(istiḥsān).* Even if God's own revelatory address to humans has been sealed, the execution of His will is dynamic and evolving in a variety of ways.

This gives us a new definition of what it means for God to be "sovereign": whatever human legislative or administrative agency that exists is not only authorized solely by divine revelation but must not take the form of independent sovereign lawmaking. Rather, man-made law must be a primarily *interpretive* activity. God's sovereignty can be seen precisely through the common metaphor of "the sleeping sovereign." God retains all moral right to legislate and command, and has in fact done so through revelation, but because that revelation is now sealed and final, it is as though God has commanded and then gone to sleep, leaving the execution of his command to his addressee. But who should be considered His deputy in this case?

What makes Mawdūdī still primarily a theorist and expositor of divine sovereignty is that he wishes to assign as much of the legislative-interpretive authority necessary for bringing God's law to life to experts, the traditionally trained scholars of Islam. When the flexibility given by the techniques of juridical interpretation are appreciated, no one can "reasonably entertain any misgiving as to the adaptability, the dynamic character, and the power of evolutionary growth of the Islamic Legal System. But it should be remembered that every Tom, Dick, and Harry is not entitled to legislate for the Islamic society. We do not recognize the right of every passerby to give verdicts on legal problems. Undoubtedly, it requires profound legal knowledge and a trained mind to enable one to speak with authority on any legal matter."[55] The expert qualifications required to speak on law include most of the traditional qualifications for an Islamic *faqīh* or *muftī:* fluency in Arabic, knowledge of the history and development of Islamic law, knowledge of Qur'ānic expression, mastery of *ḥadīth,* and sound practical legal judgment for the exercise of analogical reasoning. More advanced forms of pronouncing on the law for new circumstances *(ijtihād)* or considering the weight of equity and public interest against textualism require, in addition to technical expertise, "a developed sense of interpreting matters in the true Islamic spirit," "a complete command of the Islamic scheme of life," and "unstinted devotion and loyalty to Islam and a deep awareness of accountability before God."

So, expertise should be regarded as both technical and moral in nature. Mawdūdī's sense of the qualifications for this kind of expert legal authority is informed by his understanding of the classical Islamic legal tradition. But he is obviously acutely aware that Muslim societies are in a state of rupture with that tradition. "After centuries of stagnation and inertia, degeneration and mental slavery, we find that every aspect of our national life has been reduced to a mess." The task is restoration and renovation, not preservation of an existing order. Mawdūdī largely sees the project of regeneration through legal reform as an elite, top-down project to be pursued in the first order though a newly constituted "Academy of Law," charged with "tak[ing] stock of the entire work left behind by our ancestors in the field of law."[56]

Mawdūdī portrays the restoration of God's sovereignty as something akin to a one-time, founding, lawgiving moment. This is not surprising given that he is writing in the context of the birth of a new state created expressly as a homeland for the Muslims of South Asia. Nonetheless, the guardianship role assigned to experts is significant as a kind of general constitutional principle. Precisely because "it is not binding to accept any and every saying or expression written in a book of *fiqh,*" the resurrection and application of divine law is a productive task of political refounding. Importantly for present purposes, although some more basic, original political authority will have to "appoint a body of Islamic scholars . . . and to entrust them the task of codification of Islamic law," this act of delegation is a moral and constitutional obligation rather than an act of free constituent authority.

The guardianship role of scholarly experts in the area of lawgiving is thus extensive, if not fully sovereign. Not only are they fully responsible for creating legal norms out of revealed texts and accepted methods (both of which themselves precede political life), but they are the primary generators of new law. They first "compile [divine] commandments and laws into a Code," but then "additions to [this code] will continue to be made as fresh laws are framed by general consent or majority decision." What seems clear here is that the "general consent or majority decision" required to transform a draft legislative proposal into promulgated law is that which obtains between the scholarly experts themselves: "If and when such an exhaustive code has been compiled [by the scholars], it will be the basic book of law and all the current [premodern] books of *fiqh* will serve as commentaries for this book."[57] If this is not the final or sole word on constitutional theory, there appears here at the very least the suggestion that in principle scholars might have this authority to promulgate binding law simply on the basis of their own consensus.

Scholarly experts are not only given this kind of guardianship role when a founding legislative moment is imagined. Because "a State established on the basis of God's *de jure* sovereignty cannot legislate in contravention of the Qur'an and Sunnah even if the consensus of its people demands it,"[58] there must be a completely independent "Supreme Court [with] the inherent and original jurisdiction to entertain and decide cases challenging the validity of the legislation enacted by the Head of the State or the Central or Provincial Legislatures, if such legislation is considered to be in contravention of the letter or the spirit of the constitution."[59] Although actually existing Islamic constitutions (including that of Pakistan) tend to include secular judges, and not only classically trained *sharīʿa* judges, on such courts, the basic principle articulated here by Mawdūdī implies a kind of general right of experts in the divine law to occupy a guardianship role over political life.

One further example exemplifies the force of this right: the question of disobedience and rebellion. Mawdūdī derives from his reading of Q. 4:59 ("O you who have believed, obey God and obey the Messenger and those in authority among you. And if you disagree over anything, refer it to God and the Messenger, if you should believe in God and the Last Day"), among other principles, the right of disobedience: "The people [have] the right to differ with their rulers. In that case, the verdict of Allah of His Messenger is to be taken as final both by the rulers and the ruled."[60] What doctrine of political obligation is prescribed by this principle? It is not difficult to discern the potential for a kind of anarchy of judgment on questions of justice and fidelity to God. On this view, virtually any individual judgment that a civil law or command is repugnant to God's law authorizes anything from passive disobedience to active rebellion. This could either be seen as authorizing a kind of anti-authoritarian ethos in (Sunni) Islam or wanton violence against the state in the name of a superior understanding of God's revelation.

In the case of Mawdūdī's constitutional theory, there is some effort to contain this dissemination of the right to speak in the name of divine sovereignty. He writes that the implication of the idea that "the verdict of Allah or His Messenger is to be taken as final both by the rulers and the ruled" is that "there must be some institution for deciding such cases in the light of the Qur'an and the Sunnah." In the absence of any kind of church or canonically established office, because "the *sharī'a* does not prescribe any definite form for this, it *may* comprise a body of 'Ulama." In one of the most sensitive areas of political sovereignty, Mawdūdī's commitment to divine sovereignty inclines toward vesting authority of ultimate judgment and adjudication in the (ill-defined) class of scholarly experts in the divine law.

But he cannot quite bring himself to leave it there. Mawdūdī's theocratic and epistocratic commitments cannot even be fully articulated without invoking the specter of popular sovereignty. The ideological force behind the claim to uphold divine sovereignty is precisely that it is the only reliable and morally sound defense again the domination of humans by other humans. For this to hold, it seems to follow that the representation of divine sovereignty can never be fully and exclusively monopolized by any human agent or class of agents.

Mawdūdī's "Theo-Democracy": The Origins of Popular Sovereignty in Modern Islamist Political Theology

The need for divine sovereignty to be articulated through not only human but popular, quasi-democratic elements is not an embarrassment for the theory. For all of Mawdūdī's own claim that "Islam altogether repudiates the philosophy of popular sovereignty and rears its polity on the foundations of the sovereignty of God," the elements of his own vision that are based on various forms of popular political agency are not only points of traditional Sunni doctrine but also points of pride. Indeed, I argue here that Mawdūdī represents an important turn toward a deepening of the theological foundations of populism in Islamic political thought. This turn to populism is encapsulated by the full statement that was quoted in part above: Islam, according to Mawdūdī "rears its polity [not only] on the foundations of the sovereignty of God [but also] on the vicegerency *(Khilāfa)* of man."[61]

The People as the Source of Political Legitimacy

Mawdūdī is, of course, not an exception to the Sunni position that no ruler has a right to rule apart from some kind of authorization by the people and that all government should be seen as a delegated form of executive authority. But writing in the wake of decolonization, his language has changed. Islamic governance in general should be seen as founded on a form of contract or covenant *(ʿahd)* in which a free people is seen as the principal[62] and the executive power of an Islamic state is "constituted by the general will of the Muslims who have the right to depose it."[63]

Mawdūdī's thought now reflects far more the brute assumption of democratic legitimacy. The appointment of rulers "will *of course* be achieved through the democratic procedure of election."[64] He takes it as essentially self-evident that when it comes to the election of the head of state, this "depends entirely on the will of the general public and nobody has the right to force himself as the amir [ruler]."[65] An elected head of state cannot even claim the right to temporary emergency powers if they would include the power of suspending the constitution at will, "for during the period of suspension he would be nothing short of an autocrat."[66] His commitment to democracy in the sense that the ruler does not enjoy the power to decide on the exception is thus more robust than in some classical Western theories where the government can assume extensive discretionary powers in the shadow of the people's original "sovereignty."

Crucially, while he does derive some of these commitments from the Sunni idea that the original caliphate was "elective" *(intikhābiyya)*,[67] there is no qualifying of the "democratic" requirement of Islamic governance by the claim that it is necessarily satisfied by representatives alone (the People Who Loose and Bind). What is obligatory on the *umma* is consultation about the selection of the ruler, and then between the rulers and the people. But beyond this, the precise mode of *shūrā* has been left for Muslims to figure out. The *sharīʿa* itself "does not, therefore, lay down whether the people should be consulted directly or through their representatives; whether the representatives should be elected in general elections or through electoral colleges; whether the consultative body should have one house or two houses . . . the *sharīʿa* leaves these problems open for solution according to the needs of the time."[68] In this area, the actions of the earliest followers and successors of the prophet may be regarded as exemplary, but not normatively binding. Just because the first caliphs were not broadly elected, nor the electors themselves elected, doesn't mean rulers can't be today. The appointment of officials is subject to considerations of public interest: "We can adopt all such possible and permissible methods whereby we might be able to find out truly which persons enjoy the confidence of the masses in the greatest measure. Modern elections form one of these permissible methods."[69]

On Mawdūdī's view, the *sharīʿa* only imposes three broad conditions or restraints on how Muslims must "manage their affairs by consultation" (Q. 42:38).[70] First, he holds that God has required that (1) no collective affair can be conducted without consulting the people concerned; (2) all the people concerned should be consulted directly or through representatives (including women and non-Muslims); and (3) the consultation should be free, impartial, and genuine. Mawdūdī derives from something like the all-affected-interests principle a theory of considerable popular constituent power. If the people is the origin and effective cause of any executive power, and the *sharīʿa* has only introduced broad principles for mutual consultation, then it follows that the creation of new political and consultative institutions, and the rules governing them, will have to flow upward from the people's will.

This is a turn from exercising a role within a legal order to creating and authorizing that legal order. It is thus a recognition of the people's right to legislate within the broad canopy of the *sharīʿa*. Insofar as legislation is the archetypical attribute of sovereignty, the implication is that the people has some participation in giving form to law within an Islamic state. This presents at least two obvious questions: What is scope of the people's basic constituent authority, and what other forms of lawmaking might the people participate in?

The People's Legislative Authority

Mawdūdī has a fair amount to say about the principles governing the people's authorization of political institutions. The basic constitutional principle in question here is that whereas God has legislated with considerable specificity on many areas of law, the divine law has left many areas open and undetermined. "All administrative matters and all questions about which no explicit injunction is to be found in the *sharīʿa* are settled by consensus of opinion among the Muslims." But whereas we saw above that Mawdūdī's preference is to restrict this form of juristic interpretive activity to scholarly experts, that view does not, in fact, capture all of his commitments on the right to generate new legal norms. He writes in his early 1939 lecture that "every Muslim who is capable and qualified to give a sound opinion on matters of Islamic law, is entitled to interpret the law of God when such interpretation becomes necessary. In this sense, the Islamic polity is a democracy."[71] This doctrine represents a remarkable opening toward a political theology of limited popular sovereignty in Islamic thought.

As it happens, the area of the law that Mawdūdī is most interested in in this context is constitutional law. On his reading, the traditional Islamic constitution is uncodified in a single place and instead based on guidelines found in the Qurʾān, Sunna, precedents of the early Caliphs, and then the treatises of the great jurists. Yet, though he claims that the *sharīʿa* "has given us [only] the broad framework of . . . [Administrative and] Constitutional Law—and has left it to the discretion of Muslims to build up the details," this broad framework portrays considerable areas of constitutional law and theory as belonging to the pre-political. Mawdūdī thinks that there are canonical treatments in the divine law of the qualifications for holding public office, the status of non-Muslims, and the basic rights that an Islamic constitution must uphold.[72] He writes that "the *sharīʿa* has laid down the fundamentals" of constitutional law, but that these include answers to questions pertaining to "the basic theory of the state . . . the source of authority of its legislation . . . the guiding principles of state-policy . . . the qualifications of the rulers of an Islamic state . . . the objectives of an Islamic state . . . in whom sovereignty resides and the different organs of the state . . . the mode of distribution of power between different organs . . . the rights and duties of Muslim [and non-Muslim] citizens."[73] What is left over for popular determination is something like the institutional and administrative details of how these basic principles are incorporated. It must be said that the weight of Mawdūdī's emphasis is not on the side of popular lawmaking or constituent power, but rather on the side of a preordained constitution that constrains popular sovereignty.

Yet the remaining scope of popular constituent power should not be ignored. Mawdūdī rightly points out that historically, and in classical Islamic constitutional theory, the head of state (Imām, or caliph) was the focal point of all public authority. He appointed judges, consulted with important elite members of society, and supervised administration and justice. The Imām was not fully sovereign in the Hobbesian sense, but he represented the unity of public authority. This is the first point where Mawdūdī argues that because there are "no definite laws on [the] point" of the precise form of organizing relations between various offices, the people today "can amend or alter the details" of constitutional organization (although even here "the fundamentals will have to remain as they are"). For example, because it cannot be assumed that a head of state today will possess the same virtue as at the founding of Islam, "we can, therefore, consider restricting his administrative powers in order to safeguard against dictatorial tendencies. We may also restrain him from hearing and deciding cases, so that he may have no opportunity to obstruct the course of justice."[74] Other areas that fall within the scope of popular constituent power include the rules for electing the head of state, the procedural bylaws governing the legislature, the specific powers and status of the courts, especially to overturn laws repugnant to the *sharīʿa,* and the precise status (advisory or binding) of the legislature vis-à-vis the executive.

The last is of particular interest for present purposes. Mawdūdī finds in the earliest Islamic tradition primarily a model of consultation aiming at consensus, with final decision-making authority held by the head of state. But not only does he hold that today, given the unlikelihood of either a consultative body or the head of state attaining the virtue and wisdom of the earliest Muslims, "there is no other alternative but to restrict and to subordinate the Executive to the majority decisions of the Legislature." What is more intriguing are his views on how to reconcile potential conflict between the authority and judgment of the head of state and that of the "people of consultation." Mawdūdī imagines a kind of constitutional crisis in which "the Head of State and his advisors stick to their own individual opinions and neither of them is prepared to recede in favour of the other." In this case, he holds that "recourse may be had to a referendum, after which the one whose opinion is rejected by the public should resign."[75] Mawdūdī imagines that the ultimate authority to resolve such an emergency is none other than the people collectively, rather than a constituted political power.

A more stable and permanent version of this populism in matters of law is his proposal that when it comes to the issue of challenging laws on grounds of *sharīʿa* repugnancy, "there should be a specific provision in the Constitution that every citizen will have the right to challenge in the Supreme Court any law passed by a Legislature on the ground of its being repugnant to the teachings of the Qurʾān and the Sunna and therefore *ultra vires* of the Constitution."[76] Moreover, this is not restricted to a formal institutional mechanism. He writes that "if anything is proved to be right in the light of the Qurʾān and the Sunna, it cannot be set aside by any judge on the ground that it is in conflict with the law enacted by the legislature." But even this judicial nullification might fail, and in that case, if the people disobey the government because it has violated the *sharīʿa,* then "they will not be guilty of any crime; and it is the government whose orders must be set aside in such a case."[77] The people have some authority and discretion in authorizing new institutions, but are more enthusiastically portrayed by Mawdūdī as the agent ultimately responsible for guarding the divine mandate.

This is a quite radical form of populism in two important senses: First, the idea that popular participation in politics should extend beyond electing representatives or somehow contributing to the formation of law or policy to the right to judge and formally contest outcomes; and second, the notion that this right to represent the divine law does not just belong to the people collectively, but also radiates down to individual members, points to something very important about this popular turn in modern Islamic thought. If the people has inherited some form of political authority directly, in the absence of a church or permanent representation of God's will and judgment, the responsibility to uphold God's presence on earth is difficult to monopolize. Rather, it pulses and circulates throughout the entire *umma*, down to the last capillaries. The present case is a very weak version of this imaginary, as it only involves raising legal claims within formal institutions. But the right to partake in sovereignty as judgment of the law at the individual level is a few steps from the right to partake in sovereignty as execution of the law. We see here the seed of a belief in a kind of "sovereign believer" who might claim the right to not only passively resist impious laws but also to enforce his own understandings of God's actual intentions.

The Caliphate of Man

But if Mawdūdī is reluctant to develop the institutional forms of political agency enjoyed by the people, he represents an important turn toward inflating the people's dignity and status. It is with Mawdūdī that the theme of the universal vicegerency of God—the caliphate of man—is popularized and given its distinctly political and collective interpretation. Recall Mawdūdī's foundational statement that Islam "rears its polity on the foundations of the sovereignty of God and the vicegerency *(Khilāfa)* of man."[78] In Mawdūdī's work, this theological claim takes on great importance, and a key aspect of the dialectic between divine and popular sovereignty enters the intellectual bloodstream of modern Islamic political thought.

Mawdūdī begins by introducing a common "stewardship" claim about mankind's inheritance of authority from God: "Everything mankind has on the earth by way of powers and capacities are nothing other than gifts from God. God has put man in a position to make use of them in accordance with his wishes. In this, mankind is not the sovereign [*al-sulṭān al-mālik*[79]] himself but is the deputy [caliph] of the original sovereign."[80] Mawdūdī uses this to introduce the notion of a "collective caliphate." Without rejecting the notion that there may an office of the caliphate occupied by a single man, Mawdūdī stresses that the true, immediate vicegerency of God is inherited by the entire community of the faithful. Every individual is a participant in this caliphate, and no one can usurp this status.

Mawdūdī of course uses the concept of vicegerency precisely to distinguish the people's status from that of a sovereign. The people is God's deputy, not a fully sovereign agent. "Islam uses the term 'vicegerency' *(khilāfa)* instead of sovereignty. Because, according to Islam, sovereignty belongs to God alone, anyone who holds power and rules in accordance with the laws of God would undoubtedly be the vicegerent of the Supreme Ruler and would not be authorized to exercise any powers other than those delegated to him."[81] In his commentary on the relevant Qur'ānic verse (2:30), he is more explicit still on the subordinate status implied by the term "caliphate":

> "*Khalīfah*" or vicegerent is one who exercises the authority delegated to him by his principal, and does so in the capacity of his deputy and agent. Hence, whatever authority he possesses is not inherently his own, but is derived from, and circumscribed by, the limits set by his principal. A vicegerent is not entitled to do what he pleases, but is obliged to carry out the will of his master. If the vicegerent were either to begin thinking himself the real owner and to use the authority delegated to him in whatever manner he pleased, or if he were to acknowledge someone other than the real owner as his lord and master and to follow his directions, these would be deemed acts of infidelity and rebellion.[82]

But this doctrine of the universal caliphate should not therefore be dismissed. The force of the doctrine of the people collectively as God's caliph is that *no one else is:* "In an Islamic state, the powers of 'vicegerency' are not vested in any one individual or family or group but in the whole Muslim community when it is blessed with the possession of an independent state."[83] The popular vicegerency is thus also a rejection of theocratic forms of domination: "The theocracy built up by Islam is not ruled by any particular religious class but by the whole community of Muslims including the rank and file. The entire Muslim population runs the state in accordance with the Book of God and the practice of His Prophet. . . . I would describe this system of government as a 'theo-democracy,' that is to say a divine democratic government, because under it Muslims have been given limited popular sovereignty under the suzerainty of God."[84]

Mawdūdī is not always reluctant to compare the idea of the popular vicegerency to popular sovereignty. He claims that it "establishes democracy in an Islamic State just as 'popular sovereignty' does it in a secular state [because authority is] delegated to the Muslim community of the State as a whole and not to any particular individual or group. As a result of this, the government can be formed only with the consent of the Muslims and can function and remain in power only as long as it enjoys their confidence." Mawdūdī rightly notes that even the rightly guided Caliphs were not the "the vicegerents of God," because they saw themselves as "not directly appointed by Allah but elected by the Muslim community to wield the delegated authority on their behalf."[85]

But this is a very limited form of agency if all it involves is the right to appoint a representative to fill an office that is already itself (along with its specific powers) preordained by the divine law. What is much more intriguing is the kind of authority to represent God's own law-giving power this authorizes. If God is sovereign, and His sovereignty is primarily represented in His legislative enactments, then "those whose position it is to enforce God's law on earth should be regarded as representatives of the Supreme Ruler."[86] If there is no law outside of the agents who make it (through interpretation, enunciation, and enforcement), Mawdūdī thus comes very close to asserting that the law's authority is vested in the people collectively. But it must be said here that Mawdūdī only introduces the possibility of a form of popular control over the divine law. In his own political theory, the emphasis is starkly on the limits of the freedom of the *umma* to redefine its own essence and purposes.

What makes the people God's caliph is precisely that it has freely accepted the posited and ordained constraints of the divine law.[87] This is not just a statement about the limitations on the people's legislative authority. What is more profound is that the people *does not even exist* apart from the law. The *umma* does not exist in nature or by its own decision to form itself out of a multitude into a self-governing entity. The very existence of the *umma* is given in advance by its essence: a community dedicated to the *sharīʿa* and the covenant with God to abide by it. The *umma* cannot freely reconstitute itself under a new form of government or law. It can only destroy itself through the adoption of a different law: "If an Islamic society consciously resolves not to accept the *sharīʿa* and thinks that it will enact its own constitution and laws or borrow them from any other source in disregard of the *sharīʿa,* such a society breaks its contracts with God and forfeits its right to be called 'Islamic.'"[88] Such a state or community "can be considered sovereign only when it refuses to submit to the commands of Allah and His Messenger, which, in its turn, means the negation of its Islamic character."[89] There are thus inherent and essential limits to the *umma*'s constituent and legislative authority.

Part of the reason for this ontological constraint is that the *umma* not only preexists its formation into a sovereign body politic, but even its own collective form. It is true that in the first instance the "democratic *khilāfa*" must be seen as "the collective right of all those who accept and admit God's absolute sovereignty over themselves and adopt the Divine Code, conveyed through the Prophet, as the Law above all Laws and Regulations."[90] But the collective nature of the caliphate refers to the rights of the people over its rulers, not over its members. The caliphate is also radically individual because the acts that create this relationship between man and God (belief in and acknowledgment of God, acceptance of the obligation of the law) are individual acts. Because the *umma* itself exists through these beliefs and practices, and not through a moment of political formation, the caliphate is enjoyed not only by the collective but also by individual Muslims.

This theme comes up again and again in Mawdūdī's writings. In his earliest expression of the doctrine of the universal caliphate, he states in quick succession that "the power to rule over the earth has been promised to the whole community of believers; it has not been stated that any particular person or class among them will be raised to that position. From this it follows that all believers are repositories of the Caliphate. The Caliphate granted by God to the faithful is the popular vicegerency and not a limited one. . . . Every believer is a Caliph of God in his individual capacity. By virtue of this position he is individually responsible to God."[91] Since every individual is "the repository of the Caliphate" no any single individual can claim rights of dictatorship or suppress the rights of individual to express religious interpretations.

But at this point the powers of the individual "caliph of God" (or perhaps "sovereign believer") are not spelled out. As seen earlier, Mawdūdī does not subscribe to a particularly "protestant" conception of the law whereby any individual believer with access to the text can speak to the meaning of revelation. He continues to want as much legal authority as possible to remain in the hands of experts. Instead, at both the collective and individual level, Mawdūdī tends to emphasize the burden and responsibility that is implied by the status of the caliphate rather than the freedom of will or conscience.

The doctrine of man's vicegerency is the cornerstone of Mawdūdī's theological anthropology. What makes humans distinctly worthy of representing God on Earth is our capacity for moral responsibility.[92] Insofar as this caliphate is not only a status, dignity, or authority, but also a charge and aspiration, it follows that persons can attain to it in different measure. But this goes beyond a question of degrees of moral perfection. It bears directly on the identity and constitution of the people that is entitled to claim the status of God's vicegerent on Earth.

All humans have the same moral capacities and responsibilities. Mawdūdī even asserts that moral development can occur on a certain secular plane, within which it refers primarily to the virtues conducive to success or thriving in the world.[93] But the question of the caliphate pertains to the right to a certain kind of political authority. This in turn depends on a very specific form of moral responsibility. When

Mawdūdī speaks of the collective caliphate, this community of believers is defined as "those who have entered into a covenant with God consciously, emanating from their own will, to submit to God's rule."[94] Acknowledgment of truth and voluntary acceptance of God's covenant are, far from being arbitrary, the sole legitimate grounds for the exercise of political authority. This is also the answer to the puzzle of how Mawdūdī can speak of a political regime within which the people are so limited in their authority to choose and revise their laws as a "democracy." It is not just about the authority to choose and criticize one's rulers. Rather, it is that such a people can see themselves as fully self-governing because they can fathom no ends or laws other than the ones they have already committed to as a matter of self-constitution and self-recognition.

A Republic of Virtue

There might be something inherently paternalistic, even authoritarian, in all perfectionist conceptions of politics. Political power is legitimate when it advances true values or goods even when the subjects of political power reject those ends or goods. But perfectionist regimes can be more or less functionally authoritarian, with certain forms of epistocracy making no pretense to democratic representation or accountability. As we have seen, Mawdūdī's own constitutional theory contains much that is institutionally anti-democratic, particularly in the extensive authority he would grant to experts in the divine law.

But in Mawdūdī's vision, scholars and rulers are not just governing a passive, or politically inert, body of subjects. The community, as God's caliph, is not only the immediate source of legitimacy for political offices but is given a limited direct role in interpreting and implementing the divine law. More importantly, the people's moral development and capacities are seen as central to explaining how tyranny and domination are to be overcome. Mawdūdī does not rely solely on the supremacy of God's law in governing institutions, or the duty of obedience to authorities that can be trusted with power. Rather, the vanquishing of the human propensity to lord over other humans is attained through the formation of a moral people that refuses to be governed by man-made law.

This is the more profound implication of the doctrine of the caliphate of man. A certain kind of democracy is possible for those people already committed to specific and shared moral ends and sufficiently advanced in the knowledge and virtues that follow from these ends. The apparent contradiction between a people governing itself while being unfree to choose its own laws is resolved by positing the people's consciousness of its own emancipation through the law given to it by God. It is then that democracy is made safe for God's sovereignty: when the self-governing people wills for itself only those means and ends legislated by God. Mawdūdī's theo-democracy is thus a kind of republic, but a distinctly "republic of virtue."

If law and morality are constitutive of the very people, any balancing of power within an Islamic order must be subordinate to the principle of moral unity. The form of rule under the earliest successors to Muḥammad, on Mawdūdī's understanding of it, provides a vision of this ideal. On the one hand, there was a kind of supremacy of the caliph as "the only person to whom obedience and fealty were enjoined."[95] He imagines at the same time that the People Who Loose and Bind formed a kind of "Parliament" for the sitting caliph of the time. There was neither a strict separation between the executive and this consultative body ("he attended the Parliament himself and presided over all its sittings") nor moral divisions within it ("the whole parliament was his as long as he kept to the right path").

But it is apparent that the latter is the supreme principle. The executive's right to obedience ended as soon as he deviated from "the right path." The first locus of resistance was the notables. "As soon as he deviated, his whole party turned into opposition. Every member of his parliament had full freedom to vote for or against him on any point and even his ministers were free to oppose him if they felt impelled to do so honestly and sincerely." However, it is clear that for Mawdūdī a virtuous public is the true guarantor of morality.

He notes that the caliph was answerable before the people for both public and private acts at any time and place, citing the canonical oath of the first Caliph Abū Bakr: "Assist me when I act rightly, but if I go wrong put me on the right path. Obey me as long as I remain loyal to God and His prophet. But if I disobey God and His prophet, then there is no obligation of obedience on you." Naturally, Mawdūdī is aware that this direct form of rule cannot be compared to any modern regime type. And yet it remains the ideal around which politics should be organized. The ideal today requires precisely a moral transformation of the social body. It can "be achieved only when the society has been already developed in accordance with all the revolutionary teachings of Islam. And that is exactly why no sooner than an Islamic society deteriorated, this ideal of Government could not be fully adhered to."[96]

Certain distinctly republican ideals are in evidence: control over rulers by the people, the rule of law, and the people as the ultimate source and guarantee of a well-ordered society. This clearly does not escape Rousseau's paradox of virtue in politics (if politics makes the people virtuous, how is the people to choose virtuous government prior to being educated by a virtuous political order?). But the Islamic conception might enjoy a distinct theoretical advantage. Knowledge and practice of religion is of course the source of virtue. Insofar as the people's self-identification with the divine law preexists a specific political order, then the sovereignty of that law over politics can be imagined as arising out of a virtuous people's willing of it.

Instructive here also are Mawdūdī's recommendations for modern politics. He proposes four guiding principles if Muslims are to recreate the relationship between rulers and the people who existed at the beginning of Islam. First, rulers must be accountable to the public at large, and not only to even elected representatives. This is not only a question of the people's rights or entitlements over its entrusted officers as God's caliph, but also of how politics is most effectively constrained by law and morality. The virtuous people as a whole is a better embodiment of divine authority on Earth. Second, political parties must not be allowed to form in an Islamic state. Mawdūdī's concerns here about the evils of faction are almost Madisonian. The party system "pollutes the Government with a false sense of loyalties," and enables factions to perpetuate their hold on power. Third, the rules of government should be simple and non-confusing to ordinary people. This is not only to facilitate participation and judgment, but also to make it easy for "the people in general to find out the root-cause of the evils that might arise from time to time." Finally, public office should be limited to those possessing the moral and epistemic qualifications laid out by Islamic law.[97]

Collectively, these principles point to an ideal of collective political responsibility underpinned less by institutional design than by the exercise of moral virtue. If Islam "aims to create a State on the basis of its ideology," then only the faithful can be full citizens. "Upon the shoulders of the Muslim citizens of an Islamic State devolves the main burden of running it in accordance with Islam's best traditions; as they alone are supposed to believe in it implicitly."[98] This notion of an ideological state governed collectively by a people united in ideology is a constant from the beginning to the end of Mawdūdī's writings.[99] And indeed, this is a vision that appeals to many seeking to orient political community in a uniquely Islamic manner. In the essay I quoted from at the beginning of this chapter, Muhammad Iqbal explained that Islam stands against any form of racial, caste, or ethnic distinction between humans. But its radical equality is based on shared moral purposes: "The inner cohesion of such a nation would consist . . . in the unity of the religious and political ideal; or, in the psychological fact of 'likemindedness.' The membership of this nation, consequently, would not be determined by birth, marriage, domicile or naturalisation. It would be determined by a public declaration of 'likemindedness,' and would terminate when the individual has ceased to be likeminded with others."[100]

The path to creating this system in the first place is heavily dependent on the willingness of the faithful to assume power. A righteous leadership, a vanguard of the people, is required to first seize the means of political and cultural power. "If power and leadership are vested in God-fearing people, society moves along the right lines, and even the wicked have to follow certain rules. Good flourishes, and evils, if not altogether eradicated, are contained."[101] Although the duly constituted Islamic state rests on strict legalism, the imperative to bring about this order is so foundational a religious and moral norm that it justifies almost all means. Because "only when power in society is in the hands of the Believers and the righteous, can the objectives of Islam be realised," then "it is the primary duty of all those who aspire to please God to launch an organised struggle, sparing neither life nor property, for this purpose." The realization of God's sovereignty on Earth is in effect the authorization of "the good to possess collective organisational power."[102] This "leadership of the good" is perhaps the culmination of Mawdūdī's elaboration of the obligation to uphold divine sovereignty. As faith requires Muslims to establish and maintain "the way of life that has been ordained for the conduct of the world according to the will of God," and because this end is unattainable without the highest degree of collective effort, there must exist a God-fearing community devoted to the sole purpose of establishing and maintaining the sovereignty of God on earth."[103]

The preceding hardly does justice to the length and complexity of Mawdūdī's own political career and the pragmatism of the party he founded. But it gives us a sense of his ideal theory of sovereignty and power. The repetition in rhetoric of the exclusive sovereignty of God establishes a supreme authorization for the use of power. But it is perhaps more interesting for the related concepts and doctrines that it foregrounds. Inserting the principle of divine sovereignty into the form of the modern state and the structure of modern state–society relations requires more than insisting on the obligation of humans to obey their Creator. It requires an account of how the divine law is related to human welfare and emancipation. This in turn seems to suggest that a people must be somehow persuaded of the law's choice worthiness, which is an implicit appeal to the people's ultimate political responsibility and agency. Questions of the people's status in relation to the divine are thus forced to the surface, as are questions of the conditions under which the people at large can be seen as the true custodians of ultimate authority.

All of these concepts are present in Mawdūdī's thought, possibly coexisting in this way for the first time in the writings of a single thinker. But they are not all fully developed. Lots of Mawdūdī's writings take the form of declarations that he considers to be self-explanatory, or minimal commentary on Qur'ānic verses and *ḥadīth* reports. Concepts like the relationship of the *sharīʿa* to human nature, the caliphate of man, the relationship of the people to the public articulation of the divine law, and the kind of moral and epistemic qualities imagined in a well-ordered Islamic society receive fuller articulation in later writers, to whom we now turn.

5

The Law We Would Give Ourselves

Apart from the Ayatollah Khumaynī (Khomeini), Sayyid Quṭb (1906–1966) is perhaps the best-known Islamist intellectual of the twentieth century. His thought is synonymous with the most radical and uncompromising expression of the ideology espoused by the Muslim Brotherhood movement, and some of the core concepts of his ideology have attained notoriety far beyond the academic study of political Islam. Chief among these is precisely the concept of divine sovereignty *(ḥākimiyya)* that he adopted from Mawdūdī, along with the idea that any choice to live by anything other than divine guidance amounts to a return to the ignorance of pre-Islamic paganism *(jāhiliyya)*.[1] Because the free choice to govern oneself at the individual or collective level by standards and rules other than those given by God amounts to a conscious rejection of God's authority and thus Islam itself, Quṭb is also best known for the idea that societies or states characterized by this "*jāhilī*" rejection of God are illegitimate. But such states are also involved in a kind of warfare against Islam and Muslims, insofar as they use the means of violence to suppress Muslims' freedom to live according to God's law. Thus, Quṭb is often assigned a central place in the genealogy of ideas that was to lead to Islamist violence against

Muslim-majority states, and eventually transnational "Salafi-Jihadi" groups like al-Qāʿida and ISIS.[2]

There is no doubt that the focus on divine sovereignty is indeed Quṭb's best-known contribution to Islamist discourse. What is less clear is how much of Quṭb's writings on divine sovereignty and the universal caliphate depart from or advance those of Mawdūdī. Intellectually speaking, those concepts might not represent Quṭb's most significant contribution to modern Islamic thought on sovereignty, law, and the place of the *umma* in the modern world.

This chapter advances a different argument. Quṭb's writings are replete with a very consistent set of claims related to the practicality and ease of Islamic law and its essential harmony with human nature. These are, in fact, very old and very common claims in Islam. Early Islamic polemics against Judaism focused on the relative paucity and ease of God's demands on Muslims, for example. Muslim theologians have long referred to Islam as the "natural religion," or the "religion of human nature" *(dīn al-fiṭra)*. But as with the idea of the universal caliphate (which also has a Qurʾānic foundation), modern polemicists like Quṭb, as well as legal theorists,[3] put these claims to some novel uses. First, in Quṭb's writings there is simply an unmistakable persistence in elaborating the specific ways in which the *sharīʿa* and human nature are harmonious. Second, and more importantly, this is pitched at the level of collective application and governance rather than the perfection of individual selves.

But what does this have to do with sovereignty? Religious apologetics are an old game and have little to do with any particular form of political system. Nonetheless, I believe that the twentieth-century project to defend Islam in these specific terms (Quṭb is just one prominent example) plays a very important role in a certain kind of populist political vision. The claim is that Islam is not only easy or practical but is also fundamentally emancipatory for human selves. It brings from the ills of the soul the peak of well-being and liberation attainable on Earth. It does this not only by making demands on the ordinary human self but by accommodating the limits of human self-sacrifice. Implied by this claim is that in modernity it is up to humans to *choose* the law that best liberates them, even if they do not have an absolute right to reject that law. The perfection of the divine law, defended in this particular way, is thus an extended explanation to Muslims of how the divine law is not only obligatory on them because of God's sovereignty, but also the path to their own happiness. It is an explanation of how Muslims can be both free and governed in the modern world.

This still does not seem like an argument for popular sovereignty. But it fits into that project nonetheless. If popular sovereignty involves a kind of collective autonomy, an authorship and identification with the law, then the argument for the harmony of the *sharīʿa* with human personality in all its forms is a claim that the divine law is the law we would give ourselves. It is true that this is not an authorization for the people to reject that law and choose another in a truly sovereign fashion. But this is part of the case that the Muslim *umma* is collectively responsible for the political world (the universal caliphate) and that this responsibility carries with it the possibility of collective freedom. Thus, this defense of Islamic law is part of the utopian Islamist project to show how collective self-government is compatible with fidelity to a revealed law. Above all, it does so by shifting the emphasis from the state and its legal institutions to the formation of the kind of believing community that can assume the vicegerency of God.

From the Universal Caliphate to the Natural Religion

Quṭb absorbed the doctrine of the caliphate of man but shows reticence about some of its implications. In *Milestones,* he writes: "Islam elevates man to the position of vicegerent of God on earth, and, under certain conditions, considers the responsibilities of this vicegerency as worship of God and the purpose of man's creation. The responsibility of this vicegerency includes the material progress that comes from multiplying the bounties of God. To attain the leadership of mankind, we must have something to offer besides material progress, and this other quality can only be a faith and way of life that both promotes the benefits of modern science and technology and fulfills basic human needs."[4] Here, Quṭb largely echoes a history of Islamic political and ethical thought, going back to the medieval period, which portrays God's purpose in creating man in terms of mankind's obligations to worship Him and to civilize or cultivate the Earth *('imārat al-arḍ).*[5] A similar interpretation is given in his exegesis of the Qur'ān: "God decided to hand over the Earth's affairs and destiny to man and give him a free hand to use, develop and transform all its energies and resources for the fulfillment of God's will and purpose in creation, and to carry out the preeminent mission with which he was charged."[6]

Insofar as this collective stewardship understanding of the universal human caliphate does not emphasize a political theology of popular sovereignty within the political realm, that is partly because Quṭb is almost entirely uninterested in questions of constitutional design. He does not seriously consider technical problems of the relationship between the *umma,* the scholars and other People Who Loose and Bind, and the rulers. But there is another reason that connects with the main theme of this chapter. Quṭb does connect the caliphate of man to the relationship between the divine law and human nature. Because "man has been given the capability to take on the responsibility, and the necessary latent skills and energies to fulfil God's purpose on earth," Quṭb then deduces that "it may therefore be concluded that there is a unity or harmony between those laws [*nawāmīs; nomoi*] that govern the earth and the entire universe, and those governing man's powers and abilities."[7] This is the core theme that I explore in this chapter: the meaning of the harmony of divine law and human personality and how it connects to a specific idea of popular political agency for Quṭb. It is fitting that that he does not miss the opportunity to connect the doctrine of the universal caliphate to the idea of the divine law as human emancipation, which is a claim about the *sharī'a*'s relationship to human nature *(fiṭra).*

The claim that Islamic law is in deep and perfect harmony with the essential needs and motivations of *fiṭra* is ubiquitous in Islamic theological and juridical discourses. There are two crucial pillars of this claim, historically. As noted in the previous chapter, the first is that humans are born with an innate inclination toward pure monotheism. This innate inclination allows humans to discern the veracity of God's command, thus making it both natural and rational for humans to obey God. The second pillar is that the divine law is perfectly suited to the needs, desires, and inclinations of actual human beings—per Q. 30:30[8] it is the "natural religion," the *dīn al-fiṭra*. A variation on this claim is that humans have an innate moral sense prior to an encounter with revelation that is congruent with the teachings of revelation but also a device for interpreting it.

These points of doctrine are particularly ubiquitous across the ideological and political spectrum of modern Islamist writings on the suitability of Islamic law for all times and places despite Islam's apparent setbacks since the rise of colonialism and postcolonial imperialism. The "natural religion" doctrine is prominent in the writings of those "Modernists" or "reformers" who draw from the Islamic philosophical tradition to argue for the harmony of reason and revelation, as well as the most influential theorists of utopian Islamism, as we saw in the previous chapter on Mawdūdī. But what Mawdūdī mostly asserts Quṭb elaborates much more systematically.

The claim to Islam's compatibility with reason and the *sharī'a*'s deep harmony with human *fiṭra* seems to serve a primarily apologetic function, as a preexisting and more or less stable feature of Islam that serves to justify Islam as such against any and all other ideological, religious, or moral alternatives.[9] However, this dominant trope in Islamic writing serves two further functions. First, it is an answer to the problem of how realistic and practical normative ethics must be. Every meta-ethical theory must address the question of how ethics must "take people as they are," that is, when human behavior must be held to account by the demands of ethics and when ethics must be held to account by the facts of human nature. The "natural religion" doctrine is a device through which Islamic thinkers show how God has scaled the demandingness of morality to the inclinations of average humans. Second, and following from this, it functions as an account of the exact place of political order in Islamic moral theology.

Beyond acknowledging "ought-implies-can" constraints, it is not a formal requirement of morality that it be realistic in the sense of accommodating average human moral inclinations. It is perfectly coherent to argue that morality is precisely the articulation of ideal behavior which none but living saints will be able to fulfill. We may then discuss what we may reasonably hope for in this world, but should not confuse that with justice or morality.[10] It is particularly easy to see why a religious conception of morality might distinguish between justice or moral perfection, on the one hand, and what humans are able to achieve, on the other. Perhaps God desires that His commands should appear infinitely demanding. Perhaps the unreasonableness of God's demands is meant to serve the purpose of reminding humans of God's absolute mastery over mankind and of the limitations and imperfection, if not outright depravity, of this world. Perhaps the "divine" or the "sacred" is precisely a category of value meant to contradict the values and desires of the human or the secular.

But the claim throughout Islamic writing on law and morality, particularly among modern activists, is that God has adhered to a certain covenant. The texts comprising God's revelation reveal not only an awareness of how humans both thrive under and chafe at the constraints of morality but also a divine concern to not burden humans beyond a certain point, declared explicitly in the Qur'ān: "God never burdens a soul beyond its means" (Q. 2:286). The common claim in modern Islamic writing is that there is no essential conflict between the demands of ethics and the demands of human psychology because God has created both—the *sharīʿa* and human psychology—in perfect harmony. Humans easily fulfill the demands of morality both because they respond well to the disciplining which cultivates their higher selves—they are happiest when controlling their base desires and acting in accordance with morality—but also because demands of morality are not overly taxing. In other words, we might say that in this account of Islamic law and moral theology, not only does "ought imply can" but that ought implies can *without much difficulty.*

My argument in this chapter is that, perhaps more than the constant refrain about the obligation to obey and apply the *sharīʿa,* the discourse of Islam's harmony with human nature elucidates precisely what is political about "political Islam." It reveals the precise vision of politics offered by Islamist and the specific role of socio-political order in the attainment of moral excellence. Joined with the doctrine of the universal caliphate of man, which stresses the political agency and responsibility of the people, it is an argument also for a collective custodianship over the political, even while denying that humans have a right to legislate in a sovereign manner.

Islamic Society as Realistic Utopia in the Political Theory of Sayyid Quṭb

Quṭb is a particularly appropriate thinker to consider in this context. Born in Asyūt, Egypt, in 1906 and executed in 1966 as part of Nasser's crackdown on the Muslim Brotherhood, Quṭb remains one of the most influential articulators of both revolutionary Islamist political doctrine and the modern theology that underpins it. His work represents some of the most elaborate and sophisticated expressions of core revivalist themes. These include Islamic renewal and authenticity, the purification from religion of arbitrary practices (certain Sufism, excessive legal formalism, customary habits), a direct encounter with the texts and practices of the revelatory period, the rationalization of Islamic legal and political thought for application within the political-institutional conditions of modernity, the relevance of Islam for action and material life, and perhaps most importantly, the "natural religion" doctrine. His articulation of modern Islamist political doctrine has been profoundly influential across the entire spectrum of Islamic "Revivalist" thought, among both Sunnis and Shiʿites and both pragmatists and violent revolutionaries.[11]

Quṭb's writings developed and changed in important ways over the course of his life, even when we limit ourselves to his postwar Islamist writings.[12] I am not proposing here a comprehensive account of his entire intellectual project, especially when we bear in mind the many concerns, possibilities, and directions contained within his multivolume commentary on the Qurʾān. Nor am I doing justice to a rich historiographical account of his intellectual influences or milieu.[13] However, focusing on his most important books, which span the length of his career as an Islamic public intellectual—*Social Justice in Islam,*[14] *The Basic Principles of the Islamic Worldview,*[15] and *Milestones*—I believe that one can discern a consistent and coherent theory of the relationship between society, religion, and moral psychology.[16] This theory is central to his core concern to popularize a coherent Islamic political theology for mass consumption.

In this comprehensive theory of society, religion, and moral psychology Quṭb is not only defending Islam as the normatively required doctrine for Muslim societies, nor merely as a demonstrably superior path to strength, honor, and dignity in the face of Western domination, but also as a coherent and expressly realistic utopia grounded on a theological account of how humans adopt morality. The realism of this utopia is essential for explaining how the political order creates the conditions for individual and collective moral perfection and for authorizing collective political responsibility.

I am using the notion of a "realistic utopia," following Rawls,[17] to refer to a comprehensive theory of political life which not only posits a true doctrine of the good or the right—that is, the substance of moral obligation for persons and societies—but also contains an account of how that theory does not contradict what we know about human moral psychology. A realistic utopia is a vision of a society that is the best we can or ought to wish for and that, by virtue of its proper implementation, would remove the main perennial human obstacles to justice, morality, and the good. Crucially, it is a normative theory that has both its justification and its account of its own feasibility and perpetual stability as part of the same theory; it does not rely on myths, noble lies, or multitiered explanations to explain how the theory will be endorsed and followed by various segments of society. It is not necessary that such a theory claim that there will be no violations of the public code of justice and morality on the part of citizens, that there will be no need for coercive enforcement or that the state will wither away. However, it is crucial that the theory posit that the most harmful features of human selfishness, immorality, asociality, and conflict are socially caused, and thus that the perfect implementation of the theory will itself remove those causes and their pernicious effects on human consciousness and motivation.

This is the sense in which I want to argue that Quṭb consistently and cumulatively elaborates a theory of Islamic social order as a realistic utopia, based in large part on his use of the claim to harmony between the *sharīʿa* and *fiṭra*. His theory of Islamic social order as a realistic utopia is developed around a number of themes: (1) the need for purity and integrity within a creedal and moral system; (2) the essential practicality and worldliness of the Islamic mission; (3) the *sharīʿa*'s perfection in matching human nature, or "taking people as they are"; and thus (4) the superiority and choice-worthiness of the *sharīʿa* for modern subjects.

In addition to introducing elements of revelation and Islamic law to make his case, Quṭb consistently discusses the "*salaf*" (first generations of Muslims). We should see this as neither religious nostalgia for a unique sacred moment nor an epistemic commitment to closing the books of interpretation with the death of those who had unmediated access to the Prophet. Rather, a large part of what Quṭb's treatments of the period of the Islamic founding do is provide a model of how moral obligation and moral motivation can be realized in the same theory. The *salaf*-period for Quṭb is thus not a symbol of the agonizing gap between original charismatic perfection and present state of humanity, but exactly the opposite. It is proof of the realistic possibility of justice brought about though the actions of distinctly ordinary humans.

At the same time, by examining closely his treatment of this period alongside his theoretical-doctrinal reflections, we gain an appreciation for how Quṭb's theory is uniquely political, even in the context of modern Islamist thought. For Quṭb the harmonization of mankind's true self-interest and actual moral personality can only be realized through the security (in multiple senses of the term) offered by a perfectly just political society. Thus, Quṭb's account of the "unique Qur'anic generation" and what went wrong is also a story about the origins of human vice. The origins of sin and worldly misery are not in man's postlapsarian nature, but in the corruption of the original political order inaugurated by the Prophet Muḥammad.

Purity and Integrity

For Quṭb, the most damaging legacy of Western imperialism for Muslims was that Islam had been relegated to a purely spiritual doctrine and deprived of jurisdiction over all realms of this-worldly life. Quṭb frequently seeks to draw the distinction between Islam, for which this separation between religion and secular power is entirely alien, and other religions such as Christianity, Buddhism, and Hinduism, for which it is logical.[18] That some Muslims had been complicit in importing secular doctrines from the West (the notorious "*ḥulūl mustawrada*"—"imported solutions"—decried by Islamist groups) only made this alien imposition all the more pernicious. One of the most obnoxious features of the false consciousness from which many of his contemporaries suffered was their tendency to measure Islam by the standards of the West, whether this involved proving Islam's compatibility with secularism, democracy, human rights, or modern just war theory.

In *Basic Principles of the Islamic Worldview,* this modern dilemma is given a history. "In the history of Islam, there came a time when the original Islamic way of life, derived from the correct Islamic concept, came in contact with other ways of life and cultures predominating in the conquered lands."[19] This contact led to the sullying of the original pure Islamic "concept" with Greek philosophy, which in turn led to the "intellectual indulgence" of theology and other "tendencies alien to the Islamic concept." The early rationalist theological school of the Muʿtazilites and the later Neo-Platonic tradition of Islamic philosophy are identified as the bastard offspring of this encounter.

Elsewhere, the more or less historically based account of what went wrong in Islam given in *Social Justice in Islam* and *Basic Principles of the Islamic Worldview* is given a transhistorical interpretation in the form of Quṭb's well-known concept of *jāhiliyya.* Traditionally the term used to describe the pagan "ignorance [of God]" of the pre-Islamic Arabs, for Quṭb (following Mawdūdī), *jāhiliyya* was used in a starkly Manichean mode to identify everything in the world (ideas, concepts, lands, even persons) that was un-Islamic, insufficiently Islamic, or impurely Islamic. "When we speak of a *jāhili* society, we are not referring to conditions that might have prevailed during a particular period of history. *Jāhilī* is every society in which humans are subjugated by others."[20] *Jāhiliyya* is a permanent threat to Islamic authenticity, no less than in the time of the Prophet, and in the postcolonial world as likely to come from internal traitors as from external aggressors.[21]

Following logically from the premise that Muslims are today, and perennially, beset with the threat of ideological imperialism and the dilution of pure Islamic "concepts" with anything alien is the premise that Muslims have an obligation to discover and apply authentic Islamic solutions that by definition must be pure and integral, just as the Qur'ān urged the first Muslims "with clear determination to erase all aspects of the *jāhilī* society from which Islam saved the Muslim community, [thus] removing whatever vestiges of that society remained, and fashioning the distinctive features of the Islamic society and bringing its unique personality into sharp relief."[22]

Before any claim about Islam's distinctive features and essential superiority is advanced, the assertion on Quṭb's part is that it is a communal obligation to search for solutions derived from Muslims' own heritage. Quṭb compares "spiritual resources, intellectual capabilities, and moral and ethical traditions" to economic and political resources—no one would think of borrowing capital or importing raw materials before examining one's own stocks.[23] And yet, that is exactly what his contemporaries sought to do. This borrowing is a clear historical betrayal of Islam's spirit and origins, for the Christian divide between the spiritual and the worldly never belonged to Islam, according to Quṭb.[24] Islam's "adherents cannot be true Muslims unless they practice their faith in their social, legal, and economic relationships, [and] a society cannot be Islamic if it expels the civil and religious laws of Islam from its codes and customs."[25]

Countless further references to these themes of authenticity, integrity, and cultural purity could be cited. For sure, the extreme extent to which Quṭb stresses the need for absolute purity and isolation from other influences and standards of evaluation,[26] and his sheer consistency in doing so, recalls what some scholars have referred to as a "generic fascism" percolating in his milieu.[27] However, the premise that Islam is completely self-contained is, if anything, overshadowed in Quṭb's writings by the claim that Islam is ideally suited for application in this world because it is an essentially practical religion.

What Does It Mean for Islam to Be Practical?

The assertion of Islam's practicality is a core distinguishing feature of all twentieth-century Islamist thought. When we speak of modern

Islamist movements and thinkers as belonging to modernity, this is most clearly discernable in their repackaging of Islamic law and ethics as an accessible and attractive "system" ready to square off in battle as a fully formed, fully coherent alternative to Marxism, capitalism, and liberalism.[28] However, what is important to note about this claim is that it is not just a matter of politicizing Islam into a militant theology of liberation through praxis.[29]

Rather, what is at stake is a general claim about the nature of Islamic ethics and governance. The basic notion is that "the essential spirit of this religion is this—that practical work is religious work, for religion is inextricably bound up with life and can never exist in the isolation of consciousness in some world of conscience alone."[30] Certain obvious questions follow. What is the nature of this practical work? What is the significance of this practical work being of a religious nature? Is the point that practical work is subject to a rigorous set of religiously given moral guidelines? Or that religion endorses, and thus sacralizes, practical work as humans are wont to pursue it? Quṭb's answer is in two parts: First, that Islam is a comprehensive theory of everything, from the origins of the cosmos to the ethics of daily life; second, that Islam's ethics of this-worldly social life are deeply pragmatic and perfectly suited to all of man's needs.

The first part of the claim about Islam's essential pragmatism is well known and has largely been presented above. It is the famous claim that Islam "discusses the nature of the servitude to God that permeates both the universe and human life. It expounds the nature of the universe, of life and of man; their origin, attributes, and conditions; the relations that exist among them; and finally, the connection that links them all to the supreme divine reality. It joins this all together in a single, logical concept."[31] It is perhaps the defining feature of modern Islamism that it presents itself as a comprehensive philosophical outlook that holds self-creation and justice, private perfection and human solidarity, in a single vision. What is important for our present purposes is only the fact that Quṭb's description of Islam as a distinctly practical doctrine follows for him from Islam's metaphysical origins and absolute comprehensiveness. God has overlooked nothing in the creation of the *sharīʿa,* including the most mundane of mankind's social needs, and therefore "we should not despair of the ability of the *sharīʿa* to govern modern society."[32]

The first implication of the practicality of the religious law is thus that humans are not permitted to act in this world individually and collectively purely according to conscience, reason, or custom, even if humans are often capable of arriving at roughly sound moral judgments through intuition or inspiration. Muslims (all humans, in fact) are charged by God with obedience and with acting in accordance with the law,[33] and failing to do this, regardless of any this-worldly benefits that (post-)Muslims might attach to this false freedom, is the great crime of the modern Muslim world.

In other words, the law, as it pertains to social and political life, is demanding. References to the demands of the law are copious in Quṭb's writings. For present purposes, it suffices to note that for Quṭb it is a central task of the law not only to accommodate human desires but to confront them. "The stability that characterizes the fundamentals and values of the Islamic concept . . . protects Islam from the corruption that would befall the universe as a whole were it to be prey to the whims and passions of man, without any restraint or firm basis."[34]

It is an important point of theological principle that God's commands are not subject to human ratification, rejection, or modification and need not be immediately coherent or intelligible to humans. Rarely, however, does Quṭb describe these demands as mysterious to humans or as arbitrary for ultimate human well-being in this world. The following statement encapsulates the compatibility between the theological principle and Quṭb's political project: "God wishes that His will should customarily appear to man in the form of consistent norms and regular patterns, which men can observe, perceive and order their lives and interact with the universe accordingly. They must, however, remain aware that His will is absolute and that He does whatsoever he wishes, even if it contradicts the norms and patterns to which they are accustomed."[35] Although God could have created a painful, confusing, and seemingly arbitrary moral law, in His infinite mercy he created one that is consistent, regular, and rewarding.[36]

For this reason, even when Quṭb describes the law as onerous or demanding, the fulfillment of its strictures is rarely (if ever) presented as a genuine sacrifice for humans, still less a perpetual tragic drama of the human condition. The demands of religious morality are, at their most demanding, genuinely uplifting of the human self. They are demanding and onerous only to our baser, lower selves. To our higher selves, they are nothing but guidelines to living in accordance with what we actually want and what actually brings us happiness. Man, we are told, "by his innate nature [*fiṭra*], cannot reside in this huge world simply as an isolated and straying particle. He must establish a certain connection with this universe, guaranteeing him stability and allowing him to discern his place in the world. He needs a creed that will explain his environment and his place within that environment. This is both an innate and a perceived need."[37] "The human soul cannot live alone in deviation from the order of the universe. It cannot attain happiness while in a state of constant flight, deprived of a guide and lacking all foundation."[38] Thus: "Man attains his most elevated rank and highest position when he has attained servitude to God, for he is then in fullest conformity to his innate nature [*fiṭra*]."[39]

But second, it is not even in this sense of "*sharīʿa* as positive liberty" that Quṭb claims that the divine law "takes people as they are." Rather, it is in the sense of accommodating even people's ordinary selves. That is, the more important point for present purposes is that the demands of religious morality are presented as appropriate and beneficial even in a less exalted, more universally intuitive sense.

This theme is addressed most generally in the form of the claim that Islam not only addresses mundane life as part of its comprehensiveness but also strikes exactly the right balance between two competing realms of human life: spirituality and materialism. Christianity, for Quṭb, only addresses man's spiritual needs while neglecting his material ones.[40] Capitalism and Marxism (he sees Marxism as nothing more than the logical extension of capitalism's materialism) addresses man's material needs while neglecting his spiritual ones. Only Islam takes both equally seriously and fulfills both to the greatest possible extent. "If in any age we find a desire to overemphasize the pietistic aspect of this faith and to divorce it from the social aspect, or to divorce the social aspect from it, it will be the fault of that age rather than of Islam."[41] "It is Islam, and Islam alone, that enables man to live both for this world and for the hereafter, to work for God and to work for his own livelihood, to realize the human perfection to which his religion is pointing him while engaged in the daily activities which his function as divine vicegerent imposes on him. Nothing is asked of him in return save one thing: that he . . . worship God alone . . . [and] not go beyond the broad sphere of the permitted, which includes all the wholesome pleasures of life."[42] Quṭb presents the argument in the language of a generic, semi-Marxist ideology critique:

> We have no good grounds for any hostility between Islam and the struggle for social justice—within the bounds of the Islamic method and Law—such as the hostility which persists between Christianity and Communism. For Islam prescribes the basic principles of social justice and establishes the claim of the poor to the wealth of the rich; it lays down a just principle for power and for money and therefore has no need to drug the sentiments of men and summon them to neglect their earthly rights in favor of expectation in the Kingdom of Heaven. On the contrary, it warns those who neglect their natural rights that they will be severely punished in the next world, and it calls them "self-oppressors."[43]

But what does it mean for a religion to be practical or to give human material desires their due? What does it mean to "join [man and the universe] together in a single, logical concept, one appealing to man's essential nature [*fiṭra*], interacting with his mind and his conscience, with the totality of his being, easily and painlessly"?[44] It would seem to require one of two things. A first possibility is a conception of "human nature" which bifurcates the self into an exalted self and a baser self. On this conception, the normative theory need only prove its compatibility with this idealized conception of nature. Such a theory still leaves plenty of room for rigor and moral demandingness as would be experienced by the empirical, baser self. Islam would then be easy and painless only for our "true" selves, not always for our actual ones. A second possibility, without necessarily foregoing the first and all of its rich possibilities for closing justificatory gaps between theory and inconvenient actual human desires, is to give some consideration to the desires and limitations of the empirical, baser self. It is this second approach that involves setting limits to the demandingness of ideal morality in light of average human capacities for selflessness and deprivation.

Quṭb does indeed believe that mankind is composed of a dual nature composed equally of earthly clay and God's spirit, following a series of important Qur'ānic verses, including 38:71–72[45] and 76:3.[46] His commentary on Q. 91:7–10 is a succinct statement of his position:

> God has created man with a duality of nature and disposition. The two ingredients in his composition, earth's clay and God's spirit, form within him two equal tendencies to good or evil, to either follow divine guidance or go astray. This dual ability is deeply ingrained in him. All external factors, like divine messages, only serve to awaken his ability and help it take its chosen way.[47]

However, although we might expect a political perfectionist like Quṭb to only be interested in demonstrating compatibility between Islam and the noumenal, "higher" conception of *fiṭra,* what is worthy of keeping under consideration is the extent to which Quṭb goes in stressing Islam's regard for the empirical, baser self, for average human capacities.

Taking People as They Are

So what does it mean for a religion to be practical? In addition to allowing for flexibility in the application of the law because of the need to react to social realities, part of its practicality and superiority is the attention it pays to human psychology—human needs, desires and limitations. Quṭb's writings are replete with proclamations that the Islamic moral code not only places demands on human behavior, but also restricts those demands to what humans can bear without great stress, given certain constants about their nature. Islam is declared to be "suitable to human nature, responsive to all its aspects, and fulfilling of all its needs"[48] and to "not injure the individual . . . nor oppose human nature."[49]

As noted earlier, some accounts of this essential compatibility between *sharīʿa* and human nature are divine intentionality accounts. "God created man's nature in harmony with the universe."[50] "Islam gave a unity to all powers and abilities, it integrated all desires and inclinations and leanings, it gave a coherence to all men's efforts. In all these Islam saw one embracing unity which took in the universe, the soul and all human life."[51] "The task of living beings is not to contend with Nature, for they have grown up in her bosom, and she and they together form a part of the single universe which proceeds from the single will."[52]

It is this account that I suggested above inclines toward a positive liberty conception of the convergence between law and human interests. Islam is "a religion whose imperatives conform to human nature, enabling all man's capacities to function for the purpose for which they were created. Man is able to reach his highest levels of perfection through movement and effort, through responding to his aspirations and longings and not by subduing or suppressing them."[53] Furthermore, leaving nothing to chance, Quṭb insists that after emancipation from bondage to false gods, from fear of death and injury and from false social values, the human soul may "remain in subjection to its own self [*dhātiyya*], swayed by its pleasures and its appetites, by its desires and its longings. Thus an inner tyranny replaces the outer. . . . The soul that is thus completely freed from strangling desires is the soul that Islam seeks."[54]

However, this positive liberty account is not the only, or even the most common, explanation of how Quṭb thinks the *sharīʿa* accommodates human nature. Rather, in numerous points he stresses that when he refers to Islam's "compatibility with the nature of man . . . [it] is man as familiar to us, with all of his strengths and weaknesses, his inclinations and passions, his flesh, blood and nerves, his body, mind and soul. He is not a being as willed by some extravagant fantasy or a floating dream derived from the operations of pure logic. He is also not the being depicted as the lowest of the low by those who regard him as the creation of dumb nature or of economic forces."[55] Further:

> He is man, the real, the actual, and the path that Islam traces out for him is therefore a realistic and actual one. Its limits cor-

> respond to the limits of man's own capacities and his nature as a creature of flesh and blood, with body, reason, and spirit all intermingled in his being. Despite its loftiness, purity, idealism, and divine origin, the Islamic way of life is designed for a being living on this earth, one who eats food, walks through the market, marries and procreates, likes and dislikes, hopes and fears, and expresses all the traits of humanity that God has placed in him. It takes into account his essential nature, his capacities and talents, his virtues and vices, his strengths and weaknesses. . . . It does not depict him as a pure and translucent angel, devoid of all material aspect. It does not, therefore, despise his natural instincts and needs.[56]

It is clear that while Quṭb is confident that Islam as is has struck exactly the perfect balance between demandingness and lenience in morality, he nonetheless regards it as a serious and unavoidable obligation of morality to be responsive to an empirically observable human nature. When he writes that "a respect for humanity requires us to look at it more profoundly and with a stronger perception of the profundity of its nature [*ṭabīʿa*], the authenticity of its innate character [*fiṭra*] and its deep roots," his point is to insist that "we be more judicious, more restrained and more precise in our thinking when we try to direct it and establish systems for it. We must not let millions of years of human experience go unheeded and postulate mere theories regarding man's inclinations, nature and behavior and then apply these theories by force and coercion."[57] It is in this context that Quṭb makes this remarkable statement: "Justice demands that the social system shall conform to the desires of the individual and satisfy his inclinations—at least so far as will not injure society—as a return for his contribution to it in the way of ability and labor; in the sweat of his brow, in the labor of his thought, and in the exertion of his nerves."[58] In this, if nothing else, Quṭb's transformation of the Islamic *sharīʿa*-based political vision into a system for the modern era seems to share a core anxiety with Rawlsian and other forms of political or justificatory liberalism.

But what are these desires that Quṭb assumes are enduring in human nature and that even religion must respect and accommodate? This, of course, is the crucial question that every moral theory must answer. Every moral theory must give an account of which desires and inclinations are immoral or excessively unreasonable and must not be accommodated by morality, and which are both reasonable and perduring—"natural"—and thus may be accommodated without great harm to morality's aims.

Quṭb tends to be most understanding of mankind's limitations in the realm of material and physical desires.[59] He quotes the Qur'ān's reference to man's "love of gain" (Q. 100:8) and natural "avarice" (Q. 4:128) but observes in God's commands a "liberality with His mercy." The law is thus presumed to take nonideal facts into account. "Accordingly, when Islam comes to lay down its rules and laws, it counsels and controls, that natural 'love of gain' is not overlooked, nor is that deep natural avarice forgotten; selfishness is rebuked, avarice is dealt with by regulations and laws, [but] no duty is enjoined on man beyond his capacity."[60] "Islam does not depreciate the value of wealth or of children."[61] and "is aware of the instinct to love oneself and to love money."[62] "Man is charged to enjoy himself within boundaries . . . to give himself his due."[63] A ubiquitous theme throughout Quṭb's writings is that God has created the world for man's enjoyment, within reason, and that humans should feel no guilt about the lawful enjoyment of wealth, food, and sex. All of this is justified through dozens of Qur'ānic verses, most parsimoniously in Q. 3:14–15: "Alluring to man is the enjoyment of worldly desires through women, and children, and heaped up treasures of gold and silver, and horses of high mark, and cattle, and lands. All this may be enjoyed in the life of this world."

In addition to material and physical desires, humans have an inclination to act on their abilities and endowments and bridle at unnatural restrictions on their freedom. By way of "freeing Islam from the narrow interpretation of social justice as understood by communism," Quṭb distinguishes between moral or spiritual equality and natural equality: "We cannot deny that some individuals are born with endowments of disposition, such as healthiness, or physical integrity, or stamina; while others are born with a predisposition to sickness, or debility, or weakness."

"Is" then quickly becomes "ought" for Quṭb:

> Accordingly, to deny the existence of outstanding endowments of personality, intellect and spirit, is a piece of nonsense which is not worth discussing. So, we must reckon with all these endowments, and to all of them we must give the opportunity to produce their greatest results . . . On no account must we close off the outlet for such endowments or discourage them by making them equal in reward with lesser abilities; we must avoid shackling such gifts and stifling them, and thereby depriving of their fruits the community and the human race alike.[64]

Importantly, Quṭb does not regard this essential realism as a necessary but regrettable concession to reality, the way that some strict egalitarians regard paying doctors more money to deploy their talents as quite clearly a matter of giving in to a form of blackmail or bribery. Allowing persons to develop their talents, even at the cost of societal inequalities, is permissible because "Islam admits the reasonable [*al-maʿqūla*] causes of these [material] differences as being differences in strength and in endowment. It does not permit differences which depend on rank and station."[65]

A similar claim for the law having essentially preempted human disobedience by conceding certain inevitable human desires is given in the realm of retributive justice. In Islamic law, unpremeditated homicide is treated as a civil offense, and the victim's family is permitted to exact recompense in either money or blood. In his presentation of this feature of Islamic criminal law, Quṭb takes the scriptural foundation of this punishment for granted, commenting only on its function in light of human moral psychology. He presents the *sharīʿa* rule essentially as a concession to human inclinations, as if Islam knows that man is inclined to take revenge and thus "prescribes a principle of vengeance, awarding it as a legal right to the next of kin and permitting him to exact it in full; yet at the same time it exhorts as strongly as possible that men should forgive, forbear, and pardon."[66]

There is yet a further dimension to Quṭb's concern with human nature and the law. Throughout his writings, he reflects on the necessary conditions whereby humans will willingly conform to the demands of the moral law. His presentation of Islam as an essentially easy moral code, one that imposes no unnecessary or overly burdensome hardships to the average human self, constitutes a large part of this account. However, his writings also contain frequent speculations on when humans will be led to fulfill even these moderate demands. These reflections constitute an extended (although often unsystematic) reflection on the problems of moral motivation and the perpetual stability of a normatively justifiable system, problems which I introduced above as the core preoccupations of realistic utopian theories.

Still under the topic of property and social justice, Quṭb reflects on the psychology of ownership and redistribution per his claim that "Islam is aware of the instinct to love oneself and money . . . and treats all of this psychologically."[67] Above, it was noted that Quṭb regards differences in natural endowments as reasonable sources of social inequalities. However, he continues to discuss the stakes of failing to permit such reasonable inequalities. "The man who has the greatest abilities and who can produce the most will always overcome the law of absolute equality. Or if he cannot do that, he will hate it and resent it; in which case, either he will rebel or his intelligence will be extinguished, his abilities will atrophy, and his power of production will be lessened."[68]

Similarly, social justice is justified in terms of man's psychological needs: freedom from humiliation and protection of his self-esteem. Not only is the need for food the most humiliating need, but asking for charity causes "all one's self-esteem to leave, lost forever." "Accordingly, Islam makes the right of an individual to a competence a responsibility of the state and of the rich members of the community . . . the *zakāt* is to be received as a right, not given as a charity."[69] The concern to avoid the humiliation of the poor is certainly a moral objective in its own right, but surely also fits into a consistent pattern of searching for the conditions under which social institutions will not only be justified to persons but also under which the subjects of those institutions will be motivated to support them.

Similar reflections are forthcoming on the question of inherited wealth, always a core question for theorists of distributive justice. In Islam's law of inheritance, Quṭb sees an "equitable balance between effort and reward. The parent who works knows that the fruit of his labors will not be realized in the short and limited span of his own life, but will stretch forward to be enjoyed by his children and his grandchildren. Such a parent will give of his very best and produce as much as he can by which the welfare of the state and of the human race as a whole is served."[70] However, note that the equality and fairness of such a principle is "over and above the fact that it is in accordance with human nature [*fiṭra*] and in agreement with the fundamental inclinations of man's soul; for it is with these inclinations that Islam reckons when it establishes its whole social system."[71]

The question of the legitimate origins and extent of wealth provides Quṭb with multiple opportunities to reflect both on the extent of human moral capacities and also on the effects of inequality on the stability of a just society. He argues that Islam only permits the acquisition of property through some form of direct effort, thus prohibiting gambling and usury in addition to theft, for "there is nothing like work for reforming the soul, strengthening the body, and guarding the whole nature of man from the diseases of flabbiness, laziness and weakness."[72] Of course, these are personal virtues but ones of no small significance for others, for "excessive wealth [makes a man] drink blood and sweat in his greed, voracious in his idleness."[73] Furthermore, in shades of Ibn Khaldūn[74] and Rousseau, "the lover of luxury is flabby and weak-willed, soft, and with little virility; he cannot rely on his strength, his ambition has failed, and his generosity has vanished. To take part in *jihād* would hinder the gratification of his petty desires and forbid him his animal pleasures for a time."[75] Nonetheless, even while railing against the crime of luxury, it is still the "just middle course between luxury and deprivation"[76] that Quṭb calls for. Once again, "no matter how much it seeks to raise men above the material considerations of this world, Islam never lays obligations on them beyond their human capacities."[77]

Quṭb's argument against extreme material inequalities between members of a common society reduces to a concern for the quality of the moral relationship between social unequals.

> An excess of wealth on one side and a lack of it on the other produces a profound corruption, greater even than that produced by hatred and rancor. . . . [The effect] on the other

> side of the community, which lacks wealth, takes the form of the sale or barter of personal honor, or the form of flattery, or falsehood, or the destruction of personality—all simply to satisfy the desires of the wealthy and to pander to their false vanity. . . . All this takes no account of the personal hatreds and individual jealousies, roused by those who have immoderate wealth, in the hearts of the poor who cannot find enough for their needs. The reaction here is sometimes hatred, sometimes a feeling of degradation and debasement; such men feel their status is lowered in their own eyes and their honor sullied in the face of the power and influence of wealth. Thus they are reduced to a small and humble manhood that knows nothing but the desire to please the rich and the powerful.[78]

The previous paragraph could virtually have been written by Rousseau.[79] However, I submit that this similarity is not only a matter of a common moral sensibility (on this one question of wealth and virtue) but also a function of their shared concerns with providing an account of the perpetual stability of their realistic utopia.

Observe, thus, how Quṭb treats the problem of freedom of conscience. "Complete social justice cannot be assured, nor can its efficiency and permanence be guaranteed, unless it arises from an inner conviction of the spirit." Quṭb's concern here is not with value or epistemic pluralism, but with the conditions for the stability of a just order: "No man will claim justice by law unless he has first claimed it by instinct and by the practical methods that ensure the preservation of instinct. Similarly, society will not persevere with such legislation unless there is a belief that demands it from within and practical measures that support it from without. It is these facts that Islam has in mind in all its ordinances and laws."[80]

Of course, we should not contort his approval of Islamic law's traditional tolerance of Jews and Christians into a greater defense of freedom of conscience than it is.[81] (Indeed, this point will take on importance below.) Rather, Quṭb is primarily interested in emphasizing that an Islamic order must not only establish the right laws, but take care to cultivate the consciousness of those laws' subjects. Where he does display an interest in an innate human need for negative liberty, it is in the realm of economic behavior, the freedom (discussed earlier) to develop one's talents. Contra the Communist view: "Economic freedom in itself [here Quṭb means the freedom from poverty and deprivation] has no guarantee of permanence in society unless there is also freedom of conscience within the mind. For it produces only another form of tyranny—the repression of individual gifts and abilities and inclinations . . . a repression of the individual, inasmuch as his natural abilities are unable to find an outlet and have no opportunity of growing in competition with others."[82]

Quṭb's concern with freedom of conscience in connection with the problem of moral motivation and the stability of a just social order has a deeper dimension than the mere need for a community to socialize its members into common beliefs. This is not about the value of a "civil religion" for caulking the remaining gaps in actual citizens' devotion to the body politic that its inherent justness does not fill.

Even *Social Justice in Islam,* an early text from his Islamist phase, lacking in the militant rage of the better-known *Milestones* (written after a decade of persecution at the hands of Nasser's secular nationalist regime), is perfectly clear that the freedom of conscience sought by Islam is about "freeing the human conscience from servitude to anyone except God and from submission to any save Him."[83] For Quṭb, this emancipation from "the instinct of servitude to and worship of any of the servants of God" (i.e., other humans) is nothing less than a comprehensive emancipation from fear. When the human conscience is freed from servitude to anything but God, "and when it is filled with the knowledge that it can of itself gain complete access to God then it cannot be disturbed by any feeling of fear of life, or fear for livelihood, or fear for its station."[84]

Quṭb's interest in fear is almost exclusively political. "Fear is an ignoble instinct which lowers the individual's estimation of himself, which often makes him accept humiliation or abdicate much of his natural honor or many of his rights" and it is precisely because "Islam insists strongly that dignity and honor are the rights of man" that "it is particularly anxious to oppose the instinct of fear."[85] Without this fear, man is free to develop a certain kind of moral personality that allows the weak to demand their rights and thus provides for a moral commitment to a just social order.

At this point, Quṭb's concern with the need for an Islamic order to devote attention to the conscience and consciousness of its members reveals some important attitudes toward law and its place in Quṭb's realistic utopia. One observes here the way in which both features of realistic utopian thought converge: one, the need to provide an account of stability and, two, the concern to limit morality's demandingness on the average human conscience. Thus, I believe that one can observe in Quṭb's writings two distinct kinds of attitudes about the law and human consciousness: that Islam requires the kind of consciousness which supports law and society, but also organically creates and fosters it once the system is in place; and that Islam points beyond law to a higher consciousness and supererogatory duties.

Along the lines of the first attitude, Quṭb asserts that "the Islamic concept stirs in the conscience the desire to do good and be steadfast, dynamic and effective . . . [it] annuls and invalidates all kinds of negativism."[86] "The issue in comprehending the Qur'ān is . . . to equip the soul with emotions, perceptions and experiences similar to those that accompanied the revelation in the Qur'ān."[87] The relationship between realizing Islam as a system and individual Muslims adopting the consciousness of believers is that of a virtuous cycle. Religion naturally acts on the minds and hearts of persons in marvelous ways. Inter alia, by striking a balance "between that which inspires fear, apprehension and awe on the one hand and that which inspires security, tranquility and intimacy on the other,"[88] a religious conception is uniquely capable of filling the Muslim's heart with "comfort and a sense of security." Quṭb interprets these as distinctly social virtues: "Men proceed with their lives, moving forward on the path of God, with firm steps, open eyes, and a vigorous heart, replete with hope."[89] And yet, the creation of the social order within which persons live and act is not only supported permanently by this new consciousness[90] but is also a prerequisite for that consciousness attaining its full fruition and freedom to act.[91] Quṭb's view is perhaps something like the following: humans are more or less capable of perfecting their moral personality but require for this not only inspiration and moral education but also social and psychological security in order to fully submit to their better nature. This social and psychological security can only be provided by a political order based on and coercively enforcing in a publicized way a comprehensive moral doctrine.

Here emerges a second attitude toward law. Let us recall first a number of possibly contradictory points that have been observed at various points in this chapter. On the one hand, Quṭb is a political perfectionist of the most enthusiastic and optimistic sort. Islam promises release from all individual worldly fears and humiliations; perfect justice and solidarity in this world; and eternal salvation after it. Knowledge of these promises inspires in the believer an exalted moral consciousness and practical virtue. On the other hand, the law which man is commanded to obey in this world is consistently described as easy and undemanding. Importantly, as a theorist of a realistic utopia Quṭb is committed to both propositions.

Thus, although his vision is undoubtedly a *sharīʿa*-centered vision for the Islamic community, he at numerous points looks beyond law. For Quṭb, law is about what man can be reasonably commanded to do by God, but is not the peak of human perfection. Law sets the minimum requirements for behavior, within the limits of average persons' capacities. However, the law is not the culmination of Islamic moral ideals; Islam sets goals beyond the law for man to aspire to.

In general, Quṭb reserves detailed commentary on the specifics of the law to his multivolume exegetical work. In his political tracts, he by and large passes over specific rulings of Islamic public, criminal, and private law, as if to say that the traditional interpretations are (for the most part) manifestly correct.[92] For example, in *Social Justice in Islam,* Quṭb summarizes the entire criminal code of Islam in three short pages, barely commenting on its foundation in the revelatory texts. But he devotes chapters to the question of the spirit of the law and the human consciousness that it seeks to create. The following are characteristic statements: "Beyond [law and duty] Islam appeals to the conscience, persuading it of its responsibility and seeking to raise it above its normal scope; thus it attempts to elevate human life and to draw it ever onward and upward. It leaves a wide space between the lower level of duty, which is prescribed by the law and the higher level of conscience, which is so desirable and towards which individuals and nations have striven in every age and century."[93] Islam "leaves the minimum level of achievement to the law, while to exhortation it prescribes the achievement of the supreme level; thus it leaves for man a wide space between these two, a gap that he can overcome as best he may."[94]

The Law We Would Give Ourselves

I suggested at the beginning of this chapter that to a great extent, Quṭb's preoccupation with solving the problems of moral motivation, the stability of a just order, and the proper demandingness of the law via the claim to the *sharīʿa*'s deep harmony with human nature serves a primarily apologetic function, as a preexisting and more or less stable feature of Islam that serves to justify Islam as such against any and all other ideological, religious, or moral alternatives. Out of countless statements to this effect, the following are characteristic and sufficient to establish the present point. "By their very nature, men will turn towards Islam because it ensures a perfect balance of all the aims for which previous religions have striven and between all the passions and desires of human nature [*fiṭra bashariyya*]."[95] "Since Islam alone takes into account all the aspects of man's humanity, it is also Islam alone that can raise man to the highest level and most perfect state attained in any time or place."[96] And thus, unlike Brahmanism and Christianity, not to mention secular ideologies, only

> Islam is a religion of realism, a religion for life and movement. It is a religion for work, production, and development, a religion whose imperatives conform to human nature, enabling all man's capacities to function for the purpose for which they were created. Man is able to reach his highest levels of perfection through movement and effort, through responding to his aspirations and longings and not by subduing or suppressing them. The Islamic mode of life laid down for mankind is thus realistic in the same way that the Islamic concept is itself realistic, with respect to God, the universe, life, and man. Creedal concept and practical action are in perfect harmony in Islam.[97]

However, there is another dimension beyond the mere apologetic claim. The questions of moral motivation, the stability of a just order and the proper demandingness of the law are also about theorizing the precise way in which Islam calls for political manifestation. I believe that the fullest picture of Quṭb's views on the relationship between political order and moral motivation, and their centrality to his thought, emerges only when we pay close attention to his frequent discussions of the earliest period of Islamic history.

Paradise Lost: The Political Origins of Moral Perfection

As I have argued to this point, Quṭb's writings contain an extended and cumulative account of how Islam as a system is to be understood as a realistic utopia perfectly harmonious with human nature and thus capable of providing for its own stability if it creates and fosters humanity's innate moral personality. Quṭb's discussions of the early Islamic period are fully part of this account. They are not just an appeal to the epistemic authority of the founding understandings (a kind of religious "Originalism" or "strict constructionism"), but are more specifically a description of an actual historical model of the feasibility and realism of his politico-psychological theory. The period of the early Muslims (the *salaf*) functions for Quṭb as a historical, back-projected (rather than purely mythical or hypothetical) account of the essentially political nature of the Islamic project and of the sufficiently realistic possibility of creating a self-sustaining moral order through political order: "This precedent indicates the possibility of its own repetition."[98]

However, more importantly, this period functions for him also as a philosophical account of the origins of human vice that explains both Muslims' present woes and also why they have cause to be optimistic about the future. For Quṭb, all sin is essentially political sin in two ways. First, God's law is about action and social order in this life, and thus violation of it is a crime against the Islamic political order, a defect of civic virtue. Second, although God has balanced the natural good in humans with the natural evil in them, for Quṭb it is almost always the corruption of the social, political world that causes humans to be overpowered by their capacity for vice.

One of the features of Quṭb's theory is his belief that there is a virtuous cycle between the individual adoption of moral motives and the creation of just institutions. Just institutions need some prior willingness on the part of subjects, but the practice of living under those institutions also fosters and encourages that willingness. As noted above, these views often reveal themselves most starkly in Quṭb's treatment of the questions of distributive justice and of the relationship between individual conscience and social institutions:

> When the human conscience has come to know [that it serves none but God], it will have no need of anything to preach equality to it in words, for it will already have experienced the full meaning of equality as a reality in its own life. Moreover, it will not endure the distinctions that arise from worldly values at all. It will seek equality as its right and will strive to ensure that right; it will guard it carefully when it is gained, and it will accept no substitute for it. It will bear the responsibility of guarding and defending its equality, cost what it may in effort and sacrifice. When the establishment of equality is rooted in the conscience, when it is safeguarded by religious law, and when it is guaranteed by a sufficiency of provision, the poor and the humble will not be the only persons to desire it. Even the rich and the powerful will support it, because their conscience acknowledges those values that Islam is intent on establishing and confirming, as we have already outlined them.[99]

Immediately following this passage, Quṭb continues: "This is what actually happened in Islamic society fourteen centuries ago," that is, at the time of Islam's founding.

To be sure, part of Quṭb's telling of this story is supernatural. Plenty of credit is given to "Islam" itself in the creation of a general "spirit" of equality and justice during the founding period, and especially in the creation of motives on the part of Islam's earliest rulers.[100] What is noteworthy, though, is the sheer extent to which this is a political story and to which Quṭb seeks to deny that Muḥammad "overcame [opposition] through a one-time miracle."[101] "Medina and the establishment of the first Muslim society . . . [was] the era in which the Islamic people emerged together with their social system, in which emotions, interests and principles vitally interacted with each other . . . [and] Qur'anic verses were revealed as living pulsating realities."[102] The just, radically egalitarian, Islamic order comes about through both a revolutionary political founding and the purification of conscience and virtue.

However, as to what went wrong, Quṭb leaves no doubt. This story is one of a brief moment of perfection attained through the symbiosis of human conscience and social egalitarianism, followed by a fall brought about by political corruption. "The reason for its brevity was the outcome of chance occurrences of evil, unconnected with the nature of the system."[103] Quṭb's golden age ends not with the "Four Rightly-Guided Caliphs," but with the death of the second caliph ʿUmar and his succession by ʿUthmān instead of ʿAlī.[104] The aged and infirm ʿUthmān was unable to restrain his corrupt kinsmen (the first opponents of Muḥammad in the early Meccan period, and the later Umayyad caliphs), unleashing a period of malfeasance that plagued also the all-too-short reign of the fourth caliph, ʿAlī. The assassination of ʿUthmān led directly to the first civil war, from which emerged victorious the demon of Quṭb's story, the first Umayyad caliph, Muʿāwiya.

"Muʿāwiya's spirit differed from the true nature of Islam," we are told, and he proceeded to create an entirely new "political theory" based on the nepotistic usurpation of public resources; the dynastic inheritance of political authority; and what was worst, the social stratification of the previously egalitarian Muslim society. Muʿāwiya's greatest crime, however, was spiritual and ideological:

> We condemn Muʿāwiya not only for instituting a new system of political theory . . . but for forcing people to accept it. . . . For in Islam politics, like life in general, had always been the expression of those moral feelings that lie deep within life and that are rooted in its very nature. The existence of those feelings was a natural consequence of that constant watchfulness that Islam enjoined upon the individual conscience and of that keen moral perception that it awakens in the souls of its adherents.[105]

If Islam's political morality "was a natural consequence of that constant watchfulness that Islam enjoined upon the individual conscience," then the inverse is obviously true as well. For how could a political usurpation have undone the moral progress of Islam unless the "keen moral perception that Islam awakens in the souls of its adherents" is also predominately a function of political order? Indeed, Quṭb insists that had Islam had the chance to set deeper roots through political continuity, "there would not have followed the obliteration of the spirit of Islam that did actually take place."[106] The "calamity that broke the back of Islam"[107] was nothing other than a "chance occurrence of evil" in the form of a botched handoff of political power.

Quṭb's Salafism is thus in essence a "Paradise lost" story, but one more Rousseauvian than Miltonian.[108] The tragedy of the human condition is not innate, original sin, but the political causes of inequality and vice. Quṭb's politico-psychological interpretation of the earliest period of Islam is thus an integral part of his political theory. For Quṭb, politics must be grounded in a comprehensive Islamic morality, not merely on deontological or authenticity grounds but also on moral perfectionist grounds. Although humans have a habit of disobeying God, their innately good moral nature is capable of overpowering this habit, but only in the right political conditions.

Traditionally, Sunni religious scholars have conceived of politics and religion as mutually dependent, but not essentially the same activity. On a fairly common "developed medieval" Sunni view, political order provides for the necessary legality and material conditions in order for religious life to flourish. However, it is not commonly imagined that individual moral perfection is achieved through politics or as a result of politics, even if political life is often given sacred or theological meaning via its association with the Imamate or with *sharīʿa*. Rather, the function of law and governance is often characterized primarily as a necessary restraint on human passions: "Rational beings tend by nature to submit to a leader who would keep them from iniquity and settle their conflicts and disputes. Without rulers, men would exist in a state of utter chaos and unmitigated savagery."[109]

For Quṭb, by contrast, "politics" is indispensable for a developed moral life on the part of the individual. This is largely because (as with

Rousseau) of the utterly corrupting impact of living in an unjust society, as he makes clear through his discussions of the *salaf* period. Humans cannot merely ignore the corruptions and temptations of the external world, retreating to some inner citadel. The avarice and oppression of the powerful is a double injustice against the weak: it deprives them of their rights but also destroys the social conditions that allow them to develop their innate moral personality. Humans are innately drawn to the behavior prescribed by the law, but they can only safely give in to this innate inclination when everyone is committed in the same way.

Importantly, Quṭb's reflections on the experiences of the "unique Qur'anic generation" are not only meant to show what went wrong but also to give hope that things can be put right. Social corruption is not inevitable because the political conditions on which human vice or virtue depends are correctable though human action. Morality is, for Quṭb, a consequence not of knowledge, disposition, or motivation alone, but of the habits formed when our innate dispositions are combined with daily socialization with others in the conditions of perfected and publicized justice. The history of the *salaf* is thus part of a political account of how humans become moral and, more importantly, a foundation for rational political hope: "Knowledge of the fact [that the *salaf* were ordinary humans] . . . gives mankind a strong hope in struggling for that bright and feasible ideal. It causes mankind to trust in its own nature and inner potentialities."[110]

Ruling and Being Ruled through the *Sharīʿa*

What makes Quṭb special and his works of enduring interest is not the presence of any single constitutive building block of his thought—the thesis of harmony between *sharīʿa* and *fiṭra* or the touting of Islam's essential ease—most of which are drawn freely from the stock of mainstream modern Islamic thought. Rather, what is noteworthy and distinctly modern is the edifice that he seeks to construct out of those building blocks. Just as he views comprehensiveness as one of the essential characteristics of Islam itself, his own political theory is a sustained attempt to construct out of Islamic norms and theological beliefs a comprehensive theory of social justice, political order, and human moral motivation.

The realism of Quṭb's theory rests on his efforts to show how humans of distinctly average moral capacities will achieve moral perfection in this political order with minimal sacrifice to their essential desires and inclinations and thus do so relatively easily. At the same time, while this personal, social, and political morality is shown to be the natural, logical, and simple one for individual humans to adopt, it is not the one that human societies will naturally gravitate toward. For in society it is all too easy for the dominant to assert themselves and create oligarchies corrupting of social and political conditions. And in such conditions, humans will lack the necessary security for their innate moral personality to triumph over their baser, more ignoble instincts. Thus, the paradox that a stable just political order is a consequence of a certain social moral consensus but is also a prerequisite for such a moral consensus in the first place.

This vision is, above all, an elaborate apologia for divine sovereignty. Although Mawdūdī was far more interested in the details of what it meant to uphold divine sovereignty juridically and institutionally, Quṭb is a better guide to how Islamists have understood the emancipatory vision of restoring God's sovereignty on Earth. As such, Quṭb's is in some ways a purer vision of divine sovereignty than Mawdūdī's. He would certainly not deny that the law requires interpretation and adaptation, and that this has to be done by certain human agents. He would also not reject the classical Sunni constitutional package of a limited ruler, expert legal interpretation, and popular consultation in areas suitable for it. But the passion animating his ideal theory is a conception of the divine law as already perfect in its wisdom, constraints, and lenience.

The contribution of Quṭb's recasting of the *sharīʿa* in moral-psychological terms to a popular dimension to law and politics is that the rule of the *sharīʿa* is not only portrayed as a just law to be applied to humans (by caliphs, sultans, or scholars), but as a law through which humans in fact also govern themselves. The law is portrayed largely in organic terms; the institutional and constitutional apparatus upholding it is of vanishingly little interest to Quṭb. In some theories we have encountered, the supremacy of law is what permits the many to be ruled by the few. In other theories, offices and institutions are designed with the aim of embodying a living, vibrant law. In Quṭb, the law appears almost to have an existence and force of its own. But the implication is that the law receives this existence through its acceptance and enforcement by the divinely deputized Muslim community. The law is given entirely and exclusively by God, but it rules through the people: "Wherever an Islamic community exists which is a concrete example of the divinely-ordained system of life, it has a God-given right to step forward and take control of the political authority so that it may establish the divine system on earth."[111] Moreover, because it is a law for a people imbued with piety and virtue, but with decidedly human weaknesses and limitations, it is not a law experienced as alien, but the law that the people would give themselves. Quṭb thus manages to claim both heteronomy and autonomy, both transcendence and immanence, for the rule of *sharīʿa.*

The writings of Sayyid Quṭb represent the high point of what I have referred to as "high utopian Islamism." The influence of Quṭb on more violent strands of Islamic thought and political action is widely appreciated. It is a short step from declaring an entire state or social system to be in a state of "*jāhiliyya*" because it is not based on Islamic law, to saying that this must be because of a conscious choice on the part of those who participate in such a system to be in open rebellion against God and His law. If such societies are composed of Muslims, or former Muslims, they are thus in a state of apostasy and violent rebellion against the divine system. This amounts to an anathema, or charge of apostasy *(takfīr),* directed against all persons cooperating within such a system. As the punishment for apostasy is death in Islamic law, and the response to violent rebellion is violent suppression, then it is not difficult to see how Quṭb's views have been conducive to armed movements seeking to overthrow existing regimes.

Quṭb's own organization, the Egyptian Muslim Brotherhood, largely foreswore violence after his execution in 1966 and was able to accommodate a range of views on the question of political legitimacy.[112] However, this was not the case for more radical groups, from the 1970s organization named by outsiders "*al-Takfīr wa'l-hijra*" to the "Islamic Group" *(al-Jamā'a al-Islāmiyya)* that assassinated Egyptian president Anwār Sadāt and then waged a guerilla and terrorist campaign in Egypt throughout the 1980s and 1990s.[113] When combined with the theological preoccupations and methods of modern Salafism (which has many doctrinal criticisms of Quṭb's theology), this ideology morphs into the "Salafi-Jihadi" trend exemplified by al-Qā'ida and the "Islamic State" organization.[114] All of these groups and ideologies have their particular features, but on the concept of divine sovereignty the core template remains: God has created the universe and thus has effective mastery over everything that is in it; it is the nature of creatures to owe worship to their Creator; obedience is the truest manifestation of worship; the greatest evil a creature with free will can commit is to defy one's Creator by denying Him obedience and obeying another creature; God has freely given us a law to govern our voluntary actions no less than our involuntary ones; this law is comprehensive and regulates all human behavior individually and collectively on the basis of God's perfect wisdom and good will for humanity; to choose voluntarily to follow any other law is thus willful rebellion against God and rejection of His existence and divinity; to seek to impose such a law on other humans is the greatest evil and injustice possible as it seeks to sunder men from their Lord and Creator; and finally, our efforts to legislate are not only unlawful trespass on God's authority but are doomed to lead to misery in this world, as humans cannot possess the wisdom and knowledge of God, who gave us a law in perfect harmony with the laws of the universe for our own good and happiness. For the ideologies of many of these groups, any form of democracy became synonymous with unbelief *(kufr)*,[115] a stance that forms the backdrop for the broader Islamist defense of democracy, which is the subject of the next chapter of this book.

The period after Quṭb and the rise of violent Islamist organizations led to countless denunciations from mainstream Islamists, beginning with Muslim Brotherhood General Guide Hudaybī's "Preachers, Not Judges." The hallmark of Islamist groups in the tradition of the Brotherhood in the area of practice has also been predominantly pragmatic and accommodationist with existing regimes.[116] In the realm of theory and doctrine, Islamists after Quṭb have devoted enormous intellectual energy to the questions of legitimacy and democracy, which are, properly speaking, questions about the relationship between divine and popular sovereignty. But much of this discourse not only represents an increase in technical precision or sophistication but also in the depth of its commitment to popular sovereignty. The following chapter examines the theory of "Islamic democracy" as a regime type, with special focus on the most prominent Islamist intellectual and politician associated with the idea of Islamic democracy, the Tunisian Rāshid al-Ghannūshī.

6

A Sovereign *Umma* and a Living *Sharīʿa*

I ended the Chapter 1 of this book by synthesizing a number of different literatures in Islamic constitutional and democratic theory. These included scholarly monographs on Islamic constitutional jurisprudence *(fiqh dustūrī)* or "the principles of government" *(uṣūl al-ḥukm)* in Islam, treatises written by Islamist public intellectuals or independent intellectuals sympathetic to political Islam, and some of the texts issued officially by Islamist groups. My claim there was that, for all their differences of style, motivation, and emphasis, there are some points of general consensus that together form a kind of plateau on which modern Islamic constitutional debates are conducted.

These points of general consensus include the view that the people is, broadly-speaking, the source or origin of the legitimacy of political institutions *(maṣdar al-sulutạ̄t),* can elect and supervise political officers, and can participate in various forms of consultation and lawmaking. Similarly, it is broadly agreed that elected rulers are agents or civil servants subject to the law and limited in their authority. Moreover, although elected representatives and state officials have broad powers of legislation and policy making, what makes a political order Islamic is that all laws and enactments must be subject to *sharīʿa* review of some kind. This is what is meant when some contemporary Islamic constitutional theorists claim that the state in Islam is neither theocratic nor fully secular, but rather a "civil state" with an Islamic referent.

That some of these views require arguing for and defending should be clearer now after the subsequent chapters. The classical tradition of Islamic governance largely assumed a condominium of authority between rulers and scholars, both of whom together and separately the people were said to have a religious obligation to obey. Rulers and scholars overlapped in their authority, but can be said to have represented a different face of Islamic legal normativity. Where the scholars speak for revelation and the history of its interpretation, rulers and other public officials speak for what the public interest requires in any given moment. If these two authorities are accountable to any authority besides each other, it is to an ill-defined body of elite representatives of the community, known generically as the People Who Loose and Bind. Importantly, not only do all of these authorities rule by their own self- and mutual recognition, but this entire "constitutional" system is often said to be mandated by God.

Moving into the twentieth century, these conceptions of legitimacy did not just fall away with the modern nation-state. Islamic constitutional theory from the fall of the Ottoman Empire does not univocally reject the legitimacy of appointment to supreme political office, or even authorization of an entire regime, by a body of scholars and other notables recognizing itself as the People Who Loose and Bind. Still less is the people's legislative sovereignty universally accepted. The distinguishing feature of Islamism is that it claims to locate sovereignty solely in the divine law. Given that the technical aspects of the divine law cannot be denied, epistocratic claims to authority on the part of scholars or experts in an "Islamic state" do not vanish. Islamists like Mawdūdī and Quṭb, I have argued, introduce a political theology that leads to a form of popular sovereignty, but they are also largely responsible for the widespread skepticism or rejection of democracy in the Islamist imagination as democracy is too easily associated with radical individual and collective human freedom to choose ultimate ends and legislate around them.

I have thus argued that the "high utopian Islamism" of Mawdūdī and Quṭb bequeathed a particular ideological complex, one both radically anti-democratic and radically populist. As I noted both in the first chapter and at the end of the preceding one, much of Islamist thought since the late 1960s can be seen as navigating this complex, trying to reject the most radical implications of Quṭbist thought while being unable to completely foreswear its utopian and theocentric vision. This has often taken the form of discussing seriously the question of "Islam and democracy" and developing the view that Islam in some way sees the people as sovereign. Since the contributions of Mawdūdī and Quṭb, the political theology of the caliphate of man has only attained greater centrality and near-universal endorsement. Cumulatively, I submit, there has emerged from this body of literature a theory of an ideal regime type, which I call "Islamic democracy," that takes the doctrine of the caliphate of man as far as it can go in a democratizing direction without losing a substantive commitment to divine sovereignty.

In this chapter, I do not continue to survey the entire body of literature cited in Chapter 1 on Islamist thought after Quṭb. Instead, I focus in close and careful detail on a single thinker that I consider to be both imaginative and representative of the democratic possibility of the caliphate of man, the Tunisian intellectual and party leader Rāshid al-Ghannūshī (1941–). I do not trace genealogically in any detail the road from Quṭb to Ghannūshī, connecting all of the mixing links. And of course no single figure can claim to have articulated an authoritative theory of legitimacy or sovereignty for all Sunni Muslims. Ghannūshī's views neither absorb nor eclipse all of the texts referenced in my earlier summary. He is, however, a particularly appropriate figure to select for a few reasons.

First, he is a figure whose reputation and influence are derived in almost equal measure from his political and intellectual activities. As a leader of the Tunisian Islamist movement since the 1970s,[1] he is an important representative of the broad social movement that has pressed and thus kept alive the questions of legitimacy and sovereignty for Muslim societies. The question of divine versus popular sovereignty matters only insofar as it matters to politically engaged Muslims. It follows that the measure of the successful resolution of these foundational questions is whether it is regarded as resolved by those for whom it matters. Thus, the doctrinal and ideological developments of Islamist leaders have some special interest for us.

But not all political leaders in the Islamist movement are equally important as intellectual figures. The most important intellectual figures for Egyptian Islamists, for example, have not tended to be the General Guides or Political Bureau members. Rather, as I noted in Chapter 1, religious scholars like Muḥammad al-Ghazālī and Yūsuf al-Qaraḍāwī, or independent intellectuals like Muḥammad Salīm al-ʿAwwā, and Muḥammad ʿImāra, are the most representative of developments in Islamist ideology. In some cases, political movements have been organized around a charismatic spiritual and intellectual figure (like Morocco's ʿAbd al-Salām Yāsīn and his Justice and Charity *[al-ʿAdl wa'l- Iḥsān]* movement). Ghannūshī is not the only figure in recent decades who might fit the bill of being both intellectually and political relevant. (Ḥasan al-Turābī [d. 1932–2016] was also both an intellectual figure and political leader of global and national importance, e.g.) But Ghannūshī's influence historically and in the present is undeniable.

Third, Ghannūshī's major work, which is the main subject of this chapter, is like a delta into which have flown most of the discourses discussed to this point, from the nineteenth-century reformists through Mawdūdī and Quṭb. This doesn't mean that he has superseded or replaced all of that work (naturally), but it means that it is reasonable to accord his arguments particular relevance and salience for the interests of this book. His arguments take on the major problems of sovereignty as they have developed since the nineteenth century, while he attempts to argue for conclusions that (I will suggest) advance that debate. To point to his representativeness and centrality is partly to note that there may be more original or idiosyncratic thinkers in modern Islamic thought (e.g., Muhammad Iqbal, whom I passed over briefly in Chapter 4). But this book is primarily concerned with a genealogy of popular sovereignty within a particular discourse, which requires following a debate that has some internal coherence and shared lineage. This is valuable even if (particularly if) we are also interested in thinkers or moments that represent more radical breaks and realignments (as I will be in my conclusion).

Fourth, because he is a thinker who belongs to and is representative of late-twentieth-century political Islam, with its particular styles, sources, and modes of reasoning, but is particularly committed to the theory and practice of democracy, it is reasonable to treat his intellectual efforts as telling us something about the core questions of this book: What does it mean to be committed to popular and divine sovereignty at the same time? What conceptions of political life are involved? And what are the limits, blind spots, and paradoxes of this effort? What can we say about the ideal theory of "Islamic Democracy" as a distinct regime-type? Ghannūshī both belongs to a wider tradition attempting to theorize this and is also (on my reading) a particularly complex, fertile, and surprising thinker.

This book culminates in a certain sense here. For few thinkers is the theory of the caliphate of man as central as it is for Ghannūshī. We see here all that that doctrine is capable of doing to ground a conception of popular sovereignty. And we thus also see clearly the conditions of possibility for a regime that it is in equal measure Islamic and democratic. If that regime type is, in the end, merely an ideal, then the question becomes whether the obstacles to fulfilling its conditions of possibility are permanent or insurmountable. Or whether the means required for surmounting those obstacles in some way invalidate important claims and commitment of the theory. I think that Ghannūshī's theory does, in fact, show us the limits of a political theory that is fully Islamic and fully democratic, and in fact show us the limits of sovereignty as the organizing problem for Islam and politics.

Dignity, Responsibility, Agency: The Doctrine of the Caliphate of Man

Ghannūshī identifies the covenant of vicegerency (*ʿaqd al-istikhlāf*) as more than one theological doctrine among many, but rather as the central idea of Islamic civilization and the basic principle of Islamic political philosophy.[2] Its significance is far greater than the idea of mankind's supremacy over other creatures on Earth.[3] In Ghannūshī's treatment, man's vicegerency of God is portrayed as involving both intrinsic and extrinsic aspects. The intrinsic aspects pertain to the way that the covenant of vicegerency accounts for the ethical status, moral personality, and capacities for action that characterize humanity. The extrinsic aspects pertain to the juridical and political implications of this doctrine for the distribution of authority within the Islamic *umma*.

Ghannūshī writes that the Islamic conception of politics is based on a metaphysical account of the totality of existence, premised on the beliefs "that God is the creator and master of all existence, more knowledgeable than His creatures and the highest legislator and commander, and that man has been distinguished from the rest of God's creatures by his designation as God's deputy, through which with he has been entrusted with reason, will, freedom, responsibility and the divinely ordered path for his life."[4] The universal caliphate is the foundation for a theological anthropology that is simultaneously a fixed status, a set of moral capacities, and a charge or aspiration.

First, as to the status: mankind has already been designated by God as His deputy on Earth whatever else humans do. This entails a certain inherent dignity that Ghannūshī frequently uses to explain the Islamic approach to human rights and public liberties. The core foundation of human rights is precisely that mankind is the deputy of God on Earth, a distinguished being among God's creatures.[5] The first human right, the right to life and personal security (and an absolute prohibition on torture), is not only a legal right but a sacred obligation on society and the individual derived from man's vicegerency and dignity.[6] Similarly, more advanced rights to social welfare and security are also related to the inherent dignity of man as God's caliph. That these rights, and the institutions that sustain them, precede the state is a central point for Ghannūshī. Because divine sovereignty and the dignity enjoyed by man as God's caliph are prior to any authority held by the state, they cannot be said to depend on the state for their force and validity.[7] Importantly, while the foundation for this theological anthropological account of human dignity is based on a truth-claim about mankind's relation to God and the source of knowledge about that relation, Ghannūshī insists that the enjoyment of that dignity and its social entailments is not invalidated by a rejection of that truth-claim. Holding false beliefs about matters of God and ourselves does not destroy our *status* as dignified, divinely entrusted beings, even after death.[8]

But humans enjoy this status of inherent dignity not as passive, inert objects of beauty, but as active beings. The sign of our dignity and our status as the vicegerents of God on Earth is what we can do and how we can do it. Our capacities for moral thought and action are the signs of our vicegerency. Ghannūshī tends to focus on a certain set of moral powers in relation to the doctrine of *istikhlāf.* For Ghannūshī, the vicegerency of God is above all associated with our possession of reason, will, and freedom (he sometimes adds speech).[9] It is our capacities for reason and speech, for example, that help explain the Islamic commitment (on his understanding) to expansive protections for thought, conscience, and expression: they should not be shackled because they are part of God's endowment that makes us fit to be His vicegerent on Earth. He notes that even angels are coerced by God to be good, while humans alone have the capacity to reflect, choose, and do good or evil.

At the same time, it is important that in the Islamic conception, freedom is a trust rather than a natural endowment, and this implies our lack of radical self-sufficiency or entitlement to create our own values and norms. Obviously, the possession of capacities for reason and rational self-direction in an Islamic theological anthropology cannot be mistaken for (Aristotelian) naturalism or (Kantian) autonomy. Our capacities are a trust from a specific agent who gifted them along with a set of injunctions. What follows from the fact that our vicegerency is not a mere status, but a set of granted or gifted capacities, powers, and possibilities is that our fulfillment of this trust is measured by our realization of God's law.

For Ghannūshī this foundation represents an important alternative to Western human rights frameworks and a parallel tradition in modern Islamic thought from the nineteenth-century Salafiyya Modernist movement to the present. As opposed to the Western conception, which in Ghannūshī's account refers to nature and to man himself as the source of all legislation, the Islamic conception refers everything back to God, to the *sharīʿa,* and to the claim that man is deputized by God *(mustakhlaf),* dignified by His creator with reason, will, and freedom, and helped along the way by prophets. "This general framework for life leaves empty wide areas to be filled by man exercising his vicegerency, through which the union of freedom and obligation, unity and pluralism, is realized."[10]

Thus, the third aspect of the conception of universal vicegerency is that it is a charge. The possession of capacities and knowledge entails a responsibility to act on them and as such to attain the rank of God's caliphs with the help of revelation brought by prophets. And so the universal caliphate is not only a status or a set of capacities but an aspiration. In Aristotelian terms, being "God's caliph" represents both kinds of actuality: our possession of the capacities for reason, will, and freedom form a potentiality, or first actuality, and exercising them in the right way in accordance with our responsibility to fulfill the covenant with God represents the attainment of full caliphal status, or second actuality. In this context, Ghannūshī quotes from ʿAllāl al-Fāsī's treatise on the ultimate objectives of the divine law *(maqāṣid al-sharīʿa)* to the effect that freedom is not a natural truth or fact, but an ordained created state, a struggle, and an aspiration only achieved through worship, obedience to God, and the voluntary acceptance of obligation. In Fāsī's memorable words, "Man could not have achieved freedom without revelation, for man was not created free, but created that he might become free."[11]

Ghannūshī is explicit in portraying the universal caliphate as a charge derived from the divine law and the fundamental relationship of obligation, and thus as an aspiration. Mankind attains an even more exalted status in living up to its appointment in "bearing the responsibility to guide his ship and shape his destiny in accordance with the divine plan for his life. He is an obligated being, the servant of God . . . in this scheme, rights become sacred duties. It is not the right of God's vicegerent to abandon or neglect them. Mankind is deputized by God, charged with acting in this capacity in accordance with the will of the Sovereign."[12]

Ghannūshī thus portrays the universal caliphate as the precondition for both individual agency as well as collective political life. God's master legislation for mankind (the *sharīʿa*) presupposes a human agent that can receive this law as a moral charge, has the moral capacity to either fulfill it or neglect it, and can accept collective responsibility for its enactment. This is precisely what opens up to the extrinsic aspects of the doctrine. For if it is humanity (or even the subset of it formed by the Muslim *umma*) that it is charged with upholding God's law, then the authority of specific humans or other man-made institutions can only be derivative from this general authority.

If the intrinsic elements of the doctrine of the universal caliphate pertain to mankind's status, composition, and obligations, the extrinsic elements pertain to the power, authority, and perhaps sovereignty that follow. The right of any particular human to command and coerce another is derived solely from the authority of God's law, but as we have seen, that sovereign authority is held by humanity as a collective trust bestowed by God. No one can claim in his own right political authority, and there are severe limits to the exercise of any authorized political power. In the first place, the collective divine trustees exercise limiting and controlling power over other humans who might usurp this. But the key point is that usurpation of political power is simultaneously usurpation of divine and popular authority.

Again, Ghannūshī sees the exercise of political power by appointed authorities or institutions as inherently limited by the prior authority of the people, but largely because this prior authority is also limited, insofar as the meaning of the popular caliphate is that the people is the deputy, vicegerent, or lieutenant of the highest originating authority. And so, government may not do certain things because mankind itself may not authorize certain things. The doctrine of the universal caliphate, like theories of natural or human rights, implies a substantial limitation on popular sovereignty.

Ghannūshī's conception of Islamic human rights is based on the idea of the universal caliphate in two important ways. First, as we have seen, Islamic human rights are derived from what humans need in order to thrive qua the beings God has created us as. Humans are God's caliph in their dignity and capacities, and so enjoy entitlements to the conditions within which human excellence is realized. This is often connected to the idea of human nature *(fiṭra),* in the sense of what humans have been created to desire and to be able to endure (as seen in the previous chapter on Quṭb).

So, for example, Ghannūshī explains that Islam protects property rights because humans are naturally endowed with initiative, and it is natural for them to want have control over some amount of property and the fruits of their labor. The individual right to property is derived from mankind's status as God's deputy in that it precedes political order and is related to the conditions for human flourishing. At the same time, man's natural sociability requires that the interests of the community be given priority in cases of conflict. The covenant of vicegerency figures thus at both the individual and social level. At the individual level, human capacities are respected, and limits are placed on arbitrary government power. At the same time, there is a tradition of seeing the cultivating or civilizing of the Earth as part of man's collective duty as God's caliph.[13] Ghannūshī writes that there might be a variety of forms of organizing sovereignty over property, but it is essential to "affirm the divinely-granted right of the individual to private property, as part of the public interest and within the limits of the *sharīʿa,* as a result of his right to work and own the fruits of his labor. All of this is within the framework of the theory of universal vicegerency, without ever forgetting that the purpose of private property in Islam is to preserve the social balance and prevent the existence of class conflict over property."[14] The institution of private property is seen also as a guard against tyranny: as wealth does not flow from the sovereign grant of the state, it can be used as a check against excessive, arbitrary power.

Other examples of human rights grounded in the doctrine of vicegerency include family law (marriage precedes politics in Islam and is essential to realizing one of the core functions of mankind as God's caliph, namely cultivating the Earth);[15] the right to public education (because knowledge and learning are central to Islam, it is part of man's role as deputy of God to create popular institutions of learning and fund them through endowments); and as mentioned above, rights to social security (because man's collective status as God's caliph requires institutions that advance brotherhood, equality, justice, and mutual responsibility).[16] For present purposes, the point is that because all of these flow from the theological anthropology of the caliphate of man and are embedded in the divine law, they are not gifts of any human ruler or state apparatus, and cannot be violated by them.

But, again, humans may not legitimately authorize the violation of these rights themselves because the rights don't belong to them in a sovereign capacity. These rights are delegated to humans for safekeeping and execution. Ghannūshī writes that we should not see human rights as something owned by and originating with humans. Protecting human life, and providing for the conditions of its preservation, development, and happiness, is not a right of humans that they can dispose of or abandon through suicide, neglect, hunger, or stultification. It is a religious duty. Rights thus acquire a sanctity that forbids their abrogation or amendment even by communities collectively. Their divine source gives them a directive and obligating authority, and the derivative political task of the *umma* is to safeguard them though specific programs and institutions.

But here it is important to note a crucial theme in Islamic discussions of popular sovereignty. Because the basic principles of right and justice preexist the formation of a particular legal order, and because the people as vicegerent already exists with a moral identity and purpose prior to its unification under a state sovereign, the exercise of political power can be imagined as legitimate outside of formally authorized political structures. But this becomes very intricate, as there is a distinction between saying that the people may be a people collectively (and not just a multitude) prior to delegating power to a sovereign and saying that the authority to represent and enforce the law (possibly up to the point of wielding violence) circulates in that society prior to the institution of official coercive institutions.

For the idea of the caliphate of man at times implies not just collective popular sovereignty but a kind of "dispersed sovereignty": the circulation of the right to represent the covenant of vicegerency even at the individual level. If humanity is deputized as God's caliph, then all of the authority to represent and speak for God's law resides initially with humans collectively. But that body is composed of its members, and its members are all those who accept the lordship of God and their own trusteeship. Although (as we shall see) that body is commanded to entrust some of its members with the execution of that authority, it never irrevocably surrenders its own patrimony even when duly constituted powers are in operation. If the *umma* has a form of derived sovereignty, it never goes to sleep. And because its authority is located in the law and the idea of representing God, any member can attempt to speak for it in moments of dereliction, crisis, or emergency.

For example, consider Ghannushī's discussion of the right to private property and the evils wrought by colonial usurpation and the formation of the state. This involved, in his account, the destruction of an Islamic civil society and the creation of oligarchical control over both government and property. The Islamic ideal, as enunciated by the universal caliphate, is to distribute and disperse these powers to the greatest extent.[17] Part of the point of seeing land as the trust of all members of the society is that it is a way of achieving the dispersal of authority in society as well as a check on tyranny.[18]

When sovereignty or coercive authority has been usurped by a human ruler, opposing his violations of justice and the *sharīʿa* is not just the responsibility of a small group (the People Who Loose and Bind), but the whole *umma* on the grounds that it (and no subset of it) is the divinely appointed agent, addressed by God to enact the *sharīʿa,* and the true possessor of the trust that the ruler accepted. Insofar as (even derived) powers of sovereignty in a theological imaginary consist of the right to deploy power and judgment in the name of God, and some specific agent or power will have to engage in many forms of judgment, discretion, and the determination of the boundary between justice and tyranny, we have a clear location of this sovereign power in the people at the broadest possible level. Even if the *umma* delegates this power to decide in a contingent way to some representative body, this is always contingent and may be contested or reclaimed, and thus always involves some residual amount of divine sovereignty dispersed through the *umma* and potentially seized by some members of it in a decisionistic way.[19] From the "sovereign *umma*" it is a short distance to the "sovereign believer." Ghannūshī's version of the universal caliphate shares with many theories and theologies of popular sovereignty the claims that a higher law precedes and limits state legislative authority and that this authorizes in certain emergency scenarios ordinary members of the people to speak in the name of both the law and its own supremacy over its rulers.

So the popular caliphate is not only a theory of the sovereignty of the *umma* as a body over its rulers and political institutions (although it is that), but also of the restriction of the *umma*'s authority to whatever God has delegated and commanded. The sum of the covenant of vicegerency from the constitutional standpoint is the supremacy of God's law over any other authority, but through the consultative activities of the people. The covenant of vicegerency can thus be summarized as the "*sharīʿa* of God and consultation *(shūrā)* of the people," or "Text and consultation (*naṣṣ* and *shūrā*), reason and revelation *(ʿaql wa naql),* constraint and freedom *(iltizām wa ḥurriyya).*"

This is the problem that remains to be untangled. How are all of these various materials woven together, and what contradictions and ambiguities are produced by this attempt to do justice to divine sovereignty, the rule of law, popular sovereignty (of some kind), representation, expertise, and the residual authority of ordinary believers to speak and act as God's caliphs? I believe that the best way to do this is to proceed carefully through the distinctly divine and distinctly popular elements of this theory of legitimacy and sovereignty. For, though divine and popular sovereignty are formed from the same relationship, their elements remain conceptually distinct and often in tension. The rest of this chapter proceeds thus in two parts, focusing on the divine and popular themes in Ghannūshī's political thought in turn.

Divine Sovereignty

Divine sovereignty is obviously the background frame of reference against which all contemporary Islamist political thinkers operate. Calling into question God's cosmic and legislative sovereignty is unthinkable. But beyond the rhetorical formulation of the commitment to divine sovereignty, the elaboration of its meaning and force for political life takes a number of forms. In this section, I argue that in

Ghannūshī's political theory, divine sovereigntist themes take three forms in particular: a perfectionist vision of politics as the site for creating the optimal conditions for virtuous and flourishing Islamic lives, quite explicit declarations of the voluntarist and positivist form of the divine law, and a preservation of the idea of some form of epistocratic authority enjoyed by jurists with expertise in the divine law.

Perfectionism

This basic metaphysical foundation is used by Ghannūshī to distinguish Islamic approaches to freedom, human rights, public justification, and the state from "Western" conceptions, which he tends to see in a reductive way as all based on a kind of arbitrary, foundationless human will and purposeless philosophical anthropology.[20] Although "the idea of human rights represents an important development in human civilization and legacy of the religious and human tradition," it is still marked by the influence of the Western political and economic system, which he thinks eventually becomes trapped in the amoral will of the sovereign state. The idea of human rights is an invaluable legacy but needs to be reclaimed outside of that system.

As late as his 2012 book, *al-Dīmuqrāṭiyya wa ḥuqūq al-insān fi'l-Islām (Democracy and Human Rights in Islam),* Ghannūshī distinguished the Islamic vision of politics as being about "the unity of matter and spirit, politics and morality, this world and religion" and for "which the Islamic state is an irreplaceable means as long as people remain social by nature and as long as Islam is a comprehensive system of life that calls for constructing a social environment that allows for the greatest possible number of people to live spiritually and materially in an innate accord with the law that Islam brought." Stronger yet, in words that were written on the cusp of the democratic revolution in Tunisia: "Imagining life in accordance with the example of Islam in terms of justice, charity, piety and cooperation toward the good without establishing Islamic public authority to protect its lands, guard its frontiers and defend freedom of religion far from any form of coercion 'until there is no sedition' [Q. 8:39] is a mere deceptive fantasy, severe deviation, and fall into sin and error. In other regards, it is surrender to the enemies of Islam and giving them power over its fate."[21] This is an almost verbatim restatement of his formulation from 1993.[22]

Ghannūshī's ideas here are not original, but rather a fairly standard modern Islamist account of positive liberty. He even acknowledges his debt to Mawdūdī and Quṭb in the following formulation:

> Since Islam is a comprehensive revolution seeking to overthrow tyranny and darkness, freeing the human will from all subjection to what is not God, it would be possible for those who study Islam to summarize it in the words, "a comprehensive revolution of emancipation."[23] One should not understand from the common usage of "freedom" that it's simply about license or permissiveness. The logic of truth cannot entertain that the emancipatory message of Islam—brought to humankind from creation by thousands of prophets and messengers, in addition to their successors in the general announcement to people—would be summarized as God allowing you to do what you desire. No, Islam's conception is quite the opposite. God created you and he forbids you to follow your every ignorant whim, and he commands you to follow—as a conscious decision of your own will and design—the path that pleases Him for your life, the only one in which you will find happiness and development in this life and the next. But if you turn your back to it, you will find eternal calamity.[24]

But these themes are less developed in Ghannūshī's thought than in that of previous thinkers. He mentions many times the way that the human rights Islam guarantees are grounded in the human *fiṭra* and its understanding of human flourishing and authentic needs, but he does not elaborate a full account of the relationship between the *sharīʿa* and human psychology. Similarly, Ghannūshī does not elaborate with much precision on exactly how men are uplifted and brought closer to perfection through getting the law and statecraft right. As we will see toward the end of this chapter, he is arguably more interested in how the functioning and flourishing of the political realm depends on the virtue and moral unity of its citizenry.

What does emerge in this context is a critique of Western positivist and voluntarist theories of state sovereignty. For Ghannūshī the demand in Europe for radical popular sovereignty emerged out of a rejection of the tyranny of kings and popes. This was a distinctly Western, European problem, with the unfortunate result that the toppling of the church and absolute monarchy on behalf of the people "marked the Western state with an individualistic stamp, with a nationalist, secular and formalist spirit.[25] But he is also troubled by the radical voluntarism of the state, which at some point has to simply assert its own legal force:

> The concept of sovereignty is a legal concept, since it means to give to the law a quality of legitimacy. The law, after all, is what is issued by the ruler, the possessor of sovereignty, either in person or as a body that orders or outlaws. It is law in the sense that it is the commanding authority. From another standpoint, nothing that is commanded by someone other than the ruler has the force of law. So if the law is that which is commanded by the ruler, we need to know who the ruler is. And there is no way to know that, except through a matrix of legal rules, which in themselves need a source of legality, since sovereignty's purpose is to give the law its legitimacy.[26]

Below, in my discussion of Ghannūshī's own version of the Islamic social contract, I return to these themes and why exactly he believes that an Islamic social and political order can escape this "logical conundrum." But the other important point at present is that the radical voluntarism of state sovereignty is not only foundationless or doctrinally unacceptable from an Islamic perspective but is also associated with a kind of moral groundlessness associated with the secular state's lack of moral purpose or ethico-juridical foundation other than its own will to survive.

The legal formalism of the modern state may suffice for practical purposes, but it runs aground when the state's own purposes turn evil. Drawing on Machiavelli and Hobbes on the emergence of the modern state (as well as the French legal theorists Maurice Duverger and

Georges Burdeau), he captures the meaning of absolute state sovereignty: "This concept of the state was long centered around the existence of absolute sovereignty that had no need of legal justification for its rules; and around the necessity of submission to the state, even if its sovereignty could not be established, and no matter how much it collided with morality, religion and the law of justice."[27] Although some modern philosophers (he mentions only Hegel) imagined that the state could also be the site for the immanent development and rule of reason, "in truth, the modern wars between nation-states have been about glory and treasure, even if it was at the expense of justice and freedom. Note the clear link between those wars and this concept of the state—a 'god,' which derives its legitimacy from its own self-definition and how it sees itself as the source of all legality, yet accountable to no one else. Therefore, the representative, or representatives of its power are immune from prosecution."

From the Enlightenment vision of an alternative to "the tyranny of the Church and the feudal kings," the state itself morphed "into the basis and goal of everything, refusing any authority higher than itself and needing no justification for its decisions before anyone." Yet though the state is responsible for both the rule of law and also the grotesque, genocidal (and ecocidal) episodes of modernity, even in its softer moments (where it tries to limit itself through commitments to natural rule or human rights) "what is permanent is the dual nature of the Western state—legality and the sovereignty of the people. Fundamentally, its legality is seen in the state's submission to the law and the people's sovereignty is seen in the state's power to legislate. No authority transcends it and it will not submit to any exterior authority. . . . [Yet] the political conundrum remains in all its gravity. How can you pull back the reins of one person's will to dominate others and exploit their need to come together? There is no acceptable solution to this problem within the framework of the Western state's two essential principles—legality and the sovereignty of the people."[28]

Clearly, this is where Ghannūshī believes that the permissible adoption of certain mechanisms and devices of modern democracy and legalism needs to be supplemented by the foundational principle of divine sovereignty. The Islamic democratic system will be able to solve the paradox of legal sovereignty by positing a genuinely legitimate, self-authorizing foundation (God's will). But this leads to at least two sets of questions.

First, is it not simply begging the question to just posit that a commitment to divine sovereignty will evade the tyrannies of the state? After all, as Ghannūshī notes, those modern states have attempted, particularly in the wake of their greatest atrocities, to bind themselves to a deeper moral foundation in the form of various kinds of human and civil rights schemes. What is it about a people binding itself in principle to similar rights schemes with a divine origin that will solve the moral dilemma of sovereignty? Will it be through more sophisticated institutional checks or through a firmer ethical formation on the part of pious peoples? What is "law" doing in the Islamic context to provide both legitimacy and a moral boundary? In classical Islamic thought (arguably up to Riḍā), this was one of the core arguments for the necessity of a caliph or imām: the law needs a guarantor, and that can only be a human executive. But Ghannūshī's Islamic democratic theory appears to need a different account of what underpins the force of law if it is going to reliably guard against political tyranny and moral atrocity.

The second set of questions pertains to the form and substance of divine sovereignty. What is it, where is it found, and what form does it take? How is it received by humans, and what is the nature of its check on political self-governance? Is it a vague and flexible kind of natural law, articulated though moral principles, or is it more concrete in its legislative form?

Divine Sovereignty as Positive Law

As we have seen above, for Ghannūshī, the sum of the covenant of vicegerency from the constitutional standpoint is the sovereignty of God's law over any other authority in whatever it contains in the way of doctrines, rites, morals, and rules. Whereas Western democracy sees itself as liberating governance from authoritarianism on the basis of the concept of the rule of law and popular sovereignty, the two principles of governance in Islam are summarized as "Text and Consultation."

This double formulation is meant to summarize Islam's theocratic and democratic principles, respectively.

I ultimately argue in this chapter that the democratic principles are meant to take priority in the right conditions in Ghannūshī's theory. But the road is a complicated and obscure one, and the commitment to divine sovereignty in his doctrinal statements should not be downplayed or brushed away. Although his own presentation of his views stresses the way in which his turn back toward a "Maghrabī (North African) Islam" involved turning away from Mawdūdī and Quṭb and rehabilitating the ideas of thinkers like Khayr al-Dīn al-Tūnisī, ʿAllāl al-Fāsī, Malik Bin Nabī, and Ṭāhir Ibn ʿĀshūr, along with some post-Quṭbian Egyptian thinkers in the vein of Muḥammad Salīm al-ʿAwwā and Fatḥī ʿUthmān, both Mawdūdī and Quṭb are cited favorably, and many of their own proof-texts for divine sovereignty are restated by Ghannūshī.

Ghannūshī cites the standard Qurʾānic proof-texts for the absolute supremacy of God's will and command, and the absolute lack of freedom for humans to judge in matters settled by God: Q. 2:10; 47:33; 5:44; 4:65; 5:50 and 4:59.[29] As a commentary on these Qurʾānic verses and similar Prophetic *ḥadīth* reports, he declares starkly that "looking to revelation for judgments and submitting to them is a clear boundary between faith and disbelief. And this leads to a clear principle of creed: that God is the creator of all things and the king of kings."[30] This is in addition to a declaration of the complete ontological priority and normative supremacy of the *sharīʿa* to any human political authority, autocratic or democratic:

> If the justification for the existence of an Islamic government is the implementation of *sharīʿa,* putting God into the context of history, uniting the divine with the human, coloring life with God's hue, then it does not deserve the obedience of its citizens to its commands except to the extent that they flow from submission and adherence to *sharīʿa* and are in accord with the Legislator, or at least not in conflict with him. The Islamic state has no right, whether it is conceived as a political community that has bound itself in a covenant of loyalty and

> obedience to God or as the collection of executive, legislative, and judicial authorities, to depart from the *sharīʿa,* because the *sharīʿa,* in the language of constitutional jurisprudence, is the original, foundational authority for the community and the government.[31]

But Ghannūshī is doing more than articulating a principle of political legitimacy, legislative supremacy, or even a utopian vision for politics. He is linking those ideas to the very boundary between the sphere of fraternity and the sphere of enmity. If man's "only choices are to worship God in accordance with the covenant of vicegerency or to reject it and be ranked among the unjust, corrupt infidels," then what could the latter choice represent but a voluntary return to something akin to barbarism?[32] One would not be wrong for thinking these passages might have been written by Mawdūdī or Quṭb. He cites here Quṭb's Qurʾān commentary[33] that "there is no middle ground on this issue, no truce and no reconciliation. The believers are those who judge by what God has revealed without distorting one letter thereof, and without changing one thing contained therein. The disbelievers and those who commit injustice and immorality are those who do not judge by what God has revealed. . . . There is no middle ground between this and that."

These statements are certainly meant to sound categorical and unambiguous. But it is not entirely clear from them alone what kinds of political power and legislative forms they authorize. Even in the midst of his fulsome assertion of the absolute supremacy of divine law, he writes that this still does not make the Islamic state a theocracy because God's will is embodied in the law alone, rather than in some person, office, or institution. In a phrase that I discuss again below, he writes that "all Muslims can figure out what is clear and fixed in the text and thus what constitutes 'obedience to a creature in disobedience to the Creator.'"[34] And because this is true, divine sovereignty is presented not only as a limiting principle, as something that comes from outside all human will and is thus imposed on mankind heteronomously, but also as an empowering principle. It is precisely because the *sharīʿa* is seen as emanating from outside even the people's own will that reference to it can figure as a neutral check on tyranny. Unlike in natural or international law, which cannot provide a check on injustice issuing from popularly representative institutions, "the principles enunciated in the *sharīʿa,* as it represents the supreme and neutral authority, present a cure" to the problem of injustice and tyranny.[35]

Moreover, in the same passage in which he asserts that "it is clear that the first and primary source of the legitimacy of any ruler in Islamic political theory only derives from his complete acceptance [of the obligation] to look to God's law to judge without the slightest objection or desire to participate," he goes on to say that what is supreme and sovereign are not the specific rules of Islamic jurisprudence *(fiqh)* derived from the interpretive struggles for the jurists, but only what is general, fixed, and certain.[36] And so the question for the moment is what *else* he thinks is authorized by divine sovereignty, specifically in the realm of intermediary, expert, scholarly authority to speak for the law independent from any popular authorization or participation in lawmaking.

The Sovereignty of the Law: Expertise and Representation

Just as the obligation on the *umma* to create a "state" obligates it to appoint an executive apparatus, so does the obligation for that state to be *sharīʿa* based require "the existence of a body that executes these statutes and takes charge of this process of reference and extrapolation. This body could be a high court composed of the best judges among the jurists," for example.[37] The grounding for this is Qurʾānic in addition to rational. Q. 4:59 famously exhorts Muslims to "obey God, the Messenger, and those in authority amongst you." Ghannūshī notes (with Islamic tradition) that this is primarily a reference to the scholars of the divine law, the jurists, "the ones who 'will not agree on an error.'" According to the traditional view (as seen in Riḍā, for example), this potentially involves the right to assume the exercise of much of what might be regarded as sovereign power. For example, if the scholars agree on a point of law, it is said to attain certainty as part of the *sharīʿa.* If they agree on giving the oath of loyalty *(bayʿa)* in appointing an

Imam, then obedience becomes incumbent on all Muslims. On matters where there is no decisive revealed text, "those in authority" are presumptively authorized by the *umma* to deliberate about legislative matters on the basis of rules of interpretation and considerations of the public good. Although this is obviously not Ghannūshī's final word on the subject, he introduces as part of the terrain on which he is building his theory the traditional view of the jurists as representing the source of sovereignty and legitimacy in an Islamic political order.[38]

Because of the nature of the state project involved, it is intelligible to assert that jurists and advanced scholars inevitably form the intellectual leadership and authorizing community according to the ideal conception of Islamic governance. They can assume representation of the *umma* and the right to look after its interests. Their authorization of the ruler and contracting with him to execute the law are valid acts in Islamic law, resulting in a legitimate form of governance. This location of effective political sovereignty in the hands of the scholars is one possible implication of vesting the idea of original sovereignty in the divine law. Ghannūshī writes that "the source of sovereignty is the legislation that is taken from the Book and Sunna, if it accords with the texts and does not contradict the spirit of these two holy sources and their aims. And it is natural that there be someone to represent this sovereignty. And here we say that those one who represent it are the People Who Loose and Bind representing the entire *umma*. In that case their decisions and the laws that they issue, grounded on their expert reasoning, are correct and legitimate and are binding on the whole *umma*."[39]

He notes that a number of important twentieth-century theorists of legitimate Islamic governance explicitly grant the class of scholars the right to directly assume legislative and authorizing powers. Perhaps the founding text of modern "religiously legitimate governance" discourse, ʿAbd al-Wahhāb Khallāf's *al-Siyāsa al-sharʿiyya* declared that "it is the most senior scholars (*mujtahid*s) who inherit, acquire this authority, bound by such fixed texts as there are and the procedures of deriving new judgments from them."[40] Another thinker often quoted by Ghannūshī, Ṣubḥī ʿAbduh Saʿīd, writes that although original legislative authority is obviously God, "the derived legislative authority does not belong to the people, as amongst the non-Muslims, nor does it belong to their representatives, but only to the experts in Islamic jurisprudence."[41] The language of inheritance in Khallāf suggests a direct right to assume this authority from the logic of revelation and the purpose of governance in Islam, rather than from express appointment or delegation by the *umma*. Ṣubḥī ʿAbduh Saʿīd is even more explicit that there is a quasi-divine right of scholars to legislate for the *umma*, justified and authorized solely by the knowledge and expertise.

Ghannūshī's constitutional views are more complicated, and discussed in detail below, but the idea of expertise in the divine law persists. He opposes the view advanced, for example, by Mawdūdī that members of a representative assembly in an Islamic state must all be Muslims, but still asserts that all members of such bodies "need to submit to the political system, that is, to respect the Islamic nature of the state and not enact legislation that contravenes the sacred texts, something that could be monitored by a constitutional assembly composed of top-level jurists . . . there is no prejudice to the Islamic character of the state if the assembly has non-Muslim members, as long as the assembly, or Shūrā Council, and the rest of the state institutions work within the framework of the *sharīʿa* and under the supervision of a body of top-level jurists, which is totally independent from the state and whose mission is to monitor the constitutionality of the laws and the general conduct of the state's institutions and agents."[42]

If Ghannūshī's theory is ultimately about authorizing a semi-sovereign people to judge about how God's law bears on its temporal realities, he does not rush to that conclusion by sweeping away the idea of traditional scholarly authority. The classical account of a class of jurist-scholars who speak in the name of the divine law on the basis of their own epistocratic (not *delegated*) authority, and are thus the *umma*'s primary immediate representatives, does not immediately vanish.

We have now an adequate sense of the scope of divine sovereigntist commitments in Ghannūshī's theory that put his popular or democratic elements in context. Ghannūshī asserts the validity of divine sovereignty in the following senses: God is the unquestionable source of value and norms; this is not just a broad ethical orientation, but sets a constraint on the forms and rules of political life; many areas of basic and even specific legislation have already been decided by God if specific and clear texts exist on those matters; the nature, essence, will, and telos of the community has been fixed by the covenant of vicegerency; and finally, jurists may have some form of supra-political or pre-political legislative authority justified solely on the basis of their epistemic qualifications. What can it mean to believe, or claim to believe, in popular sovereignty in light of all this?

Popular Sovereignty

Ghannūshī's critique of modern Western political philosophy is not an absolute one, and his approach is far from the sheer antagonism infusing many Islamist writings. He acknowledges that Western representative democracy is based on human values and can protect human dignity, referring to it as the "second-best system." As we saw above, he sees democracy's radical assertion of popular sovereignty as a parochial response to the traditional struggle between a corrupt Church and absolute monarchs (as we saw in Riḍā), and the only path to the rule of law for modern Europeans was through a radical rejection of any source of sovereignty apart from the people. But Islam's traditional location of ultimate sovereignty in the divine law means for Ghannūshī that Muslims do not have go through a similar process of alienating themselves from God in order to liberate themselves from popes and kings. Moreover, it is precisely the location of sovereignty in the law and in the universal trusteeship that connects divine sovereignty to popular sovereignty. If the law is a universal trust and resource for mankind, then it is a check against political authoritarianism rather than a license for it.[43]

The practices and presuppositions of democratic politics hold both formal and substantive appeals for Ghannūshī. On the one hand, democracy is defined in terms of mechanisms and tools that themselves are neutral and can be repurposed by Muslim societies. Democracy is not like secularism, national discrimination, giving priority to profit, hedonism, domination, force, utilitarianism, or the deification of man: these cannot be used, borrowed, or transformed by Islam, but they are not necessary consequences of democracy. On the other hand, democratic mechanisms are not merely neutral means: the right to choose and remove rulers, and participate in public affairs, is an expression of human dignity.[44] In fact, on Ghannūshī's view, it is not only that modern democratic institutions and mechanisms can be of use for reviving Islamic political order, but Islam as well might represent the fulfillment of democracy's promise. Because only Islam can fully respect and develop all dimensions of human needs (material, spiritual, individual, social), democracy will find in Islam new energy and capacities to realize its objectives.

This is where the attribution of "sovereignty" to the people enters. Among the features of democracy that can be borrowed by Muslims, he lists civic equality, elections, the rotation of power on the basis of majority rule, the right of the minority opposition, the peaceful pursuit of power, and the sovereignty of the people. According to the proper understanding of Islamic constitutional theory, he believes that in the Islamic state "the *umma* . . . has supreme sovereignty, within the framework of the constitution"[45] on the basis of the covenant of divine vicegerency. If the source of the people's authority is clear and radically distinct from the Western notion of a people as self-authorizing or as creating its own identity, more interesting are the implications of this idea of a divinely transferred form of popular sovereignty. What does it do, what does it authorize, and what are its surprising implications? I track this through five problems and themes in Ghannūshī's theory: (1) political offices as civil in nature and derived from popular appointment; (2) the idea of the "people as the source of all political authorities" and the Islamic version of the social contract; (3) the scope and limits of this kind of constituent power; (4) the force of popular legislative authority and its relationship to the *sharīʿa;* and finally (5) the kind of moral unity and virtue required for popular self-government.

"The Ruler Is the People's Agent": The Bayʿa *as Popular Sovereignty*

It is important to recall that in classical Islamic constitutional theory, the "state" did not exist as a distinct, transpersonal entity. Rather, what existed was the person of the ruler, by whatever title he was known: caliph, imām, sulṭān, amīr, or generically the "*walī al-amr.*" It was possible to speak of the "caliphate," "Imamate," or "sulṭa" in the abstract, but only in reference to the office and the sum total of its activities. It is true that the office represented the idea of public authority or order, but the questions asked by classical legal and constitutional theory all pertained to the office and its holder: whether the office is necessary, how the holder of it is appointed, what qualifications he must possess, and what rights and obligations he has.

As has been discussed numerous times in this text, for Sunnis there has never been any doubt that the Caliph owes his office in some way to "election" rather than divine designation. It is thus relatively easy to say that the Islamic juridical tradition does call for the "election" of rulers and their accountability to certain elite representatives of the entire *umma* (the People Who Loose and Bind). This is a not insignificant element of democratic governance, and it might be said that the doctrinal, juridical obstacles to that amount of democracy are fewer and weaker in Sunni Islam than they might be in other traditions. It is thus not surprising that theoretical and apologetic writings on "Islam and democracy" or "Islam and constitutionalism" make much of the idea of the *bayʿa*.

For Ghannūshī, citing ʿAbd al-Razzāq al-Sanhūrī, the Imamate is a real contract, with conditions, stipulations, and an objective: namely that the contract itself be the actual source of any Imam's political authority. Moreover, it must be an actual and legally binding contract, not a hypothetical one. Ghannūshī argues that in the political practice of the Prophet and the earliest caliphs, the acceptance of the *bayʿa* signified a real contract with real conditions, and the recognition of the *umma* as the effective source of legitimate authority. The fact that the early caliphs tried to collect the *bayʿa* from the whole *umma* (as gathered in the mosque) means that they saw the *umma*, and not just the *sharīʿa* or the elite electors, as the source of their authority. Later, only the form of the caliphate contract was preserved, and not the actual content. Nonetheless, the ideal was implanted in the consciousness of Muslims that the Imam only serves at the pleasure of the *umma*, affirmed through the *bayʿa*. "What can be concluded from this is that the *umma* is the source of all authorities and has supreme sovereignty."[46]

So, the first and most important sense in which the "people is sovereign" on this theory is that the ruler isn't. "God's deputy is the *umma*, in which case the Imam is nothing other than an employee to execute their will and is responsible before them, whereas his responsibility before God is like any other Muslim (and this is the view of the majority of Muslims)."[47] "There is no legitimacy in an Islamic system that is derived from inheritance, infallibility, designation or coup."[48]

The second sense, in turn, in which the people is sovereign is that the People Who Loose and Bind are not. Of course, Ghannūshī recognizes that classical Islamic legal theory recognized that the *umma*'s elite representatives could authorize rulers in a valid and binding sense, but for him this was the traditional path to authoritarianism. He thus asks "so where is the *umma*? It is the possessor of the missing power in this conception."[49] For Ghannūshi, only Ibn Taymiyya stood firm in resisting authoritarianism in claiming that the general *bayʿa* from the people at large is necessary and decisive for appointing the caliph, with the *bayʿa* of the People Who Loose and Bind only a form of nomination. Thus, the sovereignty of the *umma* is first a matter of creating procedures for the will of the people to be genuinely effective in the authorization of political power.

A further rationale for employing the language of "sovereignty" in this context is not only that the people is the sole legitimate principal in the contract of governance but also that the appointment of an executive is a very limited delegation of authority, with specific stipulations the violation of which can permissibly lead to the people reclaiming their "sovereignty." As seen in previous chapters, it is important for Sunni scholars in particular to stress that "government is a civil authority in all regards, no different from democracy except for the superiority of the sovereignty of *sharīʿa*, or the divine legislation over all other sources of sovereignty in this system." Despite the reference to the sovereignty of the *sharīʿa* in this passage, the purpose is to stress that governance is not a sacral affair, but merely a "necessary social task for the protection of religion and the affairs of the world and those who carry it out are nothing other than the officers and servants of the people,"[50] "nothing other than the political mechanism." This view is expressly a median position between secularists who would exclude all religious considerations from politics and Shiʿa for whom political authority under a true Imām is creedal and sacral in nature.[51]

The idea of government as a contract of representation or agency *(wikāla)* between the people and the executive is standard Sunni constitutional doctrine. But in Ghannūshī's account, the doctrine of the universal caliphate gives it theological heft: "The *umma* is entitled, within the framework of this sovereignty, to appoint one amongst them to carry out the trust that would be difficult to carry out at the level of the entire society. The ruler's authority is limited by the boundaries of *sharīʿa* and the will of the *umma* for the government of God is the government of the people, and the continuation of his rule is contingent on the agreement of the people."[52] The fusion of divine and popular sovereignty are on display here: the *umma* is sovereign over the realm of worldly politics because politics is a mechanism for discharging its divinely originating obligations: "The *umma* is the one who bears the responsibility to uphold religion and its rites, and to safeguard the public interests, and is thus the possessor of supreme authority" in the realm of politics.

It is, of course, possible to hold the view that a ruler derives his authority from the people rather than from God (or by right of conquest, or by right of his virtue and merit) but that once in power he has wide ranging legislative and discretionary powers. This is the very idea of the sovereignty-government distinction. Islamic constitutional theorists differ on the extent of executive discretionary authority. Ghannūshī, though not entirely opposed to executive discretion or policy making, comes down on the far end of the rule-of-law side of the spectrum, insisting on the people's authority to constrain the ruler's prerogative. Because the obligation to obey one's government is not primarily owed to the person of the ruler but to the "ultimate lawgiver" *(ṣāḥib al-sharīʿa),* it follows that state and law are conceptually distinct. The law is prior to and foundational for the legitimacy of the state, rather than the state providing the law with its legal force and authority.[53] The constraint of the law over the ruler extends even to his core discretionary powers, which Ghannūshī describes as law and policy making "pertaining to the state or welfare of the people, relations between groups and the kind of weighing and balancing that requires formulating appropriate judgment for those states of affairs."[54]

Ghannūshī's reticence to allow for extensive executive power comes out in his critique of the well-known Palestinian Islamist thinker, the founder of the transnational Ḥizb al-Taḥrīr movement, Taqī al-Dīn al-Nabhānī, who notoriously insisted not only on the obligation of restoring the caliphate but assigned extensive legislative sovereignty to the head of state, even arguing that the caliph, should he obtain, is the supreme arbiter of disputes in Islamic law.[55] Ghannūshī frames his rejection of this strong "presidentialism" in rule of law terms. The head of state is not above the law and his own interpretive jurisprudence is not binding or decisive on religious or epistemic grounds. A command of the Imam does not "remove the legitimate disagreement" of the scholars and bind the *umma*. Even if the ruler has the scholarly expertise to engage in religious disputation and is allowed by his position to enforce commands that do not violate the *sharīʿa,* his choice of a rule in a particular case does not settle it decisively from a jurisprudential perspective. Even if the ruler has attained the rank of *mujtahid,* his judgments or rulings have no superiority to those of any other jurist from a jurisprudential standpoint. "Is it possible for us today to permit the assignment of a right to absolute *ijtihād* in all matters to the individual ruler? Can the *umma* place its entire destiny in the hand of an individual ruler who relies only on his own *ijtihād* and can dispense with the *ijtihād* of the many scholars who are elected to represent the people in the shura council?"[56] He again describes the correct role for the executive as a mere employee with a limited set of tasks.

That the ruler's rights and obligations are fixed and limited by law, and that the ruler himself does not have the authority to revise the basic rules regulating the relations between the people (principal) and himself (agent), necessarily implies ongoing powers of the *umma* over the ruler, specifically powers of oversight or supervision, advise or correction, and ultimately removal, "if he departs in a clear way from the state that qualified him on the day of his contract."[57] The shift toward a political theology of popular sovereignty grounded in the doctrine of the universal caliphate gives these powers their depth and force. "Opposing the Imam if he violates justice and the *sharīʿa* is not just the responsibility of a small group but the whole *umma* on the grounds that it is appointed and deputized, addressed by God collectively to enact the *sharīʿa,* and the possessor of the trust that the caliph accepted through the *bayʿa.*"[58] Insofar as the mandate to establish public authority itself is derived from the basic principle of the *umma* as having a responsibility to command the right and forbid the wrong, so the popular obligation to supervise and reform the execution of that public trust is an inalienable obligation of the people.

The dimensions of sovereignty at stake here involve more than just the idea that *umma* is seen as deploying God's power and judgment. Although the theory might hold that divine sovereignty provides for the rule (say, "the ruler is corrected or deposed in cases of severe violations of the *sharīʿa* or manifest infidelity"), and the role of the people is to apply and execute the rule, in reality, carrying out the rule involves the exercise of judgment and discretion in the determination of the boundary between justice and injustice, or even Islam and infidelity. It also raises the question of the representation of this power of judgment: even if Islamic political and constitutional theory allows for the people to delegate these powers to intermediate representatives, that delegation can never exhaust the popular right to revoke the authority of rulers. There is always a residual amount of this aspect of divine sovereignty dispersed through the *umma.* Because the *umma* exists prior to its being subsumed under a political authority, and because believers are addressed both individually and collectively, the exercise of the *umma*'s caliphate is not fully contained by its collective and institutionalized manifestations.

I do not want to exaggerate the extent to which Ghannūshī himself intends for this principle to authorize a radical doctrine of what might be called popular nullification or the rights of the "sovereign believer" to violently oppose public authority. He himself is quite clear that "the basic principle is that the one who possesses the right to appoint also possesses the right to remove. So, if it is the People Who Loose and Bind who appointed him, then they are called up to remove their confidence from him, announce this and appoint another," whereas if it is the *umma* that has elected him directly, then the right to depose remains a collective one. Even in this case there is a preference for this right to depose to remain delegated to representatives: "An individual or small group cannot on their own give themselves the right to replace the ruler without the people, but instead the matter is delegated to public leaders to declare the loss of legitimacy, call for civil disobedience or even for revolution."[59] But the point is that these representatives who might be called upon to judge on the questions of resistance or rebellion to duly constituted authority are not entitled to this authority apart from the confidence they enjoy from the people, are not known through a fixed, ordained status in the divine law, and are not entitled to preempt the right of the *umma* to reclaim its own right to judge. Whatever delegation of authority to representatives there might be, a residue of the original divine delegation to the people as a whole remains unalienated.

But powers of appointment and removal are not sovereignty in the full sense. The people can appoint an agent to handle its affairs, who is then answerable to it. However, can the people revoke not only the person occupying executive office, but also the constitutional order that creates and authorizes the offices themselves, including legislative powers, which are more controversial than executive? The Islamic state is based on the rule of law, but of course the law applied is in some way the divine law. This is a point of pride for Islamic political theory: the Islamic order has all of the accountability, predictability, and representativeness of democracy but applies a superior law for our this-worldly interests and attempts to assist in the securing of our next-worldly ones as well. But does this mean that the language of "sovereignty" is misused here? Beyond the mere power to appoint, shouldn't this imply something by way of the authority to create and revise new political orders?

"The People Is the Source of All Authority": The Islamic Social Contract

Discussions of the people as the principal in a contract with a delegated agent who assumes certain powers of executive leadership are often embedded in the somewhat deeper claim that "the people is the source of all authority." As I noted in my Preface, by 2011 this had become such a commonplace of Islamic thought that even Salafi parties (with a *jihādī* past) used it in their electoral manifestos. This phrase appears multiple times in Ghannūshī's treatise, for example, where he writes that the Islamic "idea of popular sovereignty is that the *umma* is the source of all authorities, the possessor of supreme sovereignty in matters of governance," and that the political order is built on the principle of the will of the people."[60] But how much more does it imply than the right to appoint individual office-holders, and how is this distinct from Western theories of popular sovereignty as absolute constituent power?

Ghannūshī's story about the founding of the state and the source of its legitimacy is representative of his complex relationship to Western democratic theory. Although he sees the Islamic state in contractual terms, he also rejects the Western social contract account of the state's legitimacy as originating completely in the free act of self-binding by persons in a state of nature. As we saw above, Ghannūshī rejects the circularity of the self-originating claims to legality: power is legitimized by legal procedures, but those laws themselves have to emerge from some procedure that also needs to justify itself. He thinks that popular will alone ("these procedures are justified because they are the ones that have been freely authorized and chosen by the people whom they will then govern") is insufficient, as the popular will itself might be evil. Ghannūshī regards popular sovereignty in the Western democratic sense as naked, free of all moral limits and human values, and thus one source of tyranny and war between peoples. The freedom of the people thus needs both a source of authorization and also moral and legal limits.

The Islamic foundation of politics is clear about both. "If original sovereignty in the Islamic state is only God's will, represented by the *sharīʿa,* then the authority of the Muslim society is as agent or representative of God, and God is the one who bestowed this sovereignty and authority on the *umma,* within the framework of His *sharīʿa,* and made the *umma* his deputy."[61] But this is therefore the grounds for doubting whether this is a theory of sovereignty, even if theorists like Ghannūshī use the word: "Man is not the possessor of original right over himself or others but is only a vicegerent or agent. He is not the possessor of (the right to) command or supreme sovereignty but is only the possessor of a right to an ordained authority by the supreme legislative authority emanating from God."[62] Ghannūshī sees a distinction between constituent power in three different kinds of regime types:

1. Theocracy: God → Ruler → People
2. Western democracy: People → Ruler
3. Islamic democracy: God → People → Ruler

He sees Islamic governance as much closer to democracy than to theocracy, but still radically constrained by divine sovereignty. Yet here Ghannūshī may be ascribing to the *umma* more sovereignty than he thinks.

This account depends on a distinction between the origins of governance as such (*ḥukm:* rule) and the origins of a regime or ruler (*ḥākim*). Governance as such—the state, including its constitutional framework—preexists all human capacities to make worldly contracts, because it is both natural and divinely ordained. He writes that "the contract is what establishes the state in Rousseau. However, in Islam, the contract of *bayʿa* does not found the state, because the Text already has, and Muslims are not free as long as they remain Muslims to apply the rules of *sharīʿa* or to invalidate them. . . . The state is an original need in human society, not an exceptional or emergency manifestation."[63] Although the idea of "divine sovereignty" might strike the critical secular reader as vague or nonsensical, here we see one clear implication of the belief in it: that the state is always already justified, requiring no further philosophical or theological grounding, and that the *umma* has no moral option of doing away with it.

But where is the principal to this original contract? Where is God as an active sovereign? The force of sovereignty in constitutional theory, even when it depends on separating sovereignty from government, is that the sovereign might wake up. God can only be the sovereign in this sense in two circumstances: either He reveals Himself to mankind again with new instructions (which Sunnis hold to be heresy, even disbelief), or He will intervene in the workings of the world and withdraw His favor from His *umma* for disobeying Him or losing faith in His providence.

Sunnis often claim to believe the second. But it is so filled with the unseen and the uncertain (What counts as disobedience in the realm of politics? Is this misfortune in fact divine recompense for our heedlessness? Is God required to help a people that help themselves?) that the claim of divine sovereignty as divine providence can only in fact function as a struggle for sovereignty within the people. Thus, though it might appear that the scope of popular "sovereignty" is limited to the power to elect persons to fill divinely ordained offices, the Islamic version of the social contract runs deeper than this once it has become popularized through the doctrine of the caliphate of man.

Ghannūshī reveals perhaps more than he means to when he writes that in Islam "popular sovereignty is limited by the authority of *sharīʿa,* which is in fact a self-limitation after this *umma* has consented to God as its Lord and Islam as its religion voluntarily and freely."[64] Note first the notion that politics begins with the people's collective essence, identity, and will already determined prior to the authorization of a new political order already. This is something that Ghannūshī simply assumes rather than argues for. This is a theory addressed to a people that already sees itself as Muslim, not a treatise on why all humans should adopt Islam and accept the covenant of vicegerency.

But, even given the acceptance of this identity, who is to judge if the people has consented to something that exceeds the authority of *sharīʿa?* The doctrine of the universal caliphate means that no representative (ruler, scholar, Looser or Binder) can claim this by right. This can only be a judgment internal to popular sovereignty itself. Ghannūshī does not state this explicitly, but he does hold that the covenant of vicegerency authorizes the people to create and revise legal norms at the constitutional and statutory level. Although it is clear that the theology of the universal caliphate limits popular sovereignty in principle to acknowledgment of the trust that has been transferred to it from God, in practice it remains an open question how much freedom that people has to create, design, and reform the legal rules for those political offices and institutions for which the people is seen as the source of legitimacy.

The Scope of Constituent Power

Ghannūshī thus moves from the classical trope of the ruler as an agent of the people to the urgency of creating a wide variety of means for expressing this popular sovereignty: not only elections, but also referenda, public opinion, journalism, and various kinds of popular assemblies. From this, it is a relatively intuitive move to argue that though government as some form of public order is required by the timeless goals of Islam, "everything else is just a means . . . The Islamic state is nothing other than the political means for realizing Islam's exalted ideal of a community founded on good and justice, realizing truth and invalidating falsehood on the entire earth."[65]

Ghannūshī discusses in some detail the traditional and modern theoretical rules from within Islamic constitutional jurisprudence on (1) the necessary qualifications of the head of state; (2) his functions, obligations, and tasks; (3) the rights owed him by the *umma*; and (4) the conditions for removing him. He takes these rules seriously as guidelines for how Islam imagines the place of political life and governance in an overall scheme of realizing the goals of religion and as a point of departure for contemporary constitutional thinking. But they are not fixed, constitutional principles and certainly not because they have been settled as such by a class of jurists on their own epistemic authority.

Thus, what is absolutely fixed in the creation of political institutions are not specific mechanisms for appointing a ruler or even the traditional rights and obligations regulating the relationship between him and the people, but the "foundational values of Islamic political order: equality, brotherhood, justice, consultation, and the commanding of right and forbidding of wrong."[66] Even in the realm of law, what is supreme and sovereign in God's law are not the particulars of Islamic jurisprudence, or even the disciplined practice of legal reasoning, but what is fixed and firm in the law because of its generality.[67] The forms government takes are secondary to the way government is only a means to the realization of these values. The scope of the *umma*'s authority to constitute new offices and orders is thus indeterminate.

Presumably this holds also for specific offices like the Imamate or caliphate. Whereas it is common in Sunni constitutional theory to say that the obligatoriness of this office is known with certainty through both reason and revelation, Ghannūshī is arguing that because any institution is a mere means to be wielded by the people, it is up to that people's judgment whether specific institutions ought to be created or authorized. Insofar as the application of universals to particulars is a form of sovereign judgment in politics, the constitution as a particular form of political life is subject to popular sovereignty.

Ghannūshī outlines some more specific parameters for the concept of popular constituent power in a discussion of the relevance of Western republican principles of the separation of powers (Montesquieu and Madison are referred to) for Islam. Under the basic principle that "supreme legitimacy both in ideology and values belongs to the Qur'ān and Sunna, which are independent from all state institutions and which provide the framework within which Islamic scholars and their institutions can carry out the task of interpreting the texts and apply them to challenges arising," he outlines a set of principles for the legitimacy of any constitutional order that involves multiple distinct branches and powers of government[68]:

1. Constitutional design is open to *ijtihād* within limits: "There is no clear and definitive Islamic text to support any of these choices [about the balance of powers within an Islamic government]. This means that this issue is amenable to several interpretations, with the proviso that the supreme legislative authority belongs to God through the Qur'ān and Sunna."
2. Islam favors cooperation and integration over a (Madisonian) conflict model: "The notion of struggle between the state

powers must be completely set aside in favor of a cooperative, mutually supportive model, which then becomes a model for all human relationships."

3. The *umma* must preserve moral unity above managing competition: "The need to concentrate powers in one hand will be much less in a believing, stable community, than in one that is unstable and even at war with itself." (Again, contra Madison in Federalist 10.)
4. Consultation (*shūrā*): "Mutual consultation entails a variety of interpretations of the *sharīʿa,* while it strongly refuses and resists the principle of conflict between Muslims as individuals and communities. It calls them to unity on the basis of creed and as social groupings."
5. All offices are accountable to the people directly: "When the head of state becomes answerable to the parliament and not to the people and the public oath of allegiance loses its constitutional meaning and becomes a mere formal ceremony, we end up considering the head of state as a mere symbol of the state's oneness and no longer truly responsible to the people. . . . This problem could be solved, however, if a constitution appointed for every state body a specific function, then its particular oath of allegiance was specifically to the *umma,* and finally if it pledged its obedience to God and his Messenger, in order to follow the constitution, respect the people's will and commit to mutual consultation."
6. The separation of powers alone is insufficient to prevent oligarchy: "By contrast, even if the Islamic system of governance decides to adopt a pluralistic form, it remains immune to creedal conflicts and special interests, because of its unitary religious nature, which favors complementarity and harmony."

What seems clear in Ghannūshī's thought on the scope of the *umma*'s constituent power is that designing specific institutional relationships is less important as a mark of the *umma*'s freedom to discover its collective will than as part of its obligation to preserve and embody its preexisting shared will and identity. As with certain republican theorists, and as introduced with Mawdūdī, the Islamic political community is primarily a republic of virtue. Its unity around shared purposes and virtues is the ultimate standard by which institutional design is judged, rather than a constitution's ability to manage conflict and prevent tyranny.

This is another way of understanding the force of divine sovereignty in Islamic thought: the idea of *sharīʿa* is not only as a set of legal rules that constitute the polity or political order in a way that constrains political action, but also as "the constituent authority for the society, the state and the civilization,"[69] defining its will and essence in a way that the pious find enabling as it also elevates to an ontological level the stakes of political and constitutional conflicts. For if "the community only exists on the basis of the Text and the Text is what gives the *umma* its legality," then not only will there be a juridical presumption against "exceeding what is clear and unambiguous in the Text,"[70] but the very commitment to Islam as a foundation for political life might be seen as the choice between the preservation or annihilation of the very people itself.

What also follows from this is that the sovereignty-government distinction from Western political theory is unlikely to map on neatly to Islamic discourses for the simple reason that there is no clear boundary between the authority of the divine law in constituting the community and its basic institutions and its authority in governing society. As a concept, or an imaginary, the *sharīʿa* is (choose your metaphor) the water in which the Muslim community swims. But this cuts both ways for the idea of popular sovereignty in Islamic democratic theory: what is imagined as an empowering or authorizing principle for the *umma*'s authority over its representatives is at the same time a limiting principle on the *umma*'s authority over itself (it cannot will otherwise than to strive to enact the *sharīʿa* in the world). Because law is prior to and foundational for the legitimacy of the state, the authority of the law is distinct from the state as an apparatus and law, and the ruler is inherently constrained by the *sharīʿa*—the rules of law—in what he commands. But the law is also both prior to and immediately constitutive of the people. The scope of the people's freedom to constitute a political order will depend entirely on how specifically that law speaks and by what practical and interpretive agency Text is brought into life.

The crucial moves, on my reading of Islamic democratic theory, consist in the way the *umma*'s authority over the representatives of the divine law is portrayed. Even in a thinker as far on the "democratic" end of the spectrum as Ghannūshī, this problem does not simply vanish. There are many points at which he seems to suggest sweeping legislative and policy authority for scholars and the People Who Loose and Bind more generally. For example: "The source of sovereignty is the legislation that is taken from the Book and Sunna, if it accords with the texts and does not contradict the spirit of these two holy sources and their aims. It is natural that there be someone to represent this sovereignty. And here we say that it is represented by the People Who Loose and Bind on behalf of the entire *umma*, and in that case their decisions and laws that they produce, building on their reasoning about it, are correct and legitimate and are binding on the whole *umma*."[71] This statement would not have been out of place in Riḍā's *The Caliphate*.

But Ghannūshī's moves in a popularizing direction even in the area of authority over the application of the *sharīʿa* within an established political order are significant. First, Ghannūshī insists that experts in the divine law only acquire any binding, enforceable authority from popular authorization: "The Islamic state is not just the rule of law, but the rule of just law. But here is the place for humans: to select people to apply the law in its details in new situations. The *umma* remains sovereign over these people."[72] Although he does not dismiss outright certain modern articulations of the idea that representative assemblies of elites, particularly jurists, might enjoy extensive authority to practice collective deliberation around the forms of governance and thus, in a way, embody sovereignty or supreme authority, those representative consultative assemblies are never self-authorizing or self-constituting in Ghannūshī's view. The *sharīʿa* itself does not determine a specific form or procedure, and so this is an undetermined area of the law eligible to change across time and place. By definition, then, it belongs to the sovereignty of the *umma* at large, as God's caliph, to decide between these various procedures.

Popular Sovereignty as Legislative Authority

In Ghannūshī's account, the people is also given substantial legislative authority within the constituted bodies. The most interesting questions pertain to the kind of law the people is seen as legislating (that is, whether there is a division between *fiqh* law and law not derived from revealed texts, but rather based on public interest), and the kind of authority the people has over experts (particularly jurists who traditionally represented divine law without the need for popular authorization or approval).

Ghannūshī's views on the legislative sovereignty of the people are developed around three primary themes: first, that God's own sovereignty is realized through a law that is flexible and requires extensive human agency to bring into force; second, that the people remains the source of any effective legislative authority that is wielded by the scholars of the divine law; third, that the people's authority over the law actually extends to the right to participate in the interpretation of the divine law and its application in particular times and places.

The *sharīʿa* itself obviously does not establish how it is to be articulated, enunciated, and enforced. The tradition of Islamic jurisprudence does not exist outside of human history and thus cannot be taken for the *sharīʿa* itself. For Ghannūshī, then, the entire tradition of Islamic legal norms and rules is not to be simply swept aside, but it is to be put in its place. The sovereignty of God should not be confused for the sovereignty of *fiqh*. The *sharīʿa* works by presenting to mankind clear standards for justice that legislators then use to guide specific lawmaking.[73] Divine sovereignty is a constraint on both politics and legislation but also, in a sense, the precondition for a kind of open-ended political life: "The *sharīʿa* is not only about ossified or frozen texts, it has not been molded in a final form once and for all, and it is also not a legal code which posits a ruling for each action or situation. Rather it creates ample space for interpretation, determination, addition, and renewal through the use of individual and collective reason, or *ijtihād*."[74]

This is in addition to the fact that the political and legal matters under consideration in a political order are not always (or even usually) issues on which the divine law speaks in a specific way or which bear on core religious concerns. Rather, on countless matters of leadership, political judgment, and managing the affairs of the world, there is no clear question of absolute right and wrong, or a religiously binding ethical norm. Classically, this was the foundation for the ruler's legislative authority, as public policy could be removed from the realm of *fiqh,* thus reducing the moral and epistemic stakes of his edicts. But in Ghannūshī's hands, part of the purpose of this move is to note that the policy-making elites in an Islamic state include not only religious scholars but also rulers, notables, holders of social power, and any kind of representatives holding secular knowledge.[75]

Here is the second dimension of the people's legislative authority: all persons holding power to deliberate on behalf of the *umma* must be authorized *by* the *umma* to deliberate about its welfare. This is obviously not an original move in Ghannūshī's thought. What is crucial is the consistency with which he emphasizes that even those who claim the authority to interpret the divine law derive their effective political and legislative authority from popular authorization. The entire dilemma of divine and popular sovereignty, and essential ambiguity in Ghannūshī's hybrid conception of sovereignty, is expressed at the end of his core exposition of the meaning of divine sovereignty:

> The foundations of this [just, divine] law are not posited by a majority of society, or a dominant class, or even a people preoccupied with its own partial interest, but only by God, the Lord of all. It is enforced, explained, and applied to new realities through new specific acts of legislation by a human body chosen and supervised by the people. The people thus has sovereignty over this body, involving appointment, supervision, and removal. This is the authority of the people, or consultation.[76]

Ghannūshī holds that a properly constituted Islamic state should guarantee that a body of top-level jurists supervise the state's legislative outputs. But this expert knowledge does not represent sovereign control: "When it comes to the legislative consultation aiming to express the *umma*'s consensus on important issues, it should be carried out by a body elected by the people, independent of the state, and composed of some of the best Islamic scholars and judges. Because everyone is allowed to gain knowledge of the *sharīʿa* and it is not limited to any class of people, there is no reason why the jurists should be those who rule the Islamic state."[77]

However, as we see here, Ghannūshī does not limit *sharīʿa*-based lawmaking to experts, and he does not limit the legislative sovereignty of the people to their periodic delegation of authority. It is here where the doctrine of the caliphate of man reaches its full force. Popular participation in government and legislation is not simply a point of legal doctrine or something granted by experts in the spaces where the divine law is silent. Rather, the divine text itself establishes the right of the people as vicegerent to participate in public affairs. Popular participation is not just the consequence of the early historical precedent and Qur'ānic reference to "consultation." Rather, *shūrā* itself is a basic principle of religion insofar as it is required by the covenant of vicegerency.[78]

The popular caliphate involves certain capacities in addition to obligations or entitlements. And so Ghannūshī writes that the acumen and judgment to figure out what is clear and fixed in the text and thus what constitutes "obedience to a creature in disobedience to the Creator" belongs to all ordinary Muslims, individually and collectively. This is another articulation of the idea discussed earlier of popular sovereignty as a kind of dispersed sovereignty. God's sovereignty is embodied in the Text and law, but also the popular judgment and interpretation that percolates throughout a Muslim society.[79]

Importantly, this popular right to engage directly with the interpretation and making of law is limited neither to matters of personal piety nor to public matters of a "secular" nature. Of course, it is easiest to argue for the latter. But the *umma*'s popular participatory legislative role is *not* limited to mundane matters. It also extends into the interpretation and application of the divine law. Ghannūshī refers to the *umma* as "the source of legislation" and notes that while God is the primary and original source of legislation, the *umma* participates in divine will through its public practice of mutual consultation. Moreover, for all the binding and constraining quality of God's eternal law, "the goal of the eternity of this final, sealing law required restricting and limiting the text of revelation to a determination of general principles and a few select particulars for organizing human relations and economics." The revealed law leaves the "filling out of the details of that framework to the legislative efforts of the *umma,* developing with time," a practice that Ghannūshī equates with the idea of universal communal consensus *(ijmāʿ)* as a source of divine law alongside revelation. This fact induces Ghannūshī to proclaim that when deliberating about political matters, "the *umma* is guided by God and acquires from His light protection against collective error."[80]

At this point, the distinction between divine and popular sovereignty seems to blur in Ghannūshī's telling. The search for a kind of collective consensus "in the Islamic *sharīʿa* is dignifying man as he is."[81] The call for this communal consensus is a clear invitation to recognize public opinion across all its differences, directions, tendencies, and inclinations within the process of legislating. And here the fusion of the divine and popular takes on a poetic character. "This human element that entered into the *sharīʿa* is part of it . . . it is no wonder if the *umma* appears with God's light or its viewpoint appears as part of prophecy and the good is what it sees as good."[82] There is an attempt, thus, to portray the human element of lawmaking not as alien to the divine, but as part of it insofar as God's sovereignty is embodied not only in Text but also in the *umma*'s public reasoning. He writes that "the human element and the *sharīʿa* are of one essence, for isn't humanity infused with God's breath just like the *sharīʿa?* Does the 'seal of prophecy' not mean the rule through mankind's own self-guidance and capability in steering the ship of his life by himself in light of the general rules for behavior [laid down by God]?"[83]

In addition to the fusion of the divine and the human, there is also an attempt to fuse the individual and the collective. As we have seen, the absence of a self-constituting body of "priests" implies a certain measure of direct, individual responsibility to engage with revelation. But the legislative dimension is most fully expressed at the collective level. Ghannūshī refers to the public, political process by which the people at large interpret, determine, add to, and renew the *sharīʿa* through the use of individual and collective reason as the moment when the "*umma*'s personality is recognized as expressed in a specific period of time and its public will to complete the law. . . . Muslims, then, decided long before Rousseau and his ilk to speak about the general will and to praise it, meaning that the people's will is free from error, as it comes from God's will, which made it a source of legislation, even if in the end it relies on the Qur'ān and Sunna."[84] The caliphate of man is fulfilled collectively when the community of the deputized believers deliberates publicly about the meaning of revealed texts, the genuine interests of the *umma*, the circumstances of the age, and the conditions for applying this or that legal norm.

This gives us an important glimpse into what Ghannūshī means by the concept of "sovereignty," what work he thinks it is doing and how it differs from the sovereignty enjoyed by God. Consider his statement that "there is no contradiction in saying that the *umma* is the source of sovereignty and that the Qur'ān and prophetic Sunna are the source of legislation. The *umma* is who understands the Book and Sunna, acts in accordance with it and reflects on its own conditions and circumstances to see what matters are for application and what matters are for suspension or amendment."[85] At least in this passage, the *umma*'s sovereign powers are related to all of the actions that relate to bringing God's will into reality. All of the powers of reception, interpretation, judgment, imagination, deliberation, application, and enforcement are held by the *umma*. If we are to compare this to the "sleeping sovereign" metaphor: here God is the sleeping sovereign who has uttered His commands and instructions at one single point in time and then left them to an agent for enforcement, and the people is God's minister, agent, or deputy, holding all powers of interpreting the sovereign's instructions, fitting them to the circumstances, and enforcing them. Barring a new sovereign intervention, the people's authority is thus irrevocable. Unless God intervenes directly to correct misguided interpretations of His will, the people can be seen as fully sovereign, and all claims to truth or authority in understanding His instructions are struggles within that sovereign body.

But this leaves a somewhat subtle question about the nature of politics and law in an Islamic society. When Ghannūshī writes that the sphere of legislation on matters not clear in revelatory texts (so called deductive or derived legislation) is the right of the *umma* and not merely the scholars or the rulers, his point is that there should not be any separation between the politics of the state and the rulings of God's law. The management of the affairs of state should be built upon the rulings of divine law, and the mission of the body of Islamic scholars should not depart from the mission of others specialized in both religious and civil law, which is to watch over the constitution.

When Ghannūshī writes that the *umma* participates in sovereignty and rulership with its legislative authority, this implies a very specific relationship to the sources and outcomes of lawmaking. In this perfectionist scheme "it is not sufficient for a citizen to follow the law because its legality emanates from a legal body, that is, an elected one, or even from the people as a whole, but it must also agree with the divine authority represented by the *sharīʿa*. Otherwise, the believer must not only refrain from applying it, but he must resist and rebel against it, according to his means. For that reason, Islam does not entrust the supervision of the state's laws to a particular body—though that too is needed—but rather to the people as a whole, who are the guarantors of God's law."[86] What holds together this imagination that divine sovereignty can be realized as popular sovereignty? Divine sovereignty as a pre-political law embodied in Text, constraining political life, only comes to life through a particular kind of collective and individual popular agency. This is an agency built on moral and epistemic commitment to fulfilling the covenant of vicegerency. The theory of popular sovereignty envisioned by the caliphate of man is thus a kind of republic of virtue.

A Republic of Virtue

Consider again the fact that Ghannūshī's theory portrays the living *sharīʿa* as that which the people "enforce, explain and apply to new realities through new specific acts of legislation." The people is not only authorized to act politically in the world, but its political acts are seen to represent the *sharīʿa*. The people's political action is not observing or abiding by the boundary between religious law and political action, but creating it.

We are thus back to the core perfectionist vision of politics that motivates the entire theory. What is democratic and populist in his vision is not that the people's will is self-justifying, providing for the legitimating ground of all subsequent political life. The people's will, as we have seen, is to a large extent given by the covenant of vicegerency. Rather, what is democratic and populist is that the people is not an object of care by some authoritative guardian. The people is the subject of its own self-direction.

The competence required to assume political responsibility for this self-direction is a matter of both collective unity of purpose and the cultivation of public virtue. The citizens and believers who make up the sovereign *umma* in this view are not just individuals who happen to find themselves within a particular territory, but are identified as those who assume responsibility for carrying out the covenant of vicegerency. The Islamic state is thus the self-governance of specific kind of collective body united by purpose and commitment. The virtue of the sovereign citizenry is also an Islamic constitutional principle because an Islamic order requires "a *passion* to lay aside the traditions and worldviews of other peoples with all the different methodologies they entail, except what is wise, and we have more wisdom than they."[87]

The idea of such a community can be seen to solve a certain set of theoretical problems in Ghannūshī's theory. First, recall his critique of Western theories of popular sovereignty. They succeeded in replacing the arbitrary rule of kings and priests with the rule of law, but a law that ultimately rested on nothing other than its own claims of legitimacy. Institutional solutions like the division of power in order to set ambition against ambition cannot guarantee that a democracy will not devolve into tyranny or evil. If the rule of law is only as good as the force that is guaranteeing it, what is it about an Islamic state resting on a divine law that makes it less susceptible to disintegration?

One of the traditional answers is that this is exactly why the Muslim community needs an Imam. Ghannūshī canvases such views in twentieth-century Islamic thought, but his own preferred view is clearly twofold: (1) the divine origin of the law makes it not only morally superior but also a more effective guard against tyranny because no human can claim a monopoly over it, as all believers can point to it as superior to the whim of the ruler;[88] and (2) the Islamic state must produce a sovereign, virtuous people who will in their daily political life act as the custodians of the rule of the law.

A first important place this aspiration to a republic of virtue manifests is in Ghannūshī's critique of (Montesquieuian/Madisonian) republican theories of the separation of powers. The Islamic state is built on the rule of law and limited government, but the unity of purpose presumed by this vision of an Islamic democracy requires an alternative theory of the relationship between the various powers and institutions of an Islamic state. The goal of any genuine Islamic political order, as established by the precedent of the Prophet's pact of governance (*ṣaḥīfa; wathīqa*) in Medina, is not merely to manage conflict between the governed or to pursue distinctly worldly political goals, but to form a political community in which all can participate in forming and pursuing a shared and common will.[89]

The institutional upshot of this view is that although the Islamic state will have various distinct powers and branches, the distinction between these institutions must never allow for distinction in overall purpose. Ghannūshī refers to James Madison's Federalist 10 as advocating the view that

> there is no escaping the necessity of muzzling these religious convictions in order to prevent the constant formation of a majority bloc in society. Rather, the state must work on dismantling that bloc so that society remains divided into a large number of parties, interests, and classes, for that is the best guarantee for freedom and democracy—and the separation of powers comes as a legal instrument spawned by the same intellectual tradition. Still, freedoms and rights, according to this view, only guarantee the tearing apart of society and the establishment of institutions competing with each other and seeking to limit each other's influence; otherwise, they will unite and oppress the people.

But, for him, Madison is not revealing some eternal insight into the working of human reason and passions "sown into the nature of man,"[90] but simply "reflect[ing] the conflict latent in their societies, the materialist philosophy, and the philosophy of humanity in rebellion against its Creator. And as long as this state of affairs endures, as long as it lacks a true human content and its solutions are focused on exterior forms of social and political organization, this political problematic will never be resolved, whether it decides on separating the powers or uniting them, since the issue is more about philosophy than social organization."[91]

The ideal of a neutral or secular state "is the influence of the errors of atheism, intellectual invasion and apostasy that leads people to have these ideas."[92] But relying merely on institutional mechanisms is also seen as an ineffective guarantee of the rule of law. He writes that Montesquieu's and Madison's focus on institutional solutions "must be supplemented by intellectual, moral and creedal principles, which must then be translated into educational methods. Such an education is rooted in a confession of God's supreme authority, as is stated in the Muslim confession of faith, which endows the human person with inner restraint and lessens the need for the intervention of this-worldly authority in a person's life. Put otherwise, the first guarantee for the public freedoms in an Islamic society is the fear of God . . . rights and freedoms come from God and have no greater guarantee than the continuing divine presence within people's consciences and lives. Thus, the restraint, as Ibn Khaldūn said, must come from within."[93]

Ghannūshī here points to the power of public opinion. In a republic of virtue, the ultimate check on tyranny are the opinions and moral courage of the sovereign believers themselves. Where institutions fail to check injustice, "public opinion begins to stir, unsheathing the weapon of commanding good and forbidding evil, with no difference between old and young, ruler or ruled, for everyone is everyone else's guardian, as the hadith goes, 'You are all shepherds and responsible over His flock.'" Popular sovereignty is thus not only represented by the people's constitutive or legislative authority, but also by its ongoing assumption of the responsibility to act as the guarantor of public liberty.

Institutions must also be so designed, and they must also be occupied by persons motivated by the same commitment and virtue. In contrast to a Madisonian republic, "even if the Islamic system of governance decides to adopt a pluralistic form, it remains immune to creedal conflicts and special interests, because of its unitary religious nature, which favors complementarity and harmony."[94] Instead, the Islamic form of republicanism is based on a kind of "flexible separation allowing for cooperation between the various organs of the state so as to lift up God's Word and incorporate it in the responsibility of all concerned." As ultimately all institutions derive their legitimacy from revelation and the *umma*'s responsibility to enact it, there can be no distinct or independent authority for political institutions than the way their existence and operation serves to support and advance this shared purpose. In the technical language of Islamic constitutional jurisprudence, this pertains to the necessary qualifications *(shurūṭ)* that must be met by elected officials. All such officials must have adequate (not expert) knowledge of Islam, but more importantly they must all hold and manifest a specific intent and motivation, namely, to pursue only the happiness of the people as understood by the grounding covenant of vicegerency.[95]

This also provides further depth to the commitment that all public offices and institutions derive their authority directly from the people, as the people is the only true and legitimate representative of divine sovereignty. When the principle of separation between state powers is taken as an objective in itself and avoids Islamic perspectives and values, it risks compromising the essence of the various oaths of allegiance made by distinct public institutions. If, for example, the executive is set up to become answerable to the parliament (as in a ministerial system of government), and not to the people directly, then the public oath of allegiance loses its constitutional meaning and becomes a mere formal ceremony. In this case the head of state becomes a mere symbol of the state's oneness and no longer truly responsible to the people, a Western model of a ceremonial presidency that is completely at odds with the Islamic office of the Imamate. Ghannūshī's solution is for the constitution to "appoint for every state body a specific function, then for its particular oath of allegiance to be specifically and directly to the *umma,* and finally to pledge its obedience to God and his Messenger, in order to follow the constitution, respect the people's will and commit to mutual consultation."[96] Ghannūshī does not limit popular sovereignty over government to rare constitutive moments.

For Ghannūshī the necessity of education for virtue thus becomes a crucial facet of his theoretical account of justice, political stability and, indeed, a matter of constitutional theory. Following his Algerian mentor Mālik Bin Nabī (Bennabi), he holds that democracy in Islam should not be seen as just a political system or assertion of popular sovereignty but as a comprehensive program for educating the people at the personal psychological, ethical, social, and political levels.[97] The ways in which the mosque features as a political, educative space and in which an Islamic state would require a comprehensive philosophy of education for political virtue (which is presently lacking) are thus treated as core constitutional questions for an Islamic state.

How should we understand the vision of politics outlined here in this theory of the Islamic state as a republic of virtue? Insofar as Ghannūshī stresses the idea of the universal caliphate and the description of politics as the *umma*'s discharging of its half of the contract of vicegerency, politics appears sacralized rather than secularized through its removal from the space of technical jurisprudence. Ghannūshī's assignment to the *umma* of the sovereign right not only to control secular rulers but also to determine what it means to "apply the *sharīʿa*," what is timeless and binding in God's law and what is always a matter of collective judgment and discretion, suggests the possibility of a popularized collapsing of *fiqh* and *siyāsa* into one kind of political and legal space inhabited by a self-governing community of sovereign believers.

But unlike in authoritarian regimes where the attempt to identify their own public policy with the legitimacy of the religious law often leads to a legitimation crisis, Ghannūshī's democratized, republican version of this attempts to avoid the oligarchic instrumentalization of divine law. For if it is "the people" unifying these spheres and sacralizing the political in this way, rather than a class of jurists with a single *primus inter pares* at the head representing this unification, the ideal of the rule of God's law need not be sacrificed at the altar of regime self-preservation. Rather, in appropriating "*sharīʿa*" for its own political action, the people vanquishes the specter of an alternative, more legitimate law haunting politics and challenging its legitimacy.

Even if we restrict ourselves to "high doctrine" (as opposed to the political culture or praxis of a party) the move from thinking about the theological bases of political sovereignty to thinking about coalitions and commitments in specific, bounded countries is not a direct one. The doctrine of the universal caliphate is ambiguous with regard to its universalism both globally and locally. It is mankind, the children of Adam, referred to in Q. 2:30: "I will create a vicegerent on earth." Yet, this covenant is one that mankind assumes the benefits and burdens of upon acknowledgment of the truth of Islam and the obligatoriness of *sharīʿa*. Thus, the sovereign community in this scheme is not "the people" as such—any people that might find themselves contracting among themselves or founding a new polis—but rather the *umma,* the believing people.

The question is not about the practical possibilities of compromise and toleration within an actually existing pluralist political system. The question pertains to the deep theory of the foundation of legitimacy and sovereignty. Are secular co-citizens of countries like Tunisia and Egypt, in the sense of co-citizens who do not begin with the covenant of vicegerency and the obligation to execute the *sharīʿa* however this is understood as the source of all political meaning, participants in this universal caliphate? If, in practice, democratic Islamists' acceptance of the institutions and practices of constitutional, parliamentary democracy appears both enduring and principled, does this signify the shedding of the political theology of the universal caliphate for another theory of politics?

7

After Islamic Democracy, after Sovereignty

If the promise of the Arab Spring, which at one point heralded an overdue wave of democratization from Tunisia through Libya and Egypt to Syria, Bahrain, and Yemen, had a tombstone, it would have two death dates. The first would be July 3, 2013, the day when Egypt's military officers (led by future President ʿAbd al-Fattāḥ al-Sīsī) removed that country's first democratically elected president, Muḥammad Mursī, and suspended the democratically ratified constitution of December 26, 2012. The second date would be June 29, 2014 (almost a year to the day after protestors filled Tahrir Square in Egypt to oust Muḥammad Mursī), when the group that had been calling itself the "Islamic State of Iraq and Syria" declared the return of the universal Islamic Caliphate, under the leadership of one Abū Bakr al-Baghdādī, now to be known by his followers as Caliph Ibrahim.

In addition to the brutal violence involved in these two different forms of counterrevolution, they also represent alternative religious ideas of authority, legitimacy, and obedience. For a certain period of time, the "Islamic State" captured media and public attention not only for its astonishing public broadcasting of its own violence but also for its attempt to capture much of the transnational discourse on sovereignty in Islam. But as the ISIS phenomenon appears to be extinguished for the moment, more relevant today as the ideological alternative to Islamic democratic discourse is another kind of anti-democratic, and also anti-Islamist, appropriation of the Islamic tradition.

Obeying the Ruler: The Anti-Politics of Authoritarian Neo-Traditionalism

From the beginning of the demonstrations of December 2010 and January 2011, there were certain scholars ready to declare all forms of public opposition to existing regimes as forbidden by the Islamic *sharīʿa,* just as scholars friendly to the uprisings (or at least hostile to the regimes they were directed against) prepared juridical defenses of the people's right to protest and remove their rulers.[1] Although the anti-democratic, counterrevolutionary efforts have not been primarily a battle about religious authority, deploying *fatwās* and speeches by what are sometimes referred to as "scholars of the state" has been a crucial part of suppressing democratic demands in general, particularly in competition with the discourse employed by scholars of the Islamist movement.

The basic anti-uprising argument is derived from the traditional Islamic juridical opposition to rebellion, or *khurūj*.[2] Rebellion against an existing ruler is deemed impermissible per se but is also associated with a series of further harms to social order, property, life, and social morality. Adnan Zulfiqar demonstrates that there are six core elements of the anti-uprising argument: (1) There are no Islamic proof-texts permitting civil unrest aiming at removing a ruler; (2) protests are a form of rebellion forbidden by a plentitude of revelatory texts; (3) such protests are a form of imitating non-Muslim, Western political action; (4) they can lead to other actions that are impermissible, like public disorder, property damage, and the mixing of genders; (5) they will almost certainly lead to violence and other forms of harm; and (6) they are futile because they incapable of leading to the restoration of the people's Islamic rights.[3]

For example, in a televised appearance in the days after Husni Mubarak's speech declaring the formation of a new government (but without himself yet resigning), Shaykh al-Azhar Aḥmad al-Ṭayyib declared that "the continuation of these demonstrations after all of the guarantees [offered by Mubarak] is a call to chaos and is forbidden in Islam because it amounts to rebellion against the state, the regime and the masses." He continued that anyone calling for more demonstrations and protests was "calling for opening the gates of hell."[4]

Wherever protests began in 2011, there were regime scholars prepared to denounce them on similar grounds. In Syria, the world-famous scholar Muḥammad Saʿīd Ramaḍān al-Būṭī, who had a long-standing close relationship with the Asad regime, took a slightly more conciliatory stance toward those calling for reform, but still condemned the aspiration to revolution. In conditions of uncertainty—both concerning the sources of recent unrest and concerning where violence might lead—Būtī called for Syrians to trust the reform process recently promised by the regime. The legal principle here was less about the need for absolute obedience to a ruler and more about "preventing harm tak[ing] precedence over attaining benefits."[5]

Between 2011 and 2013, these countries went in either one of two directions: civil war or democratic transition. The anti-political, authoritarian discourse took on new life and new importance after the Egyptian coup of July and August 2013.[6] The paradox, of course, is that before the coup the existing elected government should have itself been regarded as the "ruler" or the "holder of authority" *(walī al-amr)* to which the obligations of obedience or nonviolent counsel were due. In any event, once the deed was done, scholars ideologically inclined to the post-coup regime of ʿAbd al-Fattāḥ al-Sīsī could point simply to the fact of overwhelming force or domination as the source of actual power. This view, with some roots in classical jurisprudence, focuses on the capacity to rule and command obedience, and the exigency of restoring order at all costs. In the Egyptian case, it was most notoriously advanced by the former Grand Muftī of Egypt ʿAlī Jumʿa (2003–2013).[7]

Given the context, however, even this form of anti-democratic reasoning could not avoid some reliance on conceptions of popular sovereignty. It was not just the supreme coercive power and capacity of the army that required obedience to the new order, nor (just) that the army amounts in fact to the sovereign People Who Loose and Bind, but that the coup was in response to the call of "all of the Egyptian people" and thus was in accord with the "the will of the people."[8] In the subsequent weeks, Jumʿa's rhetoric became only more extreme, justifying the August 14, 2013, massacres on the grounds that supporters of deposed President Mursī were "*khawārij*" and "dogs of hell" who had brought the massacre on themselves for sowing unrest and chaos.[9]

But there is, if anything, an even broader and more comprehensive authoritarian agenda at stake. Since 2013, Jumʿa has been one of many pro-state authoritarian scholars who have sought to preempt a repeat of the 2011–2013 period by calling for greater order within the field of religious discourse itself. For these scholars, the roots of political unrest, characterized by the possibility of Islamist parties winning competitive and open elections, are in what he calls "chaos in the religious discourse."[10] The solution for Jumʿa is a quasi-Hobbesian one. He supported a law that would restrict any public issuing of religious legal opinions (*fatwā*s) to the official state body *(Dār al-Iftāʾ)*. This proposal is aligned with the efforts of the Egyptian Ministry of Pious Endowments *(Awqāf)* to (re-)assert control over all mosques. As one supporter of this project, a student and follower of ʿAlī Jumʿa, put it: "There has been a lot of talk over the past several years to criminalize the issuing of fatwas by non-licensed Muftis . . . this law needs to be enacted as soon as possible to give legitimate, normative institutions a fighting chance in leading Islam and Muslims away from the threat of extremism."[11] By "extremism" what is meant is anything from nonviolent political Islam to Salafi-Jihadism. Some scholars have noted that the cumulative effect of the support given by scholars like ʿAlī Jumʿa and Aḥmad al-Ṭayyib to the Sīsī government, especially their unqualified support for the violent suppression of the Muslim Brotherhood and state-led efforts to reform Azhar's curriculum by removing even the mention of controversial topics from the Islamic legal tradition, is a kind of "crisis of moral authority" for al-Azhar.[12] (However, it must be reiterated that during the transitional period in 2011, al-Azhar, including al-Ṭayyib, attempted to provide a moral framework for a democratic, inclusive constitutional transition.[13])

But the authoritarian turn in religious discourse, particularly in the form of calling for the exclusion or suppression of the Muslim Brotherhood or other Islamist parties and movements, has acquired a more organized, transnational character. Recently, efforts of the United Arab Emirates, in particular to spearhead the suppression of such organizations that they deem hostile to a more obedient relationship of religious authorities to political power, have gained attention.[14] Particularly controversial of late is its annual "Forum for Promoting Peace in Muslim Societies" (FPPMS), chaired by Mauritanian scholar ʿAbd Allāh Bin Bayya, as well as its "Council of Muslim Elders," chaired by Egyptian scholar Aḥmad al-Ṭayyib. Both institutions have served as platforms for promoting interpretations of Islamic political ethics that stress the importance of stability and "good governance" as values in Islam that take precedence over democracy and popular sovereignty. Perhaps the paradigmatic statement to this effect came in the "the summary statement" to the first Forum, in 2014, after a year of counterrevolutionary reaction. This statement declares that "democracy is not a goal in itself," that advocates of reform should focus on the goals of justice and equality before sanctifying any particular means or institutions and, most provocatively, that "democracy must not become a call in certain societies for civil war."[15]

Islamism and the Tunisian Democratic Transition

Of course, Tunisia remains the exception to the authoritarian counterrevolution against the 2011 democratic revolts. In October 2011, Tunisians elected a National Constituent Assembly (NCA) that, despite a series of political, security, and economic crises, was able to adopt a new constitution on January 26, 2014. The length of time it took the NCA to arrive at a consensus around the document, and other foundational issues of a new political order (such as a laws on transitional justice and the status of former regime officials) is a testament to the deep political and ideological divisions in Tunisia, but also to the capacity of elites both in and out of the NCA[16] to create a new political order through political bargaining alone.[17] This process is far from successfully completed. The Constitutional Court has not yet been established since the governing parties have still been unable to agree on nominees to it,[18] and some see the new system in general as less an ideological agreement to share in the formation of a new democratic society and more a kind of bargained competition over political resources through tenuous power-sharing agreements.[19] But if Nathan Brown is correct that new constitutions can attain "stability and justice" not from technocratic bargaining over interests and reasons alone but from "the ways that bargaining, short-term interest, and passions are engaged directly by the constitutional process,"[20] then the Tunisian process has the advantage at least of being forged through the passionate, even narrowly self-interested, political bargaining of democratically representative actors.

The party led by Ghannūshī, Ennahda (al-Nahḍa), which held 41% of the seats in the NCA, was central to this transitional bargaining process and thus claims a significant measure of the authorship of the new constitution. It is, to say the least, not the constitution of an Islamic republic, but rather one that reflects a political community with significant divides based on identity and competing ways of life.[21] The sole mention of Islam outside of the Preamble (which makes reference to "our people's commitment to the teachings of Islam") is that the state's religion is defined as Islam (Art. 1). But apart from the fact that the president must be Muslim (Art. 74), this is given no substance in a document that immediately also declares that the state is a "civil state based on citizenship, the will of the people, and the supremacy of law" (Art. 2) and "the people are sovereign and the source of authority, which is exercised through the peoples' representatives and by referendum" (Art. 3). Indeed, the concessions made by Ennahda on matters of religion and Islamist ideology have been widely observed. Most notable are giving up the demand for some reference to *sharīʿa* as a source or inspiration of law; the question of the language used to describe the status of women; the description of human rights as "universal"; backing down on a provision against blasphemy; and perhaps most important, agreeing to a mixed presidential-parliamentary system as opposed to the pure parliamentary system preferred by Ennahda.[22] Even an NCA member from the rival Nida Tounès (*Nidā Tūnis*) party asks "why did Ennahdha concede as much to the opposition, when it had a parliamentary majority and the possibility, with the help of some independents in the assembly, to muster the required two-thirds majority?"[23]

However, the mystery is not why a party like Ennahda would make the calculation to endorse this new constitutional order, and still less how an ideologically defined party could possibly participate in creating a constitution that does not reflect its ideal political vision. Rather, the question for this book is what the subsequent ideological and moral endorsement of this new order means for the idea of an "Islamic democracy" built on the sovereignty of a particular kind of people committed in some way to a public, deliberative creation of Islamic legal meaning and legitimacy through its own political action. Temporary political compromises need not raise this kind of intellectual or ideological crisis. But they might, particularly if the adherents of a comprehensive moral-ideological vision reveal their own belief that their ideal is in some way unrealizable, and give increasingly strong reasons for endorsing the nonideal compromise.

This book thus concludes by observing a very specific political and historical moment that generates, I submit, an important theoretical and ideological crisis. Specifically, I have in mind a certain real-world crisis of democratically inclined political Islam in which it is either brutally suppressed (in Egypt, the Gulf, Syria, and elsewhere), or has participated in a somewhat successful form of democratic transition that has resulted in a new political order that bears no resemblance to the ideal theory of an "Islamic democracy" discussed in the previous chapter. In this context, what is left of the Islamic alternative to authoritarianism on the one hand and secular democracy on the other?

It is tempting to reduce this to a question of pragmatism, compromise, or "moderation." But there is, nonetheless, something distinctive about the post-2011 condition. It is one thing to choose to accommodate or collaborate with a political order not of one's making. This can always be portrayed as a tactical decision, or a compromise, which defers to some future moment in which the ideological vision can be realized, whether through revolution, societal transformation, or a democratic refounding. But in Tunisia, the new constitutional and political order is one produced solely by the ideological and demographic divisions internal to the political community, and the Islamist party was as much a democratic author of this order as any other political formation. It is reasonable to ask what distinct theory of legitimacy and sovereignty undergirds the religious or moral commitment to this order. If something like the pluralist constitution of 2014 is not an authoritarian or colonial imposition, but rather something that reflects what the broadest segment of a particular political community can consent to, then what remains of the prior ideal theory, and what is the most sophisticated defense of the new order?

But this also raises questions about the authoritativeness of various registers or levels of discourse. Certain systematic treatises, written and published for the broad Muslim public sphere, can be presumed to represent some of the most considered reflections on sovereignty, law, and legitimacy. These works (paradigmatically Ghannūshī's *al-Ḥurriyyāt al-ʿāmma* in this book) are not merely scholarly elaborations, because they are contributions by activist intellectuals to an ongoing public discourse seeking to define the commitments of political movements. But they are also not immediate reactions to current events or political crises, where the logic of shorter-term partisan interest predominates over theoretical sophistication. They represent attempts to give the most persuasive ideal theory for Islamic government in this historical context. By contrast, much of the political discourse during and after negotiated constituent moments is ad hoc, unsystematic, and provisional. To put it bluntly: if an ideal theory of a democratic Islamic state was elaborated through complex and sophisticated treatises, does the post-utopian, nonideal order that Islamists have participated in creating need an equally complex, sophisticated and systematic theory? What would a complete political theory, or political theology, of "public freedoms in the pluralist state" look like?

Answering that completely would be the task of another book. This book closes with a few more modest goals. First, what are the ideological contours of the idea of "Muslim democracy" in contrast with the ideal Islamist theory developed in the decades prior to the 2011 revolution? How different is the nonideal, post-utopian ideology from the previous ideal theory? Second, given this knowledge of a gap between the two iterations, what kind of moral commitment or consensus undergirds the commitment to something like the 2014 constitutional order in Tunisia, again given the fact that this order was the result of free democratic negotiation rather than authoritarian imposition? Of course, this can only be speculative, and doctrinal factors are hardly the only test of democratic commitment. But insofar as there has traditionally been a very powerful alternative theory of legitimacy and sovereignty, it is worth asking how deep and persuasive the theoretical commitment to a new order might be. Finally, if something like the ideal theory of a democratic but Islamic regime remains out of reach, why is that? Are there are good theoretical reasons for thinking that the ideal form of an Islamic democracy is not only unrealized but also inherently unrealizable in the terms that the theory itself calls for?

Pluralism, Consensus, Law: "Muslim Democracy" as Nonideal Theory

The idea of a break with political Islam and its replacement by something called "Muslim democracy" did not emerge with the 2011 revolutions. Scholars have been writing about "post-Islamism" and an ideological shift to "Muslim democracy" since the mid-1990s.[24] Although it falls somewhat out of the scope of this study, it is important to note that widespread disillusionment in Iran with the project of creating an Islamic state has led to a very rich reformist discourse by religious intellectuals, many of whom were early partisans of the idea of an Islamic republic.[25] It must also be noted that the ideal theory of a "republic of virtue" that harmonizes the demands of divine and popular sovereignty always coexisted not only with deep personal pragmatism and flexibility on Ghannūshī's part but also with less perfectionist and more pluralistic aspects of his theoretical writings and the public statements of the various political formations from the Islamic Tendency Movement to al-Nahḍa.[26] So, my argument is not that there is a clean break between a pre-revolutionary, "utopian perfectionist" political thought in Ghannūshī's writings and a post-2011 "pragmatic pluralist" political thought. The two have long coexisted and it is not clear that an unambiguous unity can be established for all of Ghannūshī's theoretical reflections.

Nonetheless, although the pragmatic and pluralist elements of Ghannūshī's thought predated 2011 and the long constituent moment of Tunisian politics that culminated in the 2014 constitution, the post-2014 period is important both for some formal and official breaks with the legacy of "political Islam" and the nature of Ghannūshī's published writings. The single most important official moment is the decision of Ennahda to formally abandon the label "political Islam" and describe itself as a "Muslim Democratic" party at its May 20–22, 2016, party congress. The Concluding Statement of the congress declares that "the Ennahdha Party has in practice gone beyond all the justifications that may be used to consider it part of what is called 'political Islam,' and that this common label does not express the essence of its current identity nor reflect the substance of its future vision. Ennahdha believes its work to be within an authentic endeavor to form a broad trend of Muslim democrats who reject any contradiction between the values of Islam and those of modernity."[27] As noted by many both within[28] and without the party, this was less of a break than a ratification of long-term elements of the party's ideology and political culture.

However, this more formal and seemingly permanent turn is also a call for more substantive doctrinal reformulation. Although elements of the more radical commitment to political pluralism always existed alongside the more ideal, perfectionist elements in Ghannūshī's thought, it must be said that almost none of the elements of perfectionism and "universal caliphate" talk can be discerned in his post-2011 writings and speeches. The shift is less a matter of addition of the pluralist elements than of subtraction. Ghannūshī's postrevolutionary writings and speeches have been gathered in a number of places. One volume, *Irhāṣāt al-thawra* (*Premonitions of the Revolution*),[29] contains essays, articles, and interviews from 1999 to 2014, with the bulk originally published from 2010 on. This conclusion will draw on some of his postrevolutionary writings from this collection, particularly those from the crisis year of 2013: "Meanings and Rationales of the Post-Revolutionary Constitution," "Human Rights in Islam," "The Democratic Transition in Tunisia," "The New View of Tunisia," "From the

Founding to the Revolutionary Constitution," "Freedom of Conscience," and "The Tunisian Model Is Confirmed and Verified." Ghannūshī has also published a series of pamphlets on "the grounding of modern conceptualizations" of various core political terms: democracy, citizenship, secularism, and freedom,[30] although they often consist of short essays and interviews from before 2011. In addition to these, he has also published a number of his Friday sermons *(khuṭab)* from the post-revolutionary period.[31]

In his February 23, 2013, lecture, "Meanings and Rationales of the Post-Revolutionary Constitution," Ghannūshī asserts that the importance of a constitution consists primarily in the way that it limits the will of the ruler and makes his will subordinate to the law. This is straightforward enough and would not have been out of place in his previous accounts of the Islamic state. But whereas it will be recalled that in the previous ideal theory the limitation on the will of the ruler is but one part of the overall rule of *sharīʿa,* in his present account "the Islamic *sharīʿa only came for this purpose* of limiting the authority of the ruler and subjecting him to the law."[32] The striking nature of this remark needs little commentary. From a comprehensive moral and social order (albeit one that requires a quasi-sovereign, divinely deputized people to constantly interpret and implement), the Islamic *sharīʿa* is reduced to nothing other than the mundane, secular purpose of creating limited, nonarbitrary governance. In this view, any functioning constitutional order could be regarded as "*sharīʿa* compliant," a far cry from Ghannūshī's prior vision of a virtuous public deliberating on God's purposes and instructions with the advice and assistance of experts in the divine law.

How could this be seen as the Islamic vision of legitimacy? Throughout his many statements and articles since 2011, Ghannūshī returns time and again to what he sees as the lessons of the Prophet's covenant with the people of Medina (the *ṣaḥīfat al-Madīna*). Of course, this has long been regarded as the foundational moment of Islamic governance, although not the moment that provided authoritative precedent for jurists and theologians after the death of the Prophet. But what Ghannūshī takes as its example has undergone a remarkable transformation. As noted in Chapter 6, in *Public Freedoms in the Islamic*

State Ghannūshī uses it precisely to argue for a perfectionist vision of politics. The lesson of Medina is that politics is not merely about the (Madisonian) purposes of managing conflict or advancing worldly political goals, but to form a genuine community in which all can participate in forming and pursuing a shared and common will.

Ghannūshī developed a slightly more complex view of the significance of the *ṣaḥīfa* in the years prior to the revolution. In some essays, he views Medina as having created a kind of hybrid form of political community and membership, according to which Muslims achieved the union of moral community and political association, while the latter was offered to non-Muslims. In a 2010 article he uses the fact that the *ṣaḥīfa* of Medina involves both a confessional and a political conception of *"umma"* to argue that non-Muslims had always enjoyed "citizenship rights" in Islam, and that modern understandings of equal citizenship do not depend on a prior commitment to secularism.[33] In a later article from that same year, he again stresses that Medina was a city of multiple religious communities in which citizenship was based on shared possession of a territory, and not shared creed. But at this point he was still eager to stress that this did not mean that Islam was merely a private matter but was also "the source and reference for law and values for the community that believes in it through the institution of *shūrā*. The modern mechanisms of democracy can be identified as based on this, which moves it from being a mere source of moral values toward an institution through which the *umma* exercises its authority and power over its rulers via elected committees that represent public opinion." Within such a system, there need be no fear of Islam on grounds on freedom, as Islam is a comprehensive emancipatory resource, based on the nature that God has created us with, and is thus not any kind of imposition on it or alienation from it."[34]

But the post-2011 writings go even further in stressing that the lesson of Medina for postrevolutionary Tunisia is that Islamic governance was founded originally in circumstances of radical pluralism, precisely where a shared will or purpose among "citizens" could not be assumed. Ghannūshī writes that the first written constitution in Islam (if not the world), the *ṣaḥīfa,* codified an essentially pluralist political formation, and that "we [Muslims] are lucky that our first state was a pluralist state."[35] In a later essay, he reiterates that the founding of Medina provides Muslims with the authoritative example of founding a pluralistic political order, with citizenship (not religion) as the fundamental principle of rights and duties.[36]

The fundamental mechanism of the political order in this model is contract rather than moral formation. The *ṣaḥīfa* presents to Muslims the model of the Prophet establishing a state on the basis of contract in a religiously pluralist society, a state that establishes a civilizational model open to all mankind, capable of assimilating and incorporating all creeds, cultures, and races within a contractual and civilizational framework, without expulsion, wars of cleansing, or plans for forced assimilation.[37] In this religiously plural society, religion itself figures as a kind of dignifying of man with reason and freedom. It is not the role of the state to prove the truth of any one religion or to provide for religious conformity, but rather to recognize members as they are and to provide for peaceful coexistence, cooperation, and the development of a spirit of commonality based on equality in citizenship.[38] In this model of a political society, the purpose of governance and political life is almost exclusively "secular": protecting persons based on residence and membership (not creed), dispensing justice on the basis of equality, mutual defense, and upholding contracts.

Ghannūshī uses this understanding of Medina not only to argue for a limited conception of politics and to justify political cooperation with non-Islamic parties, but also to argue for a broad consensus model of constituent politics. What is interesting is that Ghannūshī does not merely defend these as necessary compromises given the balance of power, or as "the best we could get," or as a distinctly political choice to prioritize stability over partisan goals. Rather, he advances a view of consensus itself as the highest principle of legitimacy, particularly in constituent moments. This is most remarkable in his discussions of why they agreed to drop the *sharīʿa* clause from the constitution. He claims that the highest commitment in the drafting of the constitution was that it gain the widest possible agreement in Tunisian society, rather than the consensus sufficient for ratification. The constitution must not be seen as the constitution of a particular party, but rather of the whole country in which the entire range of political, intellectual, and social trends are found. Because it is crucial that the people and the citizens in all their orientations see themselves in it, the constitution could not be promulgated with a bare 51% majority, but must be ratified with a broader base of approval.

But here it gets tricky because a constitution must also guard and reflect the identity of the particular country it is set to govern. In the case of Tunisia, there was a consensus around an Arab, Islamic identity. Here Ghannūshī's populist (almost protestant) theology enters: "In Islam there is no church that could monopolize the interpretation of Islam. Instead, this is left to the umma and the people through its institutions that translate the meanings of this 'Arab, Islamic identity.' And so when the question of the *sharīʿa* was proposed, we found that it is a matter of disagreement. But constitutions are not adopted on the basis of what there is disagreement around but rather what there is consensus on."[39]

This, I think, is the crucial passage for understanding the move from Islamism to "Muslim democracy." Of course, Ghannūshī always knew that many contemporary Muslims did not wish to enshrine the *sharīʿa* as the governing law of their society, and yet his entire intellectual project was traditionally an interpretation of what it means for a Muslim community to govern itself by the *sharīʿa*. And in some of that previous writing, the rejection of the *sharīʿa* itself was not treated at all as a reasonable disagreement. Yet in the constitution-drafting period, the view is that it would be unreasonable or inappropriate to base so foundational a concept of legitimacy and legislative sovereignty on a controversial principle. But why? What makes disagreement about the *sharīʿa* itself reasonable or worth respecting, rather than mere disagreement on specific points of *sharīʿa?*

Ghannūshī doesn't elaborate on this question. What he does say is that "the constitution must be adopted on the basis of human values because we are a part of this humanity that crystallized and clarified a number of principles, such as the principles of democracy and human rights. We are also heirs to the principles of reform and we regard the school of reform as one of the references and authorities for our constitution and our distinctive Tunisian thought. We want to adopt a civil state in which legitimacy does not depend on anything but the people [*al-nās*], that is, from its people [*sha'b*] who are governed by it. There is no legitimacy for a ruler other than from a clear delegation and mandate, that is, through free, impartial and pluralistic elections."[40] It is not entirely clear what the deeper Islamic or principled foundation for this preference for wide consensus is, except for the repeated insistence that "We must spread freedom as much as we can, in addition to the fact that justice is one of the goals of Islam, as is freedom. . . . Constitutions came to prevent authoritarianism, not freedom, and so every orientation toward the spreading of freedom is an Islamic orientation."

He makes similar statements on the other points of disagreement. Although he thinks that Islamists were unfairly criticized over the term "*takāmul*" to refer to the nature of gender relations (he points out that it literally refers to men and women completing one another, and not that women are merely men's complements), he concedes that part of the lesson here is to "avoid all terms that stir up doubts and about which the people do not agree on the meanings of. For this reason, we advised our brothers to remove the term 'complementarity' despite the fact that we regard 'complementarity' as one of the meanings of equality and that 'they each complete each other' does not mean that 'one completes the other.' But so long as there is confusion around it, since constitutions are matters of agreement rather than disagreement," it was better to remove this language.[41]

The question of the universality of human rights has a similarly pragmatic implication for Ghannūshī. Of course, this language is sensitive because it raises questions about the universality of Islam and whether Islam has a superior approach to human rights. But "our view is that we Islamists must be happy with the general consensus of humanity that humans have rights whatever their gender or religion, and for this reason we should not object to the [idea of the] universality of human rights since this is one of the guarantees of rights and freedoms. Islam only came to realize human interests and welfare, and so anything that guarantees the welfare and rights of people is part of Islam even if there is no textual grounding for it in revelation."[42]

In a separate essay, he addresses more directly and substantively the harmony between Islamic and secular conceptions of human rights.[43] This is not particularly remarkable at this point for his defense of specific rights like freedom of conscience, freedom of religion, rights to property and to the fruits of one's labor, and the social rights (work, basic income, education, housing, even political participation), all of which he thinks are modern juridical mechanisms for defending interests that Islam also values and which are in their general direction in accord with the precepts of Islam. What is more interesting is the way that the fundamental theological foundation of his perfectionist political philosophy is deployed to defend this replacement of the *sharīʿa* with "universal" human rights.

The doctrine of the universal caliphate of mankind in this essay now refers to God's dignifying of all mankind and the fact that Islam seeks the welfare and happiness of all of humanity, not just Muslims. The individual, "negative" freedoms that underpin much modern human rights discourse are seen as squarely within the heritage of Islam as it is the foundation of the quintessential act of faith: the declaration of individual's bearing witness to God and His Messenger (the *shahāda*), which is an expression the individual's freedom and responsibility before God. If some of the specific articulations of the *sharīʿa* and human rights appear divergent, this is of little concern because Islamic law articulates the various interests and goods of mankind in a scaled, gradual way, from the fundamental and necessary to those that embellish an overall rights scheme. What matters ultimately is a convergence on the *interests themselves,* which Ghannūshī sees in modern human rights.

To conclude this section, the distinctive features of Ghannūshī's postrevolutionary, and post-Islamist, writings are (1) the view that political life must be seen primarily as a contract to jointly pursue shared worldly and social goals; (2) that the existing range of moral and political pluralism in Tunisian society must be treated as a more or less fixed fact about society; (3) that (Islamic) morality requires pursuing political agreement given the existing ideological disagreement that presently exists; and thus (4) that the "*sharīʿa*" is now an almost generic commitment to the rule of law and limited government, rather than a denser corpus of rules, methods, and principles. The arch legitimating frame for all of this is not the tradition of Islamic constitutional theory, but the lessons of the Prophet's Covenant of Medina, as Ghannūshī now understands it. There is an almost Rawlsian view of the purpose of the basic structure of society: it is to guarantee a moral conception of social life, but one which can be subject to the widest possible reasonable agreement. Controversial matters should be left aside as long as a fully just political order can be achieved without resolving them.

But this raises questions for a thinker like Ghannūshī: What kind of moral accomplishment is the 2014 Tunisian constitution, and what is the nature of its overlap with Islamic doctrines? In his postrevolutionary writings, Ghannūshī is arguing that Islamists ought to accept on principled grounds the terms of political life made possible by the 2014 constitution, despite all of the concessions that this required of them. It is true that Ghannūshī has given reasons for the acceptability of the constitution derived from plausible religious commitments, as well as sound political judgment, but his preference is to do so without reference to the prior doctrine. Even when he acknowledges that the constitution required compromises and concessions, he does not expressly say whether accepting those compromises means revising earlier views on the fundamental basis for political life.

On my reading, there are two questions in particular of interest:

1. Is the idea of *sharīʿa* permanently limited to this role of limiting government, or is this something future Tunisians might revise in different political circumstances?
2. Are non-Islamic doctrines and ways of life themselves reasonable or merely tolerable? Although Muslims may have obligations to respect the freedom of conscience of others, should differences around the fundamental acceptance or rejection of Islam be seen as something internal to reason or a failure of it?

Virtually every other principled question follows from the conception of justice and the permanence of pluralism. There are reasons to think that present constitutional compromises may have principles behind them but are still compromises. First, there is no deep account offered of why disagreement about the *sharīʿa* itself is reasonable or worth respecting. Rather, there is the observation that presently the question of *sharīʿa* is too divisive and, more intriguingly, that the objections of Tunisians to *sharīʿa* rest on misunderstandings due to the distortions of authoritarian propaganda.

Second, there is reason to believe that Ghannūshī still regards secular comprehensive doctrines as insufficient grounds for a principled moral life. In his 2013 essay on "Human Rights in Islam," he writes that the general direction of human rights declarations and international covenants are in accord with the precepts of Islam and its objectives of advancing justice, freedom, and equality in the divine dignifying of humanity, but the experience of humanity shows that humans do not live without adopting God in some fashion. "In the human soul, there is a hunger that is not satiated except by accepting God." In Ghannūshī's view, the basic defect in modern human rights declarations derived in the most part from secular philosophies is the claim that humanity can be independent of its Creator in organizing life and attaining happiness. "The result of this, despite some partial progress, is the domination of the strong over the weak, the destruction of the environment, and the fracturing of connection and compassion between humans. Whereas when human rights are based on and refer to the Creator, this gives them a kind of sanctity and makes them secure in the hearts of all believers, thus making the defense of them a religious duty with a reward for performance and a punishment for neglect. It also makes them comprehensive and positive, as God is the creator of man and is more knowledgeable of the true needs of His creatures, and it dignifies the law that protects these rights with the authority of religious conscience represented in the feelings of the believers with the eternal supervision of God."[44]

In my conversations with him, Ghannūshī gives a kind of "divine will" account of the source of radical moral pluralism.[45] For him, "the question of pluralism is an ontological question. That is, God willed it, even in matters of religion, and even to the point of denying God." But does the fact of radical pluralism, when Ghannūshī refers to pluralism even to the point of atheism as "ontological" fact, make it *reasonable*? At time he comes close to suggesting that this kind of rejection is rational: "God gave us minds and freedom so that we might disagree. The genius of it is then how we unite even through this disagreement, how we create unity. . . . This is the role of democracy, to restore unity in the midst of disagreement, to arrive at agreement through the tools that it creates." He also comes close to something like the Rawlsian burdens of judgment in speculating on why certain persons who understand Islam well are nonetheless not "guided by God" to accept it: "There are psychological reasons, since the psyche resists. There is also misleading social experience; perhaps someone has a bad experience with a Muslim man or woman. Perhaps it is vanity, or one's social interests come into play: 'What would happen if I converted, and how would my social, professional entourage look at me, and how would my interests be affected?' Many psychological, social, and material considerations come into play."

But Ghannūshī's approach to pluralism tends to focus on the general expectation of pluralism, since it is divinely willed, rather than a more specific epistemic account of why people might encounter the arguments for Islam and reasonably and rationally reject it. For example, I pressed Ghannūshī on the Kantian argument for the antinomies of reason (which has a medieval Islamic echo in philosophical considerations of equipollence in arguments for the existence of God [*takāfū' al-adilla*]), an exchange which highlighted the tension between his simultaneous acceptance of even very radical pluralism and belief in the rational demonstrability of Islam. But when asked whether something like Kant's antinomies of reason might be persuasive from an Islamic perspective, he said simply that "Kant was wrong" insofar as he claimed that reason leads to equally good reasons for a purposive creation of the world and for a nonpurposive origination of the world. "It is strange to imagine a universe without God; the mind itself cannot imagine itself [without God] if we say the mind to mean the brain, for where did it come from?"

Ghannūshī's views thus seem to place him somewhere in between an endorsement of the fact of pluralism and the fact of reasonable pluralism. Pluralism is a brute fact, decreed by God. In the right conditions, all humans could be both rationally and divinely led to true belief of God's existence and the truth of His revelation. At the same time, because pluralism is decreed by God and the natural working of the human mind both produces it and must treat it as part of the normal condition of social life, Muslims are morally and epistemically required to accept it, tolerate it, and act politically in light of it.

Thus, it is most probable that the present relationship of Islamic doctrine (as understood by Ghannūshī and others) to the 2014 constitution is as no more than a constitutional consensus that Islamists can nonetheless be content with for principled reasons (some of them "Islamic" and some of them "freestanding," derived from political experience). One possibility is that the practice of politics will make the liberal principles embedded in the 2014 constitution seem attractive and irreplaceable given the permanence of moral pluralism concerning questions of religion and lifestyle. Over a long enough period of time, the political compromises involved in accepting the constitution will be given some kind of deeper theological justification. Another possibility is that with demographic change (and perhaps political crisis), future Islamists will feel entitled to embrace the consequences of being the social majority.[46]

Is there a contradiction, or even "double-speak," in affirming freedom of conscience and political pluralism while also being willing to use the political process to defend aspects of the *sharīʿa*? For Ghannūshī, the implication of radical moral pluralism is not only restraint and toleration but also "a relationship of respect, respectful debate, and respectful proselytization."[47] But this respect is an agonistic one: difference is not only respected and accepted, but actively engaged for the purpose of persuasion. For Ghannūshī, Islam is a true comprehensive doctrine and emancipatory social system that lives in the world. Since one of the facts of the world is moral pluralism, and since it is willed by God, it must not be seen simply as a tragedy; Islam must manage it in a realistic and morally appropriate way. But there is no reason why the spread of belief in and political adherence to the true and emancipatory moral doctrine is not one of those things for which we may hope.

Similarly, Ghannūshī's political pluralism is as democratic as it is liberal. For the same reason that he argues for restraint in advancing Islamic moral aims in conditions of radical pluralism (because both politics and law must be constrained by public opinion), it is not a contradiction for him to suggest that, should the public opinion incline otherwise, laws could be crafted to reflect that. In fact, although Ghannūshī's thought contains both religious-perfectionist and liberal-pluralist elements, his deeper underlying commitment in both his ideal and non-ideal theory may be to *democracy*.

Was Islamic Democracy Impossible and Why?

With the abandonment of the label of "Islamist" for that of "Muslim democrat," and the priority of ordinary politics over high ideological politics, we are entitled to ask whether the intellectual tradition of "democratic Islamism" that was developed in an ideal form during the decades of exile from power is destined to remain just that—an ideal theory forming an intellectual tradition rather than an actually realizable regime type.

What conclusions can we draw from this for the purposes of a critical or engaged political theory? One preliminary observation may be that insofar as the ideal regime type of an "Islamic democracy" is a kind of republicanism, it confronts many of the obstacles faced by all forms of republicanism. The notion that republicanism demands too much of ordinary citizens by way of participation, knowledge, and virtue is precisely the source of the modern view that popular sovereignty can only be expressed through exceptional moments of constituent power, leaving government to elected representatives. Moreover, it places a faith in politics and the state that is simply absent in most modern societies, particularly in most Muslim ones that have high levels of alienation from the state and ruling oligarchies. But I would like to conclude by considering four (nonexclusive) factors that make the specific vision of an Islamic democracy likely to remain at the level of an ideal.

(1) The Irreversible Moral Pluralism of Modernity

Modern Islamist political thought attempts to repurpose classical Islamic legal concepts for a modern structural and institutional context. One first tension between the core assumptions of this project and modern sociological realities in Muslim societies is that Muslim-majority societies are characterized by the same fundamental challenge of pluralism as other modern societies. It is may be true that "for the great majority of Muslims today, the Sharīʿa remains a source of religious and moral authority."[48] But Muslims disagree radically on what this implies and who they want to speak in the name of the *sharīʿa.* For many (including Hallaq), this kind of pluralism is itself a tragedy that Muslims only have to face because of colonialism. But if it is true that a genuinely "Islamic" popular constituent moment is an impossibility today, that is more likely to be because of the combination of moral pluralism in Muslim societies and the irrelevance or inadequacy of the premodern Islamic legal rulings (not principles) for most social and economic policy areas. In modernity, there is reasonable disagreement about ethics, even for Muslims or those living in Muslim countries. This is a fact that cleaves the idea of an "Islamic" popular constituent power in two: either a given people is free to choose to form whatever government it wishes (in which case Islamic legal theory has nothing to say), or the freedom of the constituent moment is usurped by the prior constraints of fidelity to some pre-political Islamic social contract.

I would submit that this is particularly a problem for modern Islamic political thought precisely because of its aspiration to deep legality. Although much modern commentary has focused on the problem of "Islam and violence," the more accurate story is that the modern Islamist vision is (though not pacifist) one of consensus as the deep foundation of politics. From Riḍā's preoccupation with refounding the caliphate on purely consensual grounds to Ghannūshī's vision of a people that sees itself as God's caliph enacting a kind of dual social contract between God and it, and then it and its government, modern Islamism shares with certain kinds of liberalism precisely an embarrassment at the violent origins of politics and the violence needed to sustain it. Even the more utopian Quṭb, arguably responsible for the ease with which some more radical Islamist groups have rationalized violence, structures his reflections around a humanity that might well be conceived of as born free, that is, in its innate condition of monotheism and good (enough) moral disposition. What all of these theories have in common is beginning by simply positing the existence of an *umma,* with its essence of piety and moral unity already established. Of course, an Islamist theory of politics could acknowledge that this *umma* does not exist, but must be formed through education and coercion, as Quṭbist theories do by calling for a vanguard to take power in our present fallen times. But this is simply not the spirit of so much of modern Islamist thought before and after Quṭb, which not only rejects the violence authorized against *jāhiliyya* but also tends to imagine *jāhiliyya* away at the level of ideal theory.

Of course, the option remains for Islamic democrats to imagine an "Islamic democracy to come," a future sovereign *umma* that can express its moral unity politically, after the people has "returned" to its natural piety by a combination of removing the alien causes of disunity and gentle education. This is not a contradiction. Every democratic theory, if it hopes for more than managed competition or the minimalization of the evils that government can do, has to rest on a faith in the people becoming fit for self-rule. All that remains to be said is that because this Islamic democratic vision of self-rule involves a very deep kind of consensus about metaphysical truths and the ethical purposes of human life, it does not escape the possibility that such deep moral agreement is no longer likely in the contemporary world, at least without the kinds of coercion and limitation on freedoms of conscience and speech that Islamic democrats claim to reject. What if moral pluralism is here to stay?

(2) The Difference That Politics Makes

One response to the previous dilemma is to accept it. Islamists might argue that Islam provides for an ideal regime type, and should a self-governing community of the pious exist, it might freely choose that regime type. But the nonideal world, the world of politics, takes priority because the distinctly political goods and ills belonging to that sphere are more pressing and controlling than the aspirations of high doctrine.[49] We have seen certain post-utopian Islamist parties (particularly in Tunisia, Morocco, and Jordan) reveal preferences for political stability, the sharing of political responsibility, and even coalition building with former enemies. Of course, there are pragmatic reasons for these decisions. And even where they reflect value commitments or an acceptance of the constraints of pluralist politics, the principled grounding for this kind of politics in terms of Islamic political theory is elusive, as this chapter has argued. (Indeed, as we see have seen in Turkey, once the constraints vanish, so do the compunctions about establishing authoritarian [albeit not exactly theocratic] rule.)

Nonetheless, where Islamist parties seem to accept the constraints of existing political orders as a space for political action, this might be read as an "incompletely theorized agreement"[50] to accept the fact of political pluralism at the expense of the kind of Islamic sovereign constituent power that has become central in Islamic ideal theory. Related to this are facts about the requirements of actual government in modern states. Insofar as Islamism represented a "grand idea," it was all in the realm of moral formation of a people and a vision of legal legitimacy. But the countless areas of modern administration and policy making, particularly in societies with extremely high levels of economic and other anxieties, can simply make the concerns of Islamism seem less urgent. This is not to say that there are not laws and policies to be made in the realm of education, public morality, and otherwise promoting a conception of religious truth, and it is not to say that areas like foreign policy or economics have not been subjects of Islamist doctrinal concern.[51] But there is much less to distinguish an Islamic approach to what might be called "good governance" and economic solidarity from other approaches. And because the overwhelming task of politics is in matters of policy that are not central to the distinctive Islamist vision of the world, it is less that the practice of ordinary politics refutes the ideal theory (as I think the permanence of pluralism arguably does) and more that it simply makes it seem less important.

The above-quoted words of senior Ennahda party figure Saif Ferjani are instructive here: "Islamism ended once Ennahdha entered government and shared responsibility for social and economic provision and became accountable to the electorate and to civil society." Both parts of this statement bear dwelling on. First, power is shared, and this simply creates a practice of acknowledging the fact of pluralism, whether or not there is a deep theory of it. And second, "social and economic provision" and being "accountable to the electorate and to civil society" have ways of making a vision of politics centered on a pious people expressing a shared will that fuses both divine and human purposes simply seem less descriptive of political life, again without necessarily refuting it.

(3) The Inescapability of the Modern State

A slightly more pessimistic and critical interpretation of the preceding is that virtually all Islamist political thought occurs in the context of an existing state form that, whatever its flaws or benefits all things considered, did not emerge organically from the political history and conceptual legacy of the Islamic legal tradition. A first implication of this is that Islamist political theorists and activists operate in a context in which enormous military, security, and institutional powers are arrayed against them. The noncoercive, generative kind of constituent power they theorize is virtually impossible where these forces exist, and thus the existing apparatuses of political power constrain enormously the kind of constituent politics that can emerge.

But what of revolutionary possibilities? This has, of course, occurred in Iran and (depending on how we view events) part of Iraq and Syria governed by ISIS. But the lesson from Iran in particular (bracketing for the moment the very distinct theory of constituent power in the Shiʿa context) is precisely that it seems impossible for an Islamic regime to genuinely transform the modern state and its modes of lawmaking. For in fusing all kinds of social and political lawmaking into the same kind of sovereign law, the political is not so much reclaimed for the sacred as the sacred is reduced to the political. It is a short step from the prerevolutionary ideological claim that "the state must be run by the sacred law" to "whatever the state requires for its defense, preservation, and welfare is what the sacred law is."

The vision of Islamic democratic theory, as noted in Chapter 6, is to avoid this legitimation crisis by transforming the oligarchic instrumentalization of divine law into popular ownership of the *sharīʿa*. For if it is "the people" appropriating "*sharīʿa*" for its own political action then the politicization of religious justification of law does not need to seem instrumental or an act of domination. But in modern state forms, where it is elites, administrators, and representatives who make law, the Hobbesian effect of ultimately secularizing and vulgarizing religious law by associating it with the political seems no less likely. And so, both the vision of an open, constituent moment when the "*umma*" reconstitutes itself consensually and the vision of revolutionary transformation into a new form of public lawmaking seem precluded by the oligarchic and bureaucratic structure of the modern state and the inevitable alienation between the governors and the governed.

(4) Was Sovereignty a Mistake?

Finally, on a conceptual level, one might argue that much modern Islamist political thought has occurred against the backdrop of certain modern, post-Enlightenment political and moral assumptions: the reality of the sovereign state, the legal equality of citizens, and the moral requirement for states to claim to represent (and not only care for) a national will. The conceptual framework of the modern nation-state is one that many Islamist thinkers have gladly rushed into rather than look beyond. This has involved at least three kinds of strategies: (1) apologetics ("Islam already anticipates this set of modern legal and political categories, such as consent of the governed and government as social contract"), (2) reappropriation ("in the West the modern state is an agent of nihilism and injustice; the Islamic state will be an agent of purpose and justice"), and (3) gene-splicing, or retrofitting ("this or that post-Enlightenment political concept can be given an Islamic analogue or simply slotted in"). One possible task for a historically minded, critical comparative political theory is to explore the Frankenstein's monster that results from the attempt to simply splice in certain commanding, or even attractive, concepts to legal imaginaries without thinking deeply about their conditions of possibility.

One such concept, this book has argued, is that of sovereignty and constituent authority. Islamist political theorists have tried to democratize Islamic constitutional theory by stressing the consensual, ascending, and contractual foundations of government and arguing that they amount to a form of popular sovereignty both in the sense of constituent power and in the sense of participation in ordinary legislation. But there is no easy reconciliation between these ideas and the core Islamic idea of a pre-political law that is binding on Muslims and constraining of political life. It is the very concept of "sovereignty," which Islamist thinkers not wrongly assumed was something modern conditions required them to have a version of, that forces Islamist political theory into this aporia. It can only be resolved by accepting some version of the fact of reasonable moral pluralism (and giving up on divine sovereignty) or giving up on horizon of the modern state (and giving up on popular sovereignty).

This may indeed be a moment when the vision of both democratizing and Islamizing the modern state finally gives way to other horizons and possibilities. When Islamizing law seems less of a panacea or even a minimal condition of legitimacy, living and acting politically in such a moment is less of a challenge, perhaps, than theorizing it. Beyond subtracting Islamist idealism, even utopianism, and accommodating political reality, what are Islamic norms adding to the political?

It is possible that the most important horizon for Islamic political thought today is a post-statist, even post-sovereigntist, one. This is not just an observation imposed by the theoretical structure of this book. Alongside the claims to have moved into "post-Islamism" or "Muslim democracy," there is a nascent discourse on Islam and the political "after the state."[52] Although this may require a new generation of thinkers, it may also be a horizon that traditional Islamist thinkers themselves are best equipped to observe. This is not only because they best acquainted with the difficulty of realizing a fully Islamic public sphere, but also because they are some of the greatest witnesses of the brutality and danger of state power. Ghannūshī himself, while observing the inherent authoritarianism of any state (even an Islamic one) when it holds the society and the economic in its grip, acknowledges that the post-statist, post-sovereigntist Islamic vision may be one that focuses on society as a space for expanding the freedom from state tyranny for a variety of ways of life, not only religious ones but also materialist, secular ones. His model for this more normatively laden vision is not the Constitution of Medina, but ninth-century Baghdad which, in his telling, saw no contradiction in allowing for the flourishing of multiple ways of life and moral-intellectual communities, including those pursuing materialist and nontheist cosmologies.[53]

There is something of a "liberalism of fear" to this insight. Islamists like Ghannūshī have experienced more than their share of the awful and tyrannical power the state is capable of. And so, limiting that power, not only for the sake of the ordinary goods of nonviolence and nondomination, but for the freedom for religious ways of life to be able to flourish, is less a theoretical, doctrinal achievement than one earned by the practical, political experience of opposition to authoritarianism. In my view this potentially heralds an Islamic political thought in a new register, a *political* Islamic political thought,[54] one that is informed both by the political as its own domain of pluralism and novelty, and also by Islamists' reflection on their cumulative historical experience of political action. There need be no preset script for this register of thought (liberal, theocratic, or otherwise), but it may take place without the fantasy of sovereignty.

NOTES

ACKNOWLEDGMENTS

INDEX

Notes

Preface

1. See Bettina Gräf and Jakob Skovgaard-Petersen, *Global Mufti: The Phenomenon of Yūsuf Al-Qaraḍāwī* (New York: Columbia University Press, 2009).
2. Unpublished translation of Yahya M. Michot and Samy Metwally, "The Tahrir Square Sermon of Shaykh Yūsuf al-Qaraḍāwī" (on file with the author).
3. I often use "the people" in the singular intentionally, because the point is that the theory sees "the people" as a unitary agent or entity, with a harmonious will. It is a translation of *umma,* which is always singular.
4. For historical overviews and post-mortems, see Marc Lynch, *The Arab Uprisings: The Unfinished Revolutions of the New Middle East* (New York: PublicAffairs, 2013); and Jason Brownlee, Tarek E. Masoud, and Andrew Reynolds, *The Arab Spring: Pathways of Repression and Reform* (Oxford: Oxford University Press, 2015).
5. See Adnan A. Zulfiqar, "Revolutionary Islamic Jurisprudence: A Restatement of the Arab Spring," *New York University Journal of International Law and Politics* 49 (2017); Aria Nakissa, "The Fiqh of Revolution and the Arab Spring: Secondary Segmentation as a Trend in Islamic Legal Doctrine," *The Muslim World* 105, no. 3 (2015): 398–421; and Muʿtaz al-Khaṭīb, "al-Fiqh wa'l-dawla fi'l-thawrāt al-ʿarabiyya," *Majallat al-Tabayyun li'l-dirāsāt al-fikriyya wa'l-thaqāfiyya* (2014): 63–84.
6. First read on national television on June 20, 2011, and later published as Senior Scholars of Al-Azhar, *Wathīqat al-Azhar ḥawla mustaqbal Misr*

(Alexandria, Egypt: Library of Alexandria, 2012). See Malika Zeghal, "The 'al-Azhar Document': Further Thoughts on al-Azhar in the Revolution," *On Islam and Politics* (blog), September 1, 2011, https://onislamandpolitics.wordpress.com/2011/09/01/the-al-azhar-document-further-thoughts-on-al-azhar-in-the-revolution/.

7. Aḥmad al-Raysūnī, *Fiqh al-thawra: murājaʿāt fi'l-fiqh al-siyāsī al-islāmī* (Cairo: Dār al-Kalima, 2013).
8. Salmān al-ʿAwda, *As'ilat al-thawra* (Cairo: Dār al-Salām, 2013).
9. Waṣfī Abū Zayd, *Al-Qaraḍāwī—Al-imām Al-thā'ir: Dirāsa taḥlīliyya uṣūliyya* (n.p.: Sulṭān li'l-Nashr, 2011).
10. Samia Mehrez, ed., *Translating Egypt's Revolution: The Language of Tahrir* (New York: Oxford University Press, 2012).
11. Primary documents related to the January 2011 Tahrir Square protests (the "Tahrir Documents") are available at http://idep.library.ucla.edu/tahrir-documents/. Certain aspects of the cultural and political sensibilities of one segment of the revolutionary youth movement were portrayed in lightly fictionalized form in Omar Robert Hamilton, *The City Always Wins* (New York: Macmillan, 2017).
12. Hussein Agrama, for example, saw the Egyptian revolution (as of March 2011) as an "asecular" revolution because the Taḥrīr protests were not already built around a religious / secular antagonism and so "show[s] us that it may not be necessary to have a principled distinction between religion and politics to express an ethos of democratic sensibility." (Hussein Ali Agrama, "Asecular Revolution," *The Immanent Frame* (blog), March 11, 2011, https://tif.ssrc.org/2011/03/11/asecular-revolution/.
13. Rusha Latif, *Tahrir's Youth: Leaders of a Leaderless Revolution* (Cairo: American University Press, 2019).
14. On the central role of women activists in the Egyptian revolution, see Nermin Allam, *Women and the Egyptian Revolution: Engagement and Activism During the 2011 Arab Uprisings* (Cambridge, UK: Cambridge University Press, 2017).
15. Egyptian political scientist Yasmine Farouk observed firsthand "that the constitution making process cannot be separated from the political balance of power in which constitution making takes place" (Yasmine Farouk, "Writing the Constitution of the Egyptian Revolution: Between Social Contract and Political Contracting," *Arab Reform Initiative* Research Paper, November 2013, https://www.arab-reform.net/en/file/609/download?token=LtRUkPJi. For the view that this ordinary, bargaining feature of constitution making is actually conducive to a constitution's stability and legitimacy, see Nathan J. Brown, "Reason, Interest, Rationality, and Passion in Constitution Drafting," *Perspectives on Politics* 6, no. 4 (2008): 675–89.

16. The Egyptian constituent assembly was elected by parliament, once on March 22, 2012, and a second time on June 12, 2012, and approved a draft constitution on November 29, 2012. The Tunisian constituent assembly was popularly elected on October 23, 2011, and was replaced by the Assembly of the Representatives of the People on October 26, 2014. During this three-year period, the 217-member constituent assembly not only served as the body charged with drafting a constitution but also with forming transitional governments.
17. For a narration of some of these sentiments, see H. A. Hellyer, *A Revolution Undone: Egypt's Road Beyond Revolt* (Oxford: Oxford University Press, 2017).
18. Ennahda (al-Nahḍa) held 89 out of 217 seats in the 2011–2014 Constituent Assembly and 69 out of 217 seats in the parliament elected in 2014.
19. For example, Antonio Negri, *Insurgencies: Constituent Power and the Modern State* (Minneapolis: University of Minnesota Press, 1999); and Andreas Kalyvas, "Popular Sovereignty, Democracy, and the Constituent Power," *Constellations* 12, no. 2 (2005): 223–44. See here again Hussein Agrama: "This conception of state sovereignty contrasts with the manifestation of sovereignty that we saw in the protests. From the vantage point of the tradition of democratic legitimacy, the protests were a manifestation of pure popular sovereignty" (Agrama, "Asecular Revolution," https://tif.ssrc.org/2011/03/11/asecular-revolution/).
20. See David Kirkpatrick, *Into the Hands of Soldiers: Freedom and Chaos in Egypt and the Middle East* (New York: Viking, 2018).
21. On this phrase as an alternative to "secular state" in Egyptian public discourse, see Talal Asad, "Fear and the Ruptured State: Reflections on Egypt after Mubarak," *Social Research,* 79, no. 2 (Summer 2012), pp. 271–98, and pp. 289–91. See also the recent work of the legal theorist Jāsir ʿAwda [Jasser Auda], *al-Dawla al-madaniyya: Naḥwa tajāwuz al-istibdād wa taḥqīq maqāṣid al-sharīʿa* (Beirut: al-Shabaka al-ʿarabiyya li'l-abḥāth wa'l-nashr, 2015).
22. Nadia Marzouki, "Nahda's Return to History," *The Immanent Frame* (blog), April 30, 2012, https://tif.ssrc.org/2012/04/30/nahdas-return-to-history/.
23. The most comprehensive study of constitution making after the Arab Spring, with rigorous comparisons with previous constitutional orders, is Nimer Sultany, *Law and Revolution: Legitimacy and Constitutionalism after the Arab Spring* (Oxford: Oxford University Press, 2017).
24. For example, the 2011 party program of the Salafi Ḥizb al-Jamāʿa wa'l-tanmiya, the political wing of the terrorist "Islamic Group" *(al-Jamāʿa al-Islamiyya),* declared that among its political principles for an Islamic state was the view that it is "a state of the people, who is the source [*maṣdar*] of political authorities" (Ḥizb al-Bannāʾ wa'l-tanmiya Electoral Program, p. 5, on file with the author).

25. See, for example, Kristen Stilt, "'Islam is the Solution': Constitutional Visions of the Egyptian Muslim Brotherhood," *Texas International Law Journal* 46 (2010): 73–108.
26. Draft Constitution, Part One: The State and Society, unofficial translation by Democracy Reporting International; Arabic: http://sharek2012.dostour.eg/2012/; English: http://www.atlanticcouncil.org/images/files/egypt_draft_constitution_unofficial_translation_dri.pdf.
27. Safa Sarour, "Al-Arian: The Constitution Grants Sovereignty to the People," *Egypt Independent*, February 13, 2013, http://www.almasryalyoum.com/node/1468371.
28. "Elections Violate Islamic Law: Egypt's Mohamed El-Zawahiri," *ahramonline*, March 4, 2013, http://english.ahram.org.eg/NewsAFCON/2017/66087.aspx.
29. See, e.g., Clark Lombardi, *State Law as Islamic Law in Modern Egypt: The Incorporation of the* Shari'a *into Egyptian Constitutional Law* (Leiden: Brill, 2006).
30. As argued in Intisar Rabb, "The Least Religious Branch? Judicial Review after the Arab Spring," *UCLA Journal of International Law & Foreign Affairs* 17 (2013): 75 (in response to Ran Hirschl's *Constitutional Theocracy* (Cambridge, MA: Harvard University Press, 2010)).
31. See Hend El-Behary, "Al-Azhar scholar submit sukuk law objections to Shura Council," *Daily News Egypt*, April 25, 2013, http://www.dailynewsegypt.com/2013/04/25/al-azhar-scholars-submit-sukuk-law-objections-to-shura-council/.
32. For readers familiar with my earlier work *Islam and Liberal Citizenship: The Search for an Overlapping Consensus* (New York: Oxford University Press, 2009) or my article "What Is Comparative Political Theory?," *Review of Politics* 71, no. 4 (2009): 531–65), I should make clear that the present book is not an application of ideas expressed in those works on "engaged comparative political theory."

1. The Idea of Islamic Democracy

1. On the history of Brotherhood political participation in Egypt before 2011, see Richard P. Mitchell, *The Society of the Muslim Brothers* (Oxford: Oxford University Press, 1969); Brynjar Lia, *The Society of the Muslim Brothers in Egypt: The Rise of an Islamic Mass Movement, 1928–1942* (Reading, UK: Ithaca Press, 1998); Carrie Rosefsky Wickham, *The Muslim Brotherhood: Evolution of an Islamist Movement* (Princeton, NJ: Princeton University Press, 2013); Khalil Al-Anani, *Inside the Muslim Brotherhood: Religion, Identity, and Politics* (Oxford, UK: Oxford University Press, 2016); and Hazem Kandil, *Inside the Brotherhood* (Cambridge, UK: Polity Press, 2015).

2. Seyyed Vali Reza Nasr, *The Vanguard of the Islamic Revolution: The Jama'at-i Islami of Pakistan* (Berkley, CA: University of California Press, 1994), particularly chapter 6.
3. Generally: Seyyed Vali Reza Nasr, "Democracy and Islamic Revivalism," *Political Science Quarterly* 110, no. 2 (1995): 261–85. On Morocco see Eva Wegner, *Islamist Opposition in Authoritarian Regimes: The Party of Justice and Development in Morocco* (Syracuse, NY: Syracuse University Press, 2011). On Turkey see, for example, M. Hakan Yavuz, ed., *The Emergence of a New Turkey: Islam, Democracy, and the AK Parti* (Salt Lake City: The University of Utah Press, 2006); and William Hale and Ergun Ozbudun, eds., *Islamism, Democracy and Liberalism in Turkey: The Case of the AKP* (London: Routledge, 2009), as well as Aslı Ü. Bâli, "The Perils of Judicial Independence: Constitutional Transition and the Turkish Example," *Virginia Journal of International Law* 52 (2011): 235; "A Turkish Model for the Arab Spring?" *Middle East Law and Governance* 3, no. 1–2 (2011): 24–42; and "Courts and Constitutional Transition: Lessons from the Turkish Case," *International Journal of Constitutional Law* 11, no. 3 (2013): 666–701.
4. Melani Cammett and Pauline Jones Luong, "Is There an Islamist Political Advantage?" *Annual Review of Political Science* 17 (2014): 187–206.
5. For example, Nathan Brown, *When Victory Is Not an Option: Islamist Movements in Arab Politics* (Ithaca, NY: Cornell University Press, 2012).
6. Jocelyne Cesari, *The Awakening of Muslim Democracy: Religion, Modernity, and the State* (Cambridge, UK: Cambridge University Press, 2014), Ch. 7, "Political Opposition through Islamic Institutions."
7. "Notre voie vers la démocratie [Our path to democracy]," Collectif 18 octobre pour les droits et des libertés en Tunisie, June 15, 2010, https://goo.gl/nPTn8s.
8. Jillian Schwedler, "Can Islamists Become Moderates? Rethinking the Inclusion-Moderation Hypothesis," *World Politics* 63, no. 2 (2011): 347–76.
9. Within this literature, see Jillian M. Schwedler, *Faith in Moderation: Islamist Parties in Jordan and Yemen* (Cambridge, UK: Cambridge University Press, 2006); Mehmet Gurses, "Islamists, Democracy and Turkey: A Test of the Inclusion-Moderation Hypothesis," *Party Politics* 20, no. 4 (2014): 646–53; Janine A. Clark, "The Conditions of Islamist Moderation: Unpacking Cross-Ideological Cooperation in Jordan," *International Journal of Middle East Studies* 38, no. 4 (2006): 539–60; and Manfred Brocker and Mirjam Künkler, "Religious Parties: Revisiting the Inclusion-Moderation Hypothesis," *Party Politics* 19, no. 2 (2013): 171–86. For a view that stresses electoral incentives to radicalize rather than moderate, see Haroon K. Ullah, *Vying for Allah's Vote: Understanding Islamic Parties, Political Violence, and Extremism in Pakistan* (Washington, DC: Georgetown University Press, 2013).

10. Francesco Cavatorta and Fabio Merone, "Moderation through Exclusion? The Journey of the Tunisian Ennahda from Fundamentalist to Conservative Party," *Democratization* 20, no. 5 (2013): 857–75.
11. See Tarek Masoud, *Counting Islam: Religion, Class, and Elections in Egypt* (Cambridge, UK: Cambridge University Press, 2014).
12. Important works include Sana Abed-Kotob, "The Accommodationists Speak: Goals and Strategies of the Muslim Brotherhood of Egypt," *International Journal of Middle East Studies* 27.3 (1995): 321–39; Mona El-Ghobashy, "The Metamorphosis of the Egyptian Muslim Brothers," *International Journal of Middle East Studies* 37, no. 3 (2005): 373–95; Bruce K. Rutherford, "What Do Egypt's Islamists Want? Moderate Islam and the Rise of Islamic Constitutionalism," *Middle East Journal* 60, no. 4 (2006): 707–31; Chris Harnisch and Quinn Mecham, "Democratic Ideology in Islamist Opposition? The Muslim Brotherhood's 'Civil State,'" *Middle Eastern Studies* 45, no. 2 (2009): 189–305; Carrie Rosefsky Wickham, "The Path to Moderation: Strategy and Learning in the Formation of Egypt's Wasat Party," *Comparative Politics* (2004): 205–28; and "The Muslim Brotherhood and Democratic Transition in Egypt," *Middle East Law and Governance* 3, nos. 1–2 (2011): 204–23; and Michaelle Browers, *Political Ideology in the Arab World: Accommodation and Transformation* (Cambridge, UK: Cambridge University Press, 2009).
13. Fauzi M. Najjar, "Islam and Modern Democracy," *The Review of Politics* 20, no. 2 (1958): 164–80.
14. For a very small sample, see Gudrun Krämer, "Islamist Notions of Democracy," *Middle East Report* 183 (1993): 2–8; John L. Esposito and John O. Voll, *Islam and Democracy* (New York: Oxford University Press, 1996); Sami Zubaida, "Islam, the State and Democracy: Contrasting Conceptions of Society in Egypt," *Middle East Report* (November–December 1992): 2–10; Robin Wright, "Islam, Democracy and the West," *Foreign Affairs* no. 3 (summer 1992): 131–45; Abdou Filali-Ansary, "Muslims and Democracy," *Journal of Democracy* 10, no. 3 (1999): 18–32; Ali R. Abootalebi, "Islam, Islamists and Democracy," *Middle East Review of International Affairs* 3, no. 1 (1999): 14–24; I. William Zartman, "Islam and Democracy: The Cultural Dialectic," *Annals of the American Academy of Political and Social Science* 524 (November 1992): 181–91; and Yahya Sadowski, "The New Orientalism and the Democracy Debate," *Middle East Report* (July–August 1993): 14–21.
15. Khaled Abou El Fadl, "Islam and the Challenge of Democratic Commitment," *Fordham International Law Journal* 27 (2003): 4–71; and Joshua Cohen and Deborah Chasman, eds., *Islam and the Challenge of Democracy* (Princeton, NJ: Princeton University Press, 2004); M. A. Muqtedar Khan, ed., *Islamic Democratic Discourse: Theory, Debates, and Philosophical Perspectives* (Lanham, MD: Lexington Books, 2006); Ahmad S. Moussalli, *The*

Islamic Quest for Democracy, Pluralism, and Human Rights (Gainesville: University Press of Florida, 2001); Abdulaziz Sachedina, *The Islamic Roots of Democratic Pluralism* (New York: Oxford University Press, 2001); and Mishal Fahm al-Sulami, *The West and Islam: Western Liberal Democracy versus the System of* Shura (London: Routledge, 2003).

16. Seyyed Vali Reza Nasr, "The Rise of 'Muslim Democracy,'" *Journal of Democracy* 16, no. 2 (2005): 13–27; Anwar Ibrahim, "Universal Values and Muslim Democracy," *Journal of Democracy,* 17, no. 3 (2006): 5–12; and Cesari, *The Awakening of Muslim Democracy.*
17. Asef Bayat "The Coming of a Post-Islamist Society," *Critique: Journal for Critical Studies of the Middle East* 5, no. 9 (1996): 43–52, later developed in Bayat, *Making Islam Democratic: Social Movements and the Post-Islamist Turn* (Palo Alto, CA: Stanford University Press, 2007); *Life as Politics: How Ordinary People Change the Middle East* (Palo Alto, CA: Stanford University Press, 2013); and Bayat, ed., *Post-Islamism: The Many Faces of Political Islam* (New York: Oxford University Press, 2013).
18. Irfan Ahmad, *Islamism and Democracy in India: The Transformation of Jamaat-e-Islami* (Princeton, NJ: Princeton University Press, 2009); and "Democracy and Islam," in Seyla Benhabib and Volker Kaul, eds., *Toward New Democratic Imaginaries-İstanbul Seminars on Islam, Culture and Politics* (New York: Springer, 2016), where he calls for "shifting the debate from textual normativity to demotic praxis" (p. 125).
19. See Nathan J. Brown, *Constitutions in a Nonconstitutional World: Arab Basic Laws and the Prospects for Accountable Government* (Albany, NY: SUNY Press, 2012); Rainer Grote and Tilmann Röder, *Constitutionalism in Islamic Countries: Between Upheaval and Continuity* (Oxford, UK: Oxford University Press, 2012); and Cesari, *The Awakening of Muslim Democracy: Religion, Modernity, and the State,* particularly Ch. 3, "Islam in the Constitution."
20. "*Political Islam* does not refer to the common definition of religiously based political opposition to the state [but] is broadened to include nationalization of Islamic institutions and personnel under state ministries; usage of Islamic references in political competition by both state actors and opponents; religiously motivated social unrest or violence; and internationalization of Islam-oriented political movements or conflicts" (Cesari, *The Awakening of Muslim Democracy,* xiii).
21. See Jan Michiel Otto, ed., *Sharia Incorporated: A Comparative Overview of the Legal Systems of Twelve Muslim Countries in Past and Present* (Leiden: Leiden University Press, 2010).
22. See, for example, Robert Devereux, *The First Ottoman Constitutional Period: A Study of the Midhat Constitution and Parliament* (Baltimore, MD: Johns Hopkins Press, 1963); Carter V. Findley, *Bureaucratic Reform in the Ottoman Empire: The Sublime Porte, 1789–1922* (Princeton, NJ: Princeton University

Press, 1980); and Nader Sohrabi, *Revolution and Constitutionalism in the Ottoman Empire and Iran* (Cambridge, UK: Cambridge University Press, 2011).

23. See, for example, two important works to come out of Tunisia during the reform period, one by the Tunisian bureaucrat, historian and political theorist Aḥmad Ibn Abī al-Ḍiyāf (Bin Ḍiyāf; 1804–1874), *Itḥāf ahl al-zamān bi-akhbār mulūk Tūnis wa-ʿahd al-amān* (Tūnis, Tunisia: al-Dār al-Tūnisiyya, 1976), vol. 1 *(Muqaddima)*; and another by Khayr al-Dīn Pāsha (1822–1890), one of the great Ottoman statesmen of the nineteenth century, *Aqwam al-masālik fī maʿrifat aḥwāl al-mamālik* (Cairo: Dār al-Kitāb al-Miṣrī, 2012).
24. On the history of the 1906 Constitutional Revolution, see Janet Afary, *The Iranian Constitutional Revolution, 1906–1911* (New York: Columbia University Press, 2005); and Vanessa Martin, *Islam and Modernism: The Iranian Revolution of 1906* (London: Tauris, 1989).
25. See the English translation of the 1906 and 1907 constitutions at, for example, *Foundation for Iranian Studies*, https://fis-iran.org/en/resources/legaldoc/iranconstitution.
26. See Asghar Schirazi, *The Constitution of Iran: Politics and the State in the Islamic Republic* (London: I. B. Tauris, 1997).
27. "Annex 780, The Objectives Resolution, Article 2(a)," *The Constitution of Pakistan*, http://www.pakistani.org/pakistan/constitution/annex.html.
28. "Part VII: The Judicature; Chapter 3A: The Federal Shariat Court," *The Constitution of Pakistan*, http://www.pakistani.org/pakistan/constitution/part7.ch3A.html.
29. "Part IX: Islamic Provisions," *The Constitution of Pakistan*, http://www.pakistani.org/pakistan/constitution/part9.html.
30. "Egypt: The Constitution of the Arab Republic of Egypt 1971 (as amended up to 2007)," *WOPO*, https://wipolex.wipo.int/en/text/189854
31. See, in addition to Lombardi, *State Law as Islamic Law in Modern Egypt*, Baber Johansen, "The Relationship between the Constitution, the Sharî'a and the Fiqh: The Jurisprudence of Egypt's Supreme Constitutional Court," *Zeitschrift für ausländisches und öffentliches Recht und Völkerrecht* 64 (2004): 81–896.
32. For more general, theoretical discussions of modern Islamic constitutionalism, based partly on the experiences of the above states, see Said Arjomand, "Islamic Constitutionalism," *Annual Review of Law and Social Science* 3, no. 1 (2007): 115–40; Asifa Quraishi-Landes, "Islamic Constitutionalism: Not Secular, Not Theocratic, Not Impossible," *Rutgers Journal of Law and Religion* 16 (2015), 553–630; and many of the chapters in Grote and Röder, *Constitutionalism in Islamic Countries.*

33. ʿAbd al-Wahhāb Khallāf, *al-Siyāsa al-sharʿiyya fi'l-shu'ūn al-dustūriyya wa'l-khārijiyya wa'l-māliyya* (Cairo: Dār al-Anṣār, 1977).
34. Muḥammad Ḍiyā al-Dīn al-Rayyis, *Naẓariyyāt al-siyāsiyya al-Islāmiyya* (Cairo: Dar al-Turath, [1952] 1979).
35. Aḥmad Kamāl Abū al-Majd, *Naẓarāt ḥawla al-fiqh al-dustūrī fī al-Islām* (Cairo: Maṭbaʿat al-Azhar, 1962).
36. ʿAbbās Maḥmūd ʿAqqād, *al-Dīmuqrāṭiyya fī al-Islām* (Cairo: Dār al-Maʿārif, 1952).
37. See, for example, ʿAlī ʿAbd al-Wāḥid Wāfī, *al-Ḥurriyya al-madaniyya fi'l-Islām: muḥāḍarāt li-ʿAlī ʿAbd al-Wāḥid Wāfī* (Umm Durmān: Jāmiʿat Umm Durmān al-Islāmiyya, 1967) and ʿAbd al-Ḥakīm Ḥasan al-ʿAylī, *al-Ḥurriyyāt al-ʿāmma fi'l-fikr wa'l-niẓām al-siyāsī fi'l-Islām: dirāsa muqārana* (Cairo: Dār al-Fikr al-ʿArabī, 1974); Ṣubḥī ʿAbduh Saʿīd, *al-Sulṭa wa'l-ḥurriyya fi'l-niẓām al-Islāmī: dirāsa muqārana* (Cairo: Dār al-Fikr al-ʿArabī, 1982). The text of ʿAbd al-Ḥakīm Ḥasan al-ʿAylī is particularly widely cited in subsequent literature.
38. See, for example, Ḥāzim ʿAbd al-Mutaʿāl al-Ṣaʿīdī, *al-Naẓariyya al-Islāmiyya fi'l-dawla: maʿa al-muqārana bi-naẓariyyat al-dawla fi'l-fiqh al-dustūrī al-ḥadīth* (Cairo: Dār al-Nahḍa al-ʿArabiyya, 1986); Fatḥī Waḥīdī, *al-Fiqh al-siyāsī wa'l-dustūrī fi'l-Islām: dirāsa muqārana fī maṣādir al-niẓām al-dustūrī wa naẓariyyat al-siyāda wa tanẓīm al-dawla wa bayān ḥuqūq wa ḥurriyyāt al-insān wa-ḍamānāt taṭbīqihā fi'l-wathā'iq al-dawliyya wa'l-niẓām al-Islāmī* (Gaza: Maṭābiʿ al-Hay'a al-Khayriyya bi-Qiṭāʿ Ghazza, 1988); al-Sayyid Khalīl Haykal, *Mawqif al-fiqh al-dustūrī al-taqlīdī wa'l-fiqh al-Islāmī min binā' wa tanẓīm al-dawla* (Cairo: Dār al-Nahḍa al-ʿArabiyya, 1989); Muḥammad Kāẓim Muṣṭafawī, *Naẓariyyāt al-ḥukm wa'l-dawla: dirāsa muqārana bayna al-fiqh al-Islāmī wa'l-qānūn al-dustūrī al-waḍʿī* (Beirut: Maʿhad al-Rasūl al-Akram li'l-Sharīʿā wa'l-Dirasāt al-Islāmiyya, 2002); Vazū Muḥammad Aklī, *Durūs fi'l-fiqh al-dustūrī wa'l-nuẓum al-siyāsiyya: dirāsa muqārana* (Algiers: Dār al-Khaldūniyya li'l-nashr wa'l-tawzīʿ, 2003); Aḥmad Muḥammad Amīn, *al-Dawla al-Islāmiyya wa'l-mabādi' al-dustūriyya al-ḥadītha: dirāsa li-ahamm mabādi' al-dīmuqrāṭiyya al-gharbiyya fī ḍaw' aḥkām al-sharīʿa al-Islāmiyya* (Maktabat al-Shurūq al-Dawliyya, 2005); Ibrāhīm ʿAbd Allāh Ibrāhīm Ḥusayn, *al-Iltizāmat al-siyāsiyya li'l-ḥākim wa'l-maḥkūm fi'l-nuẓum al-siyāsiyya wa'l-qānūn al-dustūri: dirāsa muqārana maʿa al-fiqh al-Islāmī* (Cairo: Dār al-Nahḍa al-ʿArabiyya, 2009); Muḥammad Ismāʿīl Muḥammad Mashʿal, *al-Ḍawābiṭ al-munaẓẓima li'l-siyāsa al-sharʿiyya fi'l-qānūn al-idārī wa'l-dustūrī wa'l-fiqh al-Islāmī: dirāsa muqārana* (Alexandria, Egypt: Maktabat al-Wafā' al-Qānūnīyah, 2013).
39. Muḥammad Yūsuf Mūsā, *Niẓām al-ḥukm fī al-Islām* (Cairo: Dār al-Maʿrifa, 1964); ʿAlī ʿAlī Manṣūr, *Nuẓum al-ḥukm wa'l-idāra fi'l-sharīʿa al-Islāmiyya*

wa'l-qawānīn al-waḍʿiyya: muqāranāt bayna al-sharīʿa wa-al-qānūnayn al-dustūrī wa-al-idārī (Cairo: Maṭbaʿat Mukhaymar, 1965); ʿAbd al-Ḥamīd al-Mutawallī, *Mabādiʾ niẓām al-ḥukm fi'l-Islām* (Alexandria, Egypt: Manshaʾat al-Maʿārif, 1966); Ṣubḥī ʿAbduh Saʿīd, *al-Ḥākim wa uṣūl al-ḥukm fi'l-niẓām al-Islāmī: al-siyāsī wa'l-iqtiṣādī wa'l-ijtimāʿī wa'l-fikrī* (Cairo: Dār al-Fikr al-ʿArabī, 1985); Ḥusayn Fawzī al-Najjār, *al-Islām wa'l-siyāsa: baḥth fī uṣūl al-naẓariyya al-siyāsiyya wa-niẓām al-ḥukm fi'l-Islām* (Cairo: Dār al-shaʿb, 1977); ʿAbd al-Hādī Bū Ṭālib, *al-Ḥukm wa'l-sulṭa wa'l-dawla fi'l-Islām* (Casablanca, Morrocco: Munaẓẓamat al-Muʾtamar al-Islāmī, 1988: 1988); Maḥmūd ʿAbd al-Majīd Khālidī, *al-Islām wa uṣūl al-ḥukm* (Irbid: ʿĀlam al-kutub al-ḥadīth, 2005).

40. Muḥammad Yusrī Ibrāhīm, *al-Mushārakāt al-siyāsiyya al-muʿāṣira fī ḍawʾ al-siyāsa al-sharʿiyya* (Cairo: Dār al-Yusr, 2011).
41. Muḥammad Ḍiyā al-Dīn al-Rayyis, *al-Islām wa'l-khilāfa fi'l-ʿaṣr al-ḥadīth* (Cairo: Manshūrāt al-ʿAṣr al-Ḥadīth, 1973); ʿAbd al-Karīm al-Khaṭīb, *al-Khilāfa wa'l-imāma: diyānatan . . . wa-siyāsatan: dirāsa muqārana li'l-ḥukm wa'l-ḥukūma fī'l-Islām* (Cairo: Dār al-Fikr al-ʿArabī, [1963]), Ṣalāḥ al-Dīn Dabbūs, *al-Khalīfa: tawliyatuhu wa ʿazluh, ishām fī'l-naẓariyya al-dustūriyya al-Islāmiyya; dirāsa muqārana bi'l-nuẓum al-gharbīyya* (Alexandria, Egypt: Muʾassasat al-Thaqāfa al-Jāmʿiyya, [1972]); Ṣādiq Shāyif Nuʿmān, *al-Khilāfa al-Islāmiyya wa qaḍīyat al-ḥukm bi-mā anzala Allāh* (Cairo: Dār al-Salām, 2004).
42. ʿAbd al-Majīd Ḥammādī ʿĪsāwī, *al-Sulṭa al-taʾsīsiyya fi'l-qānūn al-dustūrī al-waḍʿī wa'l-fiqh al-dustūrī al-Islām: dirāsa muqārana* (Cairo: Dār al-fikr al-ʿArabī, 2015).
43. Ḥasan al-Bannā, "Niẓām al-ḥukm," *Majmūʿ rasāʾil al-Imām al-shahīd Ḥasan al-Bannā* (Cairo: al-Maktaba al-Tawfīqiyya, n.d.), 245–61.
44. Muḥammad al-Ghazālī, *al-Islām wa'l-istibdād al-siyāsī* ([Cairo]: Dār Nahḍat Miṣr, 1997).
45. Ḥasan al-Turābī, *al-Siyāsa wa'l-ḥukm: al-nuẓum al-sulṭāniyya bayna al-uṣūl wa sunan al-wāqiʿ* (Beirut: Dār al-Sāqī).
46. Yūsuf al-Qaraḍāwī, *Fiqh al-dawla fi'l-Islām: makānatuhā—maʿālimuhā—ṭabīʿatuhā, mawqifuhā min al-dīmuqrāṭiyya wa'l-taʿāddudiyya wa'l-marʾa wa ghayr al-Muslimīn* (Cairo: Dār al-Shurūq, 1997) and *al-Siyāsa al-sharʿiyya fī ḍawʾ nuṣūṣ al-sharīʿa wa maqāṣiduhā* (Cairo: Maktabat Wahba, 1998.).
47. ʿAbd al-Salām Yāsīn, *al-Shūrā wa'l-dīmuqrāṭiyya* (Beirut: Dār Lubnān li'l-Ṭibāʿa wa'l-Nashr, 2003).
48. Rāshid al-Ghannūshī, *Al-Ḥurriyyāt al-ʿāmma fi'l-dawla al-Islāmiyya* (Beirut: Markaz Dirāsāt al-Wiḥda al-ʿArabiyya, 1993).
49. Muhammad Asad, *The Principles of State and Government in Islam* (Kuala Lumpur, Malay: Islamic Book Trust, 1980).
50. Faḥmī Huwaydī, *al-Islām wa'l-dīmuqrāṭiyya* (Cairo: Markaz al-Ahrām li'l-Tarjama wa'l-Nashr, Muʾassasat al-Ahrām, 1993).

51. Muḥammad ʿImāra, *al-Islām wa falsafat al-ḥukm* (Cairo: Dār al-Shurūq, 1989); and *al-Islām wa'l-siyāsa: al-radd ʿalā shubuhāt al-ʿalmāniyyīn* (Cairo: Dār al-Tawzīʿ wa'l-Nashr al-Islāmīyyah, 1993).
52. Muḥammad Salīm al-ʿAwwa, *Fi'l-niẓām al-siyāsī li'l-dawla al-Islāmiyya* (Cairo: al-Maktab al-Miṣrī al-Ḥadīth, 1983); and *al-Niẓām al-siyāsī fi'l-Islām* (Beirut: Dār al-Fikr al-Muʿāṣir, 2004).
53. Ṭariq al-Bishrī, *Dirāsāt fi'l-Dimuqrāṭiyya al-Miṣriyya* (Cairo: Dar al-Shurūq, 1987).
54. An Arabic text of this can be found at https://bit.ly/2IfrBvx.
55. Particularly noteworthy here are the Egyptian Muslim Brotherhood's 2004 "Reform Initiative" *(Mubādirat al-Ikhwān al-Muslimīn ḥawwal mabādiʾ al-iṣlāḥ fī Miṣr)* and 2005 electoral platform, which are widely understood to be popularized distillations of the ideas introduced by many of the preceding figures, particularly Abū al-Majd, al-Shāwī, Qaraḍāwī, al-ʿAwwa, Huwaydī, and ʿImāra (see Bruce Rutherford, *Egypt after Mubarak* [Princeton, NJ: Princeton University Press, 2008], 101–8; Kristen Stilt, "'Islam Is the Solution': Constitutional Visions of the Egyptian Muslim Brotherhood," *Texas International Law Journal* 46: 73–108 [2010]). In 2004, the Syrian Muslim Brotherhood released a much more extensive "Political Program for a Future Syria" *(al-Mashrūʿ al-siyāsī li-Sūriyat al-mustaqbal).*
56. On this group and its doctrines, see the collected papers in Rafīq Ḥabīb, *Awrāq Ḥizb Al-Wasaṭ* (Cairo: Al-Ḥizb, 1996). See also Joshua Stacher, "Post-Islamist Rumblings in Egypt: The Emergence of the Wasat Party," *Middle East Journal* 56, no. 3 (2002): 415–32; Carrie Wickham, "The Path to Moderation: Strategy and Learning in the Formation of Egypt's Wasat Party," *Comparative Politics* 36, no. 2 (2004): 205–28; Augustus Richard Norton, "Thwarted Politics: The Case of Egypt's Hizb al-Wasat," in Robert W. Hefner, ed., *Remaking Muslim Politics: Pluralism, Contestation, Democratization* (Princeton, NJ: Princeton University Press, 2009), 133–60; and Browers, *Political Ideology in the Arab World,* Ch. 2, "A More Inclusive Islamism? The *Wasatiyya* Trend."
57. al-Rayyis, *Naẓariyyāt al-siyāsiyya al-Islāmiyya;* Mūsā, *Niẓām al-ḥukm fī al-Islām,* 5; al-ʿAwwa, *Fi'l-niẓām al-siyāsī li'l-dawla al-Islāmiyya,* 133; ʿImāra, *al-Islām wa falsafat al-ḥukm,* 422;ʿImāra, *al-Islām wa'l-siyāsa,* 40; and Saʿīd, *al-Ḥākim wa uṣūl al-ḥukm fi'l-niẓām al-Islāmī.*
58. al-Rayyis, *Naẓariyyāt al-siyāsiyya al-Islāmiyya;* Abū al-Majd, *Naẓarāt ḥawla al-fiqh al-dustūrī fī al-Islām,* 13; Huwaydī, *al-Islām wa'l-dīmuqrāṭiyya,* 105–7, 126.
59. Bannāʾ, "Niẓām al-ḥukm"; Khallāf, *al-Siyāsa al-sharʿiyya;* ʿAqqād, *al-Dīmuqrāṭiyya fī al-Islām,* 175; Abū al-Majd, *Naẓarāt ḥawla al-fiqh al-dustūrī fī al-Islām,* 14; and Mūsā, *Niẓām al-ḥukm fī al-Islām,* 100.
60. ʿAqqād, *al-Dīmuqrāṭiyya fī al-Islām,* 64; Abū al-Majd, *Naẓarāt ḥawla al-fiqh al-dustūrī fī al-Islām,* 21; al-Azhar Draft Islamic Constitution (Art. 16);

al-ʿAwwa, *Fi'l-niẓām al-siyāsī li'l-dawla al-Islāmiyya,* 251; Ṣaʿīdī, *al-Naẓariyya al-Islāmiyya fi'l-dawla,* 282–83; Saʿīd, *al-Ḥākim wa uṣūl al-ḥukm fi'l-niẓām al-Islāmī;* ʿImāra, *al-Islām wa'l-siyāsa,* 71–72; Huwaydī, *al-Islām wa'l-dīmuqrāṭiyya,* 103, 114, 185; Waḥīdī, *al-Fiqh al-siyāsī wa'l-dustūrī fi'l-Islām,* 36–37; and ʿĪsāwī, *al-Sulṭa al-ta'sīsiyya,* 233–36, 240–44.

61. Turābī, *al-Siyāsa wa'l-ḥukm,* 113: "*al-mujtamaʿ al-mu'min maṣdar al-sulṭān.*"
62. Abū al-Majd, *Naẓarāt ḥawla al-fiqh al-dustūrī fī al-Islām,* 22; ʿImāra, *al-Islām wa'l-siyāsa,* 13, 18, 21–24, 27–29, 36–37, 144, 211; Huwaydī, *al-Islām wa'l-dīmuqrāṭiyya,* 200; ʿĪsāwī, *al-Sulṭa al-ta'sīsiyya,* 207; and Turābī, *al-Siyāsa wa'l-ḥukm,* 119–20.
63. Bannā', "Niẓām al-ḥukm"; ʿAqqād, *al-Dīmuqrāṭiyya fī al-Islām,* 64; Abū al-Majd, *Naẓarāt ḥawla al-fiqh al-dustūrī fī al-Islām,* 15–17; al-Azhar Draft Islamic Constitution (Arts. 4, 46); al-ʿAwwa, *Fi'l-niẓām al-siyāsī li'l-dawla al-Islāmiyya,* 87, 126, 153, 248–52; al-Ṣaʿīdī, *al-Naẓariyya al-Islāmiyya fi'l-dawla,* 163; Waḥīdī, *al-Fiqh al-siyāsī wa'l-dustūrī fi'l-Islām,* 69, 247–48; ʿImāra, *al-Islām wa falsafat al-ḥukm,* 423, 472; ʿImāra, *al-Islām wa'l-siyāsa,* 31–32, 46–47; Huwaydī, *al-Islām wa'l-dīmuqrāṭiyya,* 104, 118–20, 134–41; and ʿĪsāwī, *al-Sulṭa al-ta'sīsiyya,* 206.
64. Bannā', "Niẓām al-ḥukm"; ʿAqqād, *al-Dīmuqrāṭiyya fī al-Islām,* 114–16; al-Azhar Draft Islamic Constitution (Art. 61); al-ʿAwwa, *Fi'l-niẓām al-siyāsī li'l-dawla al-Islāmiyya,* 127; ʿImāra, *al-Islām wa'l-siyāsa,* 40–41; Waḥīdī, *al-Fiqh al-siyāsī wa'l-dustūrī fi'l-Islām,* 37; and Huwaydī, *al-Islām wa'l-dīmuqrāṭiyya,* 143.
65. Abū al-Majd, *Naẓarāt ḥawla al-fiqh al-dustūrī fī al-Islām,* 26; al-Azhar Draft Islamic Constitution (Art. 2); al-ʿAwwa, *Fi'l-niẓām al-siyāsī li'l-dawla al-Islāmiyya,* 144–46; Huwaydī, *al-Islām wa'l-dīmuqrāṭiyya,* 113, 143, 186.
66. Abū al-Majd, *Naẓarāt ḥawla al-fiqh al-dustūrī fī al-Islām,* 25–26; al-ʿAwwa, *Fi'l-niẓām al-siyāsī li'l-dawla al-Islāmiyya,* 141, 152–53; ʿImāra, *al-Islām wa falsafat al-ḥukm,* 428–29; ʿImāra, *al-Islām wa'l-siyāsa,* 21, 33–37; Huwaydī, *al-Islām wa'l-dīmuqrāṭiyya,* 127, 143–44, 186.
67. al-Rayyis, *Naẓariyyāt al-siyāsiyya al-Islāmiyya;* Abū al-Majd, *Naẓarāt ḥawla al-fiqh al-dustūrī fī al-Islām,* 27–28; Amīn, *al-Dawla al-Islāmiyya wa'l-mabādi' al-dustūriyya al-ḥadītha,* 32–35; ʿImāra, *al-Islām wa'l-siyāsa,* 159; Huwaydī, *al-Islām wa'l-dīmuqrāṭiyya,* 128; and Waḥīdī, *al-Fiqh al-siyāsī wa'l-dustūrī fi'l-Islām,* 42–49.
68. Bannā', "Niẓām al-ḥukm"; ʿAqqād, *al-Dīmuqrāṭiyya fī al-Islām,* 43; Abū al-Majd, *Naẓarāt ḥawla al-fiqh al-dustūrī fī al-Islām,* 18; al-Azhar Draft Islamic Constitution (Arts. 83–84); al-ʿAwwa, *Fi'l-niẓām al-siyāsī li'l-dawla al-Islāmiyya,* 160–61, 191–98, 209–12; Huwaydī, *al-Islām wa'l-dīmuqrāṭiyya,* 208; ʿĪsāwī, *al-Sulṭa al-ta'sīsiyya,* 264–69.
69. al-ʿAwwa, *Fi'l-niẓām al-siyāsī li'l-dawla al-Islāmiyya,* 148–49; al-Ṣaʿīdī, *al-Naẓariyya al-Islāmiyya fi'l-dawla,* 282.

70. Abū al-Majd, *Naẓarāt ḥawla al-fiqh al-dustūrī fī al-Islām,* 18–19; al-Ṣaʿīdī, *al-Naẓariyya al-Islāmiyya fi'l-dawla,* 282; Huwaydī, *al-Islām wa'l-dīmuqrāṭiyya,* 115–17.
71. See, for example, al-Azhar's 1977 "Draft Islamic Constitution." See also Muhammad Asad, *The Principles of State and Government in Islam,* which includes a set of reflections on social rights and ideological goals beyond the structure of governance.

2. The Question of Sovereignty in Classical Islamic Political Thought

1. On constituent power as sovereignty, see Richard Tuck, *The Sleeping Sovereign: The Invention of Modern Democracy* (Cambridge: Cambridge University Press, 2016); and Andreas Kalyvas, "Constituent Power," *Political Concepts: A Critical Lexicon,* 3, no. 1, http://www.politicalconcepts.org/constituentpower/.
2. The ultimate right to legislate is seen as the quintessential sovereign power from the ancient Roman constitution to Hobbes, Kant, and Austin.
3. Both Bodin and Hobbes treated adjudication of the law, particularly in the last instance, as attributes of sovereignty (Jean Bodin, *On Sovereignty* (Cambridge: Cambridge University Press, 1992), 67; and Thomas Hobbes, *Leviathan,* ed. Edwin Curley (Indianapolis, IN: Hackett, 1994), Ch. XVII, "Of the Rights of Sovereigns by Institution").
4. Sovereignty as command is implied by sovereignty as lawgiving. Sovereign "political power [is] a right of making laws with penalties of death, and consequently all less penalties . . . and of employing the force of the community, in the execution of such laws" (John Locke, *Second Treatise of Government,* C. B. Macpherson, ed. (Indianapolis, IN: Hackett, 1980), 8 (§3).
5. Carl Schmitt, *Political Theology: Four Chapters on the Concept of Sovereignty,* trans. George Schwab (Chicago, IL: University of Chicago Press, 2005), 5. Schmitt's reflections have generated an industry of studying sovereignty as the exercise of violence in, around, and outside of the law. See, of course, the voluminous writings of Giorgio Agamben and Paul Kahn (particularly *Political Theology: Four New Chapters on Sovereignty* [New York: Columbia University Press, 2011]).
6. Tuck stresses in *The Sleeping Sovereign* that early modern political theorists, especially Bodin, Grotius, Pufendorf, Hobbes, Rousseau, and Sieyès, were preoccupied by the theory that democracy was only possible for moderns if popular sovereignty was limited to the right to authorize new regimes of governance, and not to exercise all powers of government directly.
7. On the gradual emergence of the idea of "the sovereignty of God" in Islamic modernity, see Muhammad Qasim Zaman, "The Sovereignty of God in Modern Islamic Thought," *Journal of the Royal Asiatic Society* 25, no. 3 (2015), 389–418.

8. See *Sunan Abī Dāwūd, Kitāb al-ʿilm* (26), *Bāb al-ḥathth ʿalā ṭalab al-ʿilm* (1), *Sunnah.com*, https://sunnah.com/abudawud/26. (I am grateful to Jonathan Brown for this specific reference.) On the rise and development of scholarly authority and charisma based on their status as the "heirs of the Prophet(s)," see Jonathan E. Brockopp, *Muhammad's Heirs: The Rise of Muslim Scholarly Communities, 622–950* (Cambridge, UK: Cambridge University Press, 2017).
9. Quoted in Khaled Abou El Fadl, "The Centrality of Sharīʿah to Government and Constitutionalism in Islam," in Rainer Grote and Tilmann Röder, eds. *Constitutionalism in Islamic Countries: Between Upheaval and Continuity* (New York: Oxford University Press, 2012), 49. Of course, there is a much more established tradition in Imāmī (Twelver) Shiʿism of that general authority in the absence of the Imām being held in trust by the scholars.
10. Abū Muḥammad, ʿAbdullāh ibn Abī Zayd al-Qayrawānī (d. 996), *Muqaddimmat al-risāla ibn Abī Zayd al-Qayrawānī,* trans. and ed. Aymān ibn Khālid (Birmingham, UK: Dār al-Sunnah, 2012), 170.
11. See Maribel Fierro, "The *Qāḍī* as Ruler," *Saber religioso y poder político en el Islam* (Madrid: Agencia Española de Cooperación Internacional, 1994): 71–116, on judges who seized power and ruled directly in Andalusian city-states in the eleventh and twelfth centuries.
12. Important thinkers in this tradition include al-Qarāfī (d. 1285), Ibn Taymiyya (d. 1328), and Ibn Qayyim al-Jawziyya (d. 1350). In his very important *Iʿlām al-muwaqqiʿīn,* Ibn al-Qayyim declares that "if a just leadership is established, through any means, then therein is the way of God . . . In fact, the purpose of God's Way is the establishment of righteousness and justice . . . so any road that establishes what is right and just is the road Muslims should follow" (quoted in Khaled Abou El Fadl, "The Centrality of Sharīʿah to Government and Constitutionalism in Islam," 42). For a collection of 15 primary texts spanning roughly a millennium on the question of the sultanate, see Yūsuf Ībish and Yāsūshī Kūsūjī [Yasushi Kosugi], eds., *al-Salṭana fi'l-fikr al-siyāsī al-Islāmī: nuṣūṣ mukhtāra wa qirāʾāt ʿalā imtidād alf ʿām* (Beirut: Dār al-Ḥamrāʾ, 1994).
13. Secondary literature on the relationship between *siyāsa* law and *fiqh* law is particularly rich for the Mamluk and Ottoman periods. On these themes under the Mamluks, see Sherman A. Jackson, *Islamic Law and the State: The Constitutional Jurisprudence of Shihāb al-Dīn al-Qarāfī* (Leiden: Brill, 1996); Kristen Stilt, *Islamic Law in Action: Authority, Discretion, and Everyday Experiences in Mamluk Egypt* (Oxford: Oxford University Press, 2011); Yossef Rapoport, "Royal Justice and Religious Law: *Siyāsah* and *Sharīʿah* under the Mamluks," *Mamluk Studies Review* 16 (2012): 71–102.
14. See Said Amir Arjomand, "The Shiʿite Hierocracy and the State in Premodern Iran: 1785–1890," *European Journal of Sociology* 22. no. 1 (1981): 40–78.

15. Halil İnalcık, "Ḳānūnnāme," in *Encyclopaedia of Islam,* 2nd ed., eds. P. Bearman, T. Bianquis, C. E. Bosworth, E. van Donzel, & W. P. Heinrichs (Leiden: Brill, 2002). For introductions and overviews, see also Imber, *Ebu's-Su'ud,* particularly Ch. 2: "The Law: *shari'a* and *qanun,*" 24–62; and Kenan İnan. "The Making of Kanun Law in the Ottoman Empire, 1300–1600," in Günther Lottes, Eero Medijainen, Jón Viðar Sigurðsson, eds., *Making, Using and Resisting the Law in European History* (Pisa: Plus-Pisa University Press, 2008): 65–75.
16. Samy Ayoub, "'The Sulṭān Says': State Authority in the Late Ḥanafī Tradition," *Islamic Law and Society* 23, no. 3 (2016): 239–78. Imber also documents the ways in which Süleyman exercised the Caliph's prerogative "to regularize legal practice, either by introducing new laws or, more often, by restricting in certain cases the powers of judges to choose between the range of solutions which were permissible within the *sharīʿa*" (Imber, *Ebu's-Su'ud,* 107).
17. See Haim Gerber, *State, Society, and Law in Islam: Ottoman Law in Comparative Perspective* (Albany, NY: SUNY Press, 1994).
18. On this trope in reference to sultans, see Ann K. S. Lambton, "Quis Custodiet Custodes: Some Reflections on the Persian Theory of Government," *Studia Islamica* 5 (1956), 125–48. It is particularly prominent outside of the juridical discourse, especially in court panegyrics and advice literature (mirrors for princes). See Louise Marlow, "Kings, Prophets and the ʿUlamāʾ in Mediaeval Islamic Advice Literature," *Studia Islamica* 81 (1995): 101–20; and Hüseyin Yılmaz, *Caliphate Redefined: The Mystical Turn in Ottoman Political Thought* (Princeton, NJ: Princeton University Press, 2018).
19. Although the practice is as old as Islamic governance itself, this particular phrase is usually attributed to the book of the Mamluk-era Ḥanbalī jurist and theologian Ibn Taymiyya (d. 1328), *Kitāb al-siyāsa al-sharʿiyya fī iṣlāḥ al-rāʿī wa'l-raʿiyya* (Beirut: Dār al-Āfāq al-Jadīda, 1983). See French translation by Henri Laoust, *Le traité de droit public d'Ibn Taimiya* (Beirut: Institut français de Damas, 1948) and English translation by Omar A. Farrukh, *Ibn Taimiyya on Public and Private Law in Islam: Or Public Policy in Islamic Jurisprudence* (Beirut: Khayats, 1966). Of note is the recent study by Ovamir Anjum, *Politics, Law and Community in Islamic Thought: The Taymiyyan Moment* (New York: Cambridge University Press, 2012). In the Ottoman period, this theory of the relationship of the sultan and the scholars was formulated in a somewhat derivative way by one Dede Cöngî Efendi (d. 1565/6 or 1566/7). See Marinos Sariyannis, *Ottoman Political Thought up to the Tanzimat: A Concise History* (Rethymno, Greece: Foundation for Research and Technology-Hellas, Institute for Mediterranean Studies, 2015), 46–47.
20. *The Study Quran: A New Translation and Commentary,* ed. and trans. Seyyed Hossein Nasr, Caner K. Dagli, Maria Massi Dakake, Joseph E. B. Lumbard, and Mohammed Rustom (New York: HarperOne, 2015), 219.

21. For a social history of the application of justice in Ottoman Cairo, see James E. Baldwin, *Islamic Law and Empire in Ottoman Cairo* (Edinburgh: Edinburgh University Press, 2017).
22. Muḥammad ibn al-Ṭayyib Bāqillānī, *Kitāb al-Tamhīd,* ed. R. J. McCarthy (Beirut: Libr. Orientale, 1957). On Bāqillānī, see also Yūsuf Ībish, *The Political Doctrine of al-Baqillani* (Beirut: American University of Beirut, Faculty of Arts and Sciences, 1966).
23. Abū Yaʿlā al-Farrāʾ, *al-Aḥkām al-sulṭāniyya,* Muḥammad Ḥāmid al-Faqqī, ed. (Beirut: Dār al-kutub al-ʿilmiyya, 2006).
24. Abū al-Ḥasan al-Māwardī, *al-Aḥkām al-sulṭāniyya wa'l-wilāyāt al-dīniyya* (Beirut: Dār al-kutub al-ʿilmiyya, 2011). English translation: *The Ordinances of Government: Al-Aḥkām al-sulṭāniyya wa'l-wilāyāt al-dīniyya,* trans. Wafaa H. Wahba (Reading, UK: Center for Muslim Contribution to Civilization / Garnet, 1996)
25. Abū al-Maʿālī al-Juwaynī, *Ghiyāth al-umam fī iltiyāth al-ẓulam* (Beirut: al-Maktaba al-ʿaṣriyya, 2007).
26. Selections from the works of these (and other) figures on the Imamate and caliphate are collected in Yūsuf Ībish, ed., *al-Khilāfa wa shurūt al-zaʿāma ʿinda ahl al-sunna wa'l-jamāʿa* (Beirut: Dār al-Ḥamrāʾ, 2003).
27. See, for example, William Montgomery Watt, *Islamic Creeds: A Selection* (Edinburgh: Edinburgh University Press, 1994); and Imām al-Ḥaramayn al-Juwayni, *Guide to Conclusive Proofs for the Principles of Belief,* trans. Paul E. Walker (Reading, UK: Garnet, 2001). The latter has an accessible and concise summary of the developed Sunnī position on many of the subjects covered in this section. For Juwaynī, the question of the Imamate is not a fundamental principle of belief itself, and so not one over which Muslims can fall into apostasy, but is a subject on which believers are at risk of falling into grave error.
28. See the various excerpts from classical Sunnī jurists on this question in Ībish, ed., *al-Khilāfa wa shurūṭ al-zaʿāma,* e.g., al-Bāqillānī, chapter from *al-Tamhīd* on "The Question of the Attributes of the Imām Whose Contract [of appointment] Is Binding," where he lists the following attributes: Qurayshī descent, knowledge sufficient for appointment as judge, good judgment and skill in matters of war and statecraft, defending the *umma* and taking vengeance on those who wrong it, righting the wrongs against the oppressed and giving them their due, capable of carrying out the *ḥudūd* punishments and pitiless in doing so (62–63).
29. Māwardī: "ʿUmar delegated the selection of the Imām to a council [*ahl al-shūrā*], the members of which were accepted by the community, as they were the leading men of the age believed to be able to validate the appointment" (Māwardī, *al-Aḥkām al-sulṭāniyya,* 11; Māwardī, *The Ordinances of*

Government, 9). See also Patricia Crone, "*Shūrā* as an Elective Institution," *Quaderni di Studi Arabi* 19 (2001), 3–39, at 8 and 39.

30. Imber cites a later Ḥanafī jurist, Ibn al-Humam (d. 1457), as arguing that if a usurper "behaves toward the people as a governor, 'Friday prayer is permissible in his presence, because rulership *(salṭana)* is thereby realized.' . . . the ruler is a person who effectively seizes and holds power, and this, it seems, is the opinion of the majority of Hanafi jurists" (Imber, *Ebu's-Su'ud,* 66).
31. On the persistence of this status into the ʿAbbāsid period even after the failed episode of the "Miḥna," see Muhammad Qasim Zaman, "The Caliphs, the ʿUlamāʾ, and the Law: Defining the Role and Function of the Caliph in the Early ʿAbbāsid Period," *Islamic Law and Society* 4, no. 1 (1997): 1–36. Zaman demonstrates that "the caliph continued to be recognized as a participant in the function of commenting on or resolving obscure matters of a legal import" (p. 1). As cited above, this was a caliphal prerogative reclaimed and put to wide use by the Ottomans from the sixteenth century.
32. See Imber, *Ebu's-Su'ud* on the efforts of the eponymous sixteenth-century jurist. See also Felicitas Opwis, "Shifting Legal Authority from the Ruler to the ʿUlamāʾ: Rationalizing the Punishment for Drinking Wine During the Saljūq Period," *Der Islam* 86, no. 1 (2011): 65–92, for the view that eleventh- and twelfth-century scholars developed Islamic legal theory in new and sophisticated ways (partly drawing on Aristotelian logic) in order to show that the divine law itself could arrive at precise answers to new problems and relied minimally on executive discretion and prerogative.
33. On these concepts and others as legal maxims, see Intisar A. Rabb, *Doubt in Islamic Law: A History of Legal Maxims, Interpretation, and Islamic Criminal Law* (New York: Cambridge University Press, 2015).
34. On this obligation in classical Islamic thought, see Michael Cook, *Commanding Right and Forbidding Wrong in Islamic Thought* (Cambridge, UK: Cambridge University Press, 2001).
35. Crone's summary seems uncontroversial: "As the Traditionalists saw it, the Prophet's guidance was dispersed in the community when he died, for he had passed his knowledge to his Companions, who passed it on to the next generation, who passed it on to their pupils, and so on. Given this dispersal, it was by sticking together that the Muslims preserved his legacy" in Patricia Crone, *God's Rule—Government and Islam: Six Centuries of Medieval Islamic Political Thought* (New York: Columbia University Press, 2005), 134.
36. Anjum, *Politics, Law, and Community in Islamic Thought,* 268–69.
37. "God has promised those of you who believe and perform righteous deeds that He will surely make them vicegerents upon Earth [*la-yastakhlifannahum*], as He caused those before them to be vicegerents [*astakhlafa*], and that He will establish for them their religion, which He has approved for them,

and that He will surely change them from a state of fear to [one of] of security . They will worship Me, not ascribing any partners unto Me. And whosoever disbelieves thereafter, it is they who are iniquitous!" (*The Study Quran*, p. 884). *The Study Quran* translates all of these instances as "vicegerent," although that begs some of the more difficult questions pertaining to the history of the interpretation of these verses, as I discuss below.

38. "And when thy Lord said to the angels: 'I am placing a vicegerent upon the earth [*jāʿil*^{un} *fi'l-arḍ*^{i} *khalīfa*^{tan}],' they said: 'Wilt Thou place therein one who will work corruption therein and shed blood, while we hymn Thy praise and call Thee holy?' He said: 'Truly I know what you know not'" (*The Study Quran*, pp. 22–22).
39. "'O David! Truly We have appointed thee as a vicegerent on Earth [*ja'lnāk*^{a} *khalīfa*^{tan} *fi'l-arḍ*^{i}]; so judge among the people with truth and follow not caprice, lest it lead thee astray from the way of God, theirs shall be a severe punishment for forgotten the Day of Reckoning" (*The Study Quran*, p. 1107).
40. See Wadād al-Qāḍī, "The Term '*Khalīfa*' in Early Exegetical Literature," *Die Welt des Islams* XXVIII (1988): 392–411, at 398.
41. See Rudi Paret, "Signification Coranique de Ḫalīfa et d'Autres Dérivés de la Racine Ḫalafa," *Studia Islamica*, no. 31 (1970): 211–17; and Sarra Tlili, *Animals in the Qur'an* (New York: Cambridge University Press, 2012), 117.
42. "He it is who appointed you vicegerents upon the earth [*jaʿalakum khalā'if*^{a} *al-arḍ*^{i}] and raised some of you by degrees above others, that He may try you in that which He has given you" (*The Study Quran*, p. 403).
43. "Or do you marvel that a reminder from your Lord should come to you by means of a man from among yourselves, so as to warn you? Remember when He made you vicegerents [*jaʿalakum khulafā'*] after the people of Noah people, and increased you amply in stature. So remember the boons of God, that haply you may prosper" (*The Study Quran*, p. 432).
44. "Remember when He made you vicegerents [*jaʿalakum khulafā'*] after ʿĀd and settled you on the earth: you build castles for yourselves on the open plain and hew dwellings in the mountains. So remember the boons of God, and behave not wickedly upon the earth, working corruption" (*The Study Quran*, p. 434).
45. Following 10:13: "We have destroyed generations before you when they did wrong, and their messengers brought them clear proofs, but they would not believe. Thus do We recompense the guilty people." Then: "Then We made you vicegerents upon the earth [*jaʿalnākum khalā'if*^{a} *fi'l-arḍ*^{i}], that We might observe how you behave" (*The Study Quran*, p. 548).
46. "Yet they denied him [Noah]. So We saved him and those with him in the ark. And We made them vicegerents [*jaʿalnākum khalā'if*^{i}], and We drowned those who denied Our signs. So observe how those who were warned fared in the end" (*The Study Quran*, p. 560).

47. "He, Who answers the one in distress when he calls upon Him and removes the evil, and Who makes you vicegerents of the earth [*yajʿalukum khulafāʾ*]? Is there a god alongside God? Little do you reflect!" (*The Study Quran*, p. 938).
48. "He it is Who appointed you vicegerents upon the earth [*jaʿalakum khalāʾif*[a] *fi'l-arḍ*[i]]. So whoever disbelieves, his disbelief is to his detriment" (*The Study Quran*, p. 1066).
49. See David L. Johnston, *Earth, Empire, and Sacred Text: Muslims and Christians as Trustees of Creation* (Bristol: Equinox Publishing, 2010).
50. Al-Qāḍi, "The Term '*Khalīfa*,'" 409.
51. Al-Qāḍi, "The Term '*Khalīfa*,'" 405.
52. Quoted in Han Hsien Liew, "The Caliphate of Adam: Theological Politics of the Qurʾānic Term *Ḫalīfa*," *Arabica* 63 (2016): 1–29, at 6. Cited also in Fritz Steppat, "God's Deputy: Materials on Islam's Image of Man," *Arabica* 36, no. 2 (1989): 163–72.
53. From Ṭabarī's commentary in his *Jāmiʿ al-bayān* on Q. 2:30, quoted in Liew, "The Caliphate of Adam," 7.
54. Steppat, "God's Deputy," 165.
55. Liew, "The Caliphate of Adam," 11–14.
56. From the commentary of al-Baghawī (d. 1122), quoted in Liew, "The Caliphate of Adam," 14.
57. Tlili, *Animals in the Qurʾan*, 117.
58. Liew, "The Caliphate of Adam," 22, paraphrasing the view of al-Aṣamm, the notorious lone voice in rejecting the obligation of the caliphate. Liew argues that the Andalusian Mālikī jurist and exegete al-Qurṭubī (d. 1272) is the "most explicit in linking the Qurʾānic *khalīfa* to the caliphate in historical reality" (24).
59. Aḥmad ibn Muḥammad ibn Miskawayh, *The Refinement of Character (Tahdhīb al-akhlāq)*, trans. Constantine K. Zurayk (Chicago, Kazi Publications, 2002), 48.
60. Abū Ḥāmid al-Ghazālī, *Mīzān al-ʿamal*, ed. ʿAlī Bū Mulḥim (Beirut: Dār wa Maktabat al-Hilāl, 1995), 72, 150, 195.
61. Ebrahim Moosa, *Ghazālī and the Poetics of Imagination* (Chapel Hill: University of North Carolina Press, 2005), 215
62. Al-Rāghib's exact dates are unknown. Recent scholarship has established that he was alive in or before the year 409/1018. See Alexander Key, "A Linguistic Frame of Mind: ar-Rāġib al-Iṣfahānī and What It Meant to Be Ambiguous.," PhD Diss., Harvard University, Cambridge, MA (2012), 32.
63. al-Rāghib al-Isfahānī, *Kitāb al-dharīʿa ilā makārim al-sharīʿa*, ed. Mahmūd Bījū (Damascus: Dār al-Iqrāʾ, 2001), 35).
64. "Thus society is necessary for the human species, for without it its existence would not be perfected nor would God's will to civilize the world with

them [*iʿmār al-ʿālam bihim*] and to make them his deputies on earth [*istikhlāfihi iyyāhum*] be realized" (Ibn Khaldūn, *al-Muqaddima: al-juzʾ al-awwal min Kitāb al-ʿibār* (Beirut: Dār al-Qalam, 1977), 34).

65. al-Iṣfahānī, *Kitāb al-dharīʿa ilā makārim al-sharīʿa,* 37.
66. al-Iṣfahānī, *Kitāb al-dharīʿa ilā makārim al-sharīʿa,* 40.
67. It is widely asserted that the interpretation by which God has deputized all of mankind as His representative, whether this means as stewards over the earth or with some kind of political authority among humans, is a strictly modern invention. See Steppat, "God's Deputy" and Tlili, *Animals in the Qur'an,* 117–22.

3. The Crisis of the Caliphate and the End of Classical Islamic Political Theory

1. See the official pamphlet, published in 1922 or 1923, *Hilafet ve hakimiyet-i milliye* (Istanbul: n.d.), later translated into Arabic by the Turkish consul in Beirut, ʿAbd al-Ghanī Sānī Bey as *al-Khilāfa wa sulṭat al-umma* (see Michelangelo Guida, "Seyyid Bey and the Abolition of the Caliphate," *Middle Eastern Studies* 44, no. 2 (2008): 275–89.)
2. Mona Hassan's study of the meaning of the caliphate for Muslims at two important periods when it was abolished has an excellent narrative of these events. See Hassan, *Longing for the Lost Caliphate: A Transregional History* (Princeton, NJ: Princeton University Press), Ch. 4, "Manifold Meanings of Loss: Ottoman Defeat, Early 1920s."
3. Quoted in Uriel Heyd, *Foundations of Turkish Nationalism: The Life and Teachings of Ziya Gökalp* (London: Luzac, 1950), 138.
4. ʿAlī ʿAbd al-Rāziq, *al-Islām wa uṣūl al-ḥukm: baḥth fi'l-khilāfa wa'l-ḥukūma fi'l-Islām* (Cairo: Maṭbaʿat Miṣr, 1925). English translation: Ali Abdel Razek, *Islam and the Foundations of Political Power,* trans. Maryam Loutfi and ed. Abdou Filali-Ansary (Edinburgh, UK: Edinburgh University Press, 2012). See also Souad T. Ali, *A Religion, Not a State: ʿAli ʿAbd Al-Raziq's Islamic Justification of Political Secularism* (Salt Lake City: University of Utah Press, 2009).
5. Muḥammad Rashīd Riḍā, *al-Khilāfa* (Cairo: al-Zahrāʾ li'l-iʿlām al-ʿarabī, 1988 [1922]).
6. Edited and reprinted in Muḥammad ʿImāra, *Maʿrakat al-Islām wa uṣūl al-ḥukm* (Cairo: Dār al-Shurūq, 1989), along with a number of primary source texts related to the controversy surrounding the publication of ʿAbd al-Rāziq's manifesto, including an extract from *al-Islām wa uṣūl al-ḥukm* and other articles by ʿAbd al-Rāziq, defending his views; proceedings from the hearing held by the Committee of Senior Scholars *(Hayʾat kibār al-ʿulamāʾ);* and their verdict, condemning the book and stripping him of his title of "Islamic scholar."

7. Muḥammad Bakhīt al-Muṭīʿī, *Ḥaqīqat al-Islām wa uṣūl al-ḥukm* (Cairo: al-Maṭbaʿa al-Salafiyya, 1925).
8. Muḥammad al-Ṭāhir bin ʿĀshūr, *Naqd ʿilmī li-kitāb al-Islām wa uṣūl al-ḥukm* (Tūnis, Tunisia: Dār Saḥnūn li'l-Nashr wa'l-Tawzīʿ, 2014).
9. A. Sanhoury, *Le Califat: son évolution vers une société des nations orientale* (Lyon, France: Imprimerie Bosc Frères & Riou, 1926). The full text of his treatise on public law was not translated into Arabic until 1989 as ʿAbd al-Razzāq Aḥmad al-Sanhūrī, *Fiqh al-khilāfa wa-taṭawwuruhā li-taṣbaḥ ʿuṣbat umam sharqīyah* (Beirut: Muʾassat al-Risāla, 2001). This translation and critical edition was carried out by Sanhūrī's daughter, Nādiya al-Sanhūrī, and her husband, a founding member of the Muslim Brotherhood and prominent legal scholar and judge in his own right, Tawfīq al-Shāwī. The translation is, in fact, not a perfectly faithful rendering of the French original. It not only includes supplementary "studies" by al-Shāwī but also some important rearrangements, excisions, additions, and choices of translation from French to Arabic that I will discuss below.
10. On this process, see Rudolph Peters, "From Jurists' Law to Statute Law or What Happens When the Shari'a Is Codified," *Mediterranean Politics* 7, no. 3 (2002): 82–95; Aharon Layish, "The Transformation of the *Sharīʿa* from Jurists' Law to Statutory Law in the Contemporary Muslim World," *Die Welt des Islams* 44, no. 1 (2004): 85–113; and Wael Hallaq, *Sharīʿa: Theory, Practice, Transformations* (Cambridge, UK: Cambridge University Press, 2009) (specifically, Ch. 15, "Hegemonic Modernity: The Middle East and North Africa during the Nineteenth and Early Twentieth Centuries").
11. For the role of *siyāsa* or *qānūn* law in nineteenth-century state modernization, see, e.g., Khaled Fahmy, *In Quest of Justice: Islamic Law and Forensic Medicine in Modern Egypt* (Oakland: University of California Press, 2018).
12. See, for example, Robert Devereux, *The First Ottoman Constitutional Period: A Study of the Midhat Constitution and Parliament* (Baltimore, MD: Johns Hopkins Press, 1963); Carter V. Findley, *Bureaucratic Reform in the Ottoman Empire: The Sublime Porte, 1789–1922* (Princeton, NJ: Princeton University Press, 1980); and Nader Sohrabi, *Revolution and Constitutionalism in the Ottoman Empire and Iran* (Cambridge, UK: Cambridge University Press, 2011).
13. His works include his memoir from his stay in Paris between 1826–1831, *Takhlīṣ al-ibrīz fī talkhīṣ Bārīz* [*Extracting Fine Gold in the Summary of Paris*] (Cairo: al-Hayʾah al-Miṣriyya al-ʿĀmma li'l-Kitāb, 1993), as well as his *Manāhij al-albāb al-miṣriyya fī mabāhij al-ādāb al-ʿaṣriyya* [*Paths for Egyptian Minds in the Joys of Contemporary Arts*] (Cairo: Dār al-Kitāb al-Miṣrī, 2012) and his reformist-pedagogical treatise, *al-Murshid al-amīn li'l-banāt wa'l-banīn* [*Trustworthy Guide for Girls and Boys*] (Cairo: Dār al-Kitāb al-Miṣrī, 2012). See the English translation of *Takhlīṣ al-ibrīz, An Imam in Paris: Account of a Stay*

in France by an Egyptian Cleric (1826–1831), trans. Daniel L. Newman (London: Saqi, 2004). Newman's introduction is an excellent overview of the history of political, intellectual, and educational reform in early nineteenth-century Egypt. See also Albert Hourani, *Arabic Thought in the Liberal Age 1798–1939* (Cambridge: Cambridge University Press, 1983 [1962]), 67–84.

14. A Tunisian bureaucrat and advisor to the royal family who penned a history of Tunisia, the introduction to which is also a formidable work of political theory (Aḥmad Ibn Abī al-Ḍiyāf, *Itḥāf ahl al-zamān bi-akhbār mulūk Tūnis wa-ʿahd al-amān* [Tūnis, Tunisia: al-Dār al-Tūnisiyya, 1976]).
15. Born in Abkhazia to a Circassian family, Khayr al-Dīn Pāsha was one of the most important Ottoman statesmen of the nineteenth century, serving as president of the Supreme Assembly *(al-Majlis al-Akbar)* of Tunisia under the first promulgated constitution in a Muslim country, as Grand Vizier/Wazīr (prime minister) of the Beylik of Tūnis, and briefly as Grand Vizier of the Ottoman Empire (1878–1879). He published a work in 1867 entitled *Aqwam al-masālik fī maʿrifat aḥwāl al-mamālik* [*The Surest Path in Knowing the Conditions of States*] (Cairo: Dār al-Kitāb al-Miṣrī, 2012), which is mostly concerned with providing an account of history, structure, and strength of European states, although his introduction makes clear that his purpose was to persuade fellow Muslims of the need and permissibility of learning from non-Muslims.
16. Described as the Young Ottoman thinker who "produced a body of political philosophy which is the only one worthy of that name among the writings of his time" (Mardin, *The Genesis of Young Ottoman Thought,* 286.) See, for example, "Wa shāwirahum fi'l-amr," *Hürriyet,* No. 4, July 20, 1868, transl. M. Şükrū Hanioğlu, in Charles Kurzman, ed., *Modernist Islam, 1840–1940* (Oxford, UK: Oxford University Press, 2002), Ch. 17.
17. Kawākibī, a Kurd from Aleppo, was a bureaucrat and journalist who eventually moved to Cairo and studied and wrote in the circle of Muḥammad ʿAbduh and Rashīd Riḍā. He is known for his books *Ṭabāʾiʿ al-istibdād wa maṣāriʿ al-istiʿbād* [*The Natures of Despotism and the Destruction of Enslavement*] (Beirut: Dār al-Nafāʾis, 2006) and *Umm al-Qurā* [*The Mother of Villages*] (Damascus: Dār al-Awāʾil, 2002), a fictional account of the first "Conference of the Islamic Renaissance *(Nahḍa).*"
18. See, for example, the contemporary Islamist intellectual Azzam Tamimi, who argues for such a genealogy in "Islam and Democracy from Tahtawi to Ghannouchi," *Theory, Culture & Society* 24, no. 2 (2007): 39–58.
19. For general introductions to Riḍā's life and intellectual trajectory, see Emad Eldin Shahin, *Through Muslim Eyes: M. Rashīd Riḍā and the West* (Herndon, VA: International Institute of Islamic Thought, 1993); and Hourani, *Arabic Thought,* Ch. IX, "Rashid Rida"; Malcolm Kerr, *Islamic Reform: The Political*

and Legal Theories of Muḥammad ʿAbduh and Rashīd Riḍā (Berkeley: University of California Press, 1966).

20. Riḍā's political writings are collected in *Maqālāt al-Shaykh Rashīd Riḍā al-siyāsiyya* (Beirut: Dār Ibn ʿArabī, 1994), 5 vol. They span from 1898 to his death in 1935.
21. On this oft-forgotten episode, see Elizabeth F. Thompson, "Rashid Rida and the 1920 Syrian-Arab Constitution: How the French Mandate Undermined Islamic Liberalism," in Cyrus Schayegh and Andrew Arsan, eds., *The Routledge Handbook of the History of the Middle East Mandates* (Abingdon, UK: Routledge, 2015); and Muḥammad Jamāl Bārūt, "Al-Muʾtamar al-Sūrī al-ʿām (1919–1920): al-dustūr al-Sūrī al-awwal," *Tabayyun* 3 (2013): 23–48. (I am grateful to Basileus Zeno for these references.)
22. On these motives in Riḍā's thought and activism, see Mahmoud Haddad, "Arab Religious Nationalism in the Colonial Era: Rereading Rashīd Riḍā's Ideas on the Caliphate," *Journal of the American Oriental Society* 117, no. 2 (1997): 253–77.
23. For some of the geopolitical causes of this turn, see John Willis, "Debating the Caliphate: Islam and Nation in the Work of Rashid Rida and Abdul Kalam Azad," *International History Review* 32, no. 4 (2010): 711–73, particularly 720–22.
24. The most extensive study of his doctrines on the caliphate probably remains that of Kerr in *Islamic Reform* (Ch. 5, "Muḥammad Rashīd Riḍā: A Revived Doctrine of the Caliphate," 153–86).
25. "God has promised those of you who believe and perform righteous deeds that He will surely make them vicegerents upon earth [*la-yastakhlifannahum*], as He caused those before them to be vicegerents [*astakhlafa*], and that He will establish for them their religion, which He has approved for them, and that He will surely change them from a state of fear to [one of] of security . They will worship Me, not ascribing any partners unto Me. And whosoever disbelieves thereafter, it is they who are iniquitous!" *The Study Quran: A New Translation and Commentary*, ed. and trans. Seyyed Hossein Nasr, Caner K. Dagli, Maria Massi Dakake, Joseph E. B. Lumbard, and Mohammed Rustom (New York: HarperOne, 2015), 884–85.
26. "He it is who appointed you vicegerents upon the earth [*jaʿalakum khalāʾif*[a] *al-arḍ*[i]] and raised some of you by degrees above others, that He may try you in that which He has given you" (*The Study Quran*, 403)
27. Riḍā, *al-Khilāfa*, 7.
28. Riḍā, *al-Khilāfa*, 64.
29. Riḍā, *al-Khilāfa*, 113.
30. Riḍā, *al-Khilāfa*, 65.

31. Thomas Hobbes, *Leviathan,* ed. Edwin Curley (Indianapolis, IN: Hackett Publishing, 1994), 110 (Ch. 18, "Of the Rights of Sovereigns by Institution").
32. Riḍā, *al-Khilāfa,* 105.
33. Riḍā, *al-Khilāfa,* 66.
34. Riḍā, *al-Khilāfa,* 121.
35. Riḍā, *al-Khilāfa,* 87.
36. Riḍā, *al-Khilāfa,* 140–41.
37. Riḍā, *al-Khilāfa,* 142.
38. On the somewhat tortured history of trying to adapt modern rights language to Islamic law, see Ebrahim Moosa, "The Dilemma of Islamic Rights Schemes," *Journal of Law and Religion* 15, no. 1/2 (2000): 185–215.
39. Riḍā, *al-Khilāfa,* 9. (Emphasis added.)
40. A candidate for the caliphate must be legally responsible, Muslim, morally upright, free, male, a *mujtahid,* and brave; he must also be possessed of sound judgment, competence, hearing, sight, and speech, and of Qurayshī lineage. Riḍā refers to al-Taftazānī's *Sharḥ al-Maqāṣid* as authority in this context (Riḍā, *al-Khilāfa,* 25).
41. The Imamate is legally valid upon the *bayʿa* given by the electors (the People Who Loose and Bind). The caliph accepts the *bayʿa* on the conditions that he will "rule by the Qurʾān and Sunna and uphold truth and justice." He is then owed obedience "in what is right" (Riḍā, *al-Khilāfa,* 32).
42. Membership in the class of "People Who Loose and Bind" is restricted to those who are morally upright, possess knowledge pertaining to who is most fit for the office, have good judgment and wisdom, and are competent to choose the most deserving candidate (Riḍā, *al-Khilāfa,* 23).
43. The Imam's general tasks include spreading the call *(daʿwa)* of truth, upholding justice, protecting religion from aggression and innovations, and consulting on everything that is not in the text. He is accountable for everything he does, and any individual person in the *umma* can confront him on an issue of error. Riḍā then lists Māwardī's ten specific public duties that the Imam is responsible for.
44. The general rule is that a ruler is only subject to removal if he has manifested clear unbelief *(kufr).* He may be resisted passively when he commands sin or injustice.
45. Riḍā, *al-Khilāfa,* 37.
46. Riḍā, *al-Khilāfa,* 25.
47. On this, see Felicitas Opwis, "Shifting Legal Authority from the Ruler to the ʿUlamāʾ: Rationalizing the Punishment for Drinking Wine During the Saljūq Period," *Der Islam* 86, no. 1 (2011): 65–92. Opwis describes how three successive jurists and theologians of this period, Juwaynī, Ghazālī, and Fakhr al-Dīn al-Rāzī (among the greatest ever produced in Islam), developed increasingly sophisticated logical and interpretive arguments for the legal

rationality of the punishment of 80 lashes, in order to show that it was a ruling that could be deduced from the texts, thus preserving the authority of the scholars (as custodians of the law) against the authority of sultans (as arbiters of the common weal).

48. Riḍā, *al-Khilāfa,* 50.
49. Riḍā, *al-Khilāfa,* 87.
50. Riḍā, *al-Khilāfa,* 112.
51. Riḍā, *al-Khilāfa,* 88.
52. Riḍā, *al-Khilāfa,* 94.
53. Riḍā, *al-Khilāfa,* 112.
54. Riḍā, *al-Khilāfa,* 102.
55. Riḍā, *al-Khilāfa,* 102–3.
56. Riḍā, *al-Khilāfa,* 39.
57. Riḍā, *al-Khilāfa,* 103.
58. Riḍā, *al-Khilāfa,* 121.
59. For example, he writes: "What [Islam] entrusted to the holders of authority in their role in deriving law—lawmaking—was not rendered absolutely free of any restriction. This was to ensure that they would not violate the *umma*'s morals by making an error in *ijtihād,* or, if corruption had overcome them, by following their passions" (Riḍā, *al-Khilāfa,* 108).
60. Riḍā, *al-Khilāfa,* 103.
61. On this theme, and the development of Riḍā's views on legal theory more generally, see Ahmad Dallal, "Appropriating the Past: Twentieth-Century Reconstruction of Pre-Modern Islamic Thought," *Islamic Law and Society* 7, no. 1 (2000): 325–58, at 355–56.
62. Riḍā, *al-Khilāfa,* 104.
63. Richard Tuck, *The Sleeping Sovereign: The Invention of Modern Democracy* (Cambridge, UK: Cambridge University Press, 2015), ix–x.
64. Riḍā, *al-Khilāfa,* 22.
65. Riḍā, *al-Khilāfa,* 141.
66. Riḍā, *al-Khilāfa,* 9.
67. Riḍā, *al-Khilāfa,* 9
68. Riḍā, *al-Khilāfa,* 153.
69. Riḍā, *al-Khilāfa,* 60.
70. Riḍā, *al-Khilāfa,* 65.
71. Riḍā, *al-Khilāfa,* 69. See also: "The cure to the illness [of disagreement about the caliphate and the most legitimate form of government], and the illnesses connected with this epidemic, is the revival of the position of the Imamate, through the return of the authority of the People Who Loose and Bind speaking for the *umma* by a majority voice, which is the ideal government for reforming the situation of the Muslims, indeed all of humanity, by combining justice and equality" (77).

72. On the history of such efforts, see Martin S. Kramer, *Islam Assembled: The Advent of the Muslim Congresses* (New York: Columbia University Press, 1986).
73. See Hassan, *Longing for the Lost Caliphate,* 174–75.
74. Elie Kedourie, "Egypt and the Caliphate 1915–1946," *Journal of the Royal Asiatic Society* 95. no. 304 (1963): 208–48, at 214–32.
75. See Hassan, *Longing for the Lost Caliphate,* 187–204, for an account of the global politics involved in convening this Congress.
76. *Maqālāt al-Shaykh Rashīd Riḍā al-siyāsiyya* (Beirut: Dār Ibn ʿArabī, 1994), 5 vol.
77. *Maqālāt al-Shaykh Rashīd Riḍā* , vol. 4, 1815.
78. For example, the Indian academic and publisher Mohammad Barakatullah (1857–1927) published a treatise in 1924, as the discussions around the convening of an international congress were beginning, in which he called for purely spiritual caliphate devoid of any temporal or material sovereignty (Mohammad Barakatullah, *The Khilafet* (London: Luzac, 1924)). Another Indian intellectual, one ʿInayātullāh Khān al-Mashriqī (1888–1963), proposed creating a joint caliphal office, occupied by five persons rather than one (Hassan, *Longing for the Lost Caliphate,* 200).
79. *Maqālāt al-Shaykh Rashīd Riḍā al-siyāsiyya,* vol. 4, 1844.
80. Ibid., vol. 4, 1921–22.
81. See ʿImāra, *Maʿrakat al-Islām wa uṣūl al-ḥukm* and the introduction to the Loutfi translation, *Islam and the Foundations of Political Power.*
82. al-Muṭīʿī, *Ḥaqīqat al-Islām wa uṣūl al-ḥukm,* 24.
83. Edited and reprinted in Muḥammad ʿImāra, *Maʿrakat al-Islām wa uṣūl al-ḥukm* (Cairo: Dār al-Shurūq, 1989), along with a number of primary source texts related to the controversy surrounding the publication of ʿAbd al-Rāziq's manifesto, including an extract from *al-Islām wa uṣūl al-ḥukm* and other articles by ʿAbd al-Rāziq defending his views, proceedings from the hearing held by the Committee of Senior Scholars *(Hayʾat kibār al-ʿulamāʾ)* and their verdict condemning the book and stripping him of his title of "Islamic scholar."
84. In ʿImāra, *Maʿrakat al-Islām wa uṣūl al-ḥukm,* 233.
85. In ʿImāra, *Maʿrakat al-Islām wa uṣūl al-ḥukm,* 270–71.
86. In ʿImāra, *Maʿrakat al-Islām wa uṣūl al-ḥukm,* 266.
87. In ʿImāra, *Maʿrakat al-Islām wa uṣūl al-ḥukm,* 422–23.
88. On Sanhūrī, see Guy Bechor, *The Sanhuri Code and the Emergence of Modern Arab Civil Law (1932 to 1949)* (Leiden: Brill, 2007); Enid Hill, "Al-Sanhuri and Islamic Law: The Place and Significance of Islamic Law in the Life and Work of ʿAbd al-Razzaq Ahmad al-Sanhuri, Egyptian Jurist and Scholar, 1895–1971," *Arab Law Quarterly* (1988): 33–64; Nabil Saleh, "Civil Codes of Arab Countries: The Sanhuri Codes," *Arab Law Quarterly* (1993): 161–67; Amr Shalakany, "Between Identity and Redistribution: Sanhuri, Genealogy and

the Will to Islamise," *Islamic Law and Society* 8. no. 2 (2001): 201–44; and Chibli Mallat, *Introduction to Middle Eastern Law* (Oxford. UK: Oxford University Press, 2009), Ch. 8, "Civil Law: Style and Substance," 244–99.

89. See Hassan, *Longing for the Lost Caliphate,* 214–17, for Sanhūrī's legacy in inspiring non-sovereign international Islamic institutions of cooperation.
90. Sanhoury, *Le Califat,* 138–41; Sanhūrī, *Fiqh al-khilāfa,* 162–63.
91. Sanhoury, *Le Califat,* 4–7; *Sanhūrī, Fiqh al-khilāfa,* 61–64.
92. Sanhoury, *Le Califat,* 6–7; *Sanhūrī, Fiqh al-khilāfa,* 66.
93. Sanhoury, *Le Califat,* 7. The Arabic translation reads. "*This has led some to claim* that the Islamic government is a government of the scholars *(al-ʿulamāʾ)*" (Sanhūrī, *Fiqh al-khilāfa,* 66–67).
94. Sanhoury, *Le Califat,* 7, fn. 6. Despite what I regard as a distortion of Sanhūrī's meaning in the main text, the translators do render this in Arabic in a footnote and add their own view that "representation by the leaders amongst the *mujtahids* is fixed and certain, because the masses of the people have recognized their leadership [*imāma*] through trust and conviction . . . without any [need for] an electoral procedure" (Sanhūrī, *Fiqh al-khilāfa,* 67).
95. Sanhoury, *Le Califat,* 18; Sanhūrī, *Fiqh al-khilāfa,* 68. For the idea of divine sovereignty in this passage, Sanhūrī writes that "Dieu seul est le dispensateur du pouvoir suprême; lui seul est Souverain," which Shāwī and N. Sanhūrī render as "*ṣāḥib al-siyāda al-ʿulyā wa mālik al-mulk.*"
96. Sanhoury, *Le Califat,* 18; Sanhūrī, *Fiqh al-khilāfa,* 68.
97. Sanhoury, *Le Califat,* 7; Sanhūrī, *Fiqh al-khilāfa,* 67.
98. Sanhoury, *Le Califat,* 18; Sanhūrī, *Fiqh al-khilāfa,* 68.
99. Sanhoury, *Le Califat,* 17, fn. 24, 18; Sanhūrī, *Fiqh al-khilāfa,* 64.
100. Sanhoury, *Le Califat,* 18; Sanhūrī, *Fiqh al-khilāfa,* 68. The translators here render Sanhūrī's "notre volonté *exprime* sa volonté divine" as "*irādat al-umma* mustamidda min *irādat Allāh*" ("the will of the *umma* is derived [or obtained] from the will of God").
101. Abdur Rahim, *The Principles of Muhammadan Jurisprudence According to the Hanafi, Maliki, Shafiʿi and Hanbali Schools* (London: Luzac, 1911).
102. See the writings of Taqī al-Dīn Nabhānī, particularly his *Niẓām al-ḥukm fiʾl-Islām* (Beirut: Dār al-Kashshāf, 1953), as well as Suha Taji-Farouki, *A Fundamental Quest: Hizb al-Tahrir and the Search for the Islamic Caliphate* (London: Grey Seal, 1996); and Reza Pankhurst, *The Inevitable Caliphate? A History of the Struggle for Global Islamic Union, 1924 to the Present* (London: Hurst, 2013), Ch. 4, "Caliphate as Liberation: Hizb ut-Tahrir—the Party of Liberation in the Post-Colonial Era."
103. See Carrie Rosefsky Wickham, *The Muslim Brotherhood: Evolution of an Islamist Movement* (Princeton, NJ: Princeton University Press, 2013), Ch. 2, "The Brotherhood's Early Years," 20–45.

4. The Sovereignty of God and the Caliphate of Man

1. Sayyid Quṭb, *Maʿālim fi'l-Ṭarīq* [Milestones] (Cairo: Dār al-Shurūq, 1964), 8.
2. "The first Arabic translation of one of Mawdūdī's works seems to have been published in Lahore in 1946, and his books started being distributed in Syria and Egypt from 1950 onward. Abū l-Ḥasan al-Nadwī (1914–1999), a noted Muslim scholar and close associate of Maududi . . . was instrumental in translating Maududi's works and in promoting them to an Arab audience. This is arguably how the Egyptian Islamist intellectual Sayyid Quṭb (1906–1966), who met al-Nadwī in Cairo in 1951 and would popularise the concept of *ḥākimiyya* in the Arab world, got acquainted with Maududi's ideas" (Stéphane Lacroix, "Ḥākimiyya," in *Encyclopaedia of Islam, Three,* eds. Kate Fleet, Gudrun Krämer, Denis Matringe, John Nawas, & Everett Rowson [Brill Reference Online, 2017]. See also John Calvert, *Sayyid Qutb and the Origins of Radical Islamism* (London: Hurst, 2010), 157–58, and James Toth, *Sayyid Qutb: The Life and Legacy of a Radical Islamic Intellectual* (Oxford: Oxford University Press, 2013), 69–70.
3. Gail Minault, *The Khilafat Movement: Religious Symbolism and Political Mobilization in India* (New York: Columbia University Press, 1982).
4. On Mawdūdī's political and intellectual career, see in particular Seyyed Vali Reza Nasr, *Mawdudi and the Making of Islamic Revivalism* (Oxford: Oxford University Press, 1996) and Roy Jackson, *Mawlana Mawdudi and Political Islam: Authority and the Islamic State* (New York: Routledge, 2011).
5. On the history of the *Jamaʿāt-i Islāmī* and Mawdūdī's leadership of it, see Seyyed Vali Reza Nasr, *The Vanguard of the Islamic Revolution: The Jamaʿat-i Islami of Pakistan* (Berkeley: University of California Press, 1994).
6. The theme of the universal caliphate in modern Islamist thought is often observed and acknowledged as a pillar of this ideological formation. See, for example, Charles J. Adams, "Mawdudi and the Islamic State," in John L. Esposito, ed., *Voices of Resurgent Islam* (Oxford: Oxford University Press, 1983), 99–133. But there are few in-depth treatments of its origins and actual significance for a philosophical theology of politics. A notable exception is David L. Johnston, who treats it from an interfaith perspective as referring to divine trusteeship (*Earth, Empire, and Sacred Text: Muslims and Christians as Trustees of Creation* [London: Equinox Publishing, 2010] or as a foundation for human rights discourse ("The Human *Khilāfa:* A Growing Overlap of Reformism and Islamism on Human Rights Discourse?" *Islamochristiana* 28 [2002]: 35–53).
7. S. M. Iqbal, "Political Thought in Islam," *The Sociological Review* 1, No. 1 (1908): 249–61, at 250.

8. See Zaman, "The Sovereignty of God," for the influence of Abul-Kalam Azad (d. 1958) and Muḥammad ʿAlī (d. 1931), the leader of the Khilafat Movement, as influential precursors to Mawdūdī.
9. "On Mawdūdī's influence on Arab thought, see, further, Fathi Osman, "Mawdūdī's Contribution to the Development of Modern Islamic Thinking in the Arabic-Speaking World," *The Muslim World,* 93 (July / October 2003), 465–85. Osman himself was an important theorist of Islam and democracy in the tradition of reformist Islamists. His books include *Min uṣūl al-fikr al-siyāsī al-Islāmī (On the Foundations of Islamic Political Thought)* (Beirut: Mu'assasat al-Risāla, 1979)
10. Abū'l-Aʿlā al-Mawdūdī, *al-Khilāfa wa'l-mulk* (Kuwait: Dār al-Qalam, 1978), 9–13. I draw from the Arabic translation of this book, originally written in Urdu in 1966.
11. Ibid., 13–15.
12. Syed Abul ʿAla ʿAla Maudoodi (henceforth: Mawdūdī), *Islamic Law and Constitution* (Jamaat-e Islami Publications, Karachi), 1955, 108–9.
13. Mawdūdī, *Islamic Law and Constitution,* 111.
14. "If, says Grotius, a private individual can alienate his liberty and turn himself into the slave of his master, why could not an entire people alienate its liberty and turn itself into the subject of a king? . . . Renouncing one's liberty is renouncing one's dignity as a man, the rights of humanity, and even its duties. There is no possible compensation for one who renounces everything" (Jean-Jacques Rousseau, *On the Social Contract,* Donald A. Cress trans. (Indianapolis, IN: Hackett Publishing, 1988), 20).
15. "That is God, your true Lord. What is there beyond truth but error? How, then, are you turned away? / Thus the Word of thy Lord came due for those who are iniquitous: truly they believe not." *The Study Quran: A New Translation and Commentary,* ed. and trans. Seyyed Hossein Nasr, Caner K. Dagli, Maria Massi Dakake, Joseph E. B. Lumbard, and Mohammed Rustom (New York: HarperOne, 2015), 553.
16. "As for anything wherein you differ, judgment thereof lies with God. That is God, my Lord. In Him do I trust and unto Him do I turn" (*The Study Quran,* 1174–75).
17. "You worship apart from Him naught but names that you have named—you and your fathers—for which God has sent down no authority. Judgment belongs to God alone. He commands that you worship none but Him. That is the upright religion, but most of mankind know not" (*The Study Quran,* 601–602).
18. "God is the best of plotters" (*The Study Quran,* p. 146).
19. "Dost thou not know that unto God belongs sovereignty over the heavens and the earth? He punishes whomsoever He will, and He forgives whomsoever He will. And God is Powerful over all things" (*The Study Quran,* p. 296).

20. "Fighting has been prescribed for you, though it is hateful to you. But it may be that you hate a thing though it be good for you, and it may be that you love a thing though it be evil for you. God knows, and you know not" (*The Study Quran*, p. 93).
21. Mawdūdī, *al-Khilāfa wa'l-mulk,* 14.
22. Mawdūdī, *al-Khilāfa wa'l-mulk,* 16–17.
23. Mawdūdī, *al-Khilāfa wa'l-mulk,* 19.
24. Mawdūdī, *al-Khilāfa wa'l-mulk,* 20.
25. Mawdudi, "Political Theory of Islam," 158. In this context, he cites the Qur'ānic verses 12:40, 3:154, 16:116, 5:44, 6:50, 4:64, 6:90, 3:79.
26. Mawdūdī, *Islamic Law and Constitution,* 79.
27. Mawdūdī, *Islamic Law and Constitution,* 87.
28. Mawdūdī, "Political Theory of Islam," 152.
29. Mawdūdī, "Political Theory of Islam," 153.
30. Mawdūdī, "Political Theory of Islam," 154.
31. Q. 25:43: "Hast thou considered the one takes his caprice as his god? Wouldst thou [O Prophet] be a guardian over him?" (*The Study Quran,* p. 897).
32. Q. 43:22: "We found our fathers upon a creed, and surely we are rightly guided in their footsteps" (*The Study Quran,* p. 1193).
33. Khurram Murad "Introduction," to *The Islamic Movement: Dynamics of Values, Power and Change,* 31.
34. Murad "Introduction," to *The Islamic Movement: Dynamics of Values, Power and Change,* 35.
35. Mawdūdī, "Political Theory of Islam," 155.
36. Mawdūdī, "Political Theory of Islam," 162.
37. John Rawls, *Political Liberalism* (New York: Columbia University Press, 1996), 55–57.
38. Mawdūdī, "Political Theory of Islam," 162–63.
39. Mawdūdī, "Political Theory of Islam," 165. See also Mawdūdī, *al-Khilāfa wa'l-mulk,* 35–36.
40. Mawdūdī, *Islamic Law and Constitution,* 127–28.
41. Mawdūdī, "Political Theory of Islam," 166.
42. Mawdūdī, *al-Khilāfa wa'l-mulk,* 36.
43. Mawdūdī, "Political Theory of Islam," 156.
44. Per Q. 7:172: "And when thy Lord took from the children of Adam, from their loins, their progeny and made them bear witness concerning themselves: 'Am I not your Lord?' they said, 'Yea, we bear witness'—lest you should say on the Day of Resurrection, 'Truly of this we were heedless'" (*The Study Quran,* p. 169). On this theme, see ʿAlī ibn ʿAbd Allāh ibn ʿAlī al-Qarnī, *al-Fiṭra: ḥaqīqatuhā wa-madhāhib al-nās fīha* (Riyadh: Dār al-Muslim li'l-nashr wa'l-tawzīʿ, 2002); Ayman Shihadeh, "The Existence of

God," in *The Cambridge Companion to Classical Islamic Theology,* ed. Tim Winter (Cambridge: Cambridge University Press, 2008), 198; Bernard G. Weiss, "Covenant and Law in Islam," in *Religion and Law: Biblical-Judaic and Islamic Perspectives,* ed. Edwin Brown Firmage, Bernard G. Weiss, John W. Welch. (Winona Lake, IN: Eisenbrauns, 1990); Bernard G. Weiss, *The Spirit of Islamic Law* (Athens, GA: University of Georgia Press, 2006), 24–37.

45. From Kant's *Critique of Practical Reason* (I.1.1.7) in Immanuel Kant, *Practical Philosophy,* Mary J. Gregor, ed. (Cambridge, UK: Cambridge University Press, 1999) 164.
46. Mawdūdī, "Political Theory of Islam," 157.
47. Mawdūdī, "Political Theory of Islam," 161.
48. Mawdūdī, "Political Theory of Islam," 163–64.
49. Mawdūdī, *Islamic Law and Constitution,* 25.
50. Mawdūdī, *Islamic Law and Constitution,* 26–27.
51. Mawdūdī, *Islamic Law and Constitution,* 119.
52. Mawdūdī, *The Islamic Movement: Dynamics of Values, Power and Change,* 99.
53. Mawdūdī, *The Islamic Movement: Dynamics of Values, Power and Change,* 99.
54. Mawdūdī, *Islamic Law and Constitution,* 34.
55. Mawdūdī, *Islamic Law and Constitution,* 36.
56. Mawdūdī, *Islamic Law and Constitution,* 57.
57. Mawdūdī, *Islamic Law and Constitution,* 63.
58. Mawdūdī, *Islamic Law and Constitution,* 117. (Emphasis added.)
59. Mawdūdī, *Islamic Law and Constitution,* 159.
60. Mawdūdī, *Islamic Law and Constitution,* 90.
61. Mawdūdī, "Political Theory of Islam," 160.
62. Mawdūdī, *al-Khilāfa wa'l-mulk,* 33.
63. Mawdūdī, "Political Theory of Islam," 161.
64. Mawdūdī, *Islamic Law and Constitution,* 56. Emphasis added.
65. Mawdūdī, *Islamic Law and Constitution,* 132.
66. Mawdūdī, *Islamic Law and Constitution,* 83, 164. See also the scholars' 22 "Basic Principles of an Islamic State," adopted in 1951. Principle 15: "The Head of State shall have no right to suspend the Constitution wholly or partly or to run the administration in any other way but on a consultative basis." (Reprinted in Mawdūdī, *Islamic Law and Constitution,* 199.)
67. Mawdūdī, *al-Khilāfa wa'l-mulk,* 49.
68. Mawdūdī, *Islamic Law and Constitution,* 83.
69. Mawdūdī, *Islamic Law and Constitution,* 137.
70. Mawdūdī, *Islamic Law and Constitution,* 83. See also Mawdūdī, *al-Khilāfa wa'l-mulk,* 22–25.
71. Mawdūdī, "Political Theory of Islam," 161.
72. In *al-Khilāfa wa'l-mulk,* Mawdūdī lists twelve rights, grounded in the *sharīʿa,* that must be codified by the state: Protection of life; protection of dignity;

protection of privacy; the right to oppose and confront injustice; the right to command the right and forbid the wrong, which includes the right to speech and criticism; freedom of assembly; freedom of conscience and belief; protection from religious persecution; freedom from collective punishment, or being held accountable for the deeds of others; due process; social rights to life's necessities; and the right to be treated as an equal by the state without discrimination.

73. Mawdūdī, *Islamic Law and Constitution,* 32.
74. Mawdūdī, *Islamic Law and Constitution,* 121–23.
75. Mawdūdī, *Islamic Law and Constitution,* 127. (Emphasis added.)
76. Mawdūdī, *Islamic Law and Constitution,* 152. (Emphasis added.)
77. Mawdūdī, *Islamic Law and Constitution,* 89.
78. Mawdūdī, "Political Theory of Islam," 159–60. (Emphasis added.)
79. Here "*mālik*" can expressed a sense of ownership as well as a sense of ruling or command. The idea is that God is the only one with original possession of authority.
80. Mawdūdī, *al-Khilāfa wa'l-mulk,* 20.
81. Mawdūdī, "Political Theory of Islam," 168.
82. Sayyid Abul Aʿlā Mawdūdī, *Towards Understanding the Qur'ān,* trans. and ed. Zafar Ishaq Ansari, (Markfield, UK: The Islamic Foundation, 1998), v. 1, 59–60.
83. Mawdūdī, *Islamic Law and Constitution,* 81.
84. Mawdūdī, "Political Theory of Islam," 160.
85. Mawdūdī, *Islamic Law and Constitution,* 82.
86. Mawdūdī, "Political Theory of Islam," 168.
87. Mawdūdī, *al-Khilāfa wa'l-mulk,* 21.
88. Mawdūdī, *Islamic Law and Constitution,* 23.
89. Mawdūdī, *Islamic Law and Constitution,* 82.
90. Mawdūdī, *Islamic Law and Constitution,* 114. (See also Mawdūdī, *al-Khilāfa wa'l-mulk,* 19–20.) Mawdūdī quotes Q. 24:55 in this context.
91. Mawdūdī, "Political Theory of Islam," 168.
92. "The distinguishing feature that makes him not only an independent being, but the *Khalīfah* (representative) of God on earth is his capacity to make moral choices and to shoulder moral responsibility" (Mawdūdī, *The Islamic Movement,* 94).
93. Mawdūdī, *The Islamic Movement,* 95.
94. Mawdūdī, *al-Khilāfa wa'l-mulk,* 34.
95. Mawdūdī, *Islamic Law and Constitution,* 137.
96. Mawdūdī, *Islamic Law and Constitution,* 138.
97. Mawdūdī, *Islamic Law and Constitution,* 139.
98. Mawdūdī, *Islamic Law and Constitution,* 142–44.

99. See Mawdūdī, *al-Khilāfa wa'l-mulk,* 35. It must be stated again that in later writings, Mawdūdī does accept that non-Muslims may serve in an elected legislature and contribute in certain secular, expert capacities so long as the compatibility of the state's laws with the *sharīʿa* is guaranteed. (Mawdūdī, *Islamic Law and Constitution,* 189.)
100. Iqbal, "Political Thought in Islam," 251.
101. Mawdūdī, *The Islamic Movement,* 77.
102. Mawdūdī, *The Islamic Movement,* 79.
103. Mawdūdī, *The Islamic Movement,* 80.

5. The Law We Would Give Ourselves

1. Two of the few book-length studies of Quṭb's thought (both by the same author) are organized around these two concepts. See Sayed Khatab, *The Political Thought of Sayyid Qutb: The Theory of Jahiliyyah* (New York: Routledge, 2006); and *The Power of Sovereignty: The Political and Ideological Philosophy of Sayyid Qutb* (New York: Routledge, 2006).
2. On the idea of Quṭb as part of the intellectual genealogy leading to global jihadism, see Gilles Kepel, *Jihad: The Trail of Political Islam* (Cambridge, MA: Belknap Press, 2002); Lawrence Wright (*The Looming Tower: Al-Qaeda and the Road to 9/11* (New York: Random House, 2006); and even the "9/11 Report" published by the US Congress.
3. The theme of the "ease of Islam" was a book authored by Rashīd Riḍā, *Yusr al-Islām wa-uṣūl al-tashrīʿ al-ʿām* (Cairo: Maṭbaʿat Al-Manār, 1928). In addition to apologetic claims that Islam *is* easy on the human self, there is a kind of juristic literature that claims that facilitation is itself a *goal* of Islamic law that jurists must seek to advance. See, most famously, Yūsuf Qaraḍāwī, *Taysīr al-fiqh fī ḍaw' al-Qur'ān wa'l-Sunnah* (Beirut: Mu'assasat al-Risāla, 1990).
4. Quṭb, *Milestones,* 8.
5. See my "Naturalizing *Sharīʿa:* Foundationalist Ambiguities in Modern Islamic Apologetics," *Islamic Law and Society,* 22, no. 1–2 (February 2015), 45–81, which outlines the history of this concept. See, for example, Ibn Khaldūn: "Thus society is necessary for the human species, for without it its existence would not be perfected nor would God's will to civilize the world with them [*iʿmār al-ʿālam bihim*] and to make them his deputies on earth [*istikhlāfihi iyyāhum*] be realized" (Ibn Khaldūn, *al-Muqaddima: al-juz' al-awwal min Kitāb al-ʿibār* [Beirut: Dār al-Qalam, 1977], 34).
6. Quṭb, *Fī Ẓilāl al-Qur'ān* (Cairo: Dar al-Shurūq, 1973–74). English translation: Sayyid Qutb, *In the Shade of the Qur'an* (18 vols.), trans. Adil Salahi and A. Shamis (Leicester, UK: The Islamic Foundation, 2002–09), vol. 1, 47.

7. Quṭb, *FZQ*, v. 1, 56; *ISQ*, v. 1, 47.
8. Q. 30:30: "Set thy face steadfastly to religion as a *ḥanīf*, in the primordial nature from God upon which He originated mankind—there is no altering the creation of God; that is the upright religion, but most of mankind know not." *The Study Quran: A New Translation and Commentary*, ed. and trans. Seyyed Hossein Nasr, Caner K. Dagli, Maria Massi Dakake, Joseph E. B. Lumbard, and Mohammed Rustom (New York: HarperOne, 2015), 991.
9. Al-Azmeh, "Islamist Revivalism and Western Ideologies," *History Workshop Journal* 32, no. 1 (1991): 44.
10. This is the crux of the debate, for example, between G. A. Cohen and all those whom he felt had been led astray by Rawlsian constructivism. Cohen's claim is that constructivism goes too far in accommodating actual human motivations and normal human moral capacities and is, thus, no longer articulating a theory of justice. (G. A. Cohen, *Rescuing Justice and Equality* [Cambridge, MA: Harvard University Press, 2008]). For an important response to G. A. Cohen's earlier formulations of his critique, see Joshua Cohen ("Taking People as They Are?" *Philosophy & Public Affairs* 30, no. 4 (2001): 363–86). On the question of feasibility and demandingness in political philosophy see also Samuel Scheffler, "Morality's Demands and Their Limits," *Journal of Philosophy* 3, no. 10 (1986): 531–37; Robert Goodin, "Demandingness as a Virtue," *Journal of Ethics* 1 (2009), 1–13; and David Estlund, "Utopophobia," *Philosophy & Public Affairs* 42, no. 2 (2014): 113–34.
11. See, for example, Yvonne Haddad, "Sayyid Qutb: Ideologue of Islamic Revival," in *Voices of Resurgent Islam*, ed. John L. Esposito (Oxford: Oxford University Press, 1983), 67–98.
12. William E. Shepard, "The Development of the Thought of Sayyid Qutb as Reflected in Earlier and Later Editions of 'Social Justice in Islam'," *Die Welt Des Islams* 32(2) 1992, 196–236; Adnan Musallam, *From Secularism to Jihad: Sayyid Qutb and the Foundations of Radical Islamism* (Westport, CT: Praeger, 2005).
13. See two recent biographies of Quṭb: James Toth, *Sayyid Qutb: The Life and Legacy of a Radical Islamic Intellectual* (New York: Oxford University Press, 2013); and John Calvert, *Sayyid Qutb and the Origins of Radical Islamism* (New York: Oxford University Press, 2009).
14. English translation Sayyid Qutb, *Social Justice in Islam*, trans. John B. Hardie and Hamid Algar, ed. Hamid Algar (Oneonta, NY: Islamic Publications International, 2000); Arabic: Sayyid Quṭb, *al-ʿAdāla al-ijtimāʿiyya fi'l-Islām* (Cairo: Dār al-Shurūq ([1949] 1995); William E. Shepard, *Sayyid Qutb and Islamic Activism: A Translation and Critical Analysis of Social Justice in Islam* (Leiden: Brill, 1996) is an excellent alternative translation, more reliable and literal for those who cannot access the Arabic original, and

contains the best critical scholarly commentary on changes across the editions.

15. English translation: Sayyid Qutb, *Basic Principles of the Islamic Worldview,* trans. Rami David (North Haledon, NJ: Islamic Publications International, 2006); Arabic: *Khaṣā'iṣ al-taṣawwur al-Islāmī wa-muqawwamātuhu* (Cairo: Dār al-Shurūq, [1960 or 1962] 1982). See the introduction to the English translation by Hamid Algar for a discussion of the text's original samizdat release during one of Quṭb's incarcerations, and hence the dispute over the precise year of its issue.
16. The views that I am reconstructing from the above texts appear throughout Quṭb's other writings as well, particularly *Hādha al-dīn* [*This Religion*] (Cairo: Dār al-Shurūq, [1961] 1974) and the series of articles reprinted after his death as *Naḥwa mujtama' Islāmī* [*Towards an Islamic Society*] (Dār al-Shurūq, [1952–1953] 1995).
17. John Rawls, *Law of Peoples* (Cambridge, MA: Harvard University Press, 2001).
18. *Social Justice in Islam,* 20; *al-'Adāla al-ijtimā'iyya fi'l-Islām,* 8.
19. *Basic Principles of the Islamic Worldview,* 6; *Khaṣā'iṣ al-taṣawwur,* 10.
20. *In the Shade of the Qur'an,* vol III, 5; *Fī Ẓilāl al-Qur'ān,* vol 1, 557.
21. Ahmad Zaki Hammad, trans., *Milestones* (Indianapolis, IN: American Trust Publications, 1990), 37–42; *Ma'ālim fi'l-ṭarīq* (Cairo: Dār al-Shurūq, 1964), 46–54.
22. *ISQ* v. III, 3; *FZQ,* v. 1, 555.
23. *Social Justice in Islam,* 19; *al-'Adāla al-ijtimā'iyya fi'l-Islām,* 7.
24. *Social Justice in Islam,* 26; *al-'Adāla al-ijtimā'iyya fi'l-Islām,* 11.
25. *Social Justice in Islam,* 26; *al-'Adāla al-ijtimā'iyya fi'l-Islām,* 11–12.
26. "Some Muslim writers, discussing the Islamic political system, labor to trace connections and similarities between it and other systems known to the ancient or modern world. . . . But Islam does not take any pride in any similarities between it and these other systems, nor is it harmed by their absence" (*Social Justice in Islam,* 114; *al-'Adāla al-ijtimā'iyya fi'l-Islām,* 75).
27. Al-Azmeh, "Islamist Revivalism and Western Ideologies," 45.
28. See, for example, William E. Shepard, "Islam as a 'System' in the Later Writings of Sayyid Qutb," *Middle Eastern Studies* 25 no. 1 (1989): 31–50; and Roxanne Euben, *Enemy in the Mirror* (Princeton, NJ: Princeton University Press, 1999), 78.
29. Although it is that. In echoes of the 11th Thesis on Feuerbach, Quṭb writes: "We are not aiming at purely cultural knowledge . . . we seek 'movement' beyond 'knowledge' . . . knowledge transforms itself into a motivating power for realizing its meaning in the real world" (*Basic Principles of the Islamic Worldview,* 6; *Khaṣā'iṣ al-taṣawwur,* 9–10).

30. *Social Justice in Islam,* 28–29; *al-ʿAdāla al-ijtimāʿiyya fi'l-Islām,* 13.
31. *Basic Principles of the Islamic Worldview,* 97; *Khaṣāʾiṣ al-taṣawwur,* 96. This quotation is taken from an entire chapter entitled "Comprehensiveness" *(al-Shumūl),* meant to designate one of seven "basic principles" or "characteristics" of the entire Islamic "concept."
32. *Social Justice in Islam,* 34; *al-ʿAdāla al-ijtimāʿiyya fi'l-Islām,* 18.
33. "Since the Islamic concept is divine and originates from God, it is the duty of all humanity to receive it, respond to it, adapt to it and apply it in real life" (*Basic Principles of the Islamic Worldview,* 73; *Khaṣāʾiṣ al-taṣawwur,* 72).
34. *Basic Principles of the Islamic Worldview,* 84; *Khaṣāʾiṣ al-taṣawwur,* 84. The entire chapter of this text, entitled "Stability" *(al-Thabāt),* is replete with this theme.
35. *Basic Principles of the Islamic Worldview,* 125; *Khaṣāʾiṣ al-taṣawwur,* 118–19.
36. "[God's] will is absolute and subject to no restraints; it creates all things simply by orienting itself to them. There is no principle governing it [obliging it: *mulzima*], nor any form imposed on it, whenever it wills to do what it wills" (*Basic Principles of the Islamic Worldview,* 123; *Khaṣāʾiṣ al-taṣawwur,* 117).
37. *Basic Principles of the Islamic Worldview,* 20; *Khaṣāʾiṣ al-taṣawwur,* 23.
38. *Basic Principles of the Islamic Worldview,* 78–79; *Khaṣāʾiṣ al-taṣawwur,* 78.
39. *Basic Principles of the Islamic Worldview,* 142; *Khaṣāʾiṣ al-taṣawwur,* 132.
40. Quṭb goes so far as to claim that Christianity "seeks to crush down the human instincts in order to encourage [spiritual] desires" (*Social Justice in Islam,* 45; *al-ʿAdāla al-ijtimāʿiyya fi'l-Islām,* 26). Quṭb believes that Islam not only protects human needs and interests, but is responsive to their *instincts,* a crucial point for this chapter.
41. *Social Justice in Islam,* 27; *al-ʿAdāla al-ijtimāʿiyya fi'l-Islām,,* 12.
42. *Basic Principles of the Islamic Worldview,* 113; *Khaṣāʾiṣ al-taṣawwur,* 109.
43. *Social Justice in Islam,* 32–33; *al-ʿAdāla al-ijtimāʿiyya fi'l-Islām,* 17.
44. *Basic Principles of the Islamic Worldview,* 97; *Khaṣāʾiṣ al-taṣawwur,* 96.
45. "Behold: I am creating a human being from clay. When I have proportioned him and breathed into him of My spirit, fall down before him prostrating!" (*The Study Quran,* 114–15).
46. "Truly we guided him upon the way, be he grateful or ungrateful" (*The Study Quran,* 1452.)
47. *In the Shade of the Qur'an,* vol. XVIII, 229; *Fī Ẓilāl al-Qurʾān,* vol. 6, 3917.
48. *Basic Principles of the Islamic Worldview,* 47; *Khaṣāʾiṣ al-taṣawwur,* 45.
49. *Social Justice in Islam,* 127; *al-ʿAdāla al-ijtimāʿiyya fi'l-Islām,,* 87.
50. *Basic Principles of the Islamic Worldview,* 149; *Khaṣāʾiṣ al-taṣawwur,* 138.
51. *Social Justice in Islam,* 42–43; *al-ʿAdāla al-ijtimāʿiyya fi'l-Islām,* 24.
52. *Social Justice in Islam,* 39–40; *al-ʿAdāla al-ijtimāʿiyya fi'l-Islām,* 22. "All these unchanging Qur'anic statements deal with an unchanging human nature. Since both are devised by the same Maker, they are able to deal with the

changing circumstances of human life and its developing stages with a flexibility that still enables man to retain his essential elements. Man has deliberately been endowed with all the necessary skills to deal with the constant flux that different life situations bring about. Hence the divine constitution for human life has been given the same degree of flexibility, because it has been made suitable for human life to the end of time" (*In the Shade of the Qur'an,* vol. III, 4; *Fī Ẓilāl al-Qur'ān* vol. 1, 556). Elsewhere Quṭb makes quite clear that "God is certainly capable of altering human nature or of creating him with a different nature" (*Basic Principles of the Islamic Worldview,* 133; *Khaṣā'iṣ al-taṣawwur,* 126).

53. *Basic Principles of the Islamic Worldview,* 200; *Khaṣā'iṣ al-taṣawwur,* 180, emphasis added). See also *Hādha al-dīn (This Religion):* "When the soul is at one with its true nature, when its needs and necessities are fulfilled, when its constructive capacities are released, then with ease and without compulsion it will flow in natural harmony with life, will ascend to the lofty summit ordained for it." *Hādha al-dīn* (Cairo: Dār al-Shurūq, [1961] 1974), 29.
54. *Social Justice in Islam,* 64–65; *al-'Adāla al-ijtimā'iyya fi'l-Islām,* 41–42.
55. *Basic Principles of the Islamic Worldview,* 195–96; *Khaṣā'iṣ al-taṣawwur,* 176.
56. *Basic Principles of the Islamic Worldview,* 196; *Khaṣā'iṣ al-taṣawwur,* 177 (emphasis added). Elsewhere Quṭb concedes "the impulses that drive men to evil, misguidance and sin" but instead of relegating them to a different part or type of human self he simply proclaims that "Islam declares them to be too weak to gain complete dominance over man" (*Basic Principles of the Islamic Worldview,* 135; *Khaṣā'iṣ al-taṣawwur,* 127).
57. *Social Justice in Islam,* 131–32; *al-'Adāla al-ijtimā'iyya fi'l-Islām,* 90.
58. *Social Justice in Islam,* 131; *al-'Adāla al-ijtimā'iyya fi'l-Islām,* 90.
59. "Islam looks at man as forming a unity whose spiritual desires cannot be separated from his bodily appetites and whose moral needs cannot be divorced from his material needs" (*Social Justice in Islam,* 45; *al-'Adāla al-ijtimā'iyya fi'l-Islām,* 26).
60. *Social Justice in Islam,* 46; *al-'Adāla al-ijtimā'iyya fi'l-Islām,* 27.
61. *Social Justice in Islam,* 61; *al-'Adāla al-ijtimā'iyya fi'l-Islām,* 38.
62. *Social Justice in Islam,* 109; *al-'Adāla al-ijtimā'iyya fi'l-Islām,* 74.
63. *Social Justice in Islam,* 80; *al-'Adāla al-ijtimā'iyya fi'l-Islām,* 53.
64. *Social Justice in Islam,* 47–48; *al-'Adāla al-ijtimā'iyya fi'l-Islām,* 28–39.
65. *Social Justice in Islam,* 48; *al-'Adāla al-ijtimā'iyya fi'l-Islām,* 29.
66. *Social Justice in Islam,* 110; *al-'Adāla al-ijtimā'iyya fi'l-Islām,* 74. This passage is not to be found in the 1995 printing of the Arabic version.
67. *Social Justice in Islam,* 109; *al-'Adāla al-ijtimā'iyya fi'l-Islām,* 74.
68. *Social Justice in Islam,* 54; *al-'Adāla al-ijtimā'iyya fi'l-Islām,* 33.
69. *Social Justice in Islam,* 66–67; *al-'Adāla al-ijtimā'iyya fi'l-Islām,* 43.
70. *Social Justice in Islam,* 84; *al-'Adāla al-ijtimā'iyya fi'l-Islām,* 56.

71. *Social Justice in Islam,* 130; *al-ʿAdāla al-ijtimāʿiyya fiʾl-Islām,* 89.
72. *Social Justice in Islam,* 143; *al-ʿAdāla al-ijtimāʿiyya fiʾl-Islām,* 99.
73. *Social Justice in Islam,* 149; *al-ʿAdāla al-ijtimāʿiyya fiʾl-Islām,* 103.
74. "Sedentary people are much concerned with all kinds of pleasures. They are accustomed to luxury and success in worldly occupations and to indulgence in worldly desires. Therefore, their souls are colored with all kinds of blameworthy and evil qualities" (Ibn Khaldun, *The Muqaddimah: An Introduction to History,* trans. Franz Rosenthal and ed. N. J. Dawood (Princeton, NJ: Princeton University Press, 2004), 94.
75. *Social Justice in Islam,* 156; *al-ʿAdāla al-ijtimāʿiyya fiʾl-Islām,* 110.
76. *Social Justice in Islam,* 160; *al-ʿAdāla al-ijtimāʿiyya fiʾl-Islām,* 113.
77. *Social Justice in Islam,* 137; *al-ʿAdāla al-ijtimāʿiyya fiʾl-Islām,* 93.
78. *Social Justice in Islam,* 136–37; *al-ʿAdāla al-ijtimāʿiyya fiʾl-Islām,* 93.
79. "The man accustomed to the ways of society is always outside himself and knows how to live only in the opinions of others. And it is, as it were, from their judgment alone that he draws the sentiment of his own existence." Rousseau, *Discourse on the Origins of Inequality,* in *Basic Political Writings of Jean-Jacques Rousseau,* trans. Donald A. Cress (Indianapolis, IN: Hackett Publishing,1987), 81.
80. *Social Justice in Islam,* 53; *al-ʿAdāla al-ijtimāʿiyya fiʾl-Islām,* 32.
81. "An objective of *jihad* is to establish the Islamic social order and defend it. It is an order that frees man from the tyranny of other men, in all its forms, by urging the submission of all to the one supreme Master" (*ISQ,* v. I, 325, 328–29; *FZQ,* v. 1, 291, 294–95).
82. *Social Justice in Islam,* 54; *al-ʿAdāla al-ijtimāʿiyya fiʾl-Islām,* 33.
83. *Social Justice in Islam,* 55; *al-ʿAdāla al-ijtimāʿiyya fiʾl-Islām,* 33.
84. *Social Justice in Islam,* 57–58; *al-ʿAdāla al-ijtimāʿiyya fiʾl-Islām,* 36.
85. *Social Justice in Islam,* 58; *al-ʿAdāla al-ijtimāʿiyya fiʾl-Islām,* 36.
86. *Basic Principles of the Islamic Worldview,* 139; *Khaṣāʾiṣ al-taṣawwur al-Islāmī wa-muqawwamātuhu* (Cairo: Dār al-Shurūq, [1960 or 1962] 1982), 129.
87. *Basic Principles of the Islamic Worldview,* 3; *Khaṣāʾiṣ al-taṣawwur,* 7.
88. *Basic Principles of the Islamic Worldview,* 144; *Khaṣāʾiṣ al-taṣawwur,* 134.
89. *Basic Principles of the Islamic Worldview,* 147; *Khaṣāʾiṣ al-taṣawwur,* 136.
90. "Society will not persevere with such [just] legislation unless there is a belief which demands it from within" (*Social Justice in Islam,* 53; *al-ʿAdāla al-ijtimāʿiyya fiʾl-Islām,* 32). "Islam places a great deal of reliance on the human conscience once it is educated; its sets it up as the guardian of the legal processes to see that they are implemented and maintained" (*Social Justice in Islam,* 95; *al-ʿAdāla al-ijtimāʿiyya fiʾl-Islām,* 64). "No renaissance of Islamic life can be effected purely by law . . . [but also] the production of a state of mind imbued with the Islamic theory of life to act as an inner motivation for establishing this form of life and to give coherence to . . . legislation. Social

justice cannot be realized until this form of life is first realized, and it cannot have any guaranteed permanence unless this form of life is built up on . . . the support of public belief and confidence in its merits" (*Social Justice in Islam,* 285; *al-'Adāla al-ijtimā'iyya fi'l-Islām,* 196–97). "True social justice was possible only when every individual of the society, whether a giver or a taker, firmly believed that this system had been legislated by God Almighty, and that by obedience to this system he would not only prosper in this world but would be rewarded in the next" (*M* 23; *MT* 26).

91. When "the human mind has come to know all this freedom of conscience; it is free from the least shadow of servility, be it to death or injury, to poverty or weakness . . . it is released from the tyranny of the values of social standing and wealth; it is saved from the humiliation of need and beggary, and it can rise superior to its desires and its bodily appetites [then] it can turn toward its One Sole Creator" (*Social Justice in Islam,* 68; *al-'Adāla al-ijtimā'iyya fi'l-Islām,* 44). Note the combination of spiritual and political conditions for the comprehensive emancipation of humans.
92. In a passing comment on the classical jurists who compiled the traditional manuals on Islamic law, Quṭb says simply that "most of their work is, in our opinion, in agreement with the spirit of Islam. But in the case of a small proportion, a certain looseness appeared in some of their works, resulting in a greater or lesser divergence from the spirit of Islam" (*Social Justice in Islam,* 34; *al-'Adāla al-ijtimā'iyya fi'l-Islām,* 18).
93. *Social Justice in Islam,* 110; *al-'Adāla al-ijtimā'iyya fi'l-Islām,* 74. As an example of this gap in practice, Quṭb here refers to the religious obligation to fight when so called by the community. He notes that the Qur'ān reveals that God was responsive to man's occasional love of comfort and reluctance to fight. Thus, the law "prescribes fighting . . . but over and above that [Islam] kindles a love for fighting by inciting the conscience to accept it, by depicting it in glowing terms, and by emphasizing its justice and the glories which it brings to a society" (*Social Justice in Islam,* 110; *al-'Adāla al-ijtimā'iyya fi'l-Islām,* 74).
94. *Social Justice in Islam,* 125; *al-'Adāla al-ijtimā'iyya fi'l-Islām,* 85.
95. *Social Justice in Islam,* 119; *al-'Adāla al-ijtimā'iyya fi'l-Islām,* 79–80.
96. *Basic Principles of the Islamic Worldview,* 196; *Khaṣā'iṣ al-taṣawwur,* 177.
97. *Basic Principles of the Islamic Worldview,* 200; *Khaṣā'iṣ al-taṣawwur,* 180–81. The entire chapter from which the previous two quotations are drawn is entitled "Realism" *(al-Waqi'īyya),* one of Quṭb's seven core "principles" or "characteristics" *(khaṣā'is)* of the Islamic worldview. See also *Social Justice in Islam:* "Islam is a perfectly practicable social system in itself; it has beliefs, laws, and a social and economic system that is under the control of both conscience and law. It offers to mankind a perfectly comprehensive theory of the universe, life, and mankind, a theory that satisfies man's intellectual needs. It offers to men a clear, broad, and deep faith, which

satisfies the conscience. It offers to society legal and economic bases that have been proved both practicable and systematic" (*Social Justice in Islam,* 317; *al-ʿAdāla al-ijtimāʿiyya fi'l-Islām,* 125).

98. *HD* 45. "It is important for us to remember that these people who realized the divine path in their lives [the *salaf*] were human beings who did not exceed the bounds of their nature [*ṭabīʿa*] or innate disposition [*fiṭra*], nor suppress their capacities. They did not impose on themselves exertion beyond their capacities, but devoted themselves to all human activities, and enjoyed all the good things of their environment and time" (*HD* 40).
99. *Social Justice in Islam,* 68; *al-ʿAdāla al-ijtimāʿiyya fi'l-Islām,* 44, emphasis added.
100. See Shahrough Akhavi, "The Dialectic in Contemporary Egyptian Social Thought: The Scripturalist and Modernist Discourses of Sayyid Qutb and Hasan Hanafi," *International Journal of Middle East Studies* 29, no. 3 (1997): 377–401, on Quṭb's reification of "Islam" as a dynamic entity or spirit in its own right.
101. *HD* 51.
102. *Basic Principles of the Islamic Worldview,* 3; *Khaṣāʾiṣ al-taṣawwur,* 7.
103. *Social Justice in Islam,* 207; *al-ʿAdāla al-ijtimāʿiyya fi'l-Islām,* 153.
104. *Social Justice in Islam,* 209; *al-ʿAdāla al-ijtimāʿiyya fi'l-Islām,* 154.
105. *Social Justice in Islam,* 215.
106. All quotations from this paragraph are from *Social Justice in Islam,* 215. All of the passages quoted in this paragraph (including the following two) were present in the 1st and 5th editions on which the Hardie/Algar translation is based. They were excised by the 7th edition (published posthumously). In an article on the changes from the 1st to the 7th editions, William Shepard notes that in Quṭb's treatment of this period of Islamic history, "the main lines of this analysis continue in the last edition, but with some interesting differences in detail" ("The Development of the Thought of Sayyid Qutb," 213). On my reading of the Hardie/Algar translation alongside a 1995 printing of the Arabic based on the 7th edition, the excised passages tend to be blunt statements about the calamity of ʿUthmān's ascension to the caliphate, such as those cited here. However, the text does indeed retain the broad outlines of the argument that the corruption of the Islamic spirit underpinning the political order was indeed a top-down political event. See Shepard, *Sayyid Qutb and Islamic Activism,* for a line-by-line comparison of the various editions.
107. *Social Justice in Islam,* 230.
108. Indeed, in another intriguing parallel with Rousseau, Quṭb observes a preservation of the pure Islamic egalitarian ethos in more "primitive," unstratified desert and rural Islamic communities.
109. Abu al-Hasan Al-Mawardi, (d. 1058), *The Ordinances of Government: al-Ahkam al-Sultaniyya wa'l-wilaya al-diniyya,* trans. Wafaa H. Wahba (Reading, UK: Garnet Publishing, 2000), 3.

110. *HD* 40.
111. Quṭb, *Milestones,* 62.
112. Barbara Zollner, *The Muslim Brotherhood: Hasan al-Hudaybi and Ideology* (New York: Routledge, 2007); Carrie Rosefsky Wickham, *The Muslim Brotherhood: Evolution of an Islamist Movement* (Princeton, NJ: Princeton University Press, 2015); and Mona El-Ghobashy, "The Metamorphosis of the Egyptian Muslim Brothers," *International Journal of Middle East Studies* 37, no. 3 (2005): 373–95.
113. In addition to Kepel, *Jihad,* see his *Muslim Extremism in Egypt: The Prophet and Pharaoh* (Berkeley, CA: University of California Press, 2003); Hisham Mubarak, "What Does the Gamaʿa Islamiyya Want?: An Interview with Talʿat Fuʾad Qasim," *Middle East Report* 198 (January–March 1996), 40–46.
114. "The notion of *ḥākimiyya* would also find its way into Salafism through the efforts of Sayyid Quṭb's brother, Muḥammad (1919–2014), who was released from jail by ʿAbd al-Nāṣir in 1971 and established himself in Saudi Arabia. Muḥammad Quṭb wrote about the imperative of *tawḥīd al-ḥākimiyya* (the belief in God's sovereignty—with all the related political and legal implications—as a key component of *tawḥīd*), merging the core concept of Salafism, *tawḥīd,* or the unity of God, with the cornerstone of his brother's political theory. *Tawḥīd al-ḥākimiyya* became one of the central concepts used by Saudi anti-regime Salafīs, in particular those of the *ṣaḥwa* movement, to challenge the Saudi monarchy by accusing it of only superficially upholding the principle of *tawḥīd*" (Lacroix, "Ḥākimiyya," EI3). See further, Joas Wagemakers, *A Quietist Jihadi: The Ideology and Influence of Abu Muhammad al-Maqdisi* (Cambridge, UK: Cambridge University Press, 2012); and Shiraz Maher, *Salafi-Jihadism: The History of an Idea* (New York: Oxford University Press, 2016).
115. For example, Abū Muḥammad al-Maqdisī, *Democracy: A Religion!* (Sprinvale South, VIC Australia: Al Furqan Islamic Information Centre, 2012) (pdf on file with author).
116. Nathan J. Brown, *When Victory Is Not an Option: Islamist Movements in Arab Politics* (Ithaca, NY: Cornell University Press, 2012); Jillian M. Schwedler, *Faith in Moderation: Islamist Parties in Jordan and Yemen* (Cambridge, UK: Cambridge University Press, 2006); and Glenn E. Robinson, "Can Islamists Be Democrats? The Case of Jordan," *The Middle East Journal* (1997): 373–87.

6. A Sovereign *Umma* and a Living *Sharīʿa*

1. On his biography, see Azzam S. Tamimi, *Rachid Ghannouchi: A Democrat within Islamism* (New York: Oxford University Press, 2001).
2. Ghannūshī, *al-Ḥurriyyāt al-ʿāmma,* 97–98. This is Ghannūshī's most important and most elaborate work of political theory, with a revised edition

published in 2015, well after the 2011 Tunisian revolution (Tūnis: Dār al-Mujtahid li'l-nashr wa'l-tawzīʿ, 2015).

3. Muhammad Asad's commentary on verse 2:30 from his translation is instructive: "The term *khalīfah*—derived from the verb *khalafa,* 'he succeeded [another]'—is used in this allegory to denote man's rightful supremacy on earth, which is most suitably rendered by the expression 'he shall inherit the earth' (in the sense of being given possession of it)." But man's rightful supremacy on earth over other creatures and its resources does not necessary imply a political community's political sovereignty—particularly of a participatory kind—over its own designated rulers. See David L. Johnston, *Earth, Empire, and Sacred Text: Muslims and Christians as Trustees of Creation* (Bristol, UK: Equinox Publishing, 2010), for the theme of vicegerency as stewardship over the earth.
4. Ghannūshī, *al-Ḥurriyyāt al-ʿāmma,* 37 (2015 ed., 35).
5. Ghannūshī, *al-Ḥurriyyāt al-ʿāmma,* 41–42 (2015 ed., 40–42). See David L. Johnston, "The Human *Khilāfa:* A Growing Overlap of Reformism and Islamism on Human Rights Discourse?" *Islamochristiana* 28 (2002): 35–53.
6. It is common for Muslim political and ethical theorists to point to the Qurʾānic verse 17:70, "and we have dignified the children of Adam," in arguments for a universal claim to dignity.
7. Ghannūshī, *al-Ḥurriyyāt al-ʿāmma,* 66 (2015 ed., 71).
8. Ghannūshī, *al-Ḥurriyyāt al-ʿāmma,* 52 (2015 ed., 54). However, it does not follow from this that certain of our beliefs or actions might not nonetheless be regarded as attacks on our own human dignity or what is referred to as "injustice to oneself" *(ẓulm al-nafs).*
9. Variations of this formulation appear at Ghannūshī, *al-Ḥurriyyāt al-ʿāmma,* 41, 52, 54, and 97. Another Tunisian Islamic political philosopher and member of Ghannūshī's movement, ʿAbd al-Majīd al-Najjār, has also written on the universal vicegerency of man. For him, it signifies the charge to implement God's intentions on earth and abiding by His rules, but this makes central humanity's capacities of reason in receiving, interpreting, and realizing God's revelation (ʿAbd Al-Majīd Najjār, *Khilāfat al-insān bayna al-waḥy wa'l-ʿaql: Baḥth fī jadaliyyat al-naṣṣ wa'l-ʿaql wa'l-wāqiʿ* [Herndon, VA: Al-Maʿhad al-ʿālamī li'l-fikr al-Islāmī, 1993]).
10. Ghannūshī, *al-Ḥurriyyāt al-ʿāmma,* 41 (2015 ed., 41).
11. Quoted in Ghannūshī, *al-Ḥurriyyāt al-ʿāmma,* 38 (2015 ed., 36). See ʿAllāl al-Fāsī, *Maqāṣid al-sharīʿa wa makārimuhā* (al-Rabāṭ: Maṭbaʿat al-Risāla, 1979),247. On the resurrection of the legal theory based on the "purposes of *sharīʿa*" derived from the Andalusian legal theorist Abū Isḥāq al-Shāṭibī (d. 1388), with a particular focus on twentieth-century Morocco and Tunisia, see Ebrahim Moosa, "Reading Shāṭibī in Rabat and Tunis," *The*

Muslim World 104, no. 4 (2014): 451–64. On Fāsī's theory as an apologetic project, similar to Quṭb's, of justifying the *sharīʿa* for modern Muslims, see my "Naturalizing *Sharīʿa:* Foundationalist Ambiguities in Modern Islamic Apologetics," *Islamic Law and Society,* 22, no. 1–2 (February 2015): 45–81.

12. Ghannūshī, *al-Ḥurriyyāt al-ʿāmma,* 41.
13. Ghannūshī again cites the Moroccan legal theorist ʿAllāl al-Fāsī in arguing for the universal caliphate as stewardship over the earth and responsibility to civilize and cultivate it *(ʿimārat al-arḍ).* "Man's ownership *(mulkiyya)* is a product *(thamra)* of his being deputized by God *(istikhlāfihi ʿan allāh).*"
14. Ghannūshī, *al-Ḥurriyyāt al-ʿāmma,* 56 (2015 ed., 59).
15. Ghannūshī, *al-Ḥurriyyāt al-ʿāmma,* 62 (2015 ed., 64–73).
16. Ghannūshī, *al-Ḥurriyyāt al-ʿāmma,* 62 (2015 ed., 72–73, adding rights to a fair trial, security and asylum).
17. Ghannūshī, *al-Ḥurriyyāt al-ʿāmma,* 66 (2015 ed., 71).
18. Ghannūshī, *al-Ḥurriyyāt al-ʿāmma,* 55 (2015 ed., 57).
19. Ghannūshī, *al-Ḥurriyyāt al-ʿāmma,* 180 (2015 ed., 203).
20. Ghannūshī relies for this critique of modern Western secularism not only on traditional Islamic sources but also on Western critics like the French convert to Islam Roger Garaudy (Ghannūshī, *al-Ḥurriyyāt al-ʿāmma,* 32–33 (2015 ed., 30–31).)
21. Rāshid al-Ghannūshī, *al-Dīmuqrāṭiyya wa ḥuqūq al-insān fi'l-Islām* (Doha: Markaz al-Jazīra li'l-dirāsat, 2012), 14.
22. "Everything else is just a means, insofar as man is social by nature and Islam is a comprehensive system for life, for creating a social environment for enabling the largest possible number of people to live spiritually and materially in accord with the law of human nature [*al-qānūn al-fiṭrī*] that came from God, that is, Islam. The Islamic state is nothing other than the political apparatus for realizing Islam's exalted ideal of a community founded on good and justice, realizing truth and invalidating falsehood on the entire earth" (Ghannūshī, *al-Ḥurriyyāt al-ʿāmma,* 93 [2015 ed., 103]).
23. Here he acknowledges that "Perhaps the first one to define Islam in this way was Mawdūdī and the martyr Sayyid Quṭb, who followed his teaching," Ghannūshī, *al-Ḥurriyyāt al-ʿāmma,* 37 (2015 ed., 35).
24. Ghannūshī, *al-Ḥurriyyāt al-ʿāmma,* 37 (2015 ed., 35).
25. Ghannūshī, *al-Ḥurriyyāt al-ʿāmma,* 39 (2015 ed., 38).
26. Ghannūshī, *al-Ḥurriyyāt al-ʿāmma,* 78 (2015 ed., 85).
27. Ghannūshī, *al-Ḥurriyyāt al-ʿāmma,* 79 (2015 ed., 86).
28. Ghannūshī, *al-Ḥurriyyāt al-ʿāmma,* 83 (2015 ed., 90).
29. Ghannūshī, *al-Ḥurriyyāt al-ʿāmma,* 98 (2015 ed., 109).
30. Ghannūshī, *al-Ḥurriyyāt al-ʿāmma,* 99 (2015 ed., 110).
31. Ghannūshī, *al-Ḥurriyyāt al-ʿāmma,* 105 (2015 ed., 117).

32. Ghannūshī, *al-Ḥurriyyāt al-ʿāmma,* 99 (2015 ed.. 110).
33. Quṭb, *Fī Ẓilāl al-Qurʾān,* v. 2., 888.
34. Ghannūshī, *al-Ḥurriyyāt al-ʿāmma,* 102 (2015 ed., 113).
35. Ghannūshī, *al-Ḥurriyyāt al-ʿāmma,* 222.
36. Ghannūshī, *al-Ḥurriyyāt al-ʿāmma,* 101 (2015 ed., 112).
37. Ghannūshī, *al-Ḥurriyyāt al-ʿāmma,* 109.
38. Ghannūshī, *al-Ḥurriyyāt al-ʿāmma,* 110–11.
39. Ghannūshī, *al-Ḥurriyyāt al-ʿāmma,* 113.
40. ʿAbd al-Wahhāb Khallāf *al-Siyāsa al-sharʿiyya,* 44–48.
41. Quoted in Ghannūshī, *al-Ḥurriyyāt al-ʿāmma,* 117.
42. Ghannūshī, *al-Ḥurriyyāt al-ʿāmma,* 125–26 (2015 ed., 140–41).
43. Ghannūshī, *al-Ḥurriyyāt al-ʿāmma,* 41.
44. Ghannūshī, *al-Ḥurriyyāt al-ʿāmma,* 77–8 (2015 ed., 84–85).
45. Ghannūshī, *al-Ḥurriyyāt al-ʿāmma,* 141 (2015 ed., 160).
46. Ghannūshī, *al-Ḥurriyyāt al-ʿāmma,* 141 (2015 ed., 160).
47. Ghannūshī, *al-Ḥurriyyāt al-ʿāmma,* 147 (2015 ed., 167).
48. Gahnnūshī, *al-Ḥurriyyāt al-ʿāmma,* 164 (2015 ed., 186).
49. Ghannūshī, *al-Ḥurriyyāt al-ʿāmma,* 150 (2015 ed., 170).
50. Ghannūshī, *al-Ḥurriyyāt al-ʿāmma,* 92–93 (2015 ed., 102–3). Again later: Islamic governance, "is a civil government in all aspects, that is, a consultative presidency only attainable through the general *bay'a,* as its source of authority is the *umma*. What happened by way of designation during the time of the Rightly-Guided Caliphs was merely nomination of candidates, but the *umma* had the final right to accept this or suggest another" (164).
51. He also notes that it is a correction to certain excesses from the Sunni tradition, whether early caliphs who claimed direct appointment by God, or even later legal theorists, like al-Qarāfī, who claimed that the ruler is God's representative on Earth (Ghannūshī, *al-Ḥurriyyāt al-ʿāmma,* 167 [2015 ed., 188]).
52. Ghannūshī, *al-Ḥurriyyāt al-ʿāmma,* 165 (2015 ed., 186).
53. Ghannūshī, *al-Ḥurriyyāt al-ʿāmma,* 105 (2015 ed., 117).
54. Ghannūshī, *al-Ḥurriyyāt al-ʿāmma,* 116 (2015 ed., 129).
55. Ghannushī is critiquing here the constitutional views set out in Taqī al-Dīn al-Nabhānī, *al-Dawla al-Islāmiyya* (Jerusalem: Ḥizb al-Taḥrīr, [1953?]).
56. Ghannūshī, *al-Ḥurriyyāt al-ʿāmma,* 118 (2015 ed., 132).
57. Ghannūshī, *al-Ḥurriyyāt al-ʿāmma,* 178 (2015 ed., 201).
58. Ghannūshī, *al-Ḥurriyyāt al-ʿāmma,* 180 (2015 ed., 203–4).
59. Ghannūshī, *al-Ḥurriyyāt al-ʿāmma,* 185 (2015 ed., 211).
60. See, for example, Ghannūshī, *al-Ḥurriyyāt al-ʿāmma,* 71. The phrase also occurs at 77, 119 (where he says that "some Islamic thinkers have gone so far as to say that Muslims are the first nation in history to say that the people is the source of authority [*sulṭān*]"), 141, 164, 165, and 186.

61. Ghannūshī, *al-Ḥurriyyāt al-ʿāmma,* 99 (2015 ed., 110).
    Ghannūshī, *al-Ḥurriyyāt al-ʿāmma,* 165 (2015 ed., 187).
62. Ghannūshī, *al-Ḥurriyyāt al-ʿāmma,* 99 (2015 ed., 110).
63. Ghannūshī, *al-Ḥurriyyāt al-ʿāmma,* 146 (2015 ed., 166).
64. Ghannūshī, *al-Ḥurriyyāt al-ʿāmma,* 169 (2015 ed., 190).
65. Ghannūshī, *al-Ḥurriyyāt al-ʿāmma,* 93 (2015 ed., 103).
66. Ghannūshī, *al-Ḥurriyyāt al-ʿāmma,* 56 (2015 ed., 58).
67. Ghannūshī, *al-Ḥurriyyāt al-ʿāmma,* 101 (2015 ed., 113).
68. All of the following are found in Ghannūshī, *al-Ḥurriyyāt al-ʿāmma,* 240–48 (2015 ed., 267–78).
69. Ghannūshī, *al-Ḥurriyyāt al-ʿāmma,* 101 (2015 ed., 113). A few pages later: "Islam is the founding authority of the *umma* and the state" (*al-Ḥurriyyāt al-ʿāmma,* 104).
70. Ghannūshī, *al-Ḥurriyyāt al-ʿāmma,* 101 (2015 ed., 113).
71. Ghannūshī, *al-Ḥurriyyāt al-ʿāmma,* 113 (2015 ed., 126).
72. Ghannūshī, *al-Ḥurriyyāt al-ʿāmma,* 106 (2015 ed., 118).
73. Ghannūshī, *al-Ḥurriyyāt al-ʿāmma,* 105 (2015 ed., 117).
74. Ghannūshī, *al-Ḥurriyyāt al-ʿāmma,* 120–21 (2015 ed., 135).
75. Ghannūshī, *al-Ḥurriyyāt al-ʿāmma,* 110 (2015 ed., 123).
76. Ghannūshī, *al-Ḥurriyyāt al-ʿāmma,* 106 (2015 ed., 117).
77. Ghannūshī, *al-Ḥurriyyāt al-ʿāmma,* 125–26 (2015 ed., 140–41).
78. Ghannūshī, *al-Ḥurriyyāt al-ʿāmma,* 105 (2015 ed., 117).
79. Ghannūshī, *al-Ḥurriyyāt al-ʿāmma,* 103 (2015 ed., 114–15).
80. Ghannūshī, *al-Ḥurriyyāt al-ʿāmma,* 119 (2015 ed., 133).
81. Ghannūshī, *al-Ḥurriyyāt al-ʿāmma,* 119 (2015 ed., 134).
82. Ghannūshī, *al-Ḥurriyyāt al-ʿāmma,* 120 (2015 ed., 134).
83. Ghannūshī, *al-Ḥurriyyāt al-ʿāmma,* 120 (2015 ed., 134).
84. Ghannūshī, *al-Ḥurriyyāt al-ʿāmma,* 121 (2015 ed., 135).
85. Ghannūshī, *al-Ḥurriyyāt al-ʿāmma,* 120 (2015 ed., 134–35).
86. Ghannūshī, *al-Ḥurriyyāt al-ʿāmma,* 221 (2015 ed., 253).
87. Ghannūshī, *al-Ḥurriyyāt al-ʿāmma,* 245–46 (2015 ed., 277). In an earlier study of Islamic democratic theory as articulated in particular by the Sudanese thinker and political leader Ḥasan al-Turābī, Aziz al-Azmeh also stresses that Islamist theories of democracy are primarily "populist" in their discomfort with liberal pluralist foundations (Aziz al-Azmeh, "Al-Azmeh, Aziz, "Populism Contra Democracy: Recent Democratist Discourse in the Arab World," in Ghassane Salamé, ed., *Democracy without Democrats? The Renewal of Politics in the Muslim World* (London: I. B. Tauris, 1994): 112–28.
88. Recall that Ghannūshī argues that because the *sharīʿa* emanates from outside the people's own will (unlike in democracies), it is thus a *neutral* check on tyranny: "One can present the principles enunciated in the *sharīʿa*

[in opposition to an errant ruler], as it represents the supreme and unbiased authority and offers a very satisfactory solution" (Ghannūshī, *al-Ḥurriyyāt al-ʿāmma,* 221 ([2015 ed., 253)]).

89. Ghannūshī, *al-Ḥurriyyāt al-ʿāmma,* 95 (2015 ed., 105–6).
90. "The latent causes of faction are thus sown in the nature of man; and we see them everywhere brought into different degrees of activity, according to the different circumstances of civil society. A zeal for different opinions concerning religion, concerning government, and many other points, as well of speculation as of practice; . . . have, in turn, divided mankind into parties, inflamed them with mutual animosity, and rendered them much more disposed to vex and oppress each other than to co-operate for their common good" (James Madison, Federalist 10. http://avalon.law.yale.edu/18th_century/fed10.asp).
91. Ghannūshī, *al-Ḥurriyyāt al-ʿāmma,* 235 (2015 ed., 266–67).
92. Ghannūshī, *al-Ḥurriyyāt al-ʿāmma,* 91 (2015 ed., 100).
93. Ghannūshī, *al-Ḥurriyyāt al-ʿāmma,* 236. It must be said here in this context, however, that Ghannūshī is not quite accurately conveying Ibn Khaldūn's views on moral restraint. For Ibn Khaldūn, men required a "restrainer" *(wāziʿ)* in social life who "must dominate them and have power and authority over them, so that no one of them will be able to attack another. This is the meaning of royal authority [*mulk*]." Ibn Khaldun, *The Muqaddimah: An Introduction to History,* trans. Franz Rosenthal, ed. by N. J. Dawood (Princeton, NJ: Princeton University Press, 2005), 47. It is true that Ibn Khaldūn held that at certain rare moments of religious conviction and piety the necessary "restraining influence" could come from purely internal motives. But even in the case of Islam, after these rare moments, the restraining forces of law and royal authority (*mulk*) were necessary for social stability.
94. Ghannūshī, *al-Ḥurriyyāt al-ʿāmma,* 247.
95. Ghannūshī, *al-Ḥurriyyāt al-ʿāmma,* 125 (2015 ed., 134).
96. Ghannūshī, *al-Ḥurriyyāt al-ʿāmma,* 246.
97. Ghannūshī, *al-Ḥurriyyāt al-ʿāmma,* 75–76 (2015 ed., 83–84).

7. After Islamic Democracy, after Sovereignty

1. For overviews of these *fatwā* wars in the 2011 period, see Adnan A. Zulfiqar, "Revolutionary Islamic Jurisprudence: A Restatement of the Arab Spring," *New York University Journal of International Law and Politics* 49 (2017): 389; and Muʿtaz al-Khaṭīb, "al-Fiqh wa'l-dawla fi'l-thawrāt al-ʿarabiyya," *Majallat al-Tabayyun li'l-dirāsāt al-fikriyya wa'l-thaqāfiyya* (2014): 63–84.
2. Muhammad al-Atawneh, "*Khurūj* in Contemporary Islamic Thought: The Case of the 'Arab Spring,'" *Ilahiyat Studies: A Journal on Islamic and Religious Studies* 7, no. 1 (2016): 27–52.

3. Zulfiqar, "Revolutionary Islamic Jurisprudence," 464.
4. Quoted in al-Khaṭīb, "al-Fiqh wa'l-dawla fi'l-thawrāt al-ʿarabiyya," *Tabayyun*, 67.
5. See both al-Khaṭīb, "al-Fiqh wa'l-dawla," 70–71; and Jawad Qureshi, "The Discourses of the Damascene Sunni Ulama during the 2011 Revolution," in *State and Islam in Baathist Syria: Confrontation or Co-Optation*, ed. Line Khatib, Raphaël Lefèvre, and Jawad Qureshi (Boulder, CO: Lynne Riener, 2012), 62–65.
6. Mohammad Fadel, "Islamic Law and Constitution-Making: The Authoritarian Temptation and the Arab Spring," *Osgoode Hall Law Journal* 53, no. 2 (2016): 472–507.
7. See David H. Warren, "Cleansing the Nation of the 'Dogs of Hell': ʿAlī Jumʿa's Nationalist Legal Reasoning in Support of the 2013 Egyptian Coup and Its Bloody Aftermath," *International Journal of Middle East Studies* 49, no. 3 (2017): 457–77, at 465–66.
8. See "ʿAli Gomaa's Message to Egyptian Security Forces Delivered Prior to the 2013 Rabaa Massacre," (Parts 1 and 2), YouTube video, 18:34, talk by Dr. ʿAli Jumʿa: member of the Board of Senior Scholars of the honorable Azhar University, posted by On the Arab Revolutions, September 20, 2014, https://www.youtube.com/watch?v=LCQqrryBy1E. See Usaama al-Azami's translation of this speech, https://www.academia.edu/19791977/Translation_of_Ali_Gomaas_Lecture_to_the_Egyptian_Armed_Forces_Summer_2013_in_the_weeks_prior_the_Rabaa_Massacre_draft.
9. See Warren, "Cleansing the Nation," and Usaama al-Azami's translation of "Ali Gomaa's Lecture to the Egyptian Armed Forces on August 18, 2013, four days after the Rabaa Massacre," https://www.academia.edu/31264955/Ali_Gomaa_s_Lecture_to_the_Egyptian_Armed_Forces_on_18_August_2013_four_days_after_the_Rabaa_Massacre_draft.
10. See the interview with ʿAlī Jumʿa by Ibrāhīm ʿUmrān in *al-Ahrām*, February 28, 2013, http://www.ahram.org.eg/NewsQ/133883.aspx.
11. Tarek Elgawhary, "Egypt's International Fatwa Conference October 2017," *Coexist Research International*, https://coexistresearch.com/egypts-international-fatwa-conference-october-2017/.
12. Masooda Bano, "At the Tipping Point: Al-Azhar's Growing Crisis of Moral Authority," *International Journal of Middle East Studies* 50 (2018): 715–34; and Masooda Bano and Hanane Benadi, "Regulating Religious Authority for Political Gains: al-Sisi's Manipulation of al-Azhar in Egypt," *Third World Quarterly* 39, no. 8 (2018): 1604–21.
13. Senior Scholars of Al-Azhar, *Wathīqat al-Azhar ḥawla mustaqbal Misr* (Alexandria, Egypt: Library of Alexandria, 2012).
14. These efforts have included declaring two American civil society organizations as "terrorist groups" and lobbying to have them and others declared as such by the United States government. See Adam Taylor, "Why the U.A.E. Is

Calling 2 American Groups Terrorists," *Washington Post,* November 17, 2014, https://www.washingtonpost.com/news/worldviews/wp/2014/11/17/why-the-u-a-e-is-calling-2-american-groups-terrorists/?utm_term=.25a7b26a3998.

15. See the text of this statement, "Inculcation of Tolerance: The Means to Countering Extremism," *The official website of His Eminence Shaykh Abdallah bin Bayyah,* February 25, 2019, http://binbayyah.net/arabic/archives/1483. For a discussion of these views, see Walaa Quisay and Thomas Parker, "On the Theology of Obedience: An Analysis of Shaykh Bin Bayyah and Shaykh Hamza Yusuf's Political Thought," *Maydan* (blog), January 8, 2019, https://www.themaydan.com/2019/01/theology-obedience-analysis-shaykh-bin-bayyah-shaykh-hamza-yusufs-political-thought/.
16. The so-called Tunisian National Dialogue Quartet won a Nobel Prize for Peace in 2015 for its role in mediating the crisis of the summer of 2013, which allowed the NCA to ultimately adopt the new constitution in January 2014.
17. On the politics of the NCA, see Sami Zemni, "The Extraordinary Politics of the Tunisian Revolution: The Process of Constitution Making," *Mediterranean Politics* 20, no. 1 (2015): 1–17; Hamadi Redissi and Rihab Boukhayatia, "The National Constituent Assembly of Tunisia and Civil Society Dynamics," EUSpring Working Paper no. 2, July 8, 2015; and Abrak Saati, "Negotiating the Post-Revolution Constitution for Tunisia: Members of the National Constituent Assembly Share Their Experiences," *International Law Research* 7, no. 1 (2018): 235–46.
18. The 2014 constitution stipulates that "the President of the Republic, the Assembly of the Representatives of the People, and the Supreme Judicial Council shall each appoint four members, three quarters of whom must be legal specialists" (Art. 118).
19. Amel Boubekeur, "Islamists, Secularists and Old Regime Elites in Tunisia: Bargained Competition," *Mediterranean Politics* 21, no. 1 (2016): 107–27.
20. Nathan J. Brown, "Reason, Interest, Rationality, and Passion in Constitution Drafting," *Perspectives on Politics* 6, no. 4 (2008): 675–89, at 676.
21. Malika Zeghal, "Competing Ways of Life: Islamism, Secularism, and Public Order in the Tunisian Transition," *Constellations* 20, no. 2 (2013): 254–74.
22. See Malika Zeghal, "Constitutionalizing a Democratic Muslim State without Shari'a: The Religious Establishment in the Tunisian 2014 Constitution," in Robert W. Hefner, ed., *Shari'a Law and Modern Muslim Ethics* (Bloomington: Indiana University Press, 2016); Monica Marks, "Convince, Coerce, or Compromise? Ennahda's Approach to Tunisia's Constitution," *Brookings Doha Center Analysis Paper* No. 10 (February 2014); and Kasper Ly Netterstrøm, "The Islamists' Compromise in Tunisia," *Journal of Democracy* 26, no. 4 (2015): 110–24.

23. Sélim Ben Abdesselem, "The Making of a Constitution: A Look Back at Tunisia's Thorny Consensus-Building Process," *ConstitutionNet,* March 26, 2014, http://constitutionnet.org/news/making-constitution-look-back-tunisias-thorny-consensus-building-process.
24. For example, Asef Bayat "The Coming of a Post-Islamist Society," *Critique: Journal for Critical Studies of the Middle East* 5, no. 9 (1996): 43–52; Seyyed Vali Reza Nasr, "The Rise of 'Muslim Democracy'," *Journal of Democracy* 16 no. 2 (2005): 13–27; Robert W. Hefner, ed., *Remaking Muslim Politics: Pluralism, Contestation, Democratization* (Princeton, NJ: Princeton University Press, 2009); and Michaelle Browers, *Political Ideology in the Arab World: Accommodation and Transformation* (Cambridge, UK: Cambridge University Press, 2009), especially chapter 2, "A More Inclusive Islamism? The *Wasatiyya* Trend."
25. These include the well-known figure of Abdolkarim Soroush (ʿAbd al-Karīm Surūsh), some of whose writings have been translated and published as Abdolkarim Soroush, *Reason, Freedom, and Democracy in Islam: Essential Writings of ʿAbdolkarim Soroush,* trans. and ed., Mahmoud Sadri and Ahmad Sadri (New York: Oxford University Press, 2000). On other reformist intellectual figures, see Tawfiq Alsaif, *Islamic Democracy and Its Limits: The Iranian Experience since 1979* (London: Saqi, 2007); Meysam Badamchi, *Post-Islamist Political Theory: Iranian Intellectuals and Political Liberalism in Dialogue* (New York: Springer, 2017); and Eskandar Sadeghi-Boroujerdi, *Revolution and Its Discontents: Political Thought and Reform in Iran* (Cambridge, UK: Cambridge University Press, 2019).
26. Ghannūshī and the other founders of the Islamic Tendency Movement stressed the people's right to choose the parties that would govern them in the first press conference after its founding. (See the transcript in *Bayānāt dhikrā al-taʾsīs l-ḥarakat al-Nahḍa al-tūnissiya* [Ennahda Publications, 2012], 10–18.
27. "Conference Concluding Statement" (on file with the author).
28. See the comments of Ennahda party member (and presently Tunisian Minister of Employment and Vocational Training) Sayida Ounissi two months before the May 2016 party congress in "Ennahda from within: Islamists or 'Muslim Democrats'?" Brookings Series "Islamists on Islamism Today," March 23, 2016, https://www.brookings.edu/research/ennahda-from-within-islamists-or-muslim-democrats-a-conversation/. Long-time Ennahda activist and party leader Said Ferjani also asserted that "Islamism ended once Ennahdha entered government and shared responsibility for social and economic provision and became accountable to the electorate and to civil society" (Said Ferjani, "The 'End of Islamism' and the Future of Tunisia," https://www.hudson.org/research/12349-the-end-of-islamism-and-the-future-of-tunisia. Ghannūshī himself presented this move to a Western

audience as "a result of 35 years of constant self-evaluation and more than two years of intense introspection and discussion at the grass-roots level" (Rached Ghannouchi, "From Political Islam to Muslim Democracy: The Ennahda Party and the Future of Tunisia," *Foreign Affairs* [September 2016]).

29. Rāshid al-Ghannūshī, *Irhāṣāt al-thawra* (Tūnis, Tunisia: Dār al-mujtahid, 2015). The title of this book ("Premonitions of the Revolution") is meant to represent Ghannūshī's response to the charge that Islamists sat out the 2011 revolution and were never devoted to a democratic, revolutionary break with the previous regime (personal communication with Ghannūshī, January 1, 2019.)
30. *Al-Dimuqrāṭiyya naḥwa ta'ṣīl li-mafāhīm mu'āṣira* (Tūnis, Tunisia: Dār al-Ṣaḥwa, 2015); *Al-Muwāṭana naḥwa ta'ṣīl li-mafāhīm mu'āṣira* (Tūnis, Tunisia: Dār al-Ṣaḥwa, 2016); *Al-'Ilmāniyya naḥwa ta'ṣīl li-mafāhīm mu'āṣira* (Tūnis, Tunisia: Dār al-Ṣaḥwa, 2016) *Al-Ḥurriyya naḥwa ta'ṣīl li-mafāhīm mu'āṣira* (Tūnis, Tunisia: Dār al-Ṣaḥwa, 2016).
31. Rāshid al-Ghannūshī, *al-Minbar: Khuṭab jum'a ba'd al-thawra* (Tūnis, Tunisia: Dār al-mujtahid 2015).
32. "Ma'ānī wa mujibāt dustūr mā ba'd al-thawra," in *Irhāṣāt al-thawra,* 227. Emphasis added.
33. "al-Islām wa'l-muwāṭana," in *Al-Muwāṭana naḥwa ta'ṣīl li-mafāhīm mu'āṣira,* 12.
34. "Ḥiwār ḥawla al-muwāṭana," in *Al-Muwāṭana naḥwa ta'ṣīl li-mafāhīm mu'āṣira,* 29.
35. "Ma'ānī wa mujibāt dustūr mā ba'd al-thawra," in *Irhāṣāt al-thawra,* 227.
36. "Ru'ā li-Tūnis al-jadīda," in *Irhāṣāt al-thawra,* 241.
37. "Dustūr Madīna," in *Al-Muwāṭana naḥwa ta'ṣīl li-mafāhīm mu'āṣira,* 58.
38. "Dustūr Madīna," in *Al-Muwāṭana naḥwa ta'ṣīl li-mafāhīm mu'āṣira,* 60.
39. "Ma'ānī wa mujibāt dustūr mā ba'd al-thawra," in *Irhāṣāt al-thawra,* 228.
40. "Ma'ānī wa mujibāt dustūr mā ba'd al-thawra," in *Irhāṣāt al-thawra,* 228.
41. "Ma'ānī wa mujibāt dustūr mā ba'd al-thawra," in *Irhāṣāt al-thawra,* 229.
42. "Ma'ānī wa mujibāt dustūr mā ba'd al-thawra," in *Irhāṣāt al-thawra,* 230
43. "Ḥuqūq al-insān fi'l-Islam," in *Irhāṣāt al-thawra,* 231–36.
44. "Ḥuqūq al-insān fi'l-Islam," in *Irhāṣāt al-thawra,* 236.
45. I conducted a series of philosophical-theological dialogues with Ghannūshī at his home in Tūnis between December 27, 2017, and January 4, 2018, and again January 1–3, 2019. These are presently being translated from Arabic for publication alongside some of his articles and essays on "Muslim democracy" (forthcoming with Oxford University Press in 2019 or 2020).
46. One telling example has emerged as I finish this manuscript. In response to the proposal of the Tunisian President's Committee on Individual Freedoms and Equality (COLIBE) to enact law guaranteeing the equality of inheritance rights, the decriminalization of homosexuality, the abolition of the death penalty, the cancellation of the dowry, and the right of women to

pass on citizenship to a foreign husband (see the Arabic report at https://colibe.org/wp-content/uploads/2018/06/Rapport-COLIBE.pdf), Ghannūshī's Ennahda party issued an official statement rejecting these changes. The head of the party's Shūrā Council, ʿAbd al-Karīm al-Hārūnī declared that the party "rejects any proposal that contradictions the constitution and the Qurʾanic texts." Hārūnī also articulates the ideal of an Islamic democracy, that the sovereign people would not violate divine will if acting with the proper virtue: "Tunisia is a civil state for a Muslim people that adheres to the teachings of the constitution and the teachings of Islam, a civil state that expresses the will of the people . . . Al-Nahḍa will participate in the defense of the rights of women related to inheritance, but within the context of proposals and laws that respect the identity of the country. . . . Al-Nahḍa supports interpretation [*al-ijtihād*] and initiatives to improve the status of women and will participate in the development of rules while adhering to the fixed teachings of Islam" (see "Al-Nahḍa tarfuḍ mubādarat al-Sabsī li'l-musāwāh bi'l-irth fī Tūnis," *al-ʿArabī al-jadīd,* August 26, 2018, https://bit.ly/2KwV2Ly).

47. From my dialogues with Ghannūshī (transcript on file with author).
48. Wael Hallaq, *The Impossible State,* x.
49. Ghannūshī was making an argument like this long before the 2011 revolt, for example, in his essay "Freedom First," which argues that political liberty and protections against tyranny are the preconditions for any other political good (Ghannūshī, "al-Ḥurriyya awwalan," in *Irhāṣāt a-thawra,* 78–82).
50. Cass R. Sunstein, "Incompletely Theorized Agreements," *Harvard Law Review* 108, no. 7 (1995): 1733–72.
51. See, famously, Muḥammad Bāqir Ṣadr, *Iqtiṣāduna* (Najaf: Maṭābiʿ Al-Nuʿmān, 1961). While written by an Iraqi Shiʿa scholar, this text had widespread influence on the entire Islamic movements.
52. See, for example, Hiba Raʾūf ʿIzzat, *al-Khiyāl al-siyāsī li'l-Islāmiyyīn: mā qabl al-dawla wa mā baʿduhā* (al-Shabaka al-ʿarabiyya, 2015), which is a study of the "Islamist political imagination" before and after the state, and the earlier cited Jāsir ʿAwda, *al-Dawla al-madaniyya,* which less a traditional claim that the Islamic state *is* a civil state and more that a non-authoritarian, civil state is what will make society safe for the development of Islamic ethics.
53. This is that theme that emerged repeatedly in my dialogues with him (transcripts on file with the author, forthcoming in translation).
54. To invoke Jeremy Waldron, "*Political* Political Theory: An Inaugural Lecture," *Journal of Political Philosophy* 21, no. 1 (2013): 1–23.

Acknowledgments

I began working in earnest on this book in late 2012. This was the height of postrevolutionary constitution-making in Egypt and Tunisia, and a period when the fate of the pro-democracy Arab revolts had not yet been written. At the time it appeared possible that the result of the democratic transition in Egypt and Tunisia (and perhaps beyond) would be not merely multi-party constitutional systems but a kind of regime inspired by longstanding Islamic theories of democracy. Such regimes would be characterized not only by the norms of parliamentary democracy or by the practice of judicial *sharīʿa* review common to many modern Muslim states, but by a vision of the legislative process and institutions of civil society reflecting popular self-governance with an Islamic reference and orientation. I imagined writing a book on the deep political theory and theology of this vision of Islamic democracy, anticipating that it might help tell the story of regimes that were long theorized but were being put into practice only for the first time.

That, in fact, is the book that I ended up writing and that is found in the preceding pages. But instead of an intellectual genealogy of a form of politics being actively created, it is now more of an obituary of a distinct ideal theory of legitimate governance, based on the supremacy of divine guidance for mankind but brought into being by the public deliberation and collective stewardship of an active and virtuous political community. That this takes the form of an obituary is largely due to repressive and brutal counter-revolution. But at its most idealistic and most sophisticated, Islamic democratic theory over the past decades has aspired to something more than merely toppling brutal and corrupt dictatorships. It has aspired to a kind of redemption of the modern sovereign state based on the assumption that, underneath the layers of state repression and venality, Muslim *societies* were both pious and capable of self-government. It is the belief in a core moral unity in Muslim societies that I believe is the core unexamined assumption of modern Islamic democratic theory, the reexamining of which would require new forms of theorizing about the state, sovereignty, and the place of Islam. This book thus aims to be both an analytic history of an idea—the idea of an Islamic democracy founded on the theological doctrine of the universal caliphate—and an argument that this idea is in tension with some fundamental facts about moral disagreement in the conditions of modernity.

In the preceding six or seven years I have accrued many debts. Gratitude is due first to my editors at Harvard University Press, Sharmila Sen and Heather Hughes, for their perfect combination of patience, encouragement, indulgence, and enthusiasm for the receipt of a finished draft. Also, in every area where their editorial eyes saw things differently from my authorial one, they were right. Every academic author should be so lucky. Much of Chapter 5 was first published as "Taking People As They Are: Islam As a 'Realistic Utopia' in the Political Theory of Sayyis Qutb," *American Political Science Review* Vol. 104, No. 1 (2010): 189–207. A revised version of this paper, in light of my developing views on the genealogy of popular sovereignty in modern Islamic thought, is reprinted here with the permission of Cambridge University Press.

Since conceiving of the idea for this book in the fall of 2012, I have presented work in progress along the way at the Middle East Legal Studies Seminar. Papers presented there in 2013, 2016, and 2018 have all in some way gone into the following pages. I am in debt to many of the interlocutors from MELSS over the years for comments on papers and general conversations. I am indebted in particular, but not exclusively, to Aslï Bâli, Salaheddin Al-Bashir, Bashir Bashir, Omar Dajani, Bahaa Ezzelarab, Abdulaziz Al Fahad, Mohamed El Fayoumy, Shafeeq Ghabra, Wael Hallaq, Nissreen Haram, Bernard Haykel, Hedayat Heikal, Choukri Hmed, Paul Kahn, Moncef Kartas, Intissar Kherigi, Darryl Li, Chibli Mallat, Nadia Marzouki, Marwan Muasher, Soli Özel, Intisar Rabb, Moussa Ramadan, Aziz Rana, Mara Revkin, Aisha Saad, Scott Shapiro, and Patrick Weil.

I have had many opportunities to present my work in progress at seminars, conferences, and lectures. One collects too many debts to count or remember, and it becomes difficult to account for the way one's approaches to a book project shift over the years. While I dread the thought of forgetting someone who has taken the time to consider and respond to my work, the following colleagues have my thanks and appreciation for comments on seminar papers or other written drafts or for engaging my questions and requests for help: Khaled Abou El Fadl, Asma Afsaruddin, Nadia Al-Bagdadi, Cemil Aydin,

Usaama Al-Azami, Rashad Ali, Ovamir Anjum, Said Arjomand, Jasser Auda, Samy Ayoub, Seyla Benhabib, Joshua Braver, Nathan Brown, Jocelyne Cesari, Jean Cohen, Joshua Cohen, Loubna El Amine, Ahmed El Shamsy, Farah El-Sharif, Dalia Fahmy, Yasmine Farouk, Michael Frazer, Pascale Ghazaleh, Eric Gregory, David Grewal, Wael Haddara, Shadi Hamid, Nader Hashemi, Clarissa Hayward, Hisham Hellyer, Khurram Hussain, Murad Idris, Turkuler Isiksel, David Kirkpatrick, Bettina Koch, Mirjam Künkler, Dunja Larise, Stephen Macedo, Charles Mathewes, Radwan Masmoudi, David Mednicoff, Eric Nelson, Alan Patten, Asifa Quraishi, Michael Rosen, Andy Sabl, Adam Sabra, Jeffrey Sachs, Karim Sadek, Rahul Sagar, Kristin Stilt, Lucas Swaine, Mairaj Syed, Nicholas Tampio, Alp Eren Topal, Richard Tuck, Nadia Urbinati, Leif Wenar, Melissa Williams, Halil Yenigun, Qasim Zaman, and Adnan Zulfiqar. I apologize to anyone I may have neglected to mention.

I was fortunate to have two workshops on various drafts of the full manuscript. My special thanks go to Michaelle Browers, Jonathan Brown, Mohammad Fadel, Ibrahim El Houdaiby, and Basileus Zeno for reading through the entire manuscript and saving me from many errors small and large. Their comments were so thoughtful, incisive, and informed that it is only by an act of faith that I proceed with the publication of this book at all. Raihan Ahmed, Creighton Coleman, Charles Mathewes, Zain Moulvi, Kyle Nicholas, Shifa Amina Noor and Jonah Schulhofer-Wohl at the University of Virginia read through a draft much closer to what is found in the subsequent pages. My only wish is that I had had their insights and suggestions at a much earlier stage. I am grateful to the Alwaleed Islamic Studies Program at Harvard and the University of Virginia for their support for these two events.

The bulk of the writing of the final drafts took place in ideal conditions. The Edmond J. Safra Center for Ethics and the Islamic Legal Studies Program at Harvard University provided the support and freedom to complete this book between 2017 and 2018. Danielle Allen and Kristin Stilt, as well as the staff and other fellows of Safra and ILSP during this period, have my gratitude and appreciation. Between 2017 and 2019 I was also supported by a long-term research grant from the International Institute of Islamic Thought. I am grateful to the IIIT, particularly Ermin Sinanović, for this support. I would also like to pay tribute here to the memory of Jamal Barzinji for his role in making the IIIT a center of creative public Islamic intellectualism.

Between 2018 and 2019 I was a visiting scholar at the Middle East Initiative of the Harvard Kennedy School of Government. This was not only an opportunity to revise drafts of this manuscript and begin work on a new project, but it bridged my transition from Safra and ILSP fellowships to taking up my present position at the University of Massachusetts. I wish to express my immense personal gratitude to Tarek Masoud for this support. He has also been a profoundly valued intellectual interlocutor for over twelve years and has sharpened many aspects of the present book over the past year.

While on the subject of ideal work conditions, I would be remiss if I did not note some of the ways in which I have escaped our present crisis of attention and distraction. First, I thank the engineers behind the Freedom app for many (but perhaps not enough) hours without access to the internet. We can choose to tie ourselves to the mast, but it's good to have the mast and the ropes. Second, I would like to thank the Massachusetts Department of Conservation and Recreation (DCR) for maintaining the electrified but otherwise off-the-grid cabins at the Savoy Mountain State Forest. Tens of thousands of words (many now on the cutting-room floor) were written in Cabin 4, in between hikes and looking for black bears, without the bane of Wi-Fi or cell reception. Speaking of western Massachusetts, my immense gratitude goes (once again) to Amel Ahmed, Angelica Bernal, and David Mednicoff for their efforts in helping me to continue my career at UMass.

This book began in 2012 when I read Rāshid al-Ghannūshī's book *Public Freedoms in the Islamic State*. I read this book because I was interested in the topic of modern Islamic legal interpretation and was curious about Ghannūshī's views on *sharīʿa* reform when he was back in Tunis after more than two decades of exile, helping to guide Tunisia's democratic transition. This book more than any other led to my appreciation for the commitment to popular sovereignty in modern Islamic thought and the particular centrality of the doctrine of the universal caliphate. The importance of his thought, and the framing of this project around the doctrine of the universal caliphate, has not changed since I began work on this project. However, I have also been extremely fortunate to discuss the ideas of this book, Ghannūshī's thought, and broader problems of democracy and moral pluralism personally with Ghannūshī himself over many hours in Tunis. These discussions have been profoundly enjoyable and a rare intellectual privilege. Ustadh Rashid also has my personal gratitude for his time, patience, and willingness to indulge my own philosophical and political preoccupations.

Tamir and Ayla were fourteen and four respectively when I began work on this book. They were a great distraction, and I thank them for my not finishing it sooner. There are more enjoyable and important things than work, and most of the time I would rather be with them. For those times when I did have to focus, I benefited enormously from the support of my family. Ayla's mother, Naz, was fantastically supportive and remains an intellectual inspiration. My love and gratitude are due also to her parents (Mahmood and Nakissa) for their help and encouragement. My parents were not only pillars of support with their grandchildren, but were the moral exemplars that I sought to emulate when grappling with a minor hardship halfway through the writing of this book. That I did not handle it worse is due to their example.

Index